Securities Disclosure in Plain English

For Wolfram Karl
With good wishes always,

Books by Bryan A. Garner

A Dictionary of Modern Legal Usage
The Elements of Legal Style
Guidelines for Drafting and Editing Court Rules
A Dictionary of Modern American Usage
Securities Disclosure in Plain English
The Winning Brief

Books edited by Bryan A. Garner

Texas, Our Texas
Black's Law Dictionary (pocket edition)
A Handbook of Basic Law Terms

Securities Disclosure in Plain English

BRYAN A. GARNER

CCH INCORPORATED
Chicago

Editorial Staff

Acquisitions Editor: Karen Clanton, J.D.

Editor: Marilynn Helt, J.D.

Cover Design: Tom O'Connor

Book Design and Production: LB Brumage

ISBN 0-8080-0321-6

4025 W. Peterson Ave.
Chicago, IL 60646-6085
1-800-248-3248
http://www.cch.com

Printed in the United States of America

For Alexandra

ACKNOWLEDGMENTS

Many people have contributed to this book, and I'm grateful to them all. Karen Clanton of CCH proposed the book to me and helped me develop its contents. Nancy Smith of the SEC helpfully suggested working with law firms for the model documents found in the appendixes—an idea that hadn't occurred to me. The law-firm contributors themselves did splendid work. Many thanks to David P. Porter of Jones, Day, Reavis & Pogue; Richard A. Boehmer of O'Melveny & Myers; and Richard D. Marshall and David Dickstein of Kirkpatrick & Lockhart.

Two plain-language experts read the entire text and made many excellent suggestions: Joseph F. Spaniol, Jr., the former Clerk of the United States Supreme Court, and Professor Joseph Kimble of the Thomas M. Cooley Law School. My heartiest thanks to both. Also, Marilynn Helt of CCH skillfully edited the manuscript. So did Karen Magnuson of Portland, Oregon—the most trusted proofreader I know.

At LawProse, Inc., I had the benefit of two keen lawyer-editors whom I am proud to call colleagues: David W. Schultz and Lance A. Cooper. They sifted through heaps of disclosure documents to find examples that were eluding me. And they sharpened the text.

I wrote the book almost entirely while in Austria in July 1998. I owe a great debt of gratitude to Professors Christoph Schreuer and Wolfram Karl of the University of Salzburg for providing me with an office as a visiting scholar. They and their university have been extraordinarily kind to me over the years.

Meanwhile, my wife, Teo, and our two daughters, Caroline and Alexandra, provided many diverting hours in Salzburg while I wasn't writing. I thank them for the joy they continually bring me.

Table of Contents

2: Audience

3: Process

4: Wording Guidelines

5: Sentences

6: Paragraphs

7: Organization

8: Design

9: Definitions

PART ONE
PLAIN-ENGLISH STYLE

Introduction

In 1996, the SEC undertook a revolutionary initiative. It declared that disclosure documents should be in plain English.

Some members of the corporate bar immediately pooh-poohed the idea, saying that this type of initiative had been tried before and had failed. They said it wouldn't go anywhere. Other members of the corporate bar cried foul, claiming that the SEC should be estopped from changing the rules: after all, the SEC had been approving legalistic forms for a long time. It wasn't fair, they said, to impose a new requirement on lawyers who had invested their entire careers in understanding the intricacies of securities law. This new requirement, they said, was burdensome and inequitable.

Exactly what was this new requirement? Merely that corporate lawyers learn how to write well—and actually do it in disclosure documents.

That can be a hard pill to swallow, especially if you've deluded yourself into thinking that you already do write well. It's a pill that causes disillusionment—something people never want for themselves.

People balk at change. They find self-justifying excuses. One of the best was this: "How can we be expected to use plain English when the SEC itself doesn't use it? Look at the SEC's regulations in the CFR!" That's a fair point, and the SEC was aware of it before anyone raised it. The SEC undertook to improve the writing it produces.

In the spring of 1997, the SEC contracted with my company, LawProse, Inc., to conduct training sessions for every SEC lawyer and accountant. I taught five six-hour sessions on plain-English legal drafting, with a focus on disclosure documents. The idea was to sensitize SEC staffers to the types of recurrent issues that arise in legal drafting. Those involved in the plain-English pilot program—especially Nancy Smith and Ann Wallace—were particularly interested in how quickly SEC lawyers could begin applying plain-English principles. They were cheered when they learned what I already knew after years of teaching continuing-legal-education courses in legal drafting: most lawyers and accountants could learn these principles and apply them quite readily. They could make a good beginning of it after only one day of training. Not only that: 90% of them were enthusiastic about plain English. After all, it would ultimately make their own jobs easier.

Of course, you can't learn it all in a day. But if you have a fair ear for the language, you can make a good start. Then again, you can lose it quite rapidly if you don't practice it. It isn't easy, but it's crucial.

Crucial to whom? you ask. That's a fair question. I'll give a double-barreled answer.

First, learning plain English is crucial to your success as a lawyer. The SEC is requiring those who write disclosure documents to retool. But even if the SEC weren't requiring this, you'd still be wise to retool because good writing is good thinking. Your documents will get better, not worse, and sound principles of drafting will lay bare many of the blunders lurking in documents that you might think you know inside and out. In other words, plain English improves not only clarity, but also accuracy and precision.

You might ask, though, how plain English can be critical to your success when it's never been critical to the success of corporate lawyers in the past. The answer is that the world is changing. Clients—especially sophisticated clients—are demanding more from their lawyers. They know now that they ought to be able to read and understand their wills, their leases, and their other contracts. And corporate clients believe, quite rightly, that they ought to be able to understand their prospectuses, their proxy statements, and the like. And even if corporate clients are somehow so misinformed as not to believe that, most investors know better.

That brings us to the second point. It's crucial to your clients that you learn to write in plain English. They'll look better in the marketplace. They'll develop a larger reservoir of goodwill. They'll have a competitive edge. They'll save time and money. Besides all that, you'll have produced documents that are legally better for the reasons outlined just above: remember that good writing is good thinking.

Be cynical about these points, if you like. Don't acquire the skill, if you don't want to. Maybe you're in the most powerful law firm in the world. But don't be surprised when prospective clients start looking at some of your old documents and then going elsewhere for representation. If you're cynical about plain English, I'd say they have good reason.

First Principles 1

§ 1 Adopt conventions that enhance clarity. Be consistent in using them.

The conventions that you adopt will mightily influence a document's clarity. If you start out with any number of false premises, you'll be sunk:

- If you use a single-column format with 9-point type, readers will find it a strain to read your document. (See § 55.)

- If you use a sans-serif typeface in the text, you'll double the strain. (See § 49.)

- If you have a decimal numbering system that involves a third level (1.1.1, 1.1.2, etc.), you'll immediately alienate many readers. (See § 46.)

- If you insist on lots of definitions for obvious terms—as by saying that *Digitropic Holdings, Inc.* is "hereinafter Digitropic"—you'll weigh down your sentences with galumphing legalisms. (See § 62.)

- If you run enumerated lists into paragraphs, you'll amass some impenetrable barriers to entry. (See § 9.)

- If you insist on using the third person exclusively, you'll make the text much less engaging. (See § 12.)

- If you organize from your own point of view and not from the reader's, you'll baffle anyone who really wants to understand. (See § 45.)

- If you stuff the cover page with relatively unimportant information, unattractively presented, you'll show just how dreadful the rest of the document is likely to be. (See § 5.)

These, unfortunately, are all conventions widely used in old-style drafting. And if you start out with any of them, you're drastically hampering yourself.

So begin by liberating yourself from some old habits. Think about the conventions that you've been using and how you might improve on them. That's mostly what this book is about.

And then once you have a good set of conventions, use a consistent format. In the pilot program, the SEC's plain-English comments often focused on inconsistencies in formatting.

§ 2 Keep the goal in mind: communicate with the public.

Adopt a relaxed, conversational tone. Remember that the primary purpose of a disclosure document is to communicate with shareholders. In preparing such a document, you're projecting a corporate image. Is it formal and distant? Or is it warm and friendly? Is it stuffy and artificial? Or is it relaxed and natural?

Most businesspeople decidedly prefer to sound warm, friendly, relaxed, and natural to their investors. You can do this while meeting all the legal requirements.

But few lawyers have learned to write that way. That's why the SEC's plain-English initiative will require transactional lawyers to learn a new way of expressing themselves—at least when it comes to disclosure documents.

To a great extent, this involves thinking in a new way. Essentially, this newly required mode of thought accepts legal thinking but disallows legalistic thinking.

Write it up the way any first-rate journalist would. If you don't know how, then start studying journalists' work in *Time*, *Newsweek*, *Fortune*, *Forbes*, *The Atlantic*, *The Economist*, and other reputable news magazines. Notice especially how the writers handle financial and legal matters. Then try to apply some of their techniques.

§ 3 Recognize that style matters. Focus on style as a means of improving the content.

If you're inclined to say that all you care about is "substance," if you routinely dismiss matters of style, then you're hopelessly naive about language—and about legal drafting.

One of my favorite techniques in training corporate lawyers—a technique I've used in many firms from coast to coast—is to take a published form and critique it for style. We'll take a commercial lease, choose some of the major provisions, and then have teams of three lawyer-participants critique one provision apiece. All they're looking at is style, but inevitably they unearth glaring substantive deficiencies—things they wouldn't have seen if they hadn't been focusing on style. (After all, the formbook authors didn't see them, and the publishers didn't see them.) This exercise is an eye-opener. You can do it with just about any formbook.

Once you've gone through that exercise, you'll have learned two important lessons. First, don't trust formbooks to supply wordings for you. Instead, use them to get ideas. Second, one of the best ways to improve content is to work hard on style. There's no substitute for it.

§ 4 Express yourself in the clearest and simplest language that the substance will allow.

Scrutinize whether some complicated ideas are worth expressing at all. If they're not, find the simplest equivalent. The following example—a 232-word sentence run together in the archaic style—runs off the rails in subpart (b). If you try to parse subpart (b), the effort will likely be for naught. It attempts to state an objective test for what is financially advantageous for most shareholders, but it's a test that most board members and most shareholders wouldn't be able to follow. It's debatable whether anyone can. The revised version says essentially the same thing at a higher level of generality, but in a much more comprehensible and commonsense way.

Example

Not this:	*But this:*
The affirmative vote of not less than 51 percent of the voting stock of an interested stockholder (defined generally as a holder of 10 percent or more of the outstanding shares of Pantheon common stock) who is a party to certain business combinations with Pantheon is required for the adoption or authorization of such business combination, unless by a two-thirds vote the disinterested members of the Pantheon board determine that: (a) the interested stockholder is the beneficial owner of not less than 80 percent of the voting stock of Pantheon and has declared its intention to vote in favor of or approve such business combination; or (b) the fair market value of the consideration per share to be received or retained by the holders of each class or series of stock of Pantheon in a business combination is equal to or greater than the consideration per share (including brokerage commissions and soliciting dealers' fees) paid by such interested stockholder in acquiring the largest number of shares of such class of stock previously acquired in any one transaction or series of related transactions, whether before or after the interested stockholder has not and will not receive the benefit, directly or indirectly (except proportionately as a stockholder), of any loans, advances, guarantees, pledges, or other financial assistance provided by Pantheon, whether in anticipation of or in connection with such business combination or otherwise. Words: 232 Sentences: 1 Average sentence length: 232	Before the business combination can go through, one of three things must happen. Each one alone is sufficient for approval: (1) if a stockholder owning at least 10 percent of Pantheon's common stock is a party to other business combinations with Pantheon, at least 51 percent of each such stockholder's voting stock approves the transaction; (2) if the Pantheon board by a two-thirds vote of its disinterested members determines that the interested stockholder is the beneficial owner of at least 80 percent of the voting stock of Pantheon and has declared its intention to approve the business combination; or (3) if the Pantheon board by a two-thirds vote of its disinterested members determines that the transaction is financially advantageous to Pantheon stockholders as a whole. Words: 125 Sentences: 5 Average sentence length: 25

§ 5 Delete unimportant information. Put relatively unimportant information toward the back of the document.

For many years, old-style drafting made disclosure documents impenetrable to the ordinary reader. It was a needle-in-the-haystack problem: the information that a reader might want was buried under so many layers of sludge that it became, in effect, irretrievable.[1] If you disclose *everything*, after all, you end up disclosing *nothing*—because nobody is dogged enough to read what you've written.

Many lawyers fear deletions, even of boilerplate, because they think that deleting something might result in increased potential for liability. The answer to this concern is threefold. First, as the SEC puts it, "Using plain English does not mean omitting important information. These rules only require you to disclose information in words investors can understand and in a format that invites them to read the document."[2] Second, plain-English disclosure should reduce potential liability because it decreases investors' misunderstandings.[3] Third, the lawyers who went through the SEC's pilot program—those with the most experience in actually preparing these documents—don't believe that their plain-English disclosures will affect potential liability.[4]

In the following example, the striking changes in cover pages show what it means to highlight the important information while subordinating the unimportant. Notice how true the old truism is: less is more. The original version is loaded with words and information having minimal value for most readers. The revised version, with its bullet lists, highlights the points most likely to be of immediate concern to most investors.

Example

Not this:

$200,000,000

Welty Gas & Electric Company

Medium-Term Notes, Series E
Due from 9 months to 30 years from Date of Issue

Welty Gas and Electric Company (the "Company") intends to sell from time to time up to $200,000,000 aggregate principal amount of its unsecured Medium-Term Notes, Series E (the "Notes"). Each Note will mature from 9 months to 30 years from the date of issue as determined by mutual agreement of the initial purchasers and the Company. The Notes may be subject to optional redemption prior to their stated maturity as indicated in an accompanying supplement to this Prospectus (the "Pricing Supplement") but will not be subject to conversion, amortization or any sinking fund.

The interest rate, or interest rate formula, for each Note will be established by the Company at the date of issuance of such Note and will be indicated in the applicable Pricing Supplement: Each interest-bearing Note will bear interest at either (a) a fixed rate (a "Fixed Rate Note") or (b) a variable rate determined by reference to an interest rate formula (a "Floating Rate Note"), which may be adjusted by adding or subtracting a Spread or multiplying by a Spread Multiplier, as indicated in the applicable Pricing Supplement. Unless otherwise indicated in the applicable Pricing Supplement, the interest rate formula for Floating Rate Notes will be the Commercial Paper Rate, the Prime Rate, the CD Rate, the Federal Funds Effective Rate, LIBOR, the Treasury Rate, or the CMT Rate. Interest rates, or interest rate formulas, are subject to change by the Company from time to time, but no such change will affect any Note previously issued or which the Company has agreed to sell. Unless otherwise indicated in the applicable Pricing Supplement, the interest payment dates for Fixed Rate Notes will be each May 1 and November 1; the interest payment dates for Floating Rate Notes will be specified in the applicable Pricing Supplement. See "DESCRIPTION OF NOTES."

The Notes will be issued in minimum denominations of $100,000 and integral multiples of $1,000 in excess thereof. Notes may be issued, as specified in the applicable Pricing Supplement, in definitive form or may be represented by a permanent global Note or Notes registered in the name of The Depository Trust Company, as depositary (the "Depositary"), or a nominee of the Depositary (each such Note represented by a permanent global Note being referred to herein as a "Book-Entry Note"). Beneficial interests in Book-Entry Notes will only be evidenced by, and transfers thereof will only be effected through, records maintained by the Depositary (with respect to its participants) and the Depositary's participants (with respect to beneficial owners). Except as described under "DESCRIPTION OF NOTES—Book-Entry Notes," owners of beneficial interests in a permanent global Note will not be entitled to receive physical delivery of Notes in definitive form and will not be considered the holders thereof.

THESE SECURITIES HAVE NOT BEEN APPROVED OR DISAPPROVED BY THE SECURITIES AND EXCHANGE COMMISSION OR ANY STATE SECURITIES COMMISSION NOR HAS THE SECURITIES AND EXCHANGE COMMISSION OR ANY STATE SECURITIES COMMISSION PASSED UPON THE ACCURACY OR ADEQUACY OF THIS PROSPECTUS. ANY REPRESENTATION TO THE CONTRARY IS A CRIMINAL OFFENSE.

	Price to Public (1)	Agents' Commission (2)(3)	Proceeds to Company (2)(4)
Per Note	100%	.125%–.750%	99.875%–99.250%
Total	$200,000,000	$250,000–$1,500,000	$199,750,000–$198,500,000

(1) Unless otherwise indicated in a Pricing Supplement, Notes will be issued at 100% of their principal amount.
(2) The Company will pay Kerbal Brothers, Kerbal Brothers Inc., and Howard, Hull & Co. (the "Agents"), as agents, a commission ranging from .125% to .750% of the principal amount of any Note, depending on its stated maturity, sold through any such Agent. The Company also may sell Notes to any Agent at a discount for resale to one or more purchasers at varying prices related to prevailing market prices at the time of resale, as determined by such Agent. In the case of Notes sold directly to investors by the Company, no discount will be allowed or commission paid.
(3) The Company has agreed to indemnify the Agents against certain civil liabilities under the Securities Act of 1933.
(4) Before deduction of expenses payable by the Company estimated at $330,000.

The Notes will be offered on a continuing basis by the Company through the Agents, each of which has agreed to use all reasonable efforts to solicit purchases of the Notes. The Company reserves the right to sell Notes directly to purchasers on its own behalf. The Company also may sell Notes to either Agent acting as principal for resale to one or more purchasers. The Company reserves the right to withdraw, cancel or modify the offer made hereby without notice. The Company or any Agent may reject any offer to purchase Notes, in whole or in part. See "PLAN OF DISTRIBUTION OF NOTES."

KERBAL BROTHERS HOWARD, HULL & CO.

September 8, 1998

But this:

Prospectus

$200,000,000

MEDIUM-TERM NOTES

SERIES E

wge

Welty Gas & Electric Co.
1400 Curtis Street
Denver, Colorado 80202
(303) 471-7188

Terms of Sale

The following terms may apply to the notes, which we may sell at one or more times. The final terms for each note will be included in a pricing supplement. For more detail, see "Description of Notes." We will receive $199,750,000 to $198,500,000 of the proceeds from the sale of the notes, after paying the agents commissions of $250,000 to $1,500,000.

- Mature 9 months to 30 years
- Fixed or floating interest rate. The floating-interest-rate formula will be based on:
  - Commercial paper rate
  - Prime rate
  - CD rate
  - Federal Funds effective rate
  - LIBOR
  - Treasury rate
  - CMT rate
- Remarketing features
- Certificate or book-entry form
- Subject to redemption and repurchase at option of WGE or holder
- Not convertible, amortizable, or subject to a sinking fund
- Interest paid on fixed-rate notes on May 1 and November 1
- Interest paid on floating-rate notes monthly, quarterly, semiannually, or annually
- Minimum denominations of $100,000, increased in multiples of $1,000

The notes have not been approved by the SEC or any state securities commission, nor have these organizations determined that this prospectus is accurate or complete. It's illegal for anyone to tell you otherwise.

KERBAL BROTHERS HOWARD, HULL & CO.

AGENTS

September 8, 1998

§ 6 Drop unnecessary complexities; simplify others.

The world is complex, that's true. And the financial world is certainly no exception. You can't eliminate complexity.

What you can eliminate, though, is *unnecessary* complexity. That's what the principle known as Occam's razor is all about. William of Occam devised a philosophical principle that simpler explanations should always be preferred over more complex ones. The same is true when you're structuring a deal: don't make it involve 12 steps if you need only 7.

Another thing. Don't just copy complex information from legal documents.[5] Explain it in clear, concise language. Paraphrase, but paraphrase accurately. Although this suggestion scares many transactional lawyers, it actually points up a problem with the initial legal documents: they ought to be worded as simply and directly as they can be. That's the mark of good drafting. If you find yourself driven to complex formulations, that's a sure sign that all is not well with the draft.

Besides, if you can't accurately paraphrase a passage, it's doubtful whether you truly understand it.

§ 7 Be as brief as clarity and readability permit.

Boil sentences down to the essential point. This tip encompasses many things. It means avoiding bizspeak. It means avoiding legalese. It means deleting clutter.

And although this is hard to do, it's well worth the effort. The following example shows Warren Buffett's translation of old-style prospectus language into plain English:[6]

Example

Not this:	*But this:*
Maturity and duration management decisions are made in the context of an intermediate maturity orientation. The maturity structure of the portfolio is adjusted in the anticipation of cyclical interest-rate changes. Such adjustments are not made in an effort to capture short-term, day-to-day movements in the market, but instead are implemented in anticipation of longer-term, secular shifts in the interest rates (i.e., shifts transcending and/or not inherent to the business cycle). Adjustments made to shorten portfolio maturity and duration are made to limit capital losses during periods when interest rates are expected to rise. Conversely, adjustments made to lengthen maturation for the portfolio's maturity and duration strategy lies in the analysis of the U.S. and global economies, focusing on levels of real interest rates, monetary and fiscal policy actions, and cyclical indicators. Words: 137 Sentences: 5 Average sentence length: 27.4	We will try to profit by correctly predicting future interest rates. When we have no strong opinion, we will generally hold intermediate-term bonds. But when we expect a major and sustained increase in rates, we will concentrate on short-term issues. And conversely, if we expect a major shift to lower rates, we will buy long bonds. We will focus on the big picture and won't make moves based on short-term considerations. Words: 74 Sentences: 5 Average sentence length: 14.8

§ 8 Illustrate points—especially mathematical calculations—with good examples.

In all types of technical writing, examples can make otherwise abstract language perfectly comprehensible. (This book, for example, would be of little help without its examples.) So when you're discussing the financial effect of a deal, *show* the reader what the effects are on given investors. Give examples. And make them easy to follow. Also, relate the examples to one another thematically whenever you can.

Example

Not this:	*But this:*
Q: Please explain what I will receive in the merger. A: In the merger, you'll receive 0.54 of a Pan-OJM ADS and $6.00 in cash in exchange for each share of Pantheon common stock you own. Pan-OJM will not issue fractional ADSs. You will instead be paid cash equal to the market value of any fractional Pan-OJM ADS you would have otherwise received.	**Q: Please explain what I will receive in the merger.** A: In the merger, you'll receive 0.54 of a Pan-OJM ADS and $6.00 in cash in exchange for each share of Pantheon common stock you own. Pan-OJM will not issue fractional ADSs. You will instead be paid cash equal to the market value of any fractional Pan-OJM ADS you would have otherwise received. *Examples* • *If you own 100 shares of Pantheon common stock, then after the merger you'll be entitled to receive 54 Pan-OJM ADSs, along with a check for $600.* • *If you own 101 shares of Pantheon common stock, then after the merger you'll be entitled to receive 54 Pan-OJM ADSs, along with a check for $606—plus the market value of 0.54 of a Pan-OJM ADS.*

§ 9 If you're listing items that can't be stated in just a couple of words, break them down into parallel provisions with cascading indents—hanging indents—from the left margin. Don't run the items into one long paragraph.

The hanging indent is perhaps the most widely overlooked tool of good drafting. It reveals structure cleanly. Because it's typographically sophisticated, don't assume you'll be able to do it immediately—it takes some setting up. But once you prepare your documents this way, you'll wonder how you ever got by with old-style methods.

The original drafts in examples A and B show typical old-style drafting—dense and uninviting. The intermediate drafts in A and B show traditional indents, with continuations of paragraphs returning to the left margin. The final versions in A and B illustrate the virtues of the hanging indent, which displays the organizational patterns much more cleanly.

Example A

Not this:

The Merger Agreement may be terminated: (a) by mutual written consent of Pantheon and OJM; (b) by either Pantheon or OJM if (i) upon a vote at the Special Meeting, any required approval of the shareholders of OJM is not obtained ("a Shareholder Termination"), (ii) the Merger has not been consummated on or before August 31, 1997, unless a failure to consummate the Merger is the result of a willful and material breach of the Merger Agreement by the party seeking to terminate the Merger Agreement (provided, however, that the passage of such period will be tolled for any part thereof (but in no event more than an additional three months) during which any party is subject to a nonfinal order, decree, ruling, or action restraining, enjoining, or otherwise prohibiting the consummation of the Merger or the calling or holding of the Special Meeting), (iii) any governmental entity has issued an order, decree, or ruling or taken any other action permanently enjoining, restraining, or otherwise prohibiting the Merger and such order, decree, ruling, or other action has become final and nonappealable, or (iv) prior to the Effective Time, the Code is amended so as to alter in any materially adverse respect any of the tax consequences prescribed by the Private Letter Ruling or Tax Opinions; (c) by Pantheon (a "Pantheon Special Termination") if (i) the OJM Board withdraws, or modifies or changes, in a manner adverse to Pantheon, its approval or recommendation of the Merger or the other transactions contemplated by the Merger Agreement and the Ancillary Agreements or recommends another offer or proposal with respect to a Third Party Acquisition, or (ii) a Third Party Acquisition has occurred or any person has entered into a definitive agreement with OJM with respect to a Third Party Acquisition; or (d) by OJM (an "OJM Special Termination") if (i) the OJM Board fails to recommend to its shareholders the approval of the transactions contemplated by the Merger Agreement, or withdraws, modifies, or changes such recommendation, in a manner permitted by the Merger Agreement, or (ii) OJM enters into an agreement with respect to a Higher Offer in a manner permitted by the Merger Agreement.

And not this:

5.3 **Termination.** The Merger Agreement may be terminated in four ways:

(A) Pantheon and OJM may, by mutual consent, agree in writing to terminate.

(B) If any of the following occurs, either Pantheon or OJM may terminate:

(1) if, upon a vote at the Special Meeting, OJM's shareholders do not approve the merger;

(2) if the merger has not been consummated by August 31, 1997, unless the failure to consummate results from a willful and material breach of the Merger Agreement by the party seeking to terminate; if, however, a party is subject to a temporary order prohibiting the consummation of the merger or the holding of the Special Meeting, the time is extended for up to three months;

(3) if a governmental entity has issued an order or taken any other action permanently prohibiting the merger—and the order or action has become final and nonappealable; or

(4) if, before the effective date of the merger, the Tax Code is amended in a way that alters in a materially adverse way any tax consequence prescribed by the private letter ruling or tax opinions.

(C) Pantheon may terminate if:

(1) the OJM Board withdraws or changes, in a manner adverse to Pantheon, its approval or recommendation of the merger or any other transaction contemplated by the Merger Agreement or any ancillary agreement or recommends another third-party acquisition; or

(2) a third-party acquisition has occurred or any person has entered into a definitive agreement with OJM with respect to a third-party acquisition.

(D) OJM may terminate if:

(1) the OJM Board fails to recommend that its shareholders approve any transaction contemplated by the Merger Agreement, or withdraws or changes the recommendation in a manner permitted by the Merger Agreement; or

(2) OJM agrees to a higher offer in a manner permitted by the Merger Agreement.

But this:

5.3 **Termination.** The merger agreement may be terminated in four ways:

(A) Pantheon and OJM may, by mutual consent, agree in writing to terminate.

(B) If any of the following occurs, either Pantheon or OJM may terminate:

(1) if, upon a vote at the special meeting, OJM's shareholders do not approve the merger;

(2) if the merger has not been consummated by August 31, 1997, unless the failure to consummate results from a willful and material breach of the merger agreement by the party seeking to terminate; if, however, a party is subject to a temporary order prohibiting the consummation of the merger or the holding of the special meeting, the time is extended for up to three months;

(3) if a governmental entity has issued an order or taken any other action permanently prohibiting the merger—and the order or action has become final and nonappealable; or

(4) if, before the effective date of the merger, the Tax Code is amended in a way that alters in a materially adverse way any tax consequence prescribed by the private letter ruling or tax opinions.

(C) Pantheon may terminate if:

(1) the OJM board withdraws or changes, in a manner adverse to Pantheon, its approval or recommendation of the merger or any other transaction contemplated by the merger agreement or any ancillary agreement or recommends another third-party acquisition; or

(2) a third-party acquisition has occurred or any person has entered into a definitive agreement with OJM with respect to a third-party acquisition.

(D) OJM may terminate if:

(1) the OJM board fails to recommend that its shareholders approve any transaction contemplated by the merger agreement, or withdraws or changes the recommendation in a manner permitted by the merger agreement; or

(2) OJM agrees to a higher offer in a manner permitted by the merger agreement.

Example B

Not this:

> *Termination Fees Payable by Pantheon.* The Merger Agreement obligates Pantheon to pay to OJM an Initial Termination Fee if (a) (i) OJM terminates the Merger Agreement because of either a Withdrawal by Pantheon or Pantheon's failure to comply (and to cure such noncompliance within 30 days' notice of the same) with certain Merger Agreement covenants relating to the holding of a stockholders' meeting, the solicitation of proxies with respect to the Pantheon Proposal, and the filing of certain documents with the Secretary of State of the State of Delaware, (ii) Pantheon terminates the Merger Agreement prior to the approval of the Pantheon Proposal by the Pantheon stockholders, upon Pantheon having received an Acquisition Proposal and the Pantheon Board having concluded that its fiduciary obligations under applicable law require that such Acquisition Proposal be accepted, or (iii) either party terminates the Merger Agreement because of the failure of Pantheon to obtain stockholder approval for the Merger Agreement and the transactions contemplated thereby at a duly held stockholders' meeting, and (b) at the time of such termination or prior to the meeting of the Pantheon stockholders there has been an Acquisition Proposal involving Pantheon or certain of its significant subsidiaries (whether or not such offer has been rejected or withdrawn prior to the time of such termination or of the meeting).

And not this:

> 5.4 *Termination Fees Payable by Pantheon.* The Merger Agreement obligates Pantheon to pay to OJM an initial termination fee of $250 million if both of the following conditions are met:
>
> (A) any of the following occurs:
>
> (1) OJM terminates the Merger Agreement because Pantheon's board withdraws its support of the merger or because Pantheon fails to comply (and fails to properly cure its noncompliance within 30 days of receiving notice) with its Merger-Agreement covenants relating to the holding of a stockholders' meeting, the solicitation of proxies on the Pantheon proposal, and the filing of certain documents with the Secretary of State of the State of Delaware;
>
> (2) Pantheon terminates the Merger Agreement before the Pantheon stockholders approve the Pantheon proposal, upon Pantheon's having received a business-combination offer involving at least 15% of Pantheon's stock and the Pantheon board's having concluded that its fiduciary obligations under applicable law require acceptance of that proposal; or
>
> (3) either party terminates the Merger Agreement on grounds that Pantheon has failed to obtain stockholder approval for the Merger Agreement and the related transactions at a duly held stockholders' meeting; and

(B) at the time of the termination or before the meeting of the Pantheon stockholders there has been a business-combination offer involving at least 15% of Pantheon's stock or that of its significant subsidiaries (whether or not the offer has been rejected or withdrawn before the termination or the meeting).

But this:

5.4 **Termination Fees Payable by Pantheon.** The merger agreement obligates Pantheon to pay to OJM an initial termination fee of $250 million if both of the following conditions are met:

(A) any of the following occurs:

(1) OJM terminates the merger agreement because Pantheon's board withdraws its support of the merger or because Pantheon fails to comply (and fails to properly cure its noncompliance within 30 days of receiving notice) with its merger-agreement covenants relating to the holding of a stockholders' meeting, the solicitation of proxies on the Pantheon proposal, and the filing of certain documents with the Secretary of State of the State of Delaware;

(2) Pantheon terminates the merger agreement before the Pantheon stockholders approve the Pantheon proposal, upon Pantheon's having received a business-combination offer involving at least 15% of Pantheon's stock and the Pantheon board's having concluded that its fiduciary obligations under applicable law require acceptance of that proposal; or

(3) either party terminates the merger agreement on grounds that Pantheon has failed to obtain stockholder approval for the merger agreement and the related transactions at a duly held stockholders' meeting; and

(B) at the time of the termination or before the meeting of the Pantheon stockholders there has been a business-combination offer involving at least 15% of Pantheon's stock or that of its significant subsidiaries (whether or not the offer has been rejected or withdrawn before the termination or the meeting).

§ 10 Put the whole document in plain English.

The SEC rules tell you that only the front and back cover pages, the summary, and the risk-factors section of a prospectus have to be in plain English.[7] But they also tell you that the entire document must be "clear, concise, and understandable."[8] You're best advised to treat this as a distinction without a difference. And in any event, you'll be writing much better if you'll simply make plain English your regular habit. So use it throughout the document.

endnotes

[1] One view is that it had become something of a game to write disclosure documents that obscured sensitive areas while not running afoul of the "buried-facts doctrine." *See Gould v. American Hawaiian Steamship Co.*, 331 F. Supp. 981 (D. Del. 1971); *Kohn v. American Metal Climax, Inc.*, 322 F. Supp. 1331 (E.D. Pa. 1970), *modified*, 458 F.2d 255 (3d Cir. 1972).

[2] *Plain English Disclosures*, Securities Act Release No. 7497, Exchange Act Release No. 39593, and Investment Company Act Release No. 23011, Fed. Sec. L. Rep. (CCH) ¶ 86,003, at 80,125, 80,132 (Jan. 28, 1998).

[3] *See id.*; *see also* Joseph Kimble, *Lawyers Need to Learn the Elements*, Nat'l L.J., Nov. 10, 1997, at A21 (describing the potential-liability argument as "a strange argument").

[4] *See Plain English Disclosures*, Fed. Sec. L. Rep. (CCH) ¶ 86,003, at 80,133.

[5] *See Plain English Disclosures*, Fed. Sec. L. Rep. (CCH) ¶ 86,003, at 80,127 (citing as a poor convention the use of "complex information copied directly from legal documents without any clear and concise explanation"); Thomas M. Clyde, *Plain English Turns the Corner: New SEC Rules for Prospectuses*, Clarity, Sept. 1998, at 9, 11 ("Prospectuses have typically just quoted significant provisions of underlying documents word for word, rather than making an effort to paraphrase and clarify them.").

[6] John Rothchild, *The War on Gobbledygook*, Time, Oct. 31, 1994, at 51.

[7] Rule 421(d)(1), 17 C.F.R. § 230.421 (1998), Fed. Sec. L. Rep. (CCH) ¶ 4265.

[8] Rule 421(b).

Audience 2

§ 11 Reject the idea that you're drafting principally for specialists.

Granted, it's probably a fiction to think that Grandma Jones (an unsophisticated investor) needs to read and understand your document. It's also a fiction to think that people can read and understand the statutes governing their conduct. Indeed, it's probably a fiction to think that even legislators can read and understand most of the statutes they pass.

That's the way of the world. No one but a tax lawyer can fathom the Internal Revenue Code. No one but an employee-benefits specialist can read and understand ERISA. No one but a bankruptcy specialist can read and understand the Bankruptcy Code. And no one but a corporate lawyer or an accountant needs to be able to read and understand your disclosure document. Right?

Wrong. The Internal Revenue Code, ERISA, and the Bankruptcy Code are drafting nightmares. To the true expert in drafting, they're abominations.

The point about widening your intended audience is that you'll draft better. It's a fiction, yes, that Grandma Jones should be able to read and understand your document. But it's a useful fiction. It will help you simplify as much as you possibly can. And if you do that, even specialists will be able to grasp your meaning more quickly.

§ 12 Use first-person pronouns (*we, our*) and second-person pronouns (*you, your*) whenever you can.

First- and second-person pronouns are personal words. They add human interest. With their friendly tone, they pull readers into the document. And in technical writing, that's especially important. Rudolf Flesch, a leading figure in plain-English circles, was one of the first to explain the need for *you*:

> Keep a running conversation with your reader. Use the second-person pronoun whenever you can. Translate everything into *you* language. *This applies to citizens over 65 = if you're over 65, this applies to you. It must be remembered that = you must remember. Many people don't realize = perhaps you don't realize*. Always write directly to *you*, the person you're trying to reach with your written message. Don't write in mental isolation; reach out to your reader.[1]

Likewise, the words *we* and *our*—in reference to your client—make corporations and other legal entities sound as if they have genuine personalities (as they typically do). Businesspeople usually appreciate this down-to-earth approach over the sterile, distancing effect of third-person prose.

Example A

Not this:	*But this:*
Whether or not *a stockholder* plans to attend a meeting, *he or she* should take the time to vote by completing and mailing the enclosed proxy card to *the Company*. If *a stockholder* signs, dates, and mails a proxy card without indicating how *he or she* wants to vote, *that stockholder's* proxy will be counted as a vote in favor of the merger. If *a stockholder* fails to return a proxy card, the effect in most cases will be a vote against the merger.	Whether or not *you* plan to attend a meeting, please take the time to vote by completing and mailing the enclosed proxy card to *us*. If *you* sign, date, and mail *your* proxy card without indicating how *you* want to vote, *your* proxy will count as a vote in favor of the merger. If *you* don't return your card, in most cases *you'll* be counted as voting against the merger.

Example B

Not this:	*But this:*
Many of *the company's* competitors and potential competitors have substantially greater resources, manufacturing and marketing capabilities, research and development staff, and production facilities than those of *the company*.	Many of *our* competitors have substantially greater resources, manufacturing and marketing capabilities, research-and-development staff, and production facilities than *we* do.

§ 13 Use contractions as you would in conversation.

Legal writers have developed a morbid fear of contractions. Maybe that's because they tend to counteract stuffiness—and legal writers everywhere tend to think they should sound stuffy. That's a major psychological cause of poor writing.

In fact, the more conversational your style is, the more readable it becomes. This doesn't mean that you should become loose and slangy in your writing—just that you should try to be relaxed and natural. And contractions contribute a lot to that effect.

Here's the test. If you would say it as a contraction, write it that way. If you wouldn't, then don't.

Example A

Not this:	*But this:*
Since most brokers *do not* participate in our advance ticket plan, tell your broker that you plan to attend the meeting and that you would like a proxy. Then simply bring that form to the meeting and *we will* give you a ticket at the door. If you *cannot* obtain a proxy in time, *we will* still give you a ticket at the door if you bring a copy of your most recent brokerage account statement showing that you own Pantheon stock.	Since most brokers *don't* participate in our advance ticket plan, tell your broker that you plan to attend the meeting and that you would like a proxy. Then simply bring that form to the meeting and *we'll* give you a ticket at the door. If you *can't* get a proxy in time, *we'll* still give you a ticket at the door if you bring a copy of your most recent brokerage account statement showing that you own Pantheon stock.

Example B

Not this:	*But this:*
You should rely only on the information incorporated by reference or provided in this prospectus or any supplement. We *have not* authorized anyone else to provide you with different information. We *are not* making an offer of these notes in any state where the offer *is not* allowed. You *should not* assume that the information in this prospectus or any supplement is accurate as of any date other than the date on the front of those documents.	You should rely only on the information incorporated by reference or provided in this prospectus or any supplement. We *haven't* authorized anyone else to provide you with different information. We *aren't* offering these notes in any state where the offer *isn't* allowed. You *shouldn't* assume that the information in this prospectus or any supplement is accurate as of any date other than the date on the front of those documents.

§ 14 Reword needlessly abstract passages.

Excessive abstractness is a prime cause of unreadable gobbledygook. The problem is that abstract words don't immediately bring anything to the reader's mind: they're imageless—nonvisual.

Good writing, though, is specific and visual. It quickly evokes images in the reader's mind. Things don't just occur. People do things, and you can tell who is doing what.

Example A

Not this:	*But this:*
In addition, during this period, Fynatel's management undertook a comprehensive strategic and financial evaluation and analysis of Borzier Insurance's business which was substantially completed in early 1998.	During this period, our managers thoroughly evaluated Borzier Insurance's business. They substantially completed their work in early 1998.

Example B

Not this:	*But this:*
The shares of OJM stock issued to Pantheon stockholders in the merger will constitute a significant proportion of the outstanding stock of OJM after the merger. Based on this significant proportion, it is expected that OJM will issue millions of OJM shares to Pantheon stockholders in the merger.	We expect that OJM will issue about 320 million shares of its stock to Pantheon shareholders in the merger. That figure will account for about 42% of OJM's outstanding stock after the merger.

endnotes

1 Rudolf Flesch, *How to Be Brief: An Index to Simple Writing* 114 (1962).

Process 3

§ 15 When using forms, be the master—not the slave.

Forms are handy. But they're dangerous when they fall into the wrong hands. They can stifle thought.

Any seasoned securities-law practitioner can recount small horror stories about disclosure documents discussing things that weren't even part of the company's business in passages that were simply remnants of earlier deals. When formbooks become too great a crutch, that's the inevitable consequence.

There's also the story—not at all apocryphal, but it's better not to name names—about the New York firm that got sued for malpractice because a secretary had inadvertently deleted a paragraph from a form contract and the lawyers hadn't caught it. The appalling thing, though, was that the secretary had done this in the early 1970s, and the mistake wasn't caught until the late 1990s. During the interim, the firm had prepared *hundreds* of documents with the selfsame error in it. The mindset apparently was, "Oh, that's just our usual form. No need to second-guess what's been working well for so long."

But second-guessing is necessary. Second-guess your forms, both from a legal standpoint and from a plain-English standpoint. Then you'll master them.

§ 16 Test a document by seeing how readily a small group of non-corporate lawyers can find the answers to common shareholder questions. Invite criticism from the participants.

Many lawyers are dubious about testing, but it's the ultimate determiner of whether your documents actually accomplish what you and your clients want them to. It can tell you which of two competing formats is better, which of two organizational approaches is sounder, what passages are most likely to trip up readers, and any number of other things.

For corporate clients, testing is fairly easy. Assemble a group of people who own stock in other companies but who don't know your client's business. Pay them a fee, if you like. Once you have a group of five or more, all you need to do is prepare carefully.

Here's how it works. Begin by tailoring your focus-group questions to the deal you're working on. If it's an IPO proxy, ask questions like these:

- What's the business? What are the main products?

- What's the company's financial history? What kind of growth patterns has it had?

- What kind of experience do the people running the company have? How much stock do they have in the company?

If it's a merger proposal, ask questions like these:

- What are the two businesses? Will they fit together well?
- What have the companies done to ensure that they'll be maximizing shareholder value?
- Who's going to be running the new company?

If it's a mutual-fund prospectus, ask questions like these:

- What type of fund is it?
- What's the fund's investment strategy? What's the primary focus?
- What's the history of the fund? What kind of performance has it had in the past? Who are the people doing the investing, and what's their track record?
- What's the cost?

Be specific. Go beyond these questions to even more particular ones that may occur to moderately sophisticated investors.

Then prepare a questionnaire posing these questions in a way that will elicit specific answers.

When you convene the focus group, explain to the participants that you're *not* testing them, but that you're testing how effective the document is. Tell them that you're operating on the principle that good writing makes readers feel smart, while bad writing makes readers feel stupid. If any of them feel stupid when searching for answers to your queries, that's not their fault. It's the fault of the writing. Tell them that the entire purpose of the exercise is to find out which parts of the document make readers feel stupid—so that you can improve it.

Make it a timed exercise. Give them 20 minutes to answer 10 right-or-wrong questions on a questionnaire. After 20 minutes, ask them to stop their work. Then ask them to discuss their impressions of the document. You'll be surprised at how illuminating the process will be. After you've gotten some general observations, ask the participants to pinpoint where they found the answers to each of the questions—and precisely what the answers were. If some went astray, find out why. This will suggest immediate edits that you can easily carry out.

You'll have asked two types of questions: impressionistic and right-or-wrong. Discuss the impressionistic ones. Use a questionnaire for the right-or-wrong ones. For those questions, don't ever expect to get 100% correct answers. That's impossible. You simply want to get as close as you can—and sometimes that may be only 85%, or even 65%.

There are more sophisticated kinds of testing—like asking readers to paraphrase some central parts of the document. Obviously, this will take more time and effort, but it can be more revealing than right-or-wrong questions and may be worth the extra effort on especially important documents.

In any event, be forewarned. Some of your colleagues will resist the idea of any kind of testing. They'll call it a colossal waste of time and money. They'll do whatever they can to dissuade you from carrying out the exercise. But once it's underway, they'll come around. Very likely, they'll be chewing their nails while the participants are reading. Once the participants begin talking about their responses, it will become apparent just how useful focus groups can be. You'll just have to work hard to overcome the initial opposition.

§ 17 Make every effort to involve a professional editor other than the initial drafter.

It's important to invite criticism—to overcome pride of authorship. But more than that, you should consider engaging a professional editor. Get a good one—someone who teaches advanced expository writing or who has graced the masthead of a major publication. Don't assume that just anyone with a degree in English knows how to write well. (That's a coin flip at best.) Instead, find someone with good, practical experience as an editor.

Then, when your editor doesn't understand the document, don't simply assume that you got the wrong person. The editor's not understanding the document—or its purpose—is a symptom that the document has some glaring deficiencies. The editor should be able to work through them.

Heed the editor's comments and recommendations. At least 75% of them should be worthwhile if you succeeded in getting a good one.

§ 18 Consider engaging a specialist in typography and design.

Legal writers know so little about this field that they don't even know that such a field exists. And even some who know about it remain impervious to its importance.

But the SEC staffers know better. In the plain-English pilot program, they repeatedly underscored the importance of page layout and typefaces. And although most of the documents in the pilot program ended up being passable, very few had a truly top-notch look.

Still, those documents looked a lot better than the old-style versions. The new-style documents show what a dramatic effect designers can have, as you'll see in the following examples.

But don't assume that the cover page is the only place where a designer comes in. A good one can steer you through problems with graphs, pictures, and the like in various parts of the document—as well as with changes in typography as they're needed throughout.

Example A

Not this:

BIEFT Corporation
Debt Securities • Preferred Stock • Depositary Shares
Common Stock • Warrants

Information contained herein is subject to completion or amendment. A registration statement relating to these securities has been filed with the Securities and Exchange Commission. These Securities may not be sold nor may offers to buy be accepted prior to the time the registration statement becomes effective. This prospectus supplement shall not constitute an offer to sell or the solicitation of an offer to buy, nor shall there be any sale of these securities in any State in which such offer, or solicitation of sale would be unlawful prior to registration or qualification under the securities laws of any State.

BIEFT Corporation ("BIEFT" or the "Company"), a Nevada corporation, may offer from time to time (a) debt securities ("Debt Securities"), which may be subordinated to other indebtedness of the Company, (b) warrants to purchase Debt Securities ("Debt Warrants"), (c) shares of preferred stock (Preferred Stock"), (d) warrants to purchase shares of Preferred Stock ("Preferred Stock Warrants"), (e) depositary shares representing entitlement to all rights and preferences of a fraction of a share of Preferred Stock of a specified series ("Depositary Shares"), (f) shares of common stock, no par value per share ("Common Stock"), or (g) warrants to purchase shares of Common Stock ("Common Stock Warrants"), all having an aggregate initial public offering price not to exceed $815,541,250 or the equivalent thereof in one or more foreign currencies, foreign currency units, or composite currencies, including European Currency Units. The Debt Warrants, Preferred Stock Warrants and Common Stock Warrants are referred to herein collectively as "Warrants," and the Debt Securities, Preferred Stock, Depositary Shares, Common Stock and Warrants are referred to herein collectively as the "Offered Securities." The Offered Securities may be offered, separately or as units with other Offered Securities, in separate series and in amounts, at prices, and on terms to be determined at or prior to the time of sale.

The Company, formerly a wholly-owned subsidiary of a Delaware corporation known as BIEFT Corporation ("Old BIEFT"), has succeeded to the hospitality, entertainment, gaming and information services businesses previously conducted by Old BIEFT. On December 19, 1995, Old BIEFT distributed to its shareholders all of the then outstanding shares of the Common Stock. The Offered Securities will not represent an ownership interest in Old BIEFT. The Company is no longer affiliated with BIEFT Industries, Inc. or BIEFT Hartford Group, Inc.

The specific terms of the Offered Securities with respect to which this Prospectus is being delivered will be set forth in an accompanying supplement to this Prospectus (a "Prospectus Supplement"), together with the terms of the offering of the Offered Securities and the initial price and the net proceeds to the Company from the sale thereof. The Prospectus Supplement will include, with regard to the particular Offered Securities, the following information: (a) in the case of Debt Securities, the specific designation, aggregate principal amount, ranking, authorized denomination, maturity, rate or method of calculation of interest, if any, and dates for payment thereof, any exchangeability, conversion, redemption, prepayment, or sinking fund provisions, the currency or currency unit in which principal, premium or interest is payable, the designation of the trustee acting under the applicable indenture, and the initial offering price; (b) in the case of Preferred Stock, the designation, number of shares, liquidation preference per share, initial public offering price, dividend rate (or method of calculation thereof), dates on which dividends shall be payable and dates from which dividends shall accrue, any redemption or sinking fund provisions, any conversion or exchange rights, and whether the Company has elected to offer the Preferred Stock in the form of Depositary Shares; (c) in the case of Common Stock, the number of shares and the terms of the offering and sale thereof; (d) in the case of Warrants, the number and terms thereof, the designation and the number of securities issuable upon exercise, the exercise price, the terms of the offering and sale thereof, and where applicable the duration and detachability thereof; and (e) in the case of all Offered Securities, whether such Offered Securities will be offered separately or as a unit with other Offered Securities. The Prospectus Supplement will also contain information, where applicable, about material United States federal income tax considerations relating to, and any listing on a securities exchange of, the Offered Securities covered by such Prospectus Supplement.

The Company may sell the Offered Securities directly, through agents designated from time to time, or through underwriters or dealers. If any agents, underwriters, or dealers are involved in the sale of the Offered Securities, the names of such agents, underwriters or dealers and any applicable commission or discounts and the net proceeds to the Company from such sale will be set forth in the applicable Prospectus Supplement.

This Prospectus may not be used to consummate sales or Offered Securities unless accompanied by a Prospectus Supplement.

THESE SECURITIES HAVE NOT BEEN APPROVED OR DISAPPROVED BY THE SECURITIES AND EXCHANGE COMMISSION OR ANY STATE SECURITIES COMMISSION. NOR HAS THE SECURITIES AND EXCHANGE COMMISSION OR ANY STATE SECURITIES COMMISSION PASSED UPON THE ACCURACY OR ADEQUACY OF THIS PROSPECTUS. ANY REPRESENTATION TO THE CONTRARY IS A CRIMINAL OFFENSE. NONE OF THE NEVADA STATE GAMING CONTROL BOARD, THE NEVADA GAMING COMMISSION, THE MISSISSIPPI GAMING COMMISSION, THE NEW JERSEY CASINO CONTROL COMMISSION OR THE INDIANA GAMING COMMISSION HAS PASSED UPON THE ACCURACY OR ADEQUACY OF THIS PROSPECTUS OR THE INVESTMENT MERITS OF THE SECURITIES OFFERED HEREBY. ANY REPRESENTATION TO THE CONTRARY IS UNLAWFUL.

The date of this Prospectus is January 12, 1998

But this:

BIEFT CORPORATION

By this prospectus, we may offer—

DEBT SECURITIES
PREFERRED STOCK
DEPOSITARY SHARES
COMMON STOCK
WARRANTS

We will provide the specific terms of these securities in supplements to this prospectus. You should read this prospectus and the supplements carefully before you invest.

BIEFT Corporation

includes—

BIEFT Altshaft Corporation
Klagenfurt International, Inc.
Pavilion Worthersee, Inc.
Wasserspiel Garden, L.P.
BIEFT Communications Services, Inc.
BIEFT World Inventories, Inc.

These securities have not been approved by the SEC, state securities commissions, Nevada State Gaming Control Board, Nevada Gaming Commission, New Jersey Casino Control Commission, Mississippi Gaming Commission, or Indiana Gaming Commission.

None of these organizations has determined that this prospectus is accurate or complete. It's illegal for anyone to tell you otherwise.

January 12, 1998

Example B

Not this:

PROSPECTUS

PBRC Master Credit Card Trust II

Asset Backed Certificates

PBRC America Bank, National Association

Seller and Servicer

The Asset Backed Certificates (collectively, the "Certificates") described herein may be sold from time to time in one or more series (each, a "Series"), in amounts, at price and off terms to be determined at the time of sale and to be set forth in a supplement to this Prospectus (a "Prospectus Supplement"). The Certificates of each Series will represent an undivided interest in PBRC Master Credit Card Trust II (the "Trust"). The Trust has been formed pursuant to a pooling and servicing agreement between PBRC America Bank, National Association ("PBRC"), as seller and servicer, and The Bank of New York, as trustee. The property of the Trust will include receivables (the "Receivables") generated from time to time in a portfolio of consumer revolving credit card accounts (the "Accounts"), all monies due in payment of the Receivables and certain other property, as more fully described herein and, with respect to any Series, in the related Prospectus Supplement. PBRC initially will own the remaining undivided interest in the Trust not represented by the Certificates issued by the Trust and will service the Receivables.

Each Series will consist of one or more classes of Certificates (each, a "Class"), one or more of which may be fixed rate Certificates, floating rate Certificates or other type of Certificates, as specified in the related Prospectus Supplement. Each Certificate will represent an undivided interest in the Trust and the interest of the Certificateholders of each Class or Series will include the right to receive a varying percentage of each month's collections with respect to the Receivables of the Trust at the times, in the manner and to the extent described herein and, with respect to any Series offered hereby, in the related Prospectus Supplement, interest and principal payments with respect to each Series offered hereby will be made as specified in the related Prospectus Supplement. One or more Classes of a Series offered hereby may be entitled to the benefits of a cash collateral account or guaranty, a collateral interest, a letter of credit, a surety bond, an insurance policy or other form of enhancement as specified in the Prospectus Supplement relating to such Series. In addition, any Series offered hereby may include one or more Classes which are subordinated in right and priority to payment of principal of, and/or interest on, one or more other Classes of such Series or another Series in each case to the extent described in the related Prospectus Supplement. Each Series of Certificates or Class thereof offered hereby will be rated in one of the four highest rating categories by at least one nationally recognized rating organization.

While the specific terms of any Series in respect of which this Prospectus is being delivered will be described in the related Prospectus Supplement, the terms of such Series will not be subject to prior review by, or consent of, the Certificateholders of any previously issued Series.

Potential investors should consider, among other things, the information set forth in "Risk Factors" beginning on page 19 herein.

THE CERTIFICATES WILL REPRESENT INTERESTS IN THE TRUST ONLY AND WILL NOT REPRESENT INTERESTS IN OR OBLIGATIONS OF PBRC AMERICA BANK, NATIONAL ASSOCIATION OR ANY AFFILIATE THEREOF. A CERTIFICATE IS NOT A DEPOSIT AND NEITHER THE CERTIFICATES NOR THE UNDERLYING ACCOUNTS OR RECEIVABLES ARE INSURED OR GUARANTEED BY THE FEDERAL DEPOSIT INSURANCE CORPORATION OR ANY OTHER GOVERNMENTAL AGENCY.

THESE SECURITIES HAVE NOT BEEN APPROVED OR DISAPPROVED BY THE SECURITIES AND EXCHANGE COMMISSION OR ANY STATE SECURITIES COMMISSION NOR HAS THE COMMISSION OR ANY STATE SECURITIES COMMISSION PASSED UPON THE ACCURACY OR ADEQUACY OF THIS PROSPECTUS. ANY REPRESENTATION TO THE CONTRARY IS A CRIMINAL OFFENSE.

Certificates may be sold by PBRC directly to purchasers, through agents designated from time to time, through underwriting syndicates led by one or more managing underwriters or through one or more underwriters acting alone. If underwriters or agents are involved in the offering of the Certificates of any Series offered hereby, the name of the managing underwriter or underwriters or agents will be set forth in the related Prospectus Supplement. If an underwriter, agent or dealer is involved in the offering of the Certificates of any Series offered hereby, the underwriter's discount, agent's commission or dealer's purchase price will be set forth in, or may be calculated from, the related Prospectus Supplement, and the net proceeds to PBRC from such offering will be the public offering price of such Certificates less such discount in the case of an underwriter, the purchase price of such Certificates less such commission in the case of an agent or the purchase price of such Certificates in the case of a dealer, and less, in each case, the other expenses of USNA associated with the issuance and distribution of such Certificates. See "Plan of Distribution."

This Prospectus may not be used to consummate sales of any Series of Certificates unless accompanied by the related Prospectus Supplement.

The date of this Prospectus is September 6, 1999.

But this:

Prospectus

PBRC Master Credit Card Trust II
Issuer

PBRC America Bank, National Association
Seller and Servicer

Asset-Backed Certificates

Look carefully at the risk factors beginning on page 10 of this prospectus.

A certificate is not a deposit, and neither the certificates nor the underlying accounts or receivables are insured or guaranteed by the Federal Deposit Insurance Corporation or any other governmental agency.

The certificates will represent interests in the trust only and will not represent interests in or obligations of PBRC or any PBRC affiliate.

This prospectus may be used to offer and sell any series of certificates only if accompanied by the prospectus supplement for that series.

The Trust—

- will be able to periodically issue asset-backed certificates in one or more series with one or more classes; and
- will own—
  - receivables in a portfolio of consumer revolving credit-card accounts;
  - payments due on those receivables; and
  - other property described in this prospectus and in the accompanying prospectus supplement.

The Certificates offered with this prospectus—

- will represent interests in the trust and will be paid only from the trust assets;
- will be rated in one of the four highest rating categories by at least one nationally recognized rating organization;
- may have one or more forms of enhancement; and
- will be issued as part of a designated series that may include one or more classes of certificates and enhancement.

The Certificateholders—

- will receive interest and principal payments from a varying percentage of credit-card-account collections.

Neither the SEC nor any state securities commission has approved these certificates or determined that this prospectus is accurate or complete. It's illegal for anyone to tell you otherwise.

September 6, 1999

§ 19 Don't defend bad writing by citing hourly rates.

If someone suggests an edit to something you've written, second-guess yourself—especially if that person happens to be an SEC staffer. When conducting training sessions for the lawyers and accountants at the SEC, I repeatedly heard the same story. It went like this. An SEC staffer would suggest a clarification in a disclosure document. A Wall Street lawyer would balk. The SEC staffer would persist. The Wall Street lawyer would then say: "Look, how much money do you make in a year? I make $900 an hour. And you think you can tell me how to do these documents?"

The lawyers who do this, of course, need even more help in human relations than they need in writing.

But the point for writers is that we must listen to how people react to the writing. If a sentence can be read in two ways, it will be. (In law, this is never a good thing.) If there are miscues in the text, some readers will go astray. If awkward phrases lurk in your sentences, some readers will stumble. All these things need straightening out. And you should welcome help from all quarters—whether it's a partner, an SEC staffer, a first-year associate, a secretary, or a high-school student.

Improving your writing means cultivating some humility.

Wording Guidelines 4

§ 20 Prefer the familiar word to the unfamiliar. Avoid legalese.

Some legalisms, of course, you'll need. If you're dealing with debentures, you're not going to be helping matters by avoiding the word *debentures*. But don't go whole hog with legalese. Sensitize yourself to the fancy but easily simplifiable legalisms that pervade most legal writing. These are the truly off-putting phrases that make ordinary people resent lawyers' writing.

This is a serious matter. In a state-bar survey in the late 1980s, California residents were asked what they cared most about in reforming the legal profession. The number-one answer had nothing to do with containing legal fees or providing legal services to the poor. The number-one answer was that legal documents need simplifying. This is an issue that affects ordinary people—all of them.

And although the profession as a whole has been slow in getting the message, the better lawyer-writers understand it well:

- "Attitudes need to change more than rules of composition need to be memorized. Lawyers must be convinced that there is no purpose, or value, in sounding archaic. This is a tall order. It will take an emotional, almost psychological, pitch to teach many attorneys that there is nothing wrong with sounding like a citizen of the second half of the 20th century. You are no less a lawyer for being understandable."—Christopher T. Lutz[1]

- "For a hundred years, good lawyers have been writing without all the garbage and in a simple, direct style."—Judge Lynn N. Hughes[2]

- "I am particularly careful to avoid jargon, and to write simply and clearly. For certain types of writing a high level of technicality is unavoidable; but in general it is the second-rate intellect that cultivates a pretentious vocabulary and a solemn and portentous style."—Judge Richard A. Posner[3]

- "The idea is to avoid any word that does not command instant understanding. Your words should be transparent vehicles that let the reader see your ideas without straining to grasp the meaning. . . . Most of the concepts you struggled to master in law school can be grasped by the average 12-year-old. It is the vocabulary training that makes it such a drudgery."—James W. McElhaney[4]

It's hardly an exaggeration to say that once you learn to write without unnecessary legalese, you'll be a better lawyer.

A List of Don'ts and Dos

Instead of:	*Say:*
as regards	about; concerning
at the present time	now
due to the fact that	because; since
during such time as	while
for a period of	for
for the duration of	during
inasmuch as	because; since
in the event that	if
notwithstanding	despite; regardless of
notwithstanding the fact that	although; even if
prior to	before
pursuant to	under; in accordance with
set forth	explain
subsequent	future; later
subsequently	later
subsequent to	after
such [+ singular noun]	this; that; the
that certain	a [this actually works!]
such time as	until
when, as, and if	when; if
with reference to	about

Example A

Not this:	*But this:*
In the event of a default by an underwriter, the standby underwriting agreement provides that, with minor exceptions, purchase commitments of the nondefaulting underwriter may be increased or the agreement may be terminated.	If an underwriter defaults, the standby underwriting agreement generally allows the nondefaulting underwriter to increase its purchase commitments or terminate the agreement.

Example B

Not this:	*But this:*
In the event of the employee's death or involuntary termination prior to the tenth anniversary of the grant date, the repurchase rights of the granting corporation shall be deemed to have lapsed ratably over a five-year period commencing with the fifth anniversary of the grant date.	If the employee dies or is fired within ten years of the grant, the granting corporation's repurchase rights will be considered to have proportionally lapsed over a five-year period starting five years after the grant.

§ 21 Avoid unnatural idioms that typify legalistic writing.

Not just words, but also sentence structures, can strike readers as legalistic. Think of the phrasings that you'd never use except in legal writing:

is entitled to effect the transaction pursuant to
the greater of this and that
each of Bob, Jane, and Mary must do this
anything in this prospectus to the contrary notwithstanding

The first three of those phrases you can put into ordinary English. The fourth is a phrase you simply shouldn't need in a disclosure document.

It's not easy, of course, learning the plain-English equivalents of legalese. For the lawyer, it's like learning a new language. As Jacques Barzun once said, "Plain English is no one's mother tongue. It has to be worked for."[5] But once you get the knack of it, you'll come to detest woolly-minded legalisms.

Example A

Not this:	*But this:*
Each of Pantheon and the Pantheon subsidiaries has duly filed all federal, state, county, and foreign tax returns required to be filed by it.	*Pantheon, as well as each of its subsidiaries,* has filed all required federal, state, county, and foreign tax returns.

Example B

Not this:	*But this:*
The Pantheon reorganization will *be effected largely pursuant to* transactions described in the master separation agreement.	The Pantheon reorganization will *take place largely through* a series of transactions described in the master separation agreement.

§ 22 Replace the word *shall*.

Unless you're quoting something that absolutely has to be quoted, you can change every *shall*. You should probably do it in all your drafting—you'll be drafting better if you do—but it's imperative in disclosure documents.

Why? Three reasons.

First, *shall* isn't really a part of standard American English. It's not a word that Americans grow up using, except in extremely limited circumstances.[6] The word strikes most readers as legalistic.

Second, *shall* doesn't do its legal job very well because it's highly ambiguous. It can mean (1) "is required to," (2) "should," (3) "may," (4) "will," or (5) "is entitled to." (For a full discussion of the ambiguities that this word gives rise to, see the second edition of *A Dictionary of Modern Legal Usage*, under "Words of Authority.")

Third, even if you insist on *shall* to denote duties, disclosure documents that refer to contractual duties are merely describing them—as opposed to creating them. So *shall* isn't the best word anyway.

In the examples that follow, you'll see several easy improvements to passages plagued with *shall*.

Example A

Not this:	*But this:*
Other capitalized terms not otherwise defined herein *shall have* the meanings given to them in the accompanying Prospectus.	Other capitalized terms not otherwise defined in this supplement *have* the meanings given to them in the accompanying prospectus.

Example B

Not this:	*But this:*
Limited Partners participating in the Consolidation *shall* relinquish any rights that they might otherwise have had to receive cash distributions from their continuation as Limited Partners of the Partnership.	Limited partners who participate in the consolidation *will* relinquish any rights they might have had to receive cash distributions from continuing as limited partners.

Example C

Not this:	*But this:*
If any event *shall* occur or any matter *shall* be brought to the attention of the General Partner that, in its judgment, materially affects one or more of the Partnerships or the Consolidation, the General Partner *shall* have the right to terminate prior to consummation of the Consolidation, modify or amend the Consolidation in order to take such event or matter into account, to exclude any Partnership from the Exchange Offer, or to take such other action as may be appropriate.	If anything happens that the general partner believes might materially affect one or more of the partnerships or the consolidation, the general partner may take any appropriate action, such as terminating the consolidation, modifying it, or excluding a partnership from the exchange offer.

§ 23 For pointing words, use *this, that, these, those,* or *the* instead of *such* or *said.*

There is more balderdash afoot about the supposed preciseness of *such* and *said* than about any other drafting convention apart from definitions (see § 62). Neither *such* nor *said* adds precision, as legal scholars and commentators have long noted.[7] The danger is that these words, when used as demonstrative adjectives (for example, *such property, said Company*), make drafters think they're being precise when they really aren't. And the terms are pure legalese: you can always improve on them with ordinary words that are every bit as precise.

Example A

Not this:	*But this:*
Net sales of $485.6 million in fiscal 1998 increased $95.5 million or 24%, from $390.1 million in fiscal 1997. The increase in *said sales* was primarily due to Pantheon's operating results for the entire fiscal 1998 period.	Our net sales increased 24% from 1997 to 1998—from $390.1 million to $485.6 million. *This increase* was primarily due to our improved operating results for the entire fiscal 1998 period.

Example B

Not this:	*But this:*
These forward-looking statements may involve known and unknown risks, uncertainties, and other factors that may cause the actual results, performance, or achievements of the Company and the Operating Partnership to be materially different from future results, performance, or achievements expressed or implied by *such* forward-looking statements.	These forward-looking statements could involve known and unknown risks, uncertainties, and other factors that might materially alter the actual results suggested by the statements. In other words, the company's or operating partnership's performance might be quite different from what *the* forward-looking statements imply.

§ 24 Replace all *here-* and *there-* legalisms.

In the first place, using *here-* and *there-* words is quite a bad habit in all drafting—even contractual drafting—because most of these terms are ambiguous. For example, *herein*, the most frequent of the *here-* words, has been held to have several meanings: "in this subparagraph," "in this paragraph," "in this subsection," "in this section," "in this article," and "anywhere in this document."[8] The *here-* or *there-* always begs the question, in this or that what? You're better off saying *in this prospectus* or *in that agreement*.

In the second place, *here-* and *there-* words are pure legal jargon. They're easily simplifiable into unambiguous terms.

Example A

Not this:	*But this:*
The following summary is qualified in its entirety by the more detailed descriptions and the financial information and statements appearing elsewhere in this prospectus supplement and the prospectus or incorporated *herein* and *therein* by reference.	The following summary is qualified by the more detailed descriptions and the financial information and statements appearing elsewhere in this prospectus supplement or in the prospectus itself, or incorporated *into either document* by reference.

Example B

Not this:	*But this:*
Except as disclosed on Schedule 4 *hereto*, all the outstanding capital stock of each of Pantheon's subsidiaries is duly authorized, validly issued, fully paid, and nonassessable.	With the minor exceptions noted on *the attached* Schedule 4, all the outstanding capital stock of Pantheon's subsidiaries is duly authorized, validly issued, fully paid, and nonassessable.

§ 25 Shun *and/or*.

This Janus-faced term, though beloved of some drafters, is virtually always unnecessary. If you were to analyze transactional documents, you'd find that 75% of the *and/ors* should be *or* and that 25% should be *and*. Look at the true meaning of the sentence, and you'll see that *and/or* makes a hash of it.

Often *and/or* means *or*:

> While we are the largest distributor in this market, some of our competitors may have greater total financial, purchasing, *and/or* [read *or*] sourcing power than we do.

But sometimes it means *and*:

> The Technology Agreement provides that any party who is a sublicensee must obtain a written agreement from each of its employees, agents, officers, *and/or* [read *and*] directors that any Technical Information will not be disclosed to third parties.

And sometimes the way to fix the problem is simply to wake up your brain from the slumber that leads to this sort of nonsense:

> "Controlling interest" means the ownership of enough outstanding voting shares in an issuing corporation to enable the acquiring person to exercise (i) one-fifth or more but less than one-third, (ii) one-third or more but less than a majority, and/or (iii) a majority of the voting power of the issuing corporation in the election of directors.

Of course, all that's saying is this:

> "Controlling interest" means the ownership of enough outstanding voting shares in an issuing corporation to enable the acquiring person to exercise at least one-fifth of the corporation's voting power in an election of directors.

Maybe you'll find some close calls with *and/or*. But on reflection, you'll see that they're not so close. If you have a long list in which *and/or* appears between the two last items, try saying *any or all of the following* in the lead-in to the list.

§ 26 Avoid multiple negatives.

Who cannot unmisgivingly say that negatives are not lacking in unmistakability when used other than sparingly?

Whenever you can recast a negative statement as a positive one without changing the meaning, do it. You'll save readers from needless mental exertion.

Example A

Not this:	*But this:*
The exercise prices of those options are determined by the board of directors and *may not be less than* the greater of the fair market value or the nominal value of the underlying ordinary shares on the date of the grant.	The board of directors determines the exercise prices of those options. But the prices must be *at least* the fair market value or the nominal value of the underlying ordinary shares on the date of the grant—whichever amount is higher.

Example B

Not this:	*But this:*
No assurances can be given that future legislative or regulatory changes will not adversely affect the Company's business.	Future legislative or regulatory changes might adversely affect the company's business.

Example C

Not this:	*But this:*
There can be no assurance that a challenge to the merger on antitrust grounds will not be made or, if such a challenge is made, that the result will not be unfavorable.	The merger might be challenged on antitrust grounds. We can't predict the result of such a challenge.

endnotes

1 "Why Can't Lawyers Write?" in *Appellate Practice Manual* 167, 177 (Priscilla A. Schwab ed., 1992).

2 As quoted in Bryan A. Garner, *Judges on Effective Writing: The Importance of Plain Language*, 73 Mich. B.J. 326, 326 (1994).

3 *How I Write*, 4 Scribes J. Legal Writing 45, 49 (1993).

4 *Writing to the Ear*, ABA J., Dec. 1995, at 74, 76.

5 As quoted in Rudolf Flesch, *The Art of Readable Writing* 1 (1949; reprint 1974).

6 *See* Bryan A. Garner, *A Dictionary of Modern American Usage* 597–98 (1998); Garner, *A Dictionary of Modern Legal Usage* 939–41 (2d ed. 1995).

7 *See, e.g.*, Peter M. Tiersma, *Legal Language* 91 (1999) ("The legal profession's long retention of *said*, *aforesaid*, *same*, and *such* cannot be justified as adding precision or clarity to the text"); Bryan A. Garner, *A Dictionary of Modern Legal Usage* 779 (2d ed. 1995) ("*Said* never lends greater precision than *the*, *this*, *that*, *these*, or *those*—in many contexts it even introduces imprecision"); *id.* at 849 ("Like *said* and *same*, [*such*] is much beloved of those who believe in the myth of precision. It therefore teems in the work of some drafters"); David Mellinkoff, *The Language of the Law* 319 (1963) ("Though some lay critics tell us that, worthless elsewhere, *said* is 'traditional' and 'permissible' in the law, it is either unnecessary or dangerous, and should be dropped").

8 *See, e.g.*, *Saulsberry v. Maddix*, 125 F.2d 430, 434 (6th Cir. 1942); *In re Pearson's Estate*, 33 P. 451, 453 (Cal. 1893); *City of Los Angeles v. Layton*, 75 Cal. Rptr. 143, 145 (Ct. App. 1969).

Sentences 5

§ 27 Use a syntactic arrangement that enhances clarity, logic, and readability.

Keep the basic sentence parts together: subject–verb–object. If the sentence is too long because the writer has tried to pack in too much information, break it up into separate sentences. If the sentence must convey complex information in the form of a list, put it at the end—after the verb. Example A illustrates the problem of putting too much into one sentence and separating the subject (*depositary*) from its verb (*has agreed*). Example B shows the equally common problem of undesirably separating the verb (*contains*) from its object (*disclosures*).

Example A

Not this:	*But this:*
The *depositary*, in order to maintain arrangements from time to time to enable persons that are considered United States residents for purposes of applicable law to receive any rebates, tax credits, or other benefits (pursuant to treaty or otherwise) relating to distributions on the Pantheon ADSs to which such persons are entitled, *has agreed* to use its best efforts that are reasonable in the circumstances.	The *depositary has agreed* to use its best efforts, as reasonable under the circumstances, to maintain arrangements that will enable U.S. residents to receive any available rebates, tax credits, and other benefits relating to the Pantheon ADSs.

Example B

Not this:	*But this:*
This document contains, and other materials filed or to be filed by Pantheon with the Securities and Exchange Commission (the "Commission"), as well as information included in oral statements or other written statements made or to be made by Pantheon, contain or will contain or include, *disclosures* which are forward-looking statements. These forward looking statements address	This *document contains disclosures* that are forward-looking statements. So do other materials that Pantheon has filed or will file with the SEC. And various other oral and written statements amount to forward-looking statements. All these statements address . . . .

§ 28 Prefer the active voice over the passive.

Notice "prefer," as opposed to "always use." The injunction to avoid passive voice should never be taken as an absolute because you'll need the passive in a small percentage of your sentences. But your overwhelming preference—your rebuttable presumption—should be to use the active voice.

Before going any further, though, we must clarify what passive voice is. Only about a third of lawyers know. "Voice," in language, refers to the relationship between the subject of the sentence and the verb. If the subject performs the action of the verb (*Pantheon consolidated the subsidiaries*), the sentence is said to be in the active voice. If the subject doesn't perform the action of the verb (*The subsidiaries were consolidated by Pantheon*), the sentence is said to be in the passive voice. It's as simple as that.

The foolproof test is this: if you see a *be*-verb (such as *is*, *are*, *was*, or *were*) followed by a verb ending in *-ed*, you've got a passive-voice construction. So all these sentences are passive:

- In 1954, ten executives *were covered* by Article XII.
- Prospective investors *are urged* to consult their own tax advisers.
- The 1997 Plan *is intended* to facilitate key employees in having a greater degree of ownership interest in the Company.

We can improve each of those sentences by changing it to active voice:

- In 1954, Article XII covered ten executives.
- We urge prospective investors to consult their own tax advisers.
- With our 1997 Plan, we intend to help key employees obtain a greater ownership interest in the Company.

Example A

Not this:	*But this:*
The instructions accompanying the subscription certificate *should be read* carefully and followed in detail.	Please follow the instructions accompanying the subscription certificate.

Example B

Not this:	*But this:*
The rights may not be sold, transferred, or exercised by any person who resides in Canada.	No Canadian resident may sell, transfer, or exercise the rights.

Example C

Not this:	*But this:*
If the merger *is completed* by Bergstrom and Portnoy prior to March 31, 1999, as a Pantheon ADS shareholder you will *be entitled* to receive the interim dividends that *are expected* to *be paid* by Pantheon on the Pantheon ordinary shares for the fiscal year ending March 31, 1999.	If Bergstrom and Portnoy complete the merger before March 31, 1999, you'll become a Pantheon ADS shareholder. Then you'll get the interim dividends that Pantheon expects to pay on its ordinary shares for the fiscal year ending March 31, 1999.

§ 29 Use the passive voice primarily to avoid an undesirable shift in emphasis from one subject to another.

Occasionally you'll encounter a sentence that seems better in the passive voice. Don't give in easily: cast it in the active voice anyway. If the result sounds bad, then try another way of expressing the thought. If that still doesn't work, then keep the passive-voice construction. Typically, this situation arises when the actor, once named, gets in the way of the information. In other words, changing from passive to active sometimes results in an unsuitable change of emphasis. For example, you're better off saying *The following information is unaudited* instead of *Our auditors haven't assessed the following information*. The focus is rightly on the information—not on the auditors.

§ 30 Avoid cluttering essential information with the inessential.

Because unnecessary detail is often cumbersome and administratively costly, include only as much detail as is necessary or helpful. Remember the French proverb: "The art of being a bore is to tell every detail."

This section illustrates itself.

§ 31 Omit every superfluous word.

Say what you need to say in the fewest possible words. That way, the text will have greater speed, clarity, and impact than it otherwise would. Experts on writing have long touted the virtues of tightening prose:

- "It is an amiable maxim that words which add nothing to the sense or to the clearness must diminish the force of the expression."—George Campbell[1]

- "Wherever we can make twenty-five words do the work of fifty, we halve the area in which looseness and disorganization can flourish, and by reducing the span of attention required we increase the force of the thought. To make our words count for as much as possible is surely the simplest as well as the hardest secret of style."—Wilson Follett[2]

- "A sentence should contain no unnecessary words, a paragraph no unnecessary sentences, for the same reason that a drawing should have no unnecessary lines and a machine no unnecessary parts."—William Strunk, Jr. and E. B. White[3]

- "Once you develop a distaste for surplus words, you will find many word-wasting idioms that can be trimmed from your sentences with no loss of meaning."—Richard C. Wydick[4]

So count your savings whenever you edit a phrase down from 12 words to 6, or even 5 down to 1. If *prior to the time when* becomes *before*—as it virtually always can—you're better off. And so is your reader.

The following examples illustrate how to transform typically wordy sentences into lean ones.

Example A

Not this:	*But this:*
While it is difficult to quantify with certainty the potential financial impact of actions regarding expenditures for environmental matters, in the opinion of management, based upon the information currently available, the ultimate liability arising from such environmental matters, taking into account established accruals for estimated liabilities, should not have a material effect on the Companies' combined financial condition. Words: 58	It's hard to calculate exactly how much it will cost to comply with environmental laws. But we believe that our total liability for environmental compliance won't materially affect our financial condition. Words: 31

Example B

Not this:	*But this:*
In considering the recommendations of the Quanco Board, shareholders should be aware that certain members of management of Quanco and of the Quanco Board have certain interests in the transactions that are in addition to the interests of shareholders generally and which may create potential conflicts of interest. Words: 48	When you consider the board's recommendations, you should realize that some board members and executives have interests that may conflict with your own interests as a shareholder. Words: 27

§ 32 Uncover so-called "buried verbs"—i.e., abstract nouns usually ending in the suffixes *-tion, -sion, -ment, -ence, -ance, -ity*—and make them into true verbs.

The problem with buried verbs—or "nominalizations," as some people call them—is fourfold: (1) they cause you to put the action in nouns, not verbs; (2) they lead to lots of *be*-verbs instead of action verbs; (3) they require additional prepositions; and (4) they make the writing more abstract than it needs to be. So if you can say *violate* instead of *is in violation of*, do it.

Example A

Not this:	*But this:*
Sales to Spritzer Bottlers have decreased as these customers have achieved substantial *completion* of full *deployment* of the company's tracking system in existing plant *locations*.	Sales to Spritzer Bottlers have decreased as these customers have substantially deployed the company's tracking system in existing plants.

Example B

Not this:	*But this:*
The *completion* of the merger will not occur unless a number of conditions are satisfied. These include: • the *approval* of the merger by the holders of a majority of the Pantheon Shares and OJM Class A common stock, voting as a single class; • the *approval* of the merger and increase in OJM's issued share capital by the holders of not less than three-fourths of the ordinary shares of OJM entitled to vote at an Extraordinary General Meeting of OJM's shareholders to be held on March 25, 1999; • the *nonexistence* of an injunction that would be a *prohibition* of the merger or which would cause a material adverse effect on either OJM or Pantheon; and • the *approval* of the relevant governmental authorities without the *imposition* of conditions that would have a material adverse effect on Pantheon, OJM, or Pan-OJM.	Pantheon and OJM will not complete the merger unless several conditions are satisfied. Those conditions include the following: • The holders of a majority of the Pantheon Shares and OJM Class A common stock must, voting as a single class, approve the merger. • The holders of at least three-quarters of OJM's ordinary shares must approve the merger and the increase in OJM's issued share capital. These shareholders will vote at an extraordinary general meeting of OJM's shareholders scheduled for March 25, 1999. • There must not be an injunction that prohibits the merger or that materially harms either OJM or Pantheon. • The relevant governmental authorities must approve the merger without imposing conditions that would materially harm Pantheon, OJM, or Pan-OJM.

§ 33 Eliminate unnecessary prepositional phrases, especially those beginning with *of.*

Sometimes, *of* course, you'll need the *of*. But test each one to see whether it's really necessary. Often you'll find that it isn't. But you must keep your wits about you: don't change *letter of credit* to *credit letter*.

The nice thing about this tip is that you'll be able to make some real headway on the computer, before printing the document out. Simply search for "[space]of[space]," scrutinizing each sentence you find. You'll probably be able to cut half the *of*s at the very least.

Example

Not this:	*But this:*
Sales *of* a significant number *of* shares *of* Pantheon common stock *in* the public market following the rights offering could have an adverse effect *on* the market price *of* the common stock *of* Pantheon.	If Pantheon sells many shares *of* common stock in the public market after the rights offering, the market price could drop.

§ 34 Use third-person pronouns (*it* and *they*) when it's natural to do so.

How can you make your prose mind-numbing? Simply repeat nouns ad nauseam without ever using a pronoun such as *it* or *them*. That will do the trick.

Mysteriously, many legal writers seem to believe that you shouldn't ever use a pronoun. Perhaps they've seen sentences in which an *it* or a *them* didn't have a clear antecedent, and they've therefore learned never to use pronouns. That's the wrong lesson because it leads to exceedingly tedious prose. The true lesson is that you must rid your text of miscues and ambiguities while retaining pronouns—well-used, unambiguous pronouns.

Example A

Not this:	*But this:*
The TORNIX bylaws permit special meetings of the stockholders of TORNIX to be called by the holders of two-thirds of the outstanding TORNIX common stock.	TORNIX's bylaws permit holders of two-thirds of *its* outstanding common stock to call a special stockholders' meeting.

Example B

Not this:	*But this:*
As of the date hereof, the income tax returns of BANTECH and the BANTECH subsidiaries have never been examined by the IRS. There are no material disputes pending, or claims asserted for, taxes or assessments upon BANTECH or any of the BANTECH subsidiaries for which BANTECH does not have adequate reserves, nor has BANTECH or any of the BANTECH subsidiaries given any currently effective waivers extending the statutory period of limitation applicable to any federal, state, county, foreign, or local income tax for any period. Words: 85 Sentences: 2 Average sentence length: 42.5	As of the date of this prospectus, the IRS has not examined the tax returns of BANTECH or *its* subsidiaries. BANTECH has enough reserves to cover pending disputes over or claims for taxes and assessments against BANTECH and *its* subsidiaries. Neither BANTECH nor any of *its* subsidiaries has given a currently effective waiver extending the statutory period of limitation applicable to any federal, state, county, foreign, or local income tax for any period. Words: 73 Sentences: 3 Average sentence length: 24.3

§ 35 Minimize parentheticals.

As used in old-style drafting, parentheticals are visual hurdles. They invite readers to leap over them, yet they sometimes contain vital information. Sometimes. They also sometimes contain needless definitions. In any event, they certainly bulk up sentences and make the writing much more cumbersome. In the pilot program, the SEC's plain-English commenters rightly objected again and again to the overuse of parentheticals.

Example A

Not this:	*But this:*
The Company is a self-administered and self-managed real-estate investment trust ("REIT") that began operations through a predecessor in 1978. At December 31, 1998, the Company owned a portfolio of 379 office and 147 industrial (including 73 service-center) properties (the "Properties"), and 729 acres (and had agreed to purchase an additional 472 acres) of undeveloped land suitable for future development (the "Development Land").	The company is a self-administered and self-managed real-estate investment trust, or REIT. We began operations through a predecessor in 1978. At the end of 1998, we owned 379 office and 147 industrial properties, including 73 service-center properties. We also owned 729 acres—and had agreed to buy an additional 472 acres—of undeveloped land suitable for future development.

Example B

Not this:	*But this:*
At the meeting ("Special Meeting"), shareholders of Pantheon will be asked to consider and vote upon a proposal (the "Distribution Proposal") to approve the distribution described in the Reorganization Agreement (as it may be amended, supplemented, or modified from time to time, the "Reorganization Agreement") to be executed by Pantheon, New Pantheon Holdings, Inc., a Missouri corporation ("New Pantheon"), Flex Inc., a Delaware corporation ("Branded Subsidiary"), and OJM, Inc., a Delaware corporation ("OJM"). Under the Reorganization Agreement, immediately prior to the Merger (as defined below), Pantheon will distribute to its shareholders on a share-for-share basis, in a nontaxable distribution (the "Distribution"), all the shares of New Pantheon. At the time of the Distribution, New Pantheon will own all the businesses, assets, and liabilities currently owned by Pantheon and its subsidiaries (collectively, the "New Pantheon Business"), other than its branded-clothing-items businesses and certain assets and liabilities related thereto (the "Branded Business") which will be acquired by OJM in the Merger.	At the special meeting, Pantheon shareholders will be asked to vote on a proposal to approve the distribution described in the reorganization agreement, as it may be changed from time to time. That agreement will be made by Pantheon; New Pantheon Holdings, Inc., a Missouri corporation; Flex Inc., a Delaware corporation; and OJM, Inc., a Delaware corporation. Under the agreement, just before the merger Pantheon will distribute to its shareholders—on a share-for-share basis and in a nontaxable distribution—all the shares of New Pantheon. At the time of the distribution, New Pantheon will own the businesses, assets, and liabilities now owned by Pantheon and its subsidiaries. The one exception is Pantheon's branded-clothing-items businesses and related assets and liabilities, all of which OJM will acquire in the merger.

§ 36 Use cross-references only when they're genuinely helpful.

Maybe you know this infamous sentence from the Internal Revenue Code:

> For purposes of paragraph (3), an organization described in paragraph (2) shall be deemed to include an organization described in section 501(c)(4), (5), or (6) which would be described in paragraph (2) if it were an organization described in section 501(c)(3).[5]

The only way to understand it is to hold in mind the several other provisions referred to—an achievement that, according to some tax-law experts, can take years of hard work.

Though disclosure documents almost never do anything so atrocious, they do often send readers elsewhere to understand something that's supposedly being discussed here and now. Better that you distill whatever it is you're saying here and now. Make it understandable here and now. And, in great moderation, tell your readers where they can find further information or original source material if they want it.

In sum, avoid sending the reader to other documents to understand a provision in the document you're writing. Make your documents self-contained. If you need to refer to another document, summarize what it is you're referring to. Do this accurately and concisely and conversationally, without simply regurgitating provisions from those other documents.

§ 37 Achieve an average sentence length of fewer than 30 words—preferably near 20.

Though sentence length isn't an absolute predictor of readability, it's a very reliable indicator. It is a major factor in most readability formulas.[6] Especially in technical prose, long sentences make for repulsive reading.

Although you'll want an average somewhere between 20 and 30 words—preferably closer to 20—you'll also want some variety. Use some sentences with 35 words and some with only 3. Variation is key to generating interest.[7]

The following examples show some ways to reduce sentence length. In Example A, it's a matter of simply inserting more periods and supplying connective words between sentences. In Example B, it's a matter of breaking a list into separate sentences and supplying signposts (*First* . . . . *Second* . . . . *Third* . . . .). Interestingly, the total number of words in B goes up in the right column. That's fine—even desirable sometimes. The left column is the work of a writer who had achieved economy at the expense of clarity and readability.

Example A

Not this:	*But this:*
The President of the United States can suspend or prohibit an acquisition of, or investment in, a U.S. company by a foreign person (such as OJM) if the President finds, after investigation, credible evidence that the foreign person might take action that threatens to impair the national security of the United States and that other provisions of existing law do not provide adequate and appropriate authority to protect the national security of the United States. Pantheon and OJM have agreed to make a voluntary filing to the Chairman of the Committee on Foreign Investment in the United States, the organization charged with administering this law, seeking a finding that the merger does not impair the national security of the United States, and this filing is expected to be made in the first quarter of 1997. Words: 135 Sentences: 2 Average sentence length: 67.5	The President of the United States can suspend or prohibit an acquisition of, or investment in, a U.S. company by a foreign person such as OJM. To do this, the President must first investigate the transaction. The President can suspend or prohibit upon finding credible evidence that (1) the foreign person might do something to impair the national security of the United States, and (2) other provisions of existing law don't provide adequate authority to protect the national security of the United States. Pantheon and OJM have agreed to make a voluntary filing to the Chairman of the Committee on Foreign Investment in the United States, the organization initially charged with deciding whether the merger impairs national security. In that filing, scheduled for the first quarter of 1997, they will seek a finding that there is no threat to national security. Words: 141 Sentences: 5 Average sentence length: 28.2

Example B

Not this:	*But this:*
Critical assumptions underlying this analysis are that a market for the Shares will develop relatively soon after the Consolidation, that equity offerings with net proceeds to the Company of $9,300,000, $9,500,000, and $20,000,000 will occur in 1998, 2000, and 2001 respectively, that the Company will assume debt of $11,200,000 in 2001, that all current debt will be refinanced at substantially the same rates as currently paid, that trailing twelve months, forward twelve months, and forward twenty-four months net earnings multiples of 30, 21, and 16, respectively, are appropriate, and by averaging the results of applying these multiples to the appropriate projected earnings one can be used to determine dilution of equity offerings and the value of the Shares.	Several critical assumptions underlie this analysis. First, we've assumed that a market for the shares will develop relatively soon after the consolidation. Second, we've assumed that an equity offering with net proceeds to the company of $9.3 million will occur in 1998, another for $9.5 million in 2000, and another for $20 million in 2001. Third, we've assumed that the company will take debt of $11.2 million in 2001. Fourth, we've assumed that all current debt will be refinanced at substantially the same rates as currently paid. Fifth, we've calculated that net earnings will be trailing for 12 months, forward for 12 months, and forward for 24 months, and that a net-earnings multiple of 30 is appropriate for the first period, 21 for the second, and 16 for the third. By averaging the results of applying these multiples to the appropriate projected earnings, we've tried to determine the dilution of equity offerings and the value of the shares.
Words: 119 Sentences: 1 Average sentence length: 119	Words: 159 Sentences: 7 Average sentence length: 22.7

§ 38 Make sure that lists are parallel.

Grammatical parallelism isn't just a point of grammar; it makes for instant understanding. By contrast, unparallel phrasing makes for miscues and double takes. Here's the key: when you have a list of items, make sure that each one matches the others grammatically—typically noun–noun–noun or verb–verb–verb. Don't mix and match.

Example A

Not this:	*But this:*
Unitech's transformation program is focused on the following: (1) unification of its business under one name—Unitech; (2) re-engineering business processes; (3) consolidation of administrative and operational functions; (4) we intend to implement a common information-technology system; and (5) the Company also plans to realign our organization to focus on target market segments.	Unitech's transformation program is focused on: (1) unifying its business under one name—Unitech; (2) re-engineering business processes; (3) consolidating administrative and operational functions; (4) implementing a common information-technology system; and (5) realigning our organization to focus on target market segments.

Example B

Not this:	*But this:*
The Credit Facility includes customary covenants and provisions that will restrict our ability to do the following: (1) merge, consolidate, or engage in certain asset sales or dispositions; (2) incurring indebtedness and enter into guarantees; (3) incurring liens and enter into sale-leaseback transactions; and (4) our ability to engage in transactions with affiliates.	The credit facility includes customary covenants and provisions that will restrict our ability to: (1) merge, consolidate, or engage in certain asset sales or dispositions; (2) incur indebtedness and enter into guarantees; (3) incur liens and enter into sale-leaseback transactions; and (4) engage in transactions with affiliates.

§ 39 Enumerate at the end of a sentence.

The core parts of the English sentence are the subject and the verb—and, optionally, the object. One key to plain English is to ensure that your readers reach the verb early on. That way, the structure of the sentence becomes transparent.

One of the worst habits that drafters develop is putting long lists of items in the subject so that the verb is delayed. This habit results in what linguists call "left-branching" sentences: ones with lots of complex information that branches out to the left side of the verb. The metaphor is that of a tree. As you read from left to right, and remembering that the trunk of the tree is the verb, imagine a sentence configured in this way:

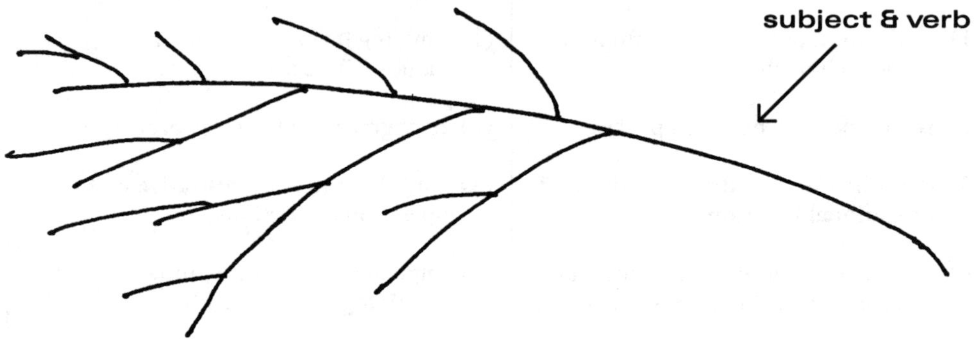

That's going to be fiendishly difficult to get through.
But imagine the tree reconfigured:

If all this talk of trees sounds abstract, look at actual examples of sentences done both ways. Here's a typical left-brancher. Look for the verb *belong*:

> Our consultants have agreed that all ideas, creations, inventions, discoveries, and improvements, whether or not patentable or copyrightable and whether or not fixed in any mode of expression or reduced to practice, that they have conceived of, alone or jointly with others, or that are suggested by or result from any work performed under our consulting agreements with them, or that relate to our actual or anticipated business, or that result from the use of our facilities, equipment, supplies, or information, belong to us as our sole and exclusive property.

And here's the same sentence done as a right-brancher, with the enumeration at the end:

> Our consultants have agreed that all of the following items belong exclusively to us: all ideas, creations, inventions, discoveries, and improvements, whether or not patentable or copyrightable and whether or not fixed in any mode of expression or reduced to practice, that they have conceived of, alone or jointly with others, or that are suggested by or result from any work performed under our consulting agreements with them, or that relate to our actual or anticipated business, or that result from the use of our facilities, equipment, supplies, or information.

Of course, writing in plain English would require anyone to simplify that sentence still further:

> Our consultants have agreed that everything they produce in their work for us will belong exclusively to us.

But if you're going to enumerate the items, they *must* appear at the end of the sentence, not at the beginning.

Here's the upshot: find the operative verb in the sentence and move it toward the front, putting your lists at the end of the sentence. Even with fairly modest lists, this technique can make a tremendous difference in readability. In the following example, the word *fix* is the operative verb. Notice how its placement changes.

Example

Not this:	*But this:*
Whenever any cash dividend or other cash distribution or distribution other than cash is made, or whenever rights shall be issued with respect to the deposited securities, or whenever for any reason the depositary causes a change in the number of Digitronic shares that are represented by each Digitronic ADS, or whenever the depositary receives notice of any meeting of holders of Digitronic shares or other deposited securities, or whenever reasonably requested by Digitronic, holders of Digitronic shares will fix a record date (which shall be as near as practicable to any corresponding record date set by Digitronic) (a) for the determination of the owners who will be (i) entitled to receive such dividend, distribution or rights, or the net proceeds of the sale thereof, or (ii) entitled to give instructions for the exercise of voting rights at any such meeting, or (b) on or after which each Digitronic ADS will represent the changed number of Digitronic shares, all subject to the provisions of the Deposit Agreement.	**7.4 Record Dates** (A) *Events triggering.* The depositary will fix a record date if: (1) a cash dividend or other cash or noncash distribution becomes payable; (2) Digitronic issues rights with respect to the deposited securities; (3) the depositary for any reason causes a change in the number of Digitronic shares that are represented by each Digitronic ADS; (4) the depositary receives notice of any meeting of holders of Digitronic shares or other deposited securities; or (5) Digitronic reasonably requests that the depositary fix a record date. (B) *Effect of the Record Date.* On the record date, the owners will determine who is entitled to receive the dividend, distribution, or net proceeds of a sale. They will also determine who is entitled to give instructions for the exercise of voting rights. After the record date, each Digitronic ADS will represent the changed number of Digitronic shares, subject to the deposit agreement.

§ 40 For lists that won't need to be cited the way contractual provisions are cited, use bullets.

Bullet dots are extraordinarily useful for directing the reader's eye from one item to the next in a list. But it's not enough simply to decide that you're going to use bullets. You need to use them well.

Here are some guidelines:

- End your introduction to the bulleted list with a colon. It serves as an anchor.

- Ensure that the size of your bullets is proportional to the size of your type. You don't want overpowering bullets; the best bullets are typically just smaller than a lowercase "o" filled in with ink.

- Adjust your tab settings so that you'll have a small tab between the bullet and the text. Space the tabs so that they look about the way you see them throughout this book—about .15 inches evenly across the line, with a larger space for a paragraph indent.

- Use a hanging indent. That is, don't allow the text to wrap under the bullet; instead, leave the bullet hanging out to the left. If you don't already know the word-processing function for this, you'll need to learn it.

- Single-space within bulleted items. If you have longish bullets, though, you may decide to double-space between them. But try to keep your bullets fairly short.

- Keep your items grammatically parallel (start each one with a verb, a noun, etc.).

- Resist the temptation to play with computer-generated boxes, arrows, check marks, and other eye-catchers. Nothing else works quite as well as a bullet.

Example

Not this:	*But this:*
The Merger Agreement also includes limitations, prohibitions, and other provisions relating to Pantheon's conduct of business during this period with respect to (a) capital projects, (b) contracts and agreements outside the ordinary course of business, (c) broker sales incentive programs, (d) trade, consumer promotions (including coupon expense and sampling) and advertising expenditures (excluding broker sales incentives) relating to the sale of branded goods, (e) inventory levels, (f) transfer or reassignment of marketing and/or research and development employees associated as of the date of the Merger Agreement primarily with the business of selling branded goods, (g) changes in or issuances, repurchases or redemption of capital stock, (h) charter or by-law amendments, (i) acquisitions and dispositions, (j) levels of indebtedness as of the effective time of the merger, (k) adoption or amendment of benefit plans or arrangements, (l) provision of information to Pantheon or its counsel, including monthly balance sheets, statements of profit and loss, and operating reports, (m) changes in accounting principles, policies, or procedures, (n) incurrence of liens, (o) actions that would impair consummation of the merger or that would impair the tax treatment thereof, (p) nonwaiver of existing standstill and confidentiality agreements, (q) transition arrangements with brokers, and (r) defense of pending litigation.	The merger agreement also includes limitations, prohibitions, and many other provisions relating to Pantheon's conduct of business during this period. These provisions deal with: • capital projects; • contracts and agreements outside the ordinary course of business; • broker sales incentive programs; • trade, consumer promotions (including coupon expense and sampling), and advertising expenditures (excluding broker sales incentives) relating to the sale of branded goods; • inventory levels; • transfer or reassignment of marketing or research-and-development employees associated as of the date of the merger agreement primarily with the business of selling branded goods; • changes in or issuances, repurchases, or redemption of capital stock; • charter or bylaw amendments; • acquisitions and dispositions; • levels of debt as of the effective time of the merger; • adoption or amendment of benefit plans or arrangements; • the flow of information to Pantheon or its counsel, including monthly balance sheets, statements of profit and loss, and operating reports; • changes in accounting principles, policies, or procedures; • incurrence of liens; • actions that would impair consummating the merger or result in an unfavorable tax treatment; • nonwaiver of existing standstill and confidentiality agreements; • transition arrangements with brokers; and • defense of pending litigation.

endnotes

[1] *Philosophy of Rhetoric* (1776) (as quoted in Alfred Ayres, *The Verbalist* vi (rev. ed. 1911)).

[2] *Modern American Usage* 14 (1966).

[3] *The Elements of Style* 23 (3d ed. 1979).

[4] *Plain English for Lawyers* 14 (4th ed. 1998).

[5] I.R.C. § 509(a) (CCH 1998).

[6] *See, e.g.*, Rudolf Flesch, *How to Write Plain English: A Book for Lawyers and Consumers* 20–27 (1979); Robert Gunning, *The Technique of Clear Writing* 32–34 (1952).

[7] Gunning, *Technique of Clear Writing* 163–64.

Paragraphs

6

§ 41 Start detesting density.

Dense writing appears formidable. People tend to put it aside, intending perhaps to get back to it when they might have more time and fortitude. But then they never do. And even if they did, they would put it aside once again because dense writing on technical subjects is deathly dull. But technical writing needn't be that way. In the right hands, it can be engaging.

One essential way to achieve this effect is to cultivate both a fear and a loathing of density. Learn to value white space, and leave a good deal of it on every page. Many techniques discussed in this book will contribute to white space:

- headings (§ 44);
- set-off lists (§ 9);
- cascading left-hand indents (§ 9);
- double columns (§ 55);
- frequent paragraphs (§ 43);
- generous margins (§ 49);
- bullets (§ 40); and
- suitable type size (§ 49).

The white space around text is what makes a page look inviting, roomy, and comfortable. The lack of it makes the page look imposing and cramped. In the following example, notice how much easier it is to read three reasonable paragraphs instead of the old-fashioned edifice.

Example

Not this:

> SECTION 7.12—*Post-Merger Blynn Star Board of Directors*. At the Effective Time, the total number of persons serving on the Board of Directors of Blynn Star shall be twenty-two (unless otherwise agreed in writing by CORPEX and Blynn Star prior to the Effective Time), half of whom shall be CORPEX Directors and half of whom shall be Blynn Star Directors (as such terms are defined below). No more than six of the

twenty-two initial Directors of Blynn Star shall be employees of CORPEX or Blynn Star; half of the employee directors shall be CORPEX Directors and half shall be Blynn Star Directors (as such terms are defined below). The persons to serve initially on the Board of Directors of Blynn Star at the Effective Time who are CORPEX Directors shall be selected solely by and at the absolute discretion of the Board of Directors of CORPEX prior to the Effective Time; and the persons to serve on the Board of Directors of Blynn Star at the Effective Time who are Blynn Star Directors shall be selected solely by and at the absolute discretion of the Board of Directors of Blynn Star prior to the Effective Time. In the event that, prior to the Effective Time, any person so selected to serve on the Board of Directors of Blynn Star after the Effective Time is unable or unwilling to serve in such position, the Board of Directors which selected such person shall designate another of its members to serve in such person's stead in accordance with the provision of the immediately preceding sentence. From and after the Effective Time and until Raoul W. Berger ceases to be the Chairman of Blynn Star, the Board of Directors of Blynn Star and each Committee of the Board of Directors of Blynn Star as constituted following each election of Directors shall consist of an equal number of CORPEX Directors and Blynn Star Directors. If, at any time during the period referred to in the immediately preceding sentence, the number of CORPEX Directors and Blynn Star Directors serving, or that would be serving following the next stockholders' meeting at which directors are to be elected, as Directors of Blynn Star or as members of any Committee of the Board of Directors of Blynn Star would not be equal, then, subject to the fiduciary duties of the Directors of Blynn Star, the Board of Directors and the Nominating Committee thereof shall nominate for election at the next stockholders' meeting at which Directors are to be elected such person or persons as may be requested by the remaining CORPEX Directors (if the number of CORPEX Directors is, or would otherwise become, less than the number of Blynn Star Directors) or by the remaining Blynn Star Directors (if the number of Blynn Star Directors is, or would otherwise become, less than the number of CORPEX Directors) to ensure that there shall be an equal number of CORPEX Directors and Blynn Star Directors. The provisions of the preceding sentence shall not apply in respect of any stockholders' meeting which takes place after the date on which Raoul W. Berger ceases to be Chairman of Blynn Star, and subsequent to such date, vacancies in the Board of Directors of Blynn Star shall be filled only by vote of the stockholders. The term "CORPEX Director" means (i) any person serving as a Director of CORPEX or of a CORPEX telephone company on the date hereof who becomes a Director of Blynn Star at the Effective Time and (ii) any person who becomes a Director of Blynn Star pursuant to the second preceding sentence and who is designated by the CORPEX Directors; and the term "Blynn Star Director" means (i) any person serving as a Director of Blynn Star on the date hereof who continues as a Director of Blynn Star at the Effective Time and (ii) any person who becomes a Director of Blynn Star pursuant to the second preceding sentence and who is designated by the Blynn Star Directors.

But this:

7.12 Post-Merger Blynn Star Board of Directors.

(A) ***Board Makeup.*** After the merger, Blynn Star's new board of directors will consist of 22 persons—11 CORPEX directors and 11 Blynn Star directors. No more than 6 of the 22 new directors will be employees of CORPEX or Blynn Star (3 from each company). Each corporation's pre-merger board will have full discretion to select its 11 directors for the post-merger board.

(B) ***Replacement Directors.*** If, before the merger, anyone selected to serve on Blynn Star's new board of directors is unable or unwilling to serve, the pre-merger board that selected that person will select a replacement.

(C) ***Equal Representation.*** As long as Raoul W. Berger is Blynn Star's chairman, Blynn Star's new board of directors—and each board committee—will consist of an equal number of CORPEX directors and Blynn Star directors. If, during this time, the number of CORPEX directors and Blynn Star directors is about to become unequal, then the new board will nominate for election as director one or more persons selected by the remaining CORPEX directors or Blynn Star directors, whichever group is about to become smaller, so that the two groups remain equal in number. Once Raoul W. Berger is no longer chairman, board vacancies will be filled by vote of the stockholders.

§ 42 Introduce and develop a single idea in each paragraph.

Good paragraphs have unity. They have topic sentences that announce the main idea to be developed in the paragraph, and then they stick to that idea. And headings (see § 44) can powerfully reinforce the unity of your paragraphs. What follows is a striking illustration of this principle.

Example

Not this:

Book-Entry System

Upon issuance, each series of Offered Securities will be represented by a global security or securities (each, a "Global Security"). Each Global Security will be deposited with, or on behalf of, Dittmar. Upon the issuance of such Global Security, Dittmar or its nominee will credit the accounts of persons held with it the respective principal or face amounts of the Offered Securities represented by such Global Security. Ownership of beneficial interests in such Global Security will be limited to persons that have accounts with Dittmar ("participants") or persons that may hold interests through participants. Ownership of beneficial interests by participants in such Global Security will be shown on, and the transfer of that ownership will be effected only through, records maintained by Dittmar. Ownership of beneficial interests in such Global Security by persons that hold through participants will be shown on, and the transfer of that ownership interest within such participant will be effected only through, records maintained by such participant. The laws of some jurisdictions require that certain purchasers of securities take physical delivery of such securities in definitive form. Such limits and such laws may impair the ability to acquire or transfer beneficial interests in such Global Security. Payment of principal of and interest on each series of Offered Securities will be made to Dittmar or its nominee, as the case may be, as the sole registered owner and holder of the Global Security for such series for all purposes under the Indenture. Neither the Operating Partnership, the Trustee, nor any agent of the Operating Partnership or the Trustee will have any responsibility or liability for any aspect of Dittmar's records relating to or payments made on account of beneficial ownership interests in such Global Security or for maintaining, supervising, or reviewing any of Dittmar's records relating to such beneficial ownership interests. The Operating Partnership has been advised by Dittmar that upon receipt of any payment of principal or of interest on any Global Security, Dittmar will immediately credit, on its book-entry registration and transfer system, the accounts of participants with payments in amounts proportionate to their respective beneficial interests in the principal or face amount of such Global Security as shown on the records of Dittmar. Payments by participants to owners of beneficial interests in such Global Security held through such participants will be governed by standing instructions and customary practices as is now the case with securities held for customer accounts registered in "street name" and will be the sole responsibility of such participants.

Neither Global Security may be transferred except as a whole by Dittmar to a nominee of Dittmar. The Global Security representing each series of Offered Securities is exchangeable for certificated Offered Securities of such series only if (x) Dittmar notifies the Operating Partnership that it is unwilling or unable to continue as depositary for such Global Security or if at any time Dittmar ceases to be a clearing agency registered under the Exchange Act and the Operating Partnership fails within 90 days thereafter to appoint a successor, (y) in the case of the Notes only, the Operating Partnership in its sole discretion determines that such Global Security shall be exchangeable, or (z) there shall have occurred and be continuing an Event of Default or an event that with the giving of notice or lapse of time, or both, would constitute an Event of Default with respect to the securities represented by such Global Security. In such event, the Operating Partnership will issue securities of the applicable series in certificated form in exchange for such Global Security. In any such instance, an owner of a beneficial interest in the Global Security will be entitled to physical delivery in certificated form of Offered Securities of such series equal in principal amount to such beneficial interest and to have such securities registered in its name. Securities so issued in certificated form will be issued in denominations of $1,000 or any larger amount that is an integral multiple thereof, and will be issued in registered form only, without coupons. Subject to the foregoing, neither Global Security is exchangeable, except for a Global Security for the same series of Offered Securities of like denomination to be registered in the name of Dittmar or its nominee.

So long as Dittmar, or its nominee, is the registered owner of a Global Security, Dittmar or such nominee, as the case may be, will be considered the sole owner or holder of the Offered Securities represented by such Global Security for the purposes of receiving payment on such securities, receiving notices, and for all other purposes of any kind under the Indenture and such securities. Beneficial interests in any of the Offered Securities will be evidenced only by, and transfer thereof will be effected only by means of and through, records maintained by Dittmar and its participants. Except as provided herein, owners of beneficial interests in any Global Security will not be entitled to be considered, and will not be considered, the Holders thereof for any purposes under the Indenture. Consequently, each person owning a beneficial interest in such Global Security must rely on the procedures of Dittmar, and, if such person is not a participant, on the procedures of the participant through which such person owns its interest, to exercise any rights of a Holder under the Indenture. Dittmar will not consent or vote with respect to the Global Security representing a series of Offered Securities. In accordance with its usual procedure, Dittmar mails an Omnibus Proxy to the Operating Partnership as soon as possible after the applicable record date. The Omnibus Proxy assigns Coebus & Co.'s (Dittmar's partnership nominee) consenting or voting rights to those participants to whose accounts the Offered Securities of a series are credited on the applicable record date (identified in a listing that is made an attachment to the Omnibus Proxy).

Words: 977
Average paragraph length: 325.6

But this:

10. Book-Entry System

10.1 ***Global securities generally.*** Once issued, each series of offered securities will be represented by a global security, which will be deposited with Dittmar. Upon the issuance of a global security, Dittmar will credit account-holders with the principal or face amounts of the offered securities represented by the global security. Ownership of a beneficial interest in a global security will be limited to Dittmar's account-holders and to those who hold interests through account-holders.

10.2 ***Record-keeping.*** An account-holder's beneficial interest in a global security will be shown on Dittmar's records. And any transfer of an interest must take place on those records. But if someone holds a beneficial interest through an account-holder, the account-holder is responsible for keeping records showing ownership as well as any transfers.

10.3 ***Legal restrictions.*** The laws of some jurisdictions require that certain buyers of securities take physical delivery of the securities. These requirements may impair the ability to acquire or transfer beneficial interests in a global security.

10.4 ***Payments; waiver of liability.*** Payment of the principal and interest on each series of offered securities will be made to Dittmar or its nominee as the sole registered owner and holder of the global security for that series for all purposes under the indenture. Neither the operating partnership nor the trustee, nor any of their agents, will be responsible or liable for any payments made on account of beneficial interests in a global security or for maintaining, supervising, or reviewing any of Dittmar's records relating to beneficial interests in a global security.

10.5 ***Crediting of accounts.*** Dittmar has advised the operating partnership that upon receipt of any payment of principal or interest on any global security, Dittmar will immediately credit, on its book-entry registration and transfer system, the accounts of participants with payments in amounts proportionate to their respective beneficial interests in the principal or face amount of the global security as shown on Dittmar's records. Payments by participants to owners of beneficial interests in the global security held through the participants will be governed by standing instructions and customary practices for securities held for customer accounts registered in "street name" and will be the sole responsibility of the participants.

10.6 ***Transfer or exchange of global securities.*** Only Dittmar or its nominee may transfer either type of global security. The global security representing each series of offered securities is exchangeable for certificated offered securities only if one of the following conditions is met:

(A) if Dittmar notifies the operating partnership that it is unwilling or unable to continue as depositary for the global security or if Dittmar ceases to be a clearing agency registered under the Exchange Act and the operating partnership does not appoint a successor within 90 days;

(B) in the case of the notes only, if the operating partnership in its sole discretion determines that the global security is exchangeable; or

(C) if an event of default—or an event that with the giving of notice or lapse of time, or both, would constitute an event of default—occurs with respect to the securities represented by the global security.

10.7 ***Exchange procedure.*** If any of the conditions in 10.6 occurs, the operating partnership will issue securities of the applicable series in certificated form in exchange for the global security. If this occurs, an owner of a beneficial interest in the global security will be entitled to physical delivery in certificated form of offered securities of the series equal in principal amount to the beneficial interest and to have the securities registered in its name. Securities issued in certificated form will be issued in denominations of $1,000 (or any larger amount that is an integral multiple of $1,000) and will be issued in registered form only, without coupons. Subject to these provisions, neither global security is exchangeable, except for a global security for the same series of offered securities of like denomination to be registered in the name of Dittmar or its nominee.

10.8 ***Record ownership.*** So long as Dittmar or its nominee is the registered owner of a global security, Dittmar or the nominee will be considered the sole owner or holder of the offered securities represented by the global security for the purposes of receiving payment and notices and for all other purposes under the indenture and the securities. Beneficial interests in any of the offered securities will be evidenced only by records maintained by Dittmar and its participants. Likewise, transfer of beneficial interests in any of the offered securities will be effected only through records maintained by Dittmar and its participants.

10.9 ***Consenting and voting rights.*** Except as otherwise provided, owners of beneficial interests in any global security will not be considered the holders of the security for any purpose under the indenture. Therefore, each person owning a beneficial interest in a global security must rely on Dittmar's procedures—or, if the person is not a participant, on the procedures of the participant through which the person owns its interest—to exercise any rights of a holder under the indenture. Dittmar will not consent or vote with respect to the global security representing a series of offered securities. In accordance with its usual procedure, Dittmar mails an omnibus proxy to the operating partnership as soon as possible after the applicable record date. The omnibus proxy assigns the consenting or voting rights of Coebus & Co.(Dittmar's partnership nominee) to those participants whose accounts the offered securities of a series are credited to on the applicable record date.

Words: 913
Average paragraph length: 76

§ 43 Strive for an average paragraph of no more than 150 words.

It's tempting to cast this injunction not as a word-count but as a sentence-count. The problem, of course, is that a maximum average of six sentences could still be horrendous if the sentences are each 80 words long. So the word-count is more reliable.

As with sentence length, you need variety in paragraph length: some slim ones and some fairly ample ones. But watch your average. And remember that there's nothing wrong with an occasional one-sentence paragraph.[1] To think that's a mistake is a monstrous superstition—a remnant of half-remembered grammar-school lessons.

Example

Not this:

Dividends
Dividend payments from Northcap's principal Insurance Subsidiaries are regulated by the insurance laws of their domiciliary states. Sun Life is domiciled in Delaware. Under the Delaware Insurance Code, an insurer domiciled in Delaware may not declare or pay a dividend or other distribution from any source other than "earned surplus" without the state insurance commissioner's prior approval. "Earned surplus" is defined as an amount equal to the unassigned funds of an insurer as set forth on its most recent statutory annual statement, including all or part of the surplus arising from unrealized capital gains or revaluation of assets. AmeriFund and Continental Care are domiciled in Texas. An insurer domiciled in Texas may pay dividends only out of "surplus profits arising from its business." Moreover, insurers domiciled in either Delaware or Texas may not pay "extraordinary dividends" without first providing the state insurance commissioner with 30 days' prior notice, during which time such commissioner may disapprove the payment. An "extraordinary dividend" is defined as a dividend whose fair market value together with that of other dividends made within the preceding 12 months exceeds the greater of (a) ten percent of the insurer's surplus as regards policy-holders as of the preceding December 31 or (b) the net gain from operations of such insurer, not including realized capital gains, for the 12-month period ending on the preceding December 31. In September 1994, Sun Life paid to Northcap an "extraordinary dividend" in the amount of $2 million. With respect to ordinary dividends payable by an insurer domiciled in Delaware, notice of any dividend must be provided to the state insurance commissioner within five business days following the declaration thereof and at least ten days prior to the payment thereof. As of December 31, 1994, Sun Life had negative statutory "earned surplus" as a result of historical statutory losses. For the foreseeable future, Sun Life has agreed to seek the approval of the Delaware insurance commissioner prior to making any dividend payments. As of December 31, 1995, Continental Care has the ability to pay to AmeriFund, without prior regulatory approval, $835,000 in dividends during 1996. As of December 31, 1995, AmeriFund has the ability to pay to Northcap, without prior regulatory approval, $1 million in dividends during 1996. In both Delaware and Texas, the state insurance commissioner reviews the dividends paid by each insurer domiciled in such commissioner's state at least once each year to determine whether they are reasonable in

relation to the insurer's surplus as regards policyholders and quality of earnings. The state insurance commissioner may issue an order to limit or disallow the payment of ordinary dividends if such commissioner finds the insurer to be presently or potentially financially distressed or troubled.

Words: 451
Average paragraph length: 451

But this:

12. Dividends

12.1 ***Dividends generally.*** Dividend payments from Northcap's principal insurance subsidiaries are regulated by the insurance laws of the states where they legally reside. Sun Life legally resides in Delaware; AmeriFund and Continental Care legally reside in Texas.

12.2 ***Ordinary dividends.*** In Delaware, an insurer may not declare or pay a dividend or other distribution from any source other than "earned surplus" without the state insurance commissioner's approval. "Earned surplus" is the amount of the insurer's unassigned funds as set forth on its most recent statutory annual statement, including all or part of the surplus arising from unrealized capital gains or revaluation of assets. In Texas, an insurer may pay dividends only out of "surplus profits arising from its business."

12.3 ***Insurance commissioner's procedures.*** In each state, the state insurance commissioner reviews at least once a year the dividends paid by an insurer to determine whether they are reasonable in relation to the insurer's surplus as regards policyholders and quality of earnings. The state insurance commissioner may issue an order limiting or disallowing the payment of ordinary dividends if the commissioner finds that the insurer is, or is about to be, in financial distress. In Delaware, notice of any ordinary dividend must be given to the insurance commissioner within five business days after the dividend is declared and at least ten days before the dividend is to be paid.

12.4 ***Extraordinary dividends.*** In both Delaware and Texas, insurers may not pay "extraordinary dividends" without first giving 30 days' notice to the state insurance commissioner, which may disapprove the payment. An "extraordinary dividend" is a dividend whose fair market value, together with that of other dividends paid during the preceding 12 months, exceeds the greater of either:

(A) 10% of the insurer's surplus as regards policyholders as of the preceding December 31; or

(B) the net gain from the insurer's operations, not including realized capital gains, for the 12-month period ending on the preceding December 31.

12.5 ***Sun Life's dividends.*** In September 1994, Sun Life paid Northcap an "extraordinary dividend" of $2 million. As of December 31, 1994, Sun Life had negative statutory "earned surplus" as a result of historical statutory losses. For the foreseeable future, Sun Life has agreed to seek the Delaware insurance commissioner's approval before paying any dividends.

12.6 ***Continental Care's dividends.*** As of December 31, 1995, Continental Care has the ability to pay AmeriFund, without prior regulatory approval, $835,000 in dividends during 1996.

12.7 ***AmeriFund's dividends.*** As of December 31, 1995, AmeriFund has the ability to pay Northcap, without prior regulatory approval, $1 million in dividends during 1996.

Words: 431
Average paragraph length: 48

§ 44 Group similar items together, preferably introducing them with parallel headings and subheadings.

Especially on the cover page, but elsewhere as well, categorize information clearly. Distinguish key information—such as price per share—from the rest of the text.

The old-style drafting model omitted headings on the cover page. The new style is to use headings to group pieces of information into highlighted categories. Again and again during the pilot program, the SEC commenters applauded cover pages that used headings in this way.

Example

Not this:

PROSPECTUS SUPPLEMENT TO PROSPECTUS DATED SEPTEMBER 5, 1998

$693,750,000

PBRC MASTER CREDIT CARD TRUST II

Class A Floating Rate Asset Backed Certificates, Series 1998-J

Class B Floating Rate Asset Backed Certificates, Series 1998-J

PBRC AMERICA BANK, NATIONAL ASSOCIATION

Seller and Servicer

Each Class A Floating Rate Asset Backed Certificate, Series 1998-J (collectively, the "Class A Certificates") and each Class B Floating Rate Asset Backed Certificate, Series 1998-J (collectively, the "Class B Certificates" and, together with the Class A Certificates, the "Certificates") will represent the right to receive certain payments from the PBRC Master Credit Card Trust II (the "Trust") created pursuant to a Pooling and Servicing Agreement between PBRC America Bank, National Association (PBRC), as seller and servicer, and The Bank of New York, as trustee.

There currently is no secondary market for the Certificates, and there is no assurance that one will develop. Potential investors should consider, among other things, the information set forth in "Risk Factors" beginning on page 19 in the Prospectus.

THE CERTIFICATES REPRESENT INTERESTS IN THE TRUST ONLY AND DO NOT REPRESENT INTERESTS IN OR OBLIGATIONS OF PBRC AMERICA BANK, NATIONAL ASSOCIATION OR ANY AFFILIATE THEREOF. A CERTIFICATE IS NOT A DEPOSIT AND NEITHER THE CERTIFICATES NOR THE UNDERLYING ACCOUNTS OR RECEIVABLES ARE INSURED OR GUARANTEED BY THE FEDERAL DEPOSIT INSURANCE CORPORATION OR ANY OTHER GOVERNMENTAL AGENCY.

THESE SECURITIES HAVE NOT BEEN APPROVED OR DISAPPROVED BY THE SECURITIES AND EXCHANGE COMMISSION OR ANY STATE SECURITIES COMMISSION NOR HAS THE SECURITIES AND EXCHANGE COMMISSION OR ANY STATE SECURITIES COMMISSION PASSED UPON THE ACCURACY OR ADEQUACY OF THIS PROSPECTUS SUPPLEMENT OR THE PROSPECTUS. ANY REPRESENTATION TO THE CONTRARY IS A CRIMINAL OFFENSE.

	Price to Public	Underwriting Discount	Proceeds to Seller(1)(2)
Per Class A Certificate	100%	0.35%	99.65%
Per Class B Certificate	100%	0.375%	99.625%
Total	$693,750,000	$2,442,187.50	$691,307,812.50

(1)Plus accrued interest, if any, at the Class A Certificate Rate or the Class B Certificate Rate, as applicable, from September 10, 1997.

(2)Before deduction of expenses estimated to be $800,000.

The Certificates are offered by, when, as and if issued by the Trust and accepted by the Underwriters and subject to the Underwriters' right to reject orders in whole or in part. It is expected that the Certificates will be delivered in book-entry form on or about December 10, 1998, through the facilities of The Depository Trust Company, Cedel Bank, Societe Anonyme, and the Euroclear System.

Underwriters of the Class A Certificates

FURMAN BROTHERS • SNIPES, FARRAR & CO. INC. • CREDIT OSTEREISCHER FIRST CINCINNATI

BIDEN, PURDY & CO. • GRIMES ALLEN & CO.

Underwriter of the Class B Certificates

FURMAN BROTHERS

the date of this Prospectus is January 6, 1998

But this:

Prospectus Supplement to Prospectus Dated September 5, 1998

PBRC Master Credit Card Trust II
Issuer

PBRC America Bank, National Association
Seller and Servicer

SERIES 1998-J
$693,750,000 Floating-Rate Asset-Backed Certificates

Look carefully at the risk factors beginning on page 10 of the prospectus.

A certificate is not a deposit, and neither the certificates nor the underlying accounts or receivables are insured or guaranteed by the Federal Deposit Insurance Corporation or any other governmental agency.

The certificates will represent interests in the trust only and will not represent interests in or obligations of PBRC or any PBRC affiliate.

This prospectus supplement may be used to offer and sell the certificates only if accompanied by the prospectus.

The Trust will issue—

	Class A Certificates	Class B Certificates
Principal amount	$ 152,654,000	$ 541,096,000
Certificate rate	One-month LIBOR plus 1% annually	One-month LIBOR plus 1% annually
Interest paid	Monthly	Monthly
First interest payment date	October 10, 1998	October 10, 1998
Scheduled principal payment date	September 9, 2028	September 9, 2028
Legal final maturity	September 9, 2028	September 9, 2028

Credit Enhancement—

The Class B Certificates are subordinated to the Class A Certificates. Subordination of the Class B Certificates provides credit enhancement for the Class A Certificates.

The Trust is also issuing a Collateral Interest in the amount of $500 million that is subordinated to the Class A Certificates and the Class B Certificates. Subordination of the Collateral Interest provides credit enhancement for both the Class A and the Class B Certificates.

Neither the SEC nor any state securities commission has approved these certificates or determined that this prospectus supplement or the prospectus is accurate or complete. It's illegal for anyone to tell you otherwise.

Underwriters of the Class A Certificates

FURMAN BROTHERS • SNIPES, FARRAR & CO. INC. • CREDIT OSTEREISCHER FIRST CINCINNATI

BIDEN, PURDY & CO. • GRIMES ALLEN & CO.

Underwriter of the Class B Certificates

FURMAN BROTHERS

January 6, 1998

endnotes

[1] For authorities debunking the false notion of never writing a one-sentence paragraph, see Eric Partridge, *Usage and Abusage* 223–24 (1942); John R. Trimble, *Writing with Style* 94 (1975).

Organization 7

§ 45 Organize to serve clarity, readability, and brevity.

Organize the document sensibly. Put information that will be important to shareholders up front, and then arrange items in descending order of importance. This point might seem so obvious as to be unnecessary. Yet many old-style forms bury critical information. For example, some annual-meeting proxy statements put the section called "Voting Procedures" way back on page 24, long after all the minutiae about particular directors. A better strategy would be to move it toward the beginning.

The cardinal rule is to organize according to the shareholders' need for information in making an investment decision. Don't organize merely by the mechanics of the transaction you're describing.

Remember: plain English is concerned with readers: what they need to know and when they need to know it. Old-style drafting was content to let readers fend for themselves.

Spill the beans up front. On the cover page, move swiftly to the transaction's effect on shareholders. In the pilot program, the SEC commenters criticized how the old-style model delayed discussing the effect on shareholders.

§ 46 Try using an easy-to-follow numbering system.

Many disclosure documents dispense with any type of formal numbering system, simply using headings instead. But then, in old-style drafting, they run in their paragraphs with enumerated items, frequently using multiple sets of (a)'s and (b)'s right next to each other, like this:

> *Assignments and Leases*. Effective as of the Distribution Date, Pantheon will (a) assign to the Branded Subsidiary all of Pantheon's rights, title, and interest in the Branded Trademarks (as defined herein) and (b) grant to the Branded Subsidiary a nonexclusive royalty-free right to use *Pantheon*, *Pantheon Foods*, and red, stylized *R* trademarks (collectively, the "Pantheon Trademarks") in the United States, its territories and possessions and the Commonwealth of Puerto Rico and military installations on packaging, promotional or advertising materials for a period of one (1) year following the Distribution Date. The "Branded Trademarks" refers to (a) all the Trademarks, other than the Pantheon Trademarks and the *Panto Flakes* and *Cookie Devil* Trademarks, previously used or currently owned by Pantheon Foods or licensed to Pantheon Foods or its subsidiaries that are or have been almost always associated with the Branded Business or intended almost always for use therein and (b) certain recipe names used in connection with snack-mix

> products produced by the Branded Business. The license term relating to the use of the Pantheon Trademarks may be extended for a period of no more than one (1) additional year for the purpose of permitting the materials that remain on hand on the one-year anniversary of the Distribution Date. The Branded Subsidiary will agree that it will (a) make reasonable efforts to conclude the use of such product packaging and promotional and advertising materials by the one-year anniversary of the Distribution Date and (b) not place any orders for such product packaging and advertising or promotional materials at any time after the one-year anniversary of the Distribution Date.

Not only is the paragraph run together in violation of § 9, but also the number one is doubled up in the "one (1)" fashion, making it look at a glance as if there's another enumeration going on; this violates § 52. Some drafters would change the second (a)–(b) set to (c)–(d). Others would resort to (x)–(y). But then what do you do with the third (a)–(b) set?

All such devices are lame attempts to fix something that a good numbering system solves. Once you're beyond the initial summary, a modified decimal numbering system can be extremely helpful. For example, the passage above might be set out in this way:

7.2 ***Assignments and Leases.***

(A) *Pantheon's duties.* Effective as of the distribution date, Pantheon will:

(1) assign to the branded subsidiary all of Pantheon's rights, title, and interest in the branded trademarks (see D);

(2) grant to the branded subsidiary a nonexclusive royalty-free right to use *Pantheon*, *Pantheon Foods*, and red stylized *R* trademarks—the Pantheon trademarks—in the United States, its territories and possessions, the Commonwealth of Puerto Rico, and military installations on packaging, promotional, or advertising materials for one year after the distribution date.

(B) *Branded subsidiary's duties.* The branded subsidiary will:

(1) make reasonable efforts to conclude the use of the product-packaging, promotional, and advertising materials by the one-year anniversary of the distribution date; and

(2) place no orders for product-packaging, advertising, or promotional materials anytime after the one-year anniversary of the distribution date.

(C) *Extension of license term.* The license term relating to the use of the Pantheon trademarks may be extended for no more than one additional year for the purpose of permitting the materials that remain on hand on the one-year anniversary of the distribution date.

(D) *Definition of "branded trademarks."* The term "branded trademarks" refers to:

(1) all the trademarks, other than the Pantheon trademarks and the *Panto Flakes* and *Cookie Devil* trademarks, that were previously used or are currently owned by Pantheon Foods or licensed to Pantheon Foods or its subsidiaries and that are or have been almost always associated with the branded business or intended almost always for use in that business; and

(2) certain recipe names used for snack-mix products produced by the branded business.

The broken-out enumerations and the greater use of headings aren't readily achievable without the numbering system. And once the numbering system is in place, it's possible to improve organization. In the preceding example, the original organization needed to be changed because it plopped a lengthy definition into the middle of the paragraph.

Old-style disclosure drafting had a low-level numbering system—that is, lots of (a)'s and (b)'s as well as (i)'s and (ii)'s—but no higher-level numbering system. To cure this defect, so that it's possible to achieve the mandate of § 9, you might adopt the following convention:

1. [Heading]
1.1 [*Subheading*]
  (A) [*Heading optional*]
    (1) [text];
    (2) [text] if both of the following conditions are met:
      (a) [text]; and
      (b) [text]; or
    (3) [text], unless either of the following occurs:
      (a) [text] upon the earlier of the following dates:
        • [text]; or
        • [text]; or
      (b) [text].
  (B) [*Heading optional*]
    (1) [text] . . . . [etc.]

Although some might say that this type of numbering system is itself legalistic, it really isn't: it appeals to the reader's yearning for sequence and orderliness. And it anchors what otherwise tends to look like floating text.

Granted, it's possible to prepare securities documents without any numbering system at all—simply by using paragraphs with headings and then bullets for lists. If you decide to forgo a numbering system, that may be fine. Most documents in the pilot program reflected that choice. But if you use any numbers at all, stick to a system such as the one illustrated above.

§ 47 Consider using a question-and-answer format.

One of the easiest, most straightforward ways to convey information to readers is to answer their most obvious questions—and to do this in a Q&A format. This format works especially well in the initial summary. (No need to number the questions, by the way.)

The most effective technique is to pose the questions using the first person *I*—as someone might do in conversation—and to answer by referring to the company as *we* and to the questioner as *you*. The text then involves the reader directly in the discussion.

Example

Not this:	*But this:*
Purpose of this Proxy Statement This Proxy Statement and the enclosed proxy card are being sent to each shareholder because Pantheon's Board of Directors is soliciting the vote of each shareholder at the 1999 Annual Meeting of Shareholders. This Proxy Statement summarizes the information that each shareholder needs to know to vote intelligently at the Annual Meeting. But a shareholder need not attend the Annual Meeting to vote his or her shares. Instead, he or she may simply complete, sign, and return the enclosed proxy card. Each share of Pantheon common stock entitles the shareholder who owns it to one vote. The proxy card indicates the number of shares of Pantheon stock owned by the recipient of this mailing. Whether a shareholder plans to attend the Annual Meeting or not, Pantheon urges each one to complete, sign, and date the enclosed proxy card and to return it promptly in the envelope provided herewith. Returning the proxy card will not affect a shareholder's right to attend the Annual Meeting and vote. A properly filled-in proxy card should be sent to Pantheon in time for the vote. Then the designated proxy will vote the shareholder's shares as directed in the proxy card. A signed card that does not specify choices will result in a vote of shares in favor of each of the proposed items. If any other matter is presented, the shareholder's proxy will vote in accordance with his or her best judgment. At the time of the printing of this Proxy Statement, the Board of Directors had no knowledge of matters that needed to be acted on at the Annual Meeting other than those discussed in this Proxy Statement.	**Why did you send me this proxy statement?** We sent you this proxy statement and the enclosed card because Pantheon's board of directors is asking for your proxy to vote at the 1999 annual meeting of shareholders. This proxy statement summarizes the information you need to know to vote intelligently at the meeting. But you don't need to attend in order to vote your shares. Instead, you may simply complete, sign, and return the enclosed proxy card. **How many votes do I have?** For each share of Pantheon stock, you get one vote. The proxy card shows the number of shares that you own. **How do I vote by proxy?** Simply complete the proxy card, date it, sign it, and return it. Your proxy—one of the persons named on your proxy card—will vote your shares as directed. If you sign the proxy card without checking the boxes showing specific choices, your proxy will vote in favor of each proposed item as follows: • "For" the election of all six nominees for director. • "For" all amendments to the Charter. • "For" the 1999 executive-incentive plan. • "For" ratification of the choice of independent auditors for 1999. If any other matter is presented, your proxy's best judgment will be used in voting. When this statement went to press, we didn't know of any other matter that needed to be acted on at the annual meeting.

§ 48 Minimize the duplication of ideas within your document.

Eliminate redundancies. In old-style drafting, it was common to build in redundancies. For example, cover pages in prospectuses would frequently repeat the number of shares to be sold several times: in the caption ("7,000,000 shares"), in the opening words of the first paragraph ("Of the 7,000,000 shares of common stock offered hereby . . ."), and in the second paragraph (same as in first paragraph). The SEC commenters rightly condemned this practice in the pilot program. In new-style drafting, it's enough to mention the number in the caption.

In terms of larger-scale organization, the plague has been repetitive disclosures that bulk up the document but don't enhance the quality of the information. Search for these repetitions and then force yourself to consolidate.

Design 8

§ 49 Design your documents to make them reader-friendly.

If the SEC's pilot program showed anything, it showed that design is every bit as important as wording. If the words are going to get read, they must be appealingly presented on the page. Yet disclosure documents have traditionally been eyesores.

Learn a thing or two about typography. Learn, for example, why sans-serif type should be confined to headings and why serifed typefaces are better for text. Learn about the relationship between type size and column width (see § 55). And learn about setting margins so that you'll have an appropriate amount of white space on the page.

You may wish to build a small collection of books on the subject, starting with these:

- Colin Wheildon, *Type & Layout* (1995).
- Robert Bringhurst, *The Elements of Typographic Style* (1997).
- Philip Brady, *Using Type Right* (1989).
- *Words into Type* (3d ed. 1974).

Glean what you can from them. Then share your newfound knowledge with colleagues. Even your litigating colleagues will benefit.

The following example typifies the benefits of sound design. The original document is a turn-off. The revised version is a friendly invitation.

Example

Not this:

Information contained herein is subject to completion or amendment. A registration statement relating to these securities has been filed with the Securities and Exchange Commission. These Securities may not be sold nor may offers to buy be accepted prior to the time the registration statement becomes effective. This prospectus supplement shall not constitute an offer to sell or the solicitation of an offer to buy, nor shall there be any sale of these securities in any State in which such offer, solicitation or sale would be unlawful prior to registration or qualification under the securities laws of any State.

PROSPECTUS

SUBJECT TO COMPLETION DATED AUGUST 21, 1998

DIATECTONICS INTERNATIONAL, LTD.

2,000,000 Shares

Diatectonics International, Ltd. ("we" or "DI"), produces computer parts that are sold to individual consumers through catalogues distributed throughout the United States and Canada. By this prospectus, we are offering you shares of DI Common Stock, no par value ("Shares").

This is our initial public offering, and no public market currently exists for DI's Shares. We estimate that the initial public offering price will be $6.01 per Share. The offering price per Share will be determined by negotiations between DI and the Representative, and may not be indicative of the market price of Shares after the Offering. Factors used to determine the initial public offering price are set forth under "Underwriting."

We will apply to have our Shares listed on The Nasdaq SmallCap System under the symbol DIG on completion of the Offering.

THIS INVESTMENT INVOLVES A HIGH DEGREE OF RISK AND IMMEDIATE AND SUBSTANTIAL DILUTION. YOU SHOULD PURCHASE UNITS ONLY IF YOU CAN AFFORD A COMPLETE LOSS. SEE "RISK FACTORS."

THESE SECURITIES HAVE NOT BEEN APPROVED OR DISAPPROVED BY THE SECURITIES AND EXCHANGE COMMISSION OR ANY STATE SECURITIES COMMISSION NOR HAS THE SECURITIES AND EXCHANGE COMMISSION OR ANY STATE SECURITIES COMMISSION PASSED UPON THE ACCURACY OR ADEQUACY OF THIS PROSPECTUS. ANY REPRESENTATION TO THE CONTRARY IS A CRIMINAL OFFENSE.

	Price to the Public	Underwriting Discounts and Commission (1)	Proceeds to the Company (2)
Per Share	$6.01	$.50	$5.51
Total (3)	$12,020,000	$1,002,000	$11,018,000

The Shares are being offered by the Underwriters when, as and if delivered to and accepted by the Underwriters and subject to various prior conditions, including their right to reject orders in whole or in part. W.B. McKee Securities, Inc. will act as representative of the Underwriters ("Representative"). We expect that Share certificates will be delivered in Dallas, Texas on or about December 21, 1998.

M.F. GRIFFIN SECURITIES, INC.

TINDAL-THOMPSON SECURITIES CORP.

the date of this Prospectus is August 21, 1998

But this:

Diatectonics International

2 Million Shares of Common Stock
$6.01 per share

Diatectonics International
1803 N. Beaston Way
Phoenix, Arizona 95201

The Offering

	Per Share	Total
Public price	$ 6.01	$12,020,000
Underwriting discounts	$ .50	$ 1,002,000
Proceeds to PCI	$ 5.51	$11,018,000

We produce computer parts that are sold to individual consumers through catalogues distributed throughout the United States and Canada.

This is our initial public offering, and no public market currently exists for our shares. The offering price may not reflect the market price of our shares after the offering.

Proposed Trading Symbols:
NASDAQ SmallCap Market℠—DIG
Boston Stock Exchange—DI

This investment involves a high degree of risk. You should purchase shares only if you can afford a complete loss. See risk factors beginning on page 5.

Neither the Securities and Exchange Commission nor any state securities commission has approved these securities or determined whether this prospectus is accurate or complete. It's illegal for anyone to tell you otherwise.

M.F. GRIFFIN SECURITIES, INC.

TINDAL-THOMPSON SECURITIES CORP.

August 21, 1998

§ 50 For long documents, prepare a table of contents and consider having an index.

In a complex document, a table of contents and an index can be invaluable. Of course, the primary aim of these devices is to help readers. But the mere exercise of preparing them will help you in your drafting. Especially with a table of contents, you'll be able to assess the document's organization better—as well as the parallel nature of headings—if you list all the major headings on one page.

§ 51 Avoid cascading left-and-right margins.

Although left-side cascading is a good thing (see § 9), the two-sided kind isn't. In old-style drafting, it was common to see cascading indents on the cover page—usually with the text in all capitals. The new-style format is to put the text in boldface, perhaps with narrower (but consistent) margins left and right.

Example

Not this:

> THESE SECURITIES HAVE NOT BEEN APPROVED OR DISAPPROVED BY THE SECURITIES AND EXCHANGE COMMISSION OR ANY STATE SECURITIES COMMISSION NOR HAS THE COMMISSION OR ANY STATE SECURITIES COMMISSION PASSED UPON THE ACCURACY OR ADEQUACY OF THIS PROSPECTUS. ANY REPRESENTATION TO THE CONTRARY IS A CRIMINAL OFFENSE.

But this:

> **Neither the SEC nor any state securities commission has approved these certificates or determined that this prospectus is accurate or complete. It's illegal for anyone to tell you otherwise.**

§ 52 Prefer numerals, not words, to denote amounts. Avoid word–numeral doublets. Generally, spell out numbers one to ten, and use numerals for numbers 11 and above. For round sums of $1 million and above, combine numerals and words such as *million, billion, trillion,* etc.

Editors used to spell out everything from 1 to 100. That's the hyperformal way—and the slow way. If you want to be solemn and stately, do that. If you want to get your information across quickly, use words only for one to ten.

But this spell-out-ten-and-under rule has several exceptions:

(1) If a passage contains some numbers below the cutoff and some above, don't mix words and numerals. If the things being counted all belong to the same category or type, use numerals consistently: *We interviewed 20 prospective managers but hired only 7.* (But: *We received shipments of 300 cars on six different days in May.*)

(2) Spell out approximations: *About a hundred employees attended that meeting.*

(3) For dollar amounts in millions and billions, use a combination of numerals plus words for round numbers (*$4 million*) and numerals for other numbers (*$4,637,888.84*).

(4) Use numerals for percentages (and use percent signs): *8%, 50%.*

(5) Spell out numbers that begin sentences: *Fifteen protesters were arrested outside the meeting hall.*

Two additional points. First, unless you're working in mathematical columns, avoid putting ".00" after a round number. Second, don't double up words and numerals, the way you do in checks and negotiable instruments. Are you really afraid that someone will fraudulently alter the number?

Example A

Not this:	*But this:*
The Pantheon Charter provides that the number of directors shall be not less than nine nor more than 19, the exact number of directors within such limits to be determined by the Pantheon board.	Our charter provides that our board must have at least 9 directors but no more than 19. Our board determines the exact number within those limits.

Example B

Not this:	*But this:*
Selling and marketing expenses for the first three months of 1998 were one hundred sixty-four thousand four hundred seventy-nine and no/100 dollars ($164,479) compared to ninety-seven thousand eight hundred ninety-three and no/100 dollars ($97,893) in 1997. The increase was due to trade-show expenses and other promotional costs incurred to introduce the Company's new products. This represents a decrease, as a percentage of sales, from thirteen percent (13%) in 1997 to six percent (6%) in 1998.	Selling and marketing expenses for the first three months of 1998 were $164,479, compared to $97,893 in 1997. The increase was due to trade-show expenses and other promotional costs incurred in introducing our new products. But as a percentage of sales, the selling and marketing expenses dropped from 13% in 1997 to 6% in 1998.

Example C

Not this:	*But this:*
No director or executive officer is expected to own more than one percent of the outstanding shares of Pantheon common stock after giving effect to the merger. The directors and executive officers of Pantheon as a group are expected to beneficially own less than one percent of the outstanding shares of Pantheon common stock after giving effect to the merger. No person is expected to beneficially own more than five percent of the outstanding shares of Pantheon common stock after giving effect to the merger.	After the merger, no one is expected to beneficially own more than 5% of Pantheon common stock. The directors and officers are expected to own less than 1%.

Example D

Not this:	*But this:*
40% of the joint venture in Shanghai is owned by the Company.	Forty percent of the joint venture in Shanghai is owned by the company. ***Or even better:*** We own 40% of the joint venture in Shanghai.

§ 53 Avoid roman numerals and romanettes.

The plain-language movement has looked askance at roman numerals. One major plain-language proponent, Judge Lynn N. Hughes of Houston, has suggested abolishing all roman numerals in legal documents. Disclosure documents would be a good place to start.

Romanettes—the lowercase roman numerals—have gained currency among corporate lawyers who habitually run their enumerations into long paragraphs (in violation of §§ 9, 41, 43). It's a habit worth kicking. Hard.

Example

Not this:	*But this:*
The Committee generally determines (i) the participants, (ii) the timing and form of award, (iii) the number of shares needed to cover an award, (iv) its terms, (v) any performance goals or conditions, (vi) adjustments to those terms, (vii) deferrals of awards, (viii) whether awards may be settled in cash or shares, (ix) transferability of any awards, and (x) cash-outs of awards.	The Committee generally determines the terms of each award, including: • the participants; • the timing and form of an award; • the number of shares needed to cover an award; • adjustments to award terms; • performance goals or conditions; • deferral of an award; • payment terms, such as whether the award is payable in cash or shares; • transferability of an award; and • cash-out of an award.

§ 54 Use a ragged right margin.

Almost all the documents that went through the SEC's pilot program had ragged right margins—and the SEC commenters were quick to point out deviations from the ragged-right preference.

To many lawyers, this preference is counterintuitive. But typography specialists insist that the flush-right margin is somewhat less readable than the ragged right. One reason is that the hills and valleys on the right side of the page make it easier for readers, after looking up from the page, to reorient themselves. To put it another way, fully justified margins give text a blocklike appearance. Yet another reason is that, if the rest of the typography isn't first-rate, a justified right margin can create potholes in the middle of the line—long gaps between words caused by the computer's spacing the line to achieve the right-side justification.

§ 55 For small print, use a double-column format. Use no more than 50–90 characters per line.

Legal documents are legendary for hiding things in the fine print. And disclosure documents are no exception.

Actually, the size of the type isn't nearly as important, all in all, as the number of characters in a line. Ideally, a line of type should accommodate 45 to 70 characters, but the "fine print" that characterizes so many legal documents often spans 150 characters to the line. In text of that kind, the reader's eye tends to get lost in mid-line or in moving from the end of one line to the beginning of the next. One way to improve a document with a large block of text—and, typically, small margins on each side—is to use a double-column format. And even in this format, if you've designed the page well, you'll be able to use hanging indents to display the various levels into which you've broken down the text.

In the following example, note how horrific the original is. It appeared just this way in the actual prospectus. Although the middle version keeps the same point size, it's much more readable because of the double columns. (Of course, many other principles discussed throughout the book also surface in this version.) The final version—back to a single-column format—shows the alternative of a larger typeface with cascading indents on the left side (see § 9). You decide which of the revised versions you prefer. But here's a tip worth considering: the double-column format is especially effective in an up-front summary even if you revert to a single column in the rest of the document.

Example

Not this:

14.1 *Authority; Noncontravention.* The Company has, and, in the case of any Ancillary Agreements (as defined in the Reorganization Agreement) executed at a later time, the Company will have, the requisite corporate power and authority (subject to the approvals described in the next sentence) to enter into this Agreement and the Ancillary Agreements and to consummate the transaction contemplated hereby and thereby. The execution and delivery of this Agreement and the Ancillary Agreements and the consummation by the Company of the transactions contemplated hereby and thereby have been duly authorized by all necessary corporate action on the part of the Company, other than, with respect to the Merger, the approval and adoption of this Agreement by the affirmative vote of the holders of Company Common Stock representing two-thirds of the shares entitled to vote (such holders of two-thirds of such shares, the "REQUISITE STOCKHOLDERS"), and formal declaration of the Distribution by the company's Board of Directors (which will occur prior to the Closing Date). This Agreement has been duly executed and delivered by the Company (excluding the Branded Subsidiary) and, assuming this Agreement constitutes a valid and binding obligation of Acquiror, constitutes a valid and binding obligation of the Company (excluding the Branded Subsidiary), enforceable against the Company (excluding the Branded Subsidiary) in accordance with its terms. Except as set forth on Schedule 3.2(c), none of the execution and delivery of the Agreement and the Ancillary Agreements or the consummation of the transactions contemplated hereby or thereby and compliance with the provisions of the Agreement and Ancillary Agreements will conflict with, or result in any violation of, or default (with or without notice or lapse of time, or both) under, or give rise to a right of termination, cancellation or acceleration of any obligation or the loss of a benefit under, or result in the creation of any adverse claim, restriction on voting or transfer, pledge, claim, lien, charge, encumbrance or security interest of any kind or nature whatsoever (collectively, "LIENS") upon any of the properties or assets of the Company (i) under its Articles of Incorporation or Bylaws, (ii) under any Contract (as defined in the Reorganization Agreement) to which the Company is a party or by which the Company or any of its assets are bound, (iii) subject to the governmental filings and other matters referred to in the following sentence, under any judgment, order, decree, statute, law, ordinance, rule or regulation applicable to the Company, or any of its properties or assets, other than, in the case of clauses (ii) and (iii), any such conflicts, violations, defaults, rights, losses or Liens, that individually or in the aggregate would not (A) have a material adverse effect on the Company, (B) materially impair the ability of the Company to perform its obligations under this Agreement or any of the Ancillary Agreements to which the Company is party or (C) prevent or materially delay the consummation of any of the transactions contemplated by this Agreement or any of the Ancillary Agreements. No consent, approval, order or authorization of, or registration, declaration or filing with, any Federal, state or local government or any court, administrative agency or declaration or filing with, any Federal, state or local government or any court, administrative agency or commission or other governmental authority or agency, or self-regulatory organization, domestic or foreign (a "GOVERNMENTAL ENTITY"), is required by or with respect to the Company in connection with the execution and delivery of this Agreement and any of the Ancillary Agreements to which it is a party or the consummation by the Company of the transactions contemplated hereby or thereby, except for (i) the filing with the Securities and Exchange Commission ("SEC") of (x) a proxy statement relating to the approval by the Company's stockholders of this Agreement (as amended or supplemented from time to time, the "PROXY STATEMENT"), (y) potentially, a registration statement on Form S-1 relating to the Distribution and (z) a registration statement on Form 10 (the "FORM 10") under, and such reports under Section 13(a) of, the Securities Exchange Act of 1934, as amended (the "EXCHANGE ACT"), as may be required in connection with this Agreement, the Ancillary Agreements and the transactions contemplated hereby and thereby, (ii) the filing of the Certificate of Merger with the Missouri Secretary of State and appropriate documents with the relevant authorities of other states in which the Company or the Branded Subsidiary is qualified to do business, (iii) expiration of the waiting period under the Hart-Scott-Rodino Antitrust Improvements Act of 1976, as amended (the "HSR ACT"), (iv) such consents, approvals, orders, authorizations, registrations, declarations and filings as are set forth on Schedule 3.2(c) and (v) such other consents, approvals, orders, authorizations, registrations, declarations and filing, the absence of which could not reasonably be expected to have a material adverse effect on the Company.

Words: 809
Sentences: 5
Average sentence length: 161.8

But this:

14.1 Authority; Noncontravention.

(A) ***Corporate power; corporate actions.*** We have the corporate power to enter into this agreement and the ancillary agreements, as well as the power to consummate those transactions. We've taken all the necessary corporate actions to consummate them, with only two exceptions. First, we must still receive the votes of two-thirds of the eligible holders of our common stock in favor of this agreement. Second, our directors must issue a formal declaration of the distribution before the closing date.

(B) ***Nature of our duties.*** We have duly executed and delivered this agreement. Assuming that it's a valid and binding obligation for the acquiror, it's also a valid and binding obligation of ours. With the exceptions noted on Schedule 3.2(c), nothing about this transaction, or related transactions, materially conflicts with or violates:

(1) our articles of incorporation;

(2) our bylaws;

(3) the various contracts to which we're a party; or

(4) any applicable law.

(C) ***Immaterial issues.*** If there were any conflict or violation of the type mentioned in (B), it would not materially:

(1) affect us in an adverse way;

(2) impair our ability to perform our obligations under this agreement or any of the ancillary agreements; or

(3) delay or prevent the consummation of any of the transactions contemplated by this agreement or any of the ancillary agreements.

(D) ***Necessary authorizations.*** Other than those listed below, we aren't required to obtain any authorization by—or to file any documents with—any governmental entity in consummating this agreement or the ancillary agreements:

(1) the SEC filings (a proxy statement, possibly a Form S-1 registration statement, a Form 10 registration statement, and related reports);

(2) a certificate of merger (and related documents) to be filed with the Missouri Secretary of State and other relevant state authorities; and

(3) the authorizations listed on Schedule 3.2(c).

(E) ***Hart-Scott-Rodino waiting period.*** We can't consummate the transactions until the expiration of the waiting period under the Hart-Scott-Rodino Antitrust Improvements Act of 1976. That waiting period will expire on January 16, 1999.

Words: 344
Sentences: 21
Average sentence length: 16.4

Or maybe this:

14.1 Authority; Noncontravention.

(A) ***Corporate power; corporate actions.*** We have the corporate power to enter into this agreement and the ancillary agreements, as well as the power to consummate those transactions. We've taken all the necessary corporate actions to consummate them, with only two exceptions. First, we must still receive the votes of two-thirds of the eligible holders of our common stock in favor of this agreement. Second, our directors must issue a formal declaration of the distribution before the closing date.

(B) ***Nature of our duties.*** We have duly executed and delivered this agreement. Assuming that it's a valid and binding obligation for the acquiror, it's also a valid and binding obligation of ours. With the exceptions noted on Schedule 3.2(c), nothing about this transaction, or related transactions, materially conflicts with or violates:

(1) our articles of incorporation;

(2) our bylaws;

(3) the various contracts to which we're a party; or

(4) any applicable law.

(C) ***Immaterial issues.*** If there were any conflict or violation of the type mentioned in (B), it would not materially:

(1) affect us in an adverse way;

(2) impair our ability to perform our obligations under this agreement or any of the ancillary agreements; or

(3) delay or prevent the consummation of any of the transactions contemplated by this agreement or any of the ancillary agreements.

(D) ***Necessary authorizations.*** Other than those listed below, we aren't required to obtain any authorization by—or to file any documents with—any governmental entity in consummating this agreement or the ancillary agreements:

(1) the SEC filings (a proxy statement, possibly a Form S-1 registration statement, a Form 10 registration statement, and related reports);

(2) a certificate of merger (and related documents) to be filed with the Missouri Secretary of State and other relevant state authorities; and

(3) the authorizations listed on Schedule 3.2(c).

(E) ***Hart-Scott-Rodino waiting period.*** We can't consummate the transactions until the expiration of the waiting period under the Hart-Scott-Rodino Antitrust Improvements Act of 1976. That waiting period will expire on January 16, 1999.

Words: 344
Sentences: 21
Average sentence length: 16.4

§ 56 Use headings to enhance readability.

The more complicated the subject matter, the simpler and more overt you should make the structure. The best way to do this is to use informative, easily accessible headings. They need to be clear to the nonspecialist. So translate them into language that Uncle Bob and Aunt Louise can understand.

Example

Not this:	*But this:*
The proposed amended Plan differs from the existing one in the following principal ways: • **Section 162(m).** The plan incorporates changes necessary to qualify under the exemption from income taxes imposed by Section 162(m) of the Internal Revenue Code discussed below. • **Rule 16b-3.** The plan incorporates changes occasioned by the SEC's amendments to Rule 16b-3 under the Securities Exchange Act of 1934. Generally that rule change relaxed some restrictions on the form of plans, such as permitting transferability of awards, discussed below, and removing restrictions on holding awards for 6 months.	The proposed amended plan differs from the existing one in several ways. The main ways are as follows: • **Tax Qualification.** The plan incorporates changes necessary to qualify under the exemption from income taxes imposed by Section 162(m) of the Internal Revenue Code. • **Short-Swing Profits.** The plan incorporates changes resulting from the SEC's amendments to Rule 16b-3 under the Securities Exchange Act of 1934. Generally, that rule change relaxed some restrictions on the form of plans, such as permitting awards to be transferred and removing restrictions on holding awards for six months.

§ 57 Use tables, charts, and other graphics—but only if they're immediately understandable to the ordinary reader.

Make sure that your graphs and diagrams are easily accessible and almost instantly comprehensible. Even old-style disclosure documents used graphs and diagrams. The problem was that they often meant very little to anyone other than accountants. "That's fine," say some accountants, "because we know what we're looking for." But it's not fine for anyone else.

§ 58 Ban the all-caps style in legends. And avoid contagious capitalization.

Text set in all capitals is unreadable. As the SEC says: "Using all capitalized letters for the legends does not give them proper prominence. Rather, it makes them hard to read. A well-designed cover page that does not crowd the legends with other text can give them the prominence they need."[1] Consider the typical old-style legend:

> THESE SECURITIES HAVE NOT BEEN APPROVED OR DISAPPROVED BY THE SECURITIES AND EXCHANGE COMMISSION OR ANY STATE SECURITIES COMMISSION NOR HAS THE SECURITIES AND EXCHANGE COMMISSION OR ANY STATE SECURITIES COMMISSION PASSED UPON THE ACCURACY OR ADEQUACY OF THIS PROSPECTUS SUPPLEMENT OR THE ACCOMPANYING PROSPECTUS. ANY REPRESENTATION TO THE CONTRARY IS A CRIMINAL OFFENSE.

The reason it's unreadable is that if all the characters are the same size, those characters have fewer identifying characteristics: the brain has to work harder to differentiate the characters and therefore to see what words are being used.

Even if you change to initial capitals, you can't say there's much of an improvement in readability:

> These Securities Have Not Been Approved or Disapproved by the Securities and Exchange Commission or Any State Securities Commission Nor Has the Securities and Exchange Commission or Any State Securities Commission Passed upon the Accuracy or Adequacy of This Prospectus Supplement or the Accompanying Prospectus. Any Representation to the Contrary Is a Criminal Offense.

You're better off using ordinary sentences in boldface type. In the following example, the text is also cleaned up a little:

> **Neither the SEC nor any state securities commission has approved these certificates or determined that this prospectus is accurate or complete. It's illegal for anyone to tell you otherwise.**

Capitalization, though, isn't just an outmoded way to highlight text. It's also the traditional way of showing which words you've defined. The problem is that some drafters define and capitalize terms that couldn't possibly be confused by anybody. So in the pilot program, the SEC plain-English commenters again and again warned drafters not to capitalize common nouns such as *merger agreement*, *ordinary shares*, and *annual meeting*. Initial capitals are almost as reader-unfriendly as all caps: they create visual hiccups.

The tendency to use initial capitals stems partly from the tendency to overdefine. Once you minimize definitions (see § 62), you'll eliminate many capitals.

§ 59 Avoid underlining as a means of highlighting text.

In traditional typewriting, you have two ways to emphasize text: using capitals and underlining. But with enhanced typographic capabilities, underlining has become outmoded. Several better techniques are available for emphasis, such as changing the type size and using boldface type.

Example

Not this:	*But this:*
Limited Partners of the Partnership desiring to tender their Interests in the Partnership pursuant to the Exchange Offer must vote such Interests in favor of the Proposal described above. Limited Partners of the Partnership desiring to vote in favor of the Proposal described above must tender their Interests in the Partnership pursuant to the Exchange Offer.	**If you're a limited partner and you want to vote for the proposal, you must tender your partnership interests in accordance with the exchange offer. Likewise, if you want to tender your partnership interests under the exchange offer, you must vote your interests in favor of the proposal.**

§ 60 Make the cover page self-contained. Don't allow text to spill over to a second page.

Some of the SEC's comments during the pilot program criticized cover pages with text that continued beyond the first page. As a result, the SEC decided to amend Item 501 to require that the cover-page text be limited to one page.[2] So you're no longer allowed to put "(continued on next page)" anywhere on the cover page. Whatever needs to be there should be there.

§ 61 Use trademarks, logos, and other identifying features to personalize the prospectus. Consider using color graphics inside the front and back covers.

Of course, trading symbols are required under the securities laws.[3] But even if they weren't, it would be a good idea to use them on the cover pages of disclosure documents. They are identifying features that immediately distinguish one prospectus or proxy statement from another.[4]

And with the reduced clutter of cover pages, they become even more prominent.

Pictures are also valuable both in generating reader interest and in reinforcing corporate identity. The two examples that follow appeared in prospectuses that had excellent graphics inside the front and back covers. Example A appeared inside the front cover of the Boddie-Noell Properties, Inc. prospectus that offered 2.5 million shares of common stock in December 1997. Example B appeared inside the back cover of a Photran Corporation prospectus that offered 2 million shares of common stock in May 1996.

Example A

BNP

BODDIE-NOELL PROPERTIES, INC.

A Real Estate Investment Trust

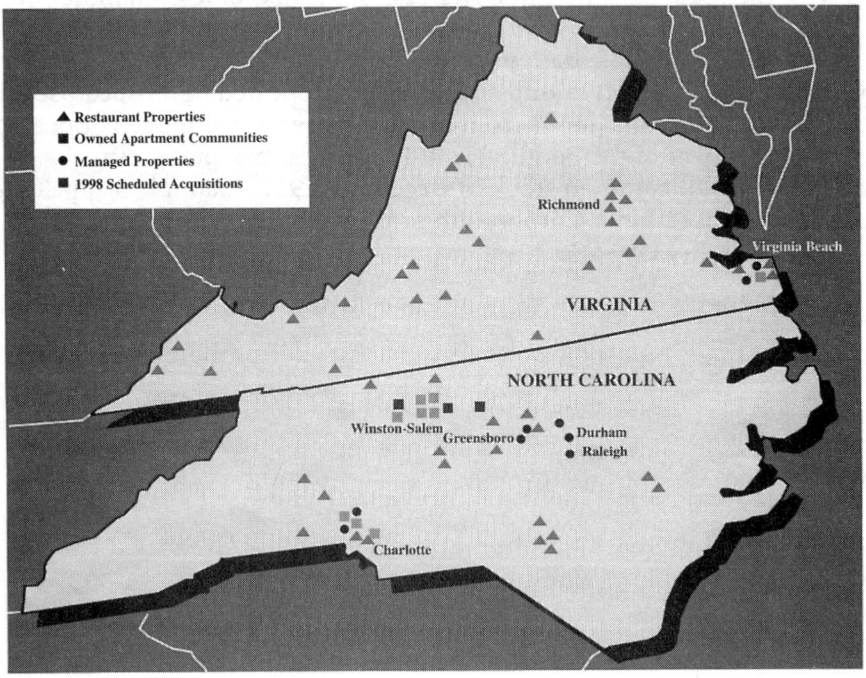

Assets by Cost

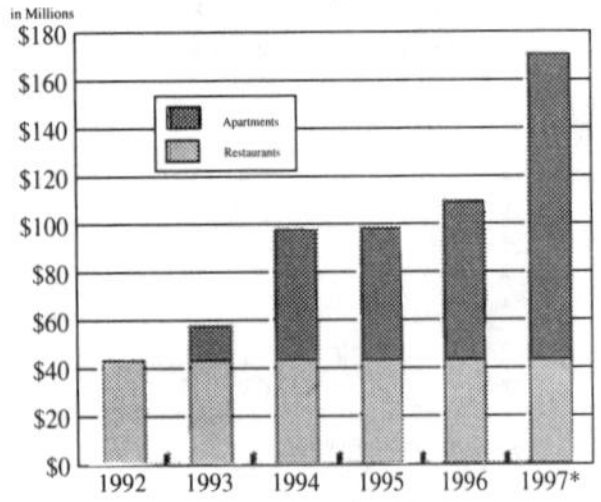

* At September 30, Pro Forma

Revenue Growth

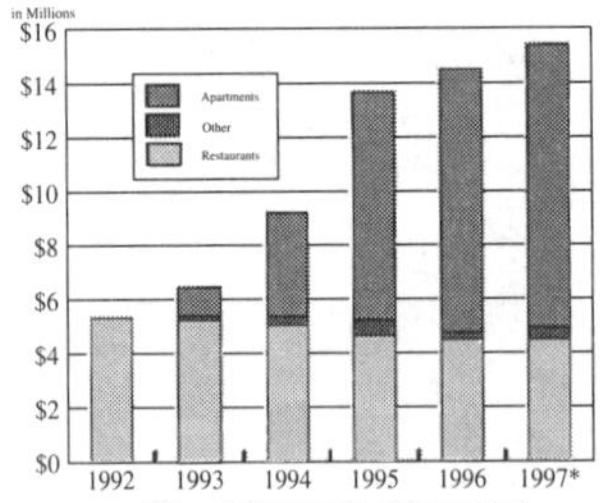

* Through September 30, 1997, Annualized

Apartment Units Owned

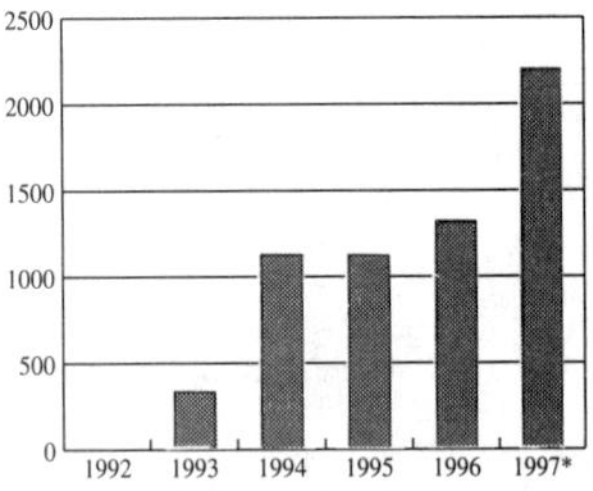

* At September 30, Pro Forma

In connection with an underwritten offering, the SEC rules permit the underwriters to engage in transactions that stabilize the price of our common stock. These transactions may include purchases for the purpose of fixing or maintaining the price of the common stock at a level that is higher than the market would dictate in the absence of such transactions.

Example B

Photran Products

PCO® ITO Glass for Flat Panel Displays

PCO brand electrically conductive Indium Tin Oxide coated glass. This material is a key component in most types of flat panel displays.

ZeroRay™ Glare and Radiation Filters

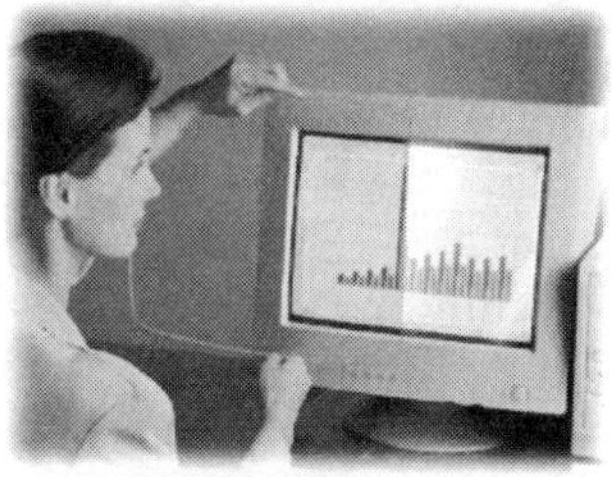

ZeroRay glare and radiation filters provide an advanced solution for controlling glare and radiation from computer monitors, televisions and other display devices without loss of screen brightness.

UVAR™ Low Reflection and UV Light Blocking Eyeglass Lenses

UVAR eyeglass lenses feature a combination of low reflection, ultraviolet light blocking, chemical and mechanical durability and ease of cleaning. In addition, UVAR ophthalmic lenses contribute to improved night vision.

PMAX® Ultra High Reflection Optical Grade Mirrors for use in Copy Machines, Laser Scanners and Projection Televisions

PMAX front surface high performance optical grade mirrors are used where reflected light must be maximized in optical systems.

ArtGlas™ Low Reflection and UV Light Blocking Picture Framing Glass

ArtGlas eliminates virtually all glare and blocks 100% of the ultraviolet portion of sunlight and artificial light. Ultraviolet light is a major cause of irreversible damage to artwork, photographs, carpets and drapes.

PHOTRAN

endnotes

1 *Plain English Disclosures*, Fed. Sec. L. Rep. (CCH) ¶ 86,003, at 80,129.

2 *See id.*

3 *See* Item 501 of Regulation S–K, 17 C.F.R. § 229.501 (1998).

4 *See Plain English Disclosures*, Fed. Sec. L. Rep. (CCH) ¶ 86,003, at 80,128 (where the SEC states that "we intend . . . to give you the flexibility you need to design a cover page tailored to your company and the offering").

Definitions 9

§ 62 Work hard to draft without definitions.

Keep to a minimum (hereinafter "Minimize") all definitional words, especially those in the form of midsentence parentheticals (hereinafter collectively "Defined Terms"). Most Defined Terms serve as shorthand forms for the person doing the writing (hereinafter "the Writer"). But they're typically roadblocks (hereinafter "Roadblocks" or "Impediments") for the people who do the reading (hereinafter "Readers"), who undoubtedly wish that the Roadblocks were Minimized. If a writer uses an Impediment such as a Defined Term without first ensuring that clarity and precision (hereinafter collectively "Accurate Readability") have been improved, the Writer is likely to seem willfully obscure to naive Readers (hereinafter "Naive Readers") and doltish to more sophisticated Readers (hereinafter "Sophisticated Readers"). The resulting mishmash (hereinafter "Mishmash") will drive all types of Readers, whether Naive Readers or Sophisticated Readers, away from the document (hereinafter "Repulsive Effect") precisely because the Mishmash and the effects relating thereto, including but not limited to the Repulsive Effect (hereinafter collectively the "Concomitant Effects"), are inconsistent with Accurate Readability.

Write that way if you must. But you needn't. And you shouldn't.

The advice contained in that initial paragraph—if you took the time to figure it out—is quite counterintuitive to most transactional lawyers, who have come to believe that the more you define terms, the better. Experts in the field of drafting have long held the opposite view:

- "[A] definition . . . often creates more problems than it solves."—Lord Reid[1]

- "[D]efinitions don't belong in a legal document. If they just echo the dictionary, they are pointless—like section 441(d) of the Internal Revenue Code, which says, 'For purposes of this subtitle, the term "calendar year" means a period of 12 months ending on December 31.' If they *don't* echo the dictionary but sneak in something extra, they're a piece of trickery and should always be replaced by a straightforward explanation in the text of the document."—Rudolf Flesch[2]

- "In the realm of definitions, it is usually wise to try to be a minimalist, in other words, to try to convey everything you have to say clearly without using definitions at all."—Barbara Child[3]

The following example shows how readily you can draft clear passages without definitions. Notice how eliminating the definitions results in improved organization. Notice also that the left-hand column uses the defined term *Representative*, which in the actual prospectus was defined 36 pages before this passage. A LawProse staffer took ten minutes searching in vain for the definition of *Representative.* (Would an investor spend that much time?) In the end, all the term means is *underwriters' representative*—an easy enough thing to say explicitly.

Example

Not this:	*But this:*
3.4 Bridge Financing In October 1998, the Company obtained bridge financing (the "Bridge Financing") which consisted of the issuance of Bridge Notes in an aggregate principal amount of $4 million (the "Bridge Notes") and warrants to purchasers of the Bridge Notes to purchase 400,000 shares of the Company's Common Stock, and a warrant to the Representative as selling agent to purchase 40,000 shares of the Company's Common Stock (collectively, the "Bridge Warrants"). The Bridge Financing was used for the acquisition of capital equipment and construction of facility improvements. The Bridge Notes bear interest from the date of issue at a rate of 11.75% per annum, payable at maturity. The Bridge Notes are payable in full on the earlier of October 15, 1999, or the closing date of this Offering.	**3.4 Bridge Financing** In October 1998, we obtained bridge financing to acquire capital equipment and to improve our facilities. The financing consisted of: (A) bridge notes in an aggregate principal amount of $4 million, bearing interest from the date of issue at a rate of 11.75% per year, payable at maturity (either October 15, 1999, or the closing date of this offering, whichever is earlier); (B) warrants to buyers of the bridge notes to buy 400,000 shares of our common stock; and (C) warrants to the underwriters' representative as our selling agent to buy 40,000 shares of our common stock.

§ 63 Define terms in only two circumstances: (1) when you need to clarify a term of uncertain meaning; and (2) when you need to avoid duplicating long swaths of verbiage for which a shorthand term is available.

This guideline states the test for defining terms in contractual drafting. It appears here only because it might conceivably apply to securities documents. Having looked for examples of justifiable definitions, I haven't found any—apart from the arguable need to define *we* and *you*. So I can't illustrate the need. Perhaps Flesch's quotation in § 62, despite its seeming hyperbole, isn't an overstatement at all.

§ 64 If you define a term, use an everyday shorthand name for it. Avoid alien-sounding acronyms.

Remember that you're writing English—plain English—not some hybrid language full of terms you make up. And to the extent that you must define terms, choose words that are both descriptive and immediately comprehensible.

In Example A, "GBFSH1" refers to the Griffin-Buck Family Steakhouse #1. A similar acronym denotes each of the numbers up to 5. The result is a mishmash of GBFSH's. Just by using the word *Restaurant* as opposed to *GBFSH*, you've enhanced clarity for the vast majority of readers.

Example B has two problems. First, the reader is served a huge bowl of alphabet soup: ten acronyms are introduced in a single sentence. Second, the example's first acronym, "NFL," is likely to cause a miscue with most readers—at least those who watch TV in the fall. Moral: don't use an acronym that carries some other popular meaning.

One other thing about Example B. If you don't have the shorthand acronyms, how are you supposed to refer to Westbrook Marketing Corporation or Precision Dialing Services, Inc. a second time? Do you have to use the full name over and over? The answer, of course, is no. Simply say *Westbrook Marketing* and *Precision Dialing*. And do it without the heavy-handedness of saying, in your first mention, "Westbrook Marketing Corporation ('Westbrook Marketing')," etc. Give your reader an ounce of credit for having some candlepower.

Example A

Not this:	*But this:*
On December 14, 1997, GBFSH1, GBFSH2, and GBFSH3 distributed all of their cash available for distribution (net of reserves) of $32,000 (or $40 per Interest), $32,000 (or $36 per Interest), and $36,000 (or $36 per Interest), respectively, to their Limited Partners. GBFSH4 and GBFSH5 had no cash available for distribution at July 31, 1998. Limited Partners in GBFSH1, GBFSH2, and GBFSH3 all have invested in the Griffin-Buck Family Steakhouse concept in a substantially earlier phase of that concept than did the Limited Partners in GBFSH4 and GBFSH5.	On December 14, 1997, Restaurants #1–3 distributed all of their cash available for distribution (net of reserves) to their limited partners. Restaurant #1 distributed $32,000 (or $40 per interest); Restaurant #2 distributed $32,000 (or $36 per interest); and Restaurant #3 distributed $36,000 (or $36 per interest). Restaurants #4 and #5 had no cash available for distribution on July 31, 1998. Limited partners in Restaurants #1–3 all invested in the Griffin-Buck Family Steakhouse concept at a substantially earlier phase of that concept than the limited partners in Restaurants #4 and #5.

Example B

Not this:	But this:
The Company's wholly owned subsidiaries and affiliated companies include National Foundation Life Insurance Company ("NFL"), National Financial Insurance Company ("NFIC"), American Insurance Company of Illinois ("AICI"), Westbrook National Life Insurance Company ("WNL") and together with NFL, NFIC and AICI (the "Insurance Subsidiaries"), Foundation Financial Services, Inc. ("FFS"), Westbrook Marketing Corporation ("WMC"), Precision Dialing Services, Inc. ("PDS"), Westbrook Printing Services, Inc. ("WPS"), Westbrook Funding Corporation ("WFC"), LifeStyles Marketing Group, Inc. ("LifeStyles Marketing"), Senior Benefits, LLC ("Senior Benefits"), American Senior Security Plans, LLC ("ASSP") and Health Care-One Insurance Agency, Inc. ("Health Care-One").	The company's wholly owned subsidiaries and affiliated companies include: • National Foundation Life Insurance Company; • National Financial Insurance Company; • American Insurance Company of Illinois; • Westbrook National Life Insurance Company; • Foundation Financial Services, Inc.; • Westbrook Marketing Corporation; • Precision Dialing Services, Inc.; • Westbrook Printing Services, Inc.; • Westbrook Funding Corporation; • LifeStyles Marketing Group, Inc.; • Senior Benefits, LLC; • American Senior Security Plans, LLC; and • Health Care-One Insurance Agency, Inc.

§ 65 To the extent that you define terms, collect the definitions at the back of the document.

Transactional lawyers are accustomed to putting definitions at the beginning of their contracts—sometimes 2 pages but sometimes as much as 30 pages of intertwined, heavily cross-referenced, often incomprehensible definitions that would make any lexicographer blush. Businesspeople tend to detest this practice, but the lawyers say this in their own defense: how can you read the document if you don't know what the terms mean?

It's not a good defense. No one—not even the lawyer—slogs dutifully through the definitions before reading a document. Not, that is, unless the reader is an expert in the field who knows precisely what to look for in a given definition. And that reader, who isn't the primary audience for disclosure documents anyway, can just as readily flip to the back of the document to consult the definition.

Almost all the documents that were part of the SEC's pilot program for plain-English disclosure reflected the move-the-definitions-to-the-back approach.

endnotes

1 *Brutus v. Cozens,* [1972] 3 W.L.R. 521, 525.

2 *How to Write Plain English: A Book for Lawyers and Consumers* 68–69 (1979).

3 *Drafting Legal Documents* 356 (2d ed. 1992).

Conclusion

Plain-English drafting isn't easy. It requires hard work—just as all good writing does. In the end, though, if you acquire this skill, not only will you be writing much better than most transactional lawyers have done in the past, you'll also be thinking better. Plain English is good mental hygiene.

And this skill, this mental habit, is more in demand than ever. Not only are securities documents now required to be in plain English. So are franchise agreements[1] and, in many states, consumer contracts and insurance policies.[2]

Progress is being made on other fronts, too. Article 9 of the Uniform Commercial Code has been revised into plain English and sent to the states for adoption.[3] What's more, the entire federal government has gotten into the act. The federal courts are now producing plain-English court rules.[4] And the President signed an official memorandum requiring federal agencies to start using plain English in all new documents by October 1, 1998.[5]

The legal profession is changing. The way people communicate with each other is changing. As the world becomes increasingly complex, and as information about our world becomes increasingly complex, people are yearning for a little simplicity. Simple words. Direct sentences. Intelligibility.

Don't ever oversimplify. Just say things as simply as you can.

endnotes

1 *Uniform Franchise Offering Circular—1993 Guidelines*, Bus. Franchise Guide (CCH) ¶ 5750.

2 *See* Joseph Kimble, *Plain English: A Charter for Clear Writing*, 9 Thomas M. Cooley L. Rev. 1, 32–35 (1992).

3 *See* Steven O. Weise, *Plain English Comes to the Uniform Commercial Code*, Clarity, Sept. 1998, at 20.

4 *See* Bryan A. Garner, *Guidelines for Drafting and Editing Court Rules* (Admin. Office of the U.S. Courts, 1996); Garner, *The Substance of Style in Federal Rules*, Clarity, Sept. 1998, at 15.

5 *See The Recent Presidential Memorandum on Plain Language*, 6 Scribes J. Legal Writing 39 (1996–1997).

Select Bibliography

Cutts, Martin. *The Plain English Guide*. Oxford: Oxford Univ. Press, 1995.

Eagleson, Robert. *Writing in Plain English*. Canberra: Australian Government Publishing Service, 1990.

Flesch, Rudolf. *How to Write Plain English: A Book for Lawyers and Consumers*. New York: Harper & Row, 1979.

Garner, Bryan A. *A Dictionary of Modern American Usage*. New York: Oxford Univ. Press, 1998.

Garner, Bryan A. *A Dictionary of Modern Legal Usage*. 2d ed. New York: Oxford Univ. Press, 1995.

Garner, Bryan A. *The Elements of Legal Style*. New York: Oxford Univ. Press, 1991.

Gunning, Robert. *The Technique of Clear Writing*. New York: McGraw-Hill, 1952.

Kimble, Joseph. "Answering the Critics of Plain Language," 5 *Scribes J. Legal Writing* 51 (1994–1995).

Kimble, Joseph. "Writing for Dollars, Writing to Please," 6 *Scribes J. Legal Writing* 1 (1996–1997).

Wydick, Richard C. *Plain English for Lawyers*. 4th ed. Durham, N.C.: Carolina Academic Press, 1998.

PART TWO
PLAIN-ENGLISH FILINGS

Though based on real filings, the following documents are fictional. No actual offer or solicitations were ever made with them—or ever will be. Any similarity of names to those in real filings is coincidental and unintentional.

Mutual-Fund Prospectus and Profile

Drafters:

Richard D. Marshall
David Dickstein
Kirkpatrick & Lockhart LLP
1251 Avenue of the Americas
45th Floor
New York, New York 10020-1104

Editorial Consultants:

LawProse, Inc.
5949 Sherry Lane, Suite 1280
Dallas, Texas 75225-8008

INVESTMENT HORIZONS
Growth and Value Fund

Prospectus
September 5, 1998

Neither the SEC nor any state securities commission has approved these securities or determined if this prospectus is truthful or complete. It's illegal for anyone to tell you otherwise.

RISK/RETURN SUMMARY

Investment Goal

Our goal is to provide you with investment returns that consistently outperform the Standard & Poor's 500 Index. We measure your investment returns by adding together your capital appreciation and income from the Fund.

Principal Investment Strategies

We invest Fund assets in growth and undervalued domestic securities. We use a company's financial health and stock price to determine its value. We use a company's expected earnings to indicate its future growth. We reduce potential risks by placing no more than 10% of the Fund's assets in any one stock or industry.

Principal Risks

Investing in securities is inherently risky, and there is no guarantee that we will achieve our investment goals. In fact, you could lose money by investing in the Fund. The principal risks include:

- **Market Risks**. The price of particular securities may fall because of declines in the stock market regardless of the success of the individual companies' businesses.
- **Diversification Risks**. We may invest in securities not listed in the Standard and Poor's 500 Index. There is a chance that these securities will perform poorly, which may enable the Standard and Poor's 500 Index to outperform the Fund.
- **Undervalued Securities**. The Fund often purchases securities that the market undervalues in relation to their actual worth. We assume that the market will ultimately recognize the actual worth of these companies, thus causing their stock prices to rise. The market may, however, indefinitely undervalue these securities, causing their prices to remain the same or even decline.
- **Low Dividends**. The Fund often purchases the securities of companies that expect their earnings to rise. These stocks typically pay little if any dividends. Securities that pay small dividends are risky because their stock prices often decline in market downturns.

Past Performance

The bar chart and performance table below indicate some of the risks of investing in the Fund. The bar chart shows the changes in the Fund's performance from year to year over a 10-year period. The performance table shows how the Fund's average annual returns for 1, 5, and 10 years compare with those of the Standard and Poor's 500 Index, a broad measure of market performance. When you review these charts, be aware that past investment performance does not necessarily indicate how the Fund will perform in the future.

A Decade of Year-End Returns

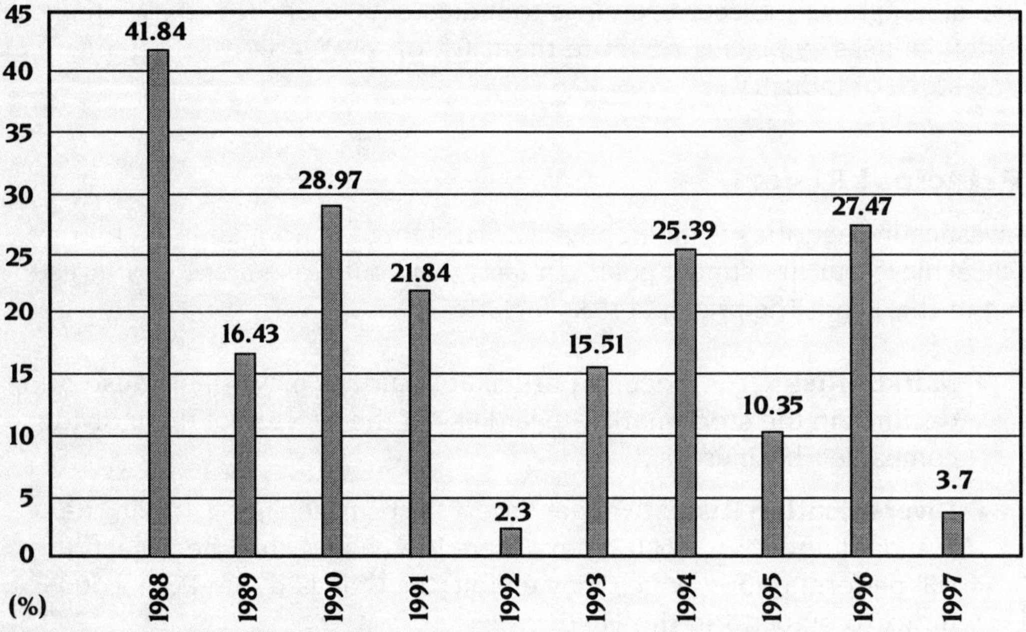

During the period shown above, the best quarter was the second quarter of 1988, when the Fund produced a 36% return. The worst quarter was the third quarter of 1992, when the Fund produced a -8% return.

Average Annual Returns

	1 year (1997)	5 years (1993–1997)	10 years (1988–1997)
Fund	3.70%	16.48%	19.38%
S&P 500	22.50%	13.37%	16.42%

Shareholder Fees and Expenses

Investors pay certain fees and expenses in connection with investing in mutual funds. This table describes the fees and expenses that you may pay if you buy and hold shares of the Investment Horizons Growth and Value Fund. Shareholder fees are paid directly from your investment. Annual Fund operating expenses are deducted from Fund assets.

Shareholder Fees (fees paid directly from your investment)	
Maximum sales charge (load) imposed on purchases (as a percentage of offering price)	None
Maximum deferred sales charge (load) (as a percentage of offering price)	None
Maximum sales charge (load) imposed on reinvested dividends (as a percentage of offering price)	None
Redemption fee (as a percentage of amount redeemed)	None
Exchange fee	None
Annual Fund Operating Expenses (expenses deducted from Fund assets)	
Management fees	0.90%
Distribution (12b-1) and service fees	0.20%
Other expenses	0.00%
Total annual Fund operating expenses	1.10%

Expense Example

The example below is intended to help you compare the cost of investing in the Fund with the cost of investing in other mutual funds. The example assumes that:

- you invest $10,000 in the Fund for the time periods indicated;
- your investment has a 5% return each year; and
- the Fund's operating expenses remain the same.

Although your actual costs may be higher or lower, under these assumptions your costs would be:

Number of years	1	3	5	10
	$170	$425	$760	$1,705

These figures would remain the same regardless of whether you sold your shares at the end of a period.

INVESTMENT OBJECTIVES AND PRINCIPAL INVESTMENT STRATEGIES

Investment Goal

Our goal is to provide investment returns that consistently outperform the Standard & Poor's 500 Index. We measure your investment returns by adding together your capital appreciation and income from the Fund. Our goal may change without shareholder approval.

Principal Investment Strategies

We invest in a blend of growth and undervalued domestic stocks that are likely to generate returns better than those of the Standard & Poor's 500 Index. Generally, we select stocks for the Fund by following a two-step process:

(A) **Ranking Stocks**: Our analysts identify and rank stocks on an industry-by-industry basis. Within each industry we rank companies according to their:

- **Price**. The price of the stock in comparison to our view of the company's actual worth.
- **Expected Earnings**. The company's expected future earnings.
- **Financial Health**. The company's assets and liabilities.

(B) **Reducing Risk**: We buy and sell stocks that have our highest rankings. The portfolio manager reduces risk by placing no more than 10% of the Fund's assets in any one stock or industry.

Ordinarily, we'll apply our principal investment strategies when making investment decisions. Occasionally, we may need to abandon our principal investment strategies and take temporary defensive positions in response to adverse market, economic, or political conditions. Investing in temporary defensive positions diminishes the chances of achieving our investment goals.

We may engage in active and frequent trading to achieve our principal investment strategies. This may increase your capital-gains distributions, which in turn would increase your tax liability. Frequent trading will also increase our transaction costs, which may reduce the Fund's investment performance.

MANAGEMENT

Investment Horizons Management is the investment adviser for the Fund. Our company began doing business in 1937. We provide investment advice exclusively to mutual funds. We currently manage 40 mutual funds with combined assets of over $70 billion.

We provide the following advisory services to the Investment Horizons Growth and Equity Fund:

- The making of all investment decisions.
- The placing of all orders for purchases and sales of Fund securities.
- The administering of the Fund's other affairs, including the furnishing of office space, preparing or assisting in preparing materials for regulatory bodies, and overseeing the Fund's custodial and accounting services.
- The distributing of the Fund's shares to investors.

During 1997 we received 0.9% of the Fund's average net assets for our services.

Peter Williams is the portfolio manager for the Fund. Mr. Williams joined Investment Horizons Management's staff in 1982, and he began managing the Fund in 1986.

Our mailing address is:

Investment Horizons Management
4020 North LaSalle Street
Chicago, Illinois 60601

SHAREHOLDER INFORMATION

Pricing of Fund Shares

The price at which you buy and sell Fund shares is the Fund's net asset value (NAV) per share. The NAV per share is generally calculated at the close of the regular trading session of the New York Stock Exchange (usually 4:00 p.m. EST). The Fund's shares will not be priced on days when the New York Stock Exchange is closed. The last quoted market prices of the Fund's holdings determine its NAV per share. If market prices are not available for particular securities, we will value them at a price we think is fair.

Once the Fund accepts your order, the purchase price will be the NAV per share calculated immediately after the order is accepted. You pay no sales load for buying or selling Fund shares.

Procedures for Buying Fund Shares

The minimum investment requirements for the Fund are:

	Opening the Account	Adding to the Account
Regular accounts	$5,000	$100
IRAs	$1,000	$100

We reserve the right to change these minimum investment amounts at any time. Also, we can refuse any purchase order that might adversely affect the Fund's operations.

You may buy Fund shares in any of these ways:

By telephone

Call 1-800-555-5555 to buy shares of the Fund. You must send us your payment within three business days of your order. To meet this deadline, you may send a check by overnight mail or wire payment, or you may make an electronic transfer through your bank.

By mail

Mail your application and check to:

Investment Horizons Management
Fund Purchases
4020 North LaSalle Street
Chicago, Illinois 60601

If you purchase additional shares of the Fund, you must send a completed investment slip together with a check that has your account number on it.

By the Internet

Our website address is www.invhor.com. Follow the application instructions on the website.

Procedures for Selling Fund Shares

You may sell up to $300,000 of Fund shares per day. You will receive the sale proceeds within five business days after we accept your sell order.

We won't accept any sell orders until:

- you return all certificates representing the shares being sold; and
- you completely pay for any outstanding debts you owe for the shares being sold.

You may sell Fund shares in any of these ways:

By telephone

Call 1-800-555-5555 and give your name, account number, the name of the Fund, and the dollar amount or number of shares you want to sell. Then send us any certificates representing the shares being redeemed.

By mail

Complete a redemption form and send it to:

Investment Horizons Management
Fund Redemption Center
4020 North LaSalle Street
Chicago, Illinois 60601

You must sign the redemption form exactly as your name appears on the account. Include any certificates for the shares being sold with your redemption form.

Fund Distributions

Each year (usually in December), the Fund distributes dividends from net investment income and net capital gains from investment transactions. We will automatically reinvest the distributions in additional shares of the Fund, unless you choose to receive them in cash. If you prefer cash, you must notify us in writing at least five days before the date of each distribution. There are no fees or sales charges on reinvestments.

Taxes

Any sale or exchange of Fund shares, and all Fund distributions, are taxable regardless of whether they are paid in cash or by reinvestment in additional Fund shares.

For federal income-tax purposes:

Short-term capital gains means distributions you receive for shares sold up to 12 months after buying them;

Long-term capital gains means distributions you receive for shares sold after holding them for at least 12 months.

Dividends from taxable net investment income and distributions of net short-term capital gains are taxable as ordinary income. Distributions of net long-term capital gains are taxable as long-term capital gains. We will send you tax statements every January describing the taxes that you owe for investing in the Fund during the previous calendar year.

The tax information provided here is quite general. We urge you to consult your tax adviser about federal, state, and local tax consequences.

Rule 12b-1 Fees

The Fund maintains a 12b-1 plan that allows it to pay distribution fees for the sale and distribution of its shares. The Fund pays out of its assets 0.2% each year in 12b-1 fees. Over time, these fees will increase the cost of your investment and may cost you more than paying other types of sales charges.

Investor Services

We provide you with a number of services to help you manage your account:

- **Information Services**. Our telephone representatives are available 24 hours a day, 365 days a year, to provide the information or service you need. To reach us, call 1-800-555-5555.
- **Fund Transfer Services**. You may transfer money by phone from your Fund account to your bank account. We will complete most transactions within two business days.
- **Automatic Investment Services**. You may direct us to automatically invest preset amounts from your various bank accounts in Fund shares. These automatic investments may be made on a monthly or quarterly basis.
- **Exchange Services**. You may make regular exchanges of Investment Horizons Growth and Value Fund shares for shares of our other funds.

FINANCIAL HIGHLIGHTS

The following table shows the Fund's financial performance for the past five years. Certain information reflects financial results for a single Fund share. The total returns in the table represent the rate that an investor would have earned on an investment in the Fund (assuming reinvestment of all dividends and distributions). AccuStat Accounting audited this information (except for the six-month period ended June 30, 1998). Their report, along with the Fund's financial statements, are included in the Statement of Additional Information, which is available upon request.

	Six Months Ended June 30,	Year Ended December 31,				
	1998	1997	1996	1995	1994	1993
Per-Share Data ($)						
Net asset value, beginning of period	$28.46	$28.88	$24.42	$24.00	$19.31	$18.91
Investment operations:						
Investment income—net	.08	.19	.17	.21	.23	.29
Net realized and unrealized gains on investments	12.00	.85	5.97	2.16	4.65	2.62
Total from investment operations	12.08	1.04	6.14	2.37	4.88	2.91
Distributions:						
Dividends from investment income—net	(.22)	(.11)	(.20)	(.25)	(.04)	(.31)
Dividends from net realized gain on investments	(1.43)	(1.35)	(1.48)	(1.70)	(.15)	(2.20)
Total distributions	(1.65)	(1.46)	(1.68)	(1.95)	(.19)	(2.51)
Net asset value, end of period	$38.89	$28.46	$28.88	$24.42	$24.00	$19.31
Total return (%)	43.92%	3.70%	27.47%	10.35%	25.39%	15.51%
Ratios/Supplemental Data (%)						
Ratio of expenses to average net assets	1.06%	1.06%	1.04%	1.10%	1.09%	1.00%
Ratio of net investment income to average net assets	.50%	.91%	.91%	1.09%	(.14%)	.11%
Portfolio turnover rate	112.32%	137.38%	268.40%	242.75%	194.59%	90.03%
Net assets, end of period (in thousands of dollars)	$508,562	$471,660	$418,240	$372,313	$463,323	$569,791

ADDITIONAL INFORMATION

Please contact us to obtain free additional information about the Fund or to make shareholder inquiries. On request, we'll also send you the following documents about the Fund, at no charge.

Annual and Semiannual Report

Additional information about the Fund's investments is available in the Fund's annual and semiannual reports to shareholders. In each annual report, you will find a discussion of the market conditions and investment strategies that significantly affected the Fund's performance during its last fiscal year.

Statement of Additional Information (SAI)

The SAI includes additional information about the Fund, its business operations, and its policies. The SAI is incorporated by reference into this prospectus.

You may review and copy additional information about the Fund, including the SAI, at the Securities and Exchange Commission's Public Reference Room in Washington, DC. To obtain information on the operation of the Public Reference Room, call 1-800-SEC-0330.

You also may obtain copies of these documents and other information about the Fund from the SEC by sending a duplication fee and written request to the Public Reference Section of the SEC, Washington, DC 20549-6009, or free of charge from the SEC's website at www.sec.gov.

To contact us:

Investment Horizons Management
4020 North LaSalle Street
Chicago, Illinois 60601
1-800-555-5555
www.invhor.com

SEC File No. 811-37232

INVESTMENT HORIZONS
Growth and Value Fund

Fund Profile
September 5, 1998

This profile summarizes key information about the Fund. The Fund's prospectus contains more information about the Fund, including a detailed description of the risks associated with investing in the Fund—risks that you should consider before you invest. You may get the prospectus and other information about the Fund at no cost by calling 1-800-555-5555 or by visiting our website at www.invhor.com.

Investment Goal

Our goal is to provide you with investment returns that consistently outperform the Standard & Poor's 500 Index. We measure your investment returns by adding together your capital appreciation and income from the Fund.

Principal Investment Strategies

We invest Fund assets in growth and undervalued domestic securities. We use a company's financial health and stock price to determine its value. We use a company's expected earnings to indicate its future growth. We reduce potential risks by placing no more than 10% of the Fund's assets in any one stock or industry.

Annual and Semiannual Reports: Additional information about the Fund's investments is available in the Fund's annual and semi-annual reports to shareholders. In the Fund's annual report, you will find a discussion of the market conditions and investment strategies that significantly affected the Fund's performance during its last fiscal year. You may obtain either or both of these reports at no cost by calling 1-800-555-5555.

Principal Risks

Investing in securities is inherently risky, and there is no guarantee that we will achieve our investment goals. In fact, you could lose money by investing in the Fund. The principal risks include:

- **Market Risks.** The price of particular securities may fall because of declines in the stock market regardless of the success of the individual companies' businesses.
- **Diversification Risks.** We may invest in securities not listed in the Standard and Poor's 500 Index. There is a chance that these securities will perform poorly, which may enable the Standard and Poor's 500 Index to outperform the Fund.
- **Undervalued Securities.** The Fund often purchases securities that the market undervalues in relation to their actual worth. We assume that the market will ultimately recognize the actual worth of these companies, thus causing their stock prices to rise. The market may, however, indefinitely undervalue these securities, causing their prices to remain the same or even decline.

- **Low Dividends.** The Fund often purchases the securities of companies that expect their earnings to rise. These stocks typically pay little, if any, dividends. Securities that pay small dividends are risky because their stock prices often decline in market downturns.

Past Performance

The bar chart and performance table below indicate some of the risks of investing in the Fund. The bar chart shows the changes in the Fund's performance from year to year over a 10-year period. The performance table shows how the Fund's average annual returns for 1, 5, and 10 years and the most recent calendar quarter compare with those of the Standard and Poor's 500 Index, a broad measure of market performance. When you review these charts, be aware that past investment performance does not necessarily indicate how the Fund will perform in the future.

A Decade of Year-End Returns

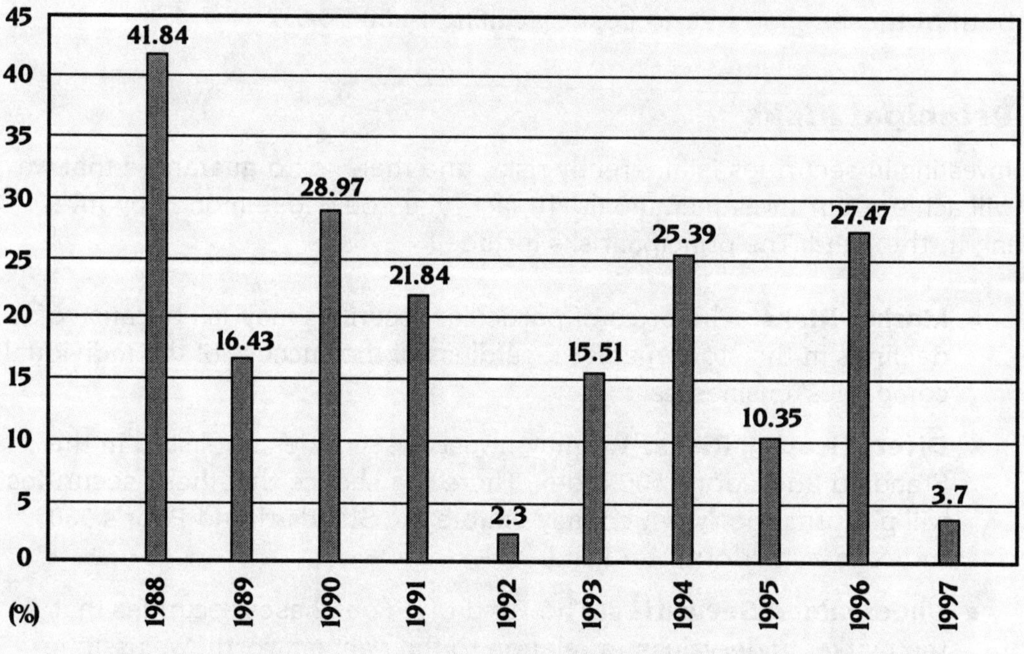

During the period shown above, the best quarter was the second quarter of 1988, when the Fund produced a 36% return. The worst quarter was the third quarter of 1992, when the Fund produced a -8% return.

Average Annual Returns

	Quarter (Apr.-Jun. '98)	1 Year (1997)	5 Years (1993-1997)	10 Years (1988-1997)
Fund	43.92%	3.70%	16.48%	19.38%
S&P 500	17.63%	22.50%	13.37%	16.42%

Shareholder Fees and Expenses

Investors pay certain fees and expenses in connection with investing in mutual funds. This table describes the fees and expenses that you may pay if you buy and hold shares of the Investment Horizons Growth and Value Fund. Shareholder fees are paid directly from your investment. Annual Fund operating expenses are deducted from Fund assets.

Shareholder Fees (fees paid directly from your investment)	
Maximum sales charge (load) imposed on purchases (as a percentage of offering price)	None
Maximum deferred sales charge (load) (as a percentage of offering price)	None
Maximum sales charge (load) imposed on reinvested dividends (as a percentage of offering price)	None
Redemption fee (as a percentage of amount redeemed)	None
Exchange fee	None
Annual Fund Operating Expenses (expenses deducted from Fund assets)	
Management fees	0.90%
Distribution (12b-1) and service fees	0.20%
Other expenses	0.00%
Total annual Fund operating expenses	1.10%

Expense Example

The example below is intended to help you compare the cost of investing in the Fund with the cost of investing in other mutual funds. The example assumes that:

- you invest $10,000 in the Fund for the time periods indicated;
- your investment has a 5% return each year; and
- the Fund's operating expenses remain the same.

Although your actual costs may be higher or lower, under these assumptions your costs would be:

Number of years	1	3	5	10
	$170	$425	$760	$1,705

These figures would remain the same regardless of whether you sold your shares at the end of a period.

Management

Investment Horizons Management is the investment adviser for the Fund. Our company began in 1937. It provides investment advice exclusively to mutual funds. We currently manage 40 mutual funds with combined assets of over $70 billion. Peter Williams is the portfolio manager for the Fund. Mr. Williams joined Investment Horizons Management's staff in 1982, and he began managing the Fund in 1986.

Buying Fund Shares

The minimum investment requirements for the Fund are:

	Opening the Account	Adding to the Account
Regular accounts	$5,000	$100
IRAs	$1,000	$100

We reserve the right to change these minimum investment amounts at any time. Also, we can refuse any purchase order that may adversely affect the Fund's operations. You pay no sales load for buying or selling Fund shares.

Selling Fund Shares

You may sell up to $300,000 of Fund shares on any day we are open for business. You will receive the sale proceeds within five business days after we accept your sell order.

We won't accept any sell orders until:

- you return all certificates representing the shares being sold; and
- you completely pay for any outstanding debts you owe for the shares being sold.

You may sell Fund shares in any of these ways:

By telephone

Call 1-800-555-5555 and give your name, account number, the name of the Fund, and the dollar amount or number of shares you want to sell. Then send us any certificates representing the shares being redeemed.

By mail

Complete a redemption form and send it to:

Investment Horizons Management
Fund Redemption Center
4020 North LaSalle Street
Chicago, Illinois 60601

You must sign the redemption form exactly as your name appears on the account. Include any certificates for the shares being sold with your redemption form.

Fund Distributions and Tax Information

Each year (usually in December), the Fund distributes dividends from net investment income and net capital gains from investment transactions. We will automatically reinvest the distributions in additional shares of the Fund, unless you choose to receive them in cash. If you prefer cash, you must notify us in writing at least five days before the date of each distribution. There are no fees or sales charges on reinvestments.

Any sale or exchange of Fund shares, and all Fund distributions, are taxable regardless of whether they are paid in cash or by reinvestment in additional Fund shares. These sales, exchanges, and distributions may be taxed as regular income or capital gains. The rates you pay on capital gains depend on the length of time the Fund held its assets.

Investor Services

We provide you with a number of services to help you manage your account:

- **Information Services.** Our telephone representatives are available 24 hours a day, 365 days a year, to provide the information you need. To reach us, call 1-800-555-5555.
- **Fund Transfer Services.** You may transfer money by phone from your Fund account to your bank account. We will complete most transactions within two business days.
- **Automatic Investment Services.** You may direct us to automatically invest preset amounts from your various bank accounts in Fund shares. These automatic investments may be made on a monthly or quarterly basis.
- **Exchange Services.** You may make regular exchanges of Investment Horizons Growth and Value Fund shares for shares of our other funds.

IPO Prospectus (Red Herring)

Drafter:	David P. Porter Jones, Day, Reavis & Pogue North Point 901 Lakeside Avenue Cleveland, Ohio 44114-1190
Editorial Consultants:	LawProse, Inc. 5949 Sherry Lane, Suite 1280 Dallas, Texas 75225-8008

PROSPECTUS

for the initial public offering for sale of:

5,000,000 Shares of Common Stock

of

OSR INC

	Per Share	Total
Initial Offering Price to the Public	$	$
Underwriting Discounts	$	$
Proceeds to OSR Inc., net of Underwriting Discounts	$	$

We're the largest retailer of eyewear products and optometric services in the United States.

This is our initial public offering. No public market currently exists for our shares. We will list our shares on the New York Stock Exchange under the symbol "**OSR**." We estimate that the initial offering price to the public will be between $12 and $14 per share. But this initial offering price may not reflect the market price after the initial offering.

Investing in our common stock involves risks. See "Risk Factors" (page 9).

We intend to grant an option for an additional 750,000 shares of our common stock to our underwriters — exercisable until December 15, 1998 — to fulfill overallotments that might occur during this offering. The numerical share information in this prospectus doesn't include the shares to be issued if our underwriters exercise this option.

Neither the SEC nor any state securities commission has approved or disapproved our securities or determined that this prospectus is truthful or complete. It's illegal for anyone to tell you otherwise.

Underwriters

Lapin Brothers Incorporated **Gruenewald Securities Corporation**

October 1, 1998

The information in this prospectus isn't complete. It might change. We're not allowed to sell the common stock offered by this prospectus until the registration statement that we have filed with the SEC becomes effective. This prospectus isn't an offer to sell our common stock — and doesn't solicit offers to buy — in any state where the offer or sale isn't permitted.

TABLE OF CONTENTS

1 SUMMARY OF OUR OFFERING

This summary highlights important information about our business and about this offering. Because it's a summary, it doesn't contain all the information you should consider before investing in the common stock. So please read the entire prospectus.

OSR Inc., an Ohio corporation, was founded in 1984 to acquire a specialty retailing business that had begun operations in 1946. Our optical retail operations date back to 1959. Our principal executive offices are at 100 Main Street, Cleveland, Ohio 44114, (216) 123-4567. Our fiscal year ends on the Saturday that falls closest to January 31. Fiscal years are identified in this prospectus by the calendar year in which they begin; for example, the fiscal year that ended January 29, 1994 is referred to as 1993.

1.1 Our Business

We're the largest retailer of eyewear products and optometric services in the United States. We operate as "Lucid Optical" and "Ferrier Optical" through licensed departments in Lucid and Ferrier department stores. We also offer comprehensive eyecare benefits to major employers and healthcare providers through our managed vision-care programs. Here are some highlights of our business:

- Our eyewear product lines include a broad selection of prescription eyeglasses, contact lenses, and accessories within the price range and categories desired by the middle-market customers who shop at our principal host stores, Lucid and Ferrier.

- More than 960 of our 1,000 optical retail stores feature an on-site optometrist to provide eye exams. Our level of personal service is competitive with that of private optometrists.

- Because each of our optical retail stores is computer-linked to our own centralized manufacturing labs, we can provide next-day delivery on most eyewear. Our centralized labs allow us to manufacture products of a more consistent quality, at a lower per-unit cost, and with lower capital and inventory investments, than is possible through competing optical superstores that have in-store labs.

1.2 Our Operating Results

We've been in the optical retail business for almost 40 years. During that time, we've had a strong record of increasing sales and operating income. Here are some financial highlights:

- Our profits of $30.7 million in 1997 were 24.3% higher than in 1996, and 134% higher than in 1995.

- In 1997, sales at stores that had been open throughout 1996 and 1997 increased 5%, and our operating income rose 14% over 1996. In the last ten fiscal years, our combined store sales grew at a compound annual rate of 4%, reaching $628.5 million in 1997. Our operating income grew at a compound annual rate of 12%, reaching $49 million in 1997. For additional discussion, see sections 1.5 and 5.

1.3 Our Growth Strategies

We believe that, as the average age of the U.S. population increases, the optical-products and vision-care markets will also grow. We plan to take part in this growth by developing the following areas of our business:

(A) **Freestanding optical stores.** We opened 9 freestanding "Lucid Optical" stores during 1997 in markets where we already had existing in-store Lucid optical departments and where Lucid has a large credit-card customer base. These factors provide advertising support for our expansion. We expect to have some 35 freestanding stores open by the end of 1998. About 400 more potential locations meet our criteria for freestanding Lucid stores.

(B) **Managed vision-care program.** Our managed vision-care program offers comprehensive managed eyecare benefits to major employers and healthcare organizations. We're now the exclusive provider of vision-care benefits to over 25 million members plus their dependents. Our established national network of retail locations, together with our proven ability to administer a national managed vision-care program, makes our program particularly attractive to corporate and other benefit-plan sponsors.

(C) **Expansion within existing and into new host stores.** We think there are opportunities for opening additional optical departments within our existing host stores. We hope to acquire more locations in our existing host stores, as well as in new ones. In 1997, we acquired 107 optical locations in Ferrier stores where competitors had been operating. And we have opened optical departments on a test basis in two new host stores: Westview and Park Ridge.

(D) **New retailing concepts.** In 1997, we opened five fashion-sunglass boutiques called "Sunshine" within Lucid stores, focusing on the rapidly growing premium-sunglass market. We plan to expand our test of this concept at selected locations in 1998 and 1999.

1.4 The Offering

(A) Common stock offered	5,000,000 shares — 4,000,000 in the United States and 1,000,000 internationally. We expect to give the underwriters an overallotment option for an additional 750,000 shares.
(B) Proposed symbol and trading market	**"OSR"** on the New York Stock Exchange
(C) Use of proceeds	We will use the proceeds of this offering to reduce our debt and to pay the offering's expenses. Assuming an offering price to the public of $13, we would have about $59.5 million in net

proceeds, after expenses. We plan to use the net proceeds to redeem or otherwise retire the 11-1/4% First Mortgage Notes due 2006 issued by our wholly owned subsidiary, OpTech, to finance the construction of our Memphis centralized manufacturing facility.

1.5 Selected Financial Data

The following financial information summarizes the more complete historical financial information at the end of this prospectus. Our independent public accountants, Phelps & Skidmore, have audited it. You should read the information below along with all other financial information and analysis in this prospectus. Please don't assume that the results below indicate results we'll achieve in the future.

	Fiscal Year Ended				
	Jan. 29, 1994	**Jan. 28, 1995**	**Feb. 3, 1996**	**Feb. 1, 1997**	**Jan. 31, 1998**
Statement of Operations Data:					
Net sales	$401.5	$428.1	$472.9	$528.0	$628.5
Gross profit	296.3	304.0	332.0	363.7	427.3
Operating expenses	241.5	258.5	281.2	305.5	359.1
Depreciation and amortization	13.8	13.6	13.5	14.9	18.6
Income (loss) from operations	25.6	31.9	37.2	43.0	49.0
Interest expense	23.0	22.3	23.2	23.2	23.2
Income tax provision	4.1	4.1	2.3	(4.9)	(4.9)
Income (loss) from continuing operations	(1.5)	5.5	13.1	24.7	30.7
Earnings per share	—	1.09	2.47	4.65	5.79
Other Financial Data:					
Number of stores open at end of period	880	900	925	950	1,000
Comparable stores sales growth	3.8%	4.3%	4.2%	4.5%	5.0%
Balance Sheet Data:					
Current assets	$100.0	$112.3	$126.1	$141.6	$148.3
Total assets	213.7	234.8	257.9	283.3	298.2
Current liabilities	88.6	91.3	94.1	92.0	108.5
Long-term debt	242.3	240.3	238.3	184.4	180.2
Total stockholders' equity	(117.2)	(96.8)	(75.1)	3.3	5.5

2 RISK FACTORS

Please carefully consider the following risk factors before deciding to invest in the common stock.

2.1 Risks Associated with Our Financial Position

(A) We have a high level of debt. Although the net proceeds of this offering will increase our stockholder's equity and reduce our consolidated indebtedness (pro forma for the offering), our consolidated long-term debt at January 31, 1998 would have been $65 million and our stockholder's equity would have been $120.8 million. Also, because we own all our operating assets through wholly owned subsidiaries, we must rely on those subsidiaries for all of our cash flow. Although OSR Inc. itself has no indebtedness, our subsidiaries are highly leveraged, and their debt-service requirements are substantial. If we cannot pay our debts on time or obtain acceptable alternative terms, there would be a material adverse effect on us and our stockholders. Although we expect our subsidiaries will be able to pay their debts as they become due out of cash flow from operations, or will be able to refinance or repay their debt through the sale of assets, this expectation is subject to a variety of factors that could cause us to be unable to pay our subsidiaries' debt, including:

(1) factors that affect our actual operating performance, such as:

(a) the impact of competition on our sales volume and pricing;

(b) our relationship with Lucid and Ferrier, and their performance;

(c) any external economic factor that might adversely affect the level of consumer spending on optical products;

(d) our ability to maintain adequate cash resources for capital improvements and expansions; and

(e) our ability to identify and stock the optical merchandise attractive to consumers;

(2) factors that affect the credit and equity markets and that may make refinancing more difficult, such as:

(a) interest-rate variability;

(b) stock-market swings; and

(c) credit shortages that might affect our access to commercial banks and other lending sources;

(3) factors affecting our ability to sell assets, such as:

(a) the attractiveness of those assets to potential buyers;

(b) our limited amounts of long-life property and equipment;

(c) our ability to sell subsidiary operations as a going concern; and

(d) economic factors that affect buyers and their ability to finance a purchase; and

(4) factors that accelerate the obligation to repay the indebtedness, such as certain events that would be considered a change in control of OSR Inc.

(B) Our growth may be constrained by restrictive debt covenants. Our subsidiaries' debt agreements contain a variety of restrictive covenants that may limit our ability to grow, including restrictions on the amount of additional debt that our subsidiaries may incur, and restrictions on mergers and sales of assets that could adversely affect the use of our resources.

2.2 Business Factors that May Adversely Affect Our Operations

(A) We face the pressures of a competitive industry. Although we're the largest optical retailer in the United States, we have a relatively small share (about 6%) of the overall U.S. optical retail market. We compete with many other chain optical companies and many independent optometrists and opticians. Our industry is highly competitive: we face pressures on pricing and in obtaining choice retail locations. We also face mounting pressure from the consolidation of our industry, which is increasingly experiencing mergers and acquisitions. Some of our competitors might have greater financial resources than we do, enhancing their competitive strength.

(B) We must maintain and expand our relationships with our host stores. As we operate more than 90% of our stores under short-term licenses from Lucid and Ferrier, we depend on continuing our relationship with those host stores, and on their continuing strength as major retailers that attract customers to our locations. Our licenses with Lucid and Ferrier can be canceled on 60–90 days' notice. Although during our 40-year relationship with Lucid and Ferrier we have never had a licensed location terminated other than in the context of a store closing, relocation, or major remodeling, we can't guarantee that we'll be able to maintain this track record or our good relations with our host stores. During 1997, we derived $350 million in sales and $40.5 million in income from operations from our Ferrier business. Ferrier is currently operating under the protection of the bankruptcy laws, and we can't assure you that we won't be hurt by their difficulties. We envision expanding our positions with Lucid and Ferrier and developing new relationships with other host retail operators. But we can't assure you that these plans will be realized.

2.3 Other Factors that May Adversely Affect Our Financial Results

(A) Our business is seasonal. We sell more products and services during the first three quarters of the year, and sell less during the fourth quarter.

(B) We can't ensure year-2000 compliance. We're working with a consulting firm to assess and resolve the potential impact of the year 2000 on the ability of our computer systems to accurately process date-sensitive information. Any system that recognizes a date using "00" as the year 1900 rather than the year 2000 might fail. We're working to identify all computer systems and hardware that include embedded microprocessor technology. We'll also identify critical third parties with whom we do business regarding their year-2000 readiness. About 90% of our hardware devices and software applications have been identified and evaluated, and we have contacted most of our critical suppliers, host stores, and managed-care partners. We expect to complete this process in early 1999. Then we'll complete a comprehensive plan that will include:

- an estimate of the total year-2000 costs;
- a timeline for completion of any required modifications; and
- a contingency plan to address the risks of failing to be year-2000 ready and to identify actions that can reduce those risks.

We use over 500 computer systems, many of which have been installed recently as part of our major systems overhaul begun in 1997. We've already modified many of our software applications. We can't accurately estimate the costs of assessing and resolving our year-2000 issues, which include internal staff costs as well as outside consulting and other expenses. And despite our progress to date, we can't assure you that we'll avoid year-2000 problems or that their impact will be slight. Our biggest concern is the uncertainties involving our third-party suppliers, over whom we have little control. If we or critical third parties, such as our suppliers, host stores, or managed vision-care partners, cannot find timely and cost-effective solutions to year-2000 problems, we might suffer.

2.4 Other Factors that May Adversely Affect Our Common Stock

(A) **There may be no active public market for our common stock.** Because this is the initial public offering of our common stock, we can't assure you that there will be an active public market for our shares. And the stock market — especially the market for our shares — may be highly volatile because of general market conditions, as well as factors relating to our own performance and our ability to meet market expectations.

(B) **We don't plan to pay dividends.** We don't expect to pay dividends on common stock anytime soon. We expect to use all earnings, and the proceeds from this offering, to pay outstanding debt and to develop our business. Our board will decide on any future payment of dividends, depending on our results of operations, financial condition, capital requirements, and any other relevant factors. We are also constrained in the amount of dividends that we can pay by the restrictive covenants of our subsidiaries' indentures, which limit the amount of dividends that they can pay us.

(C) **You will experience dilution.** You'll experience immediate and substantial dilution in net tangible book value. Our deficit in net tangible book value as of January 31, 1998, was $100 million — or $20 per share. After giving effect to the offering at an assumed offering price to the public of $13 per share, and our planned use of the offering proceeds as though both had occurred on January 31,

1998, our deficit in tangible book value at that date would have been $40 million. This results in an immediate increase in net tangible book value to our existing stockholders of $16 per share and an immediate dilution to you of $9 per share.

(D) **We are subject to provisions that may affect changes in control.** Our corporate charter documents, the provisions of our subsidiaries' debt agreements, and Ohio's corporate laws could deter transactions involving the acquisition of us or could delay and prevent changes in control or management of us. After the offering, about 35% of our common stock will be owned by Carl Greco. Because our certificate of incorporation requires affirmative approval by 70% of our stockholders for certain actions, such as mergers or amendments to our certificate of incorporation, Carl Greco would be able to prevent approval of these actions.

3 FORWARD-LOOKING STATEMENTS

3.1 In General

This prospectus contains statements that plan for or anticipate the future. Forward-looking statements include statements about the future of the optical products and vision-care industry, statements about our future business plans and strategies, and most other statements that are not historical in nature. In this prospectus, forward-looking statements are generally identified by the words "anticipate," "plan," "believe," "expect," "estimate," and the like. Because forward-looking statements involve future risks and uncertainties, there are factors that could cause actual results to differ materially from those expressed or implied. For example, a few of the uncertainties that could affect the accuracy of forward-looking statements, besides the specific factors identified in section 2, include:

(A) changes in general economic and business conditions affecting the vision-care industry;

(B) our ability to recover, identify, and stock merchandise that appeals to our customers;

(C) technical developments that make our products or services obsolete;

(D) our costs in the pricing of our products;

(E) the level of demand for our products; and

(F) changes in our business strategies.

3.2 No "Safe Harbor"

The Private Securities Litigation Reform Act of 1995, which provides a "safe harbor" for similar statements by existing public companies, does not apply to our offering.

4 CAPITALIZATION

We'll use the net proceeds of the offering to reduce our level of indebtedness by redeeming or otherwise retiring some of the 11-1/4% First Mortgage Notes due 2006 issued by our wholly owned subsidiary, OpTech. The following table shows our capitalization as of January 31, 1998, and is adjusted to account for the offering.

	January 31, 1998	
	Actual	Pro Forma as Adjusted for the Offering
Cash and cash equivalent	$50,000	$50,000
Long-term debt (including current maturities):		
11-1/4% First Mortgage Notes due 2006	180,000	120,000
9-7/8% Notes due 2007	100,000	100,000
Other debt	5,500	5,500
Total debt	285,500	225,500
Stockholders' equity:		
Common stock, 50,000,000 shares authorized:		
Capital in excess of par value	4,000	5,000
Total stockholders' equity	5,500	69,500
Total capitalization	291,000	291,000

5 MANAGEMENT'S DISCUSSION AND ANALYSIS OF FINANCIAL CONDITION AND RESULTS OF OPERATIONS

5.1 Overview

The following is a discussion of certain factors affecting our results for the three fiscal years ending January 31, 1998 and our liquidity and capital resources. This discussion should be read along with our consolidated financial statements and their notes, which can be found on page F-1 of this prospectus [not included].

As a reminder, our fiscal year ends on the Saturday that falls closest to January 31. The years mentioned throughout this prospectus are fiscal years.

5.2 Results of Operations

(A) Comparison of 1997 and 1996.

(1) ***Net sales.*** Our net sales increased 19% in 1997, from $528 million to $628.5 million. At the end of 1997 we operated 1,000 optical retail locations, versus 950 locations at the end of 1996. The increase in net sales was due to a sales increase of 5% for stores that were open in both years and the additional optical retail locations opened during 1996 and 1997. Our expansion included 107 Ferrier locations acquired from a competitor for $4 million in May 1997. We believe that we benefited from a general increase in consumer spending on optical products and services during the year. But we can't assure you that this trend will continue.

(2) ***Gross margin.*** Our gross margin dropped to 65.9% in 1997 from 68% in 1996, primarily as a result of the growth in optical sales.

(3) ***Operating expenses.*** Our operating expenses increased 17.6% in 1997, from $305.5 million to $359.1 million. Although decreasing as a percentage of sales, our payroll costs increased 30% to $101 million, largely because of new stores, as well as $5 million paid as part of an in-store bonus program. And our advertising expenses grew 7% to $29.5 million as we expanded our television marketing in three cities to test new concepts. Because we feel the new advertising concepts worked well, we anticipate increased levels of advertising costs during 1997. Our store-occupancy expense increased 9% to $110 million in 1997 from $100.9 million in the prior year, but decreased as a percentage of our sales from 18% to 17.5% despite scheduled rent increases of $4 million for older stores as well as $5.1 million in additional rents from the new stores. We, like other retailers generally, are facing rising real-estate costs as the real-estate industry recovers from its earlier recession.

(4) ***Income from operations.*** Our income from operations increased 14% in 1997, from $34 million to $39 million. This increase was primarily a result of the increased comparable store sales and our reduction of operating expenses as a percentage of sales that resulted from lower payroll, store occupancy, and advertising expenses as a percentage of sales.

(5) ***Interest expense.*** Our interest expense in 1997 of $23.2 million was comparable to that of 1996. We expect that this cost will be less in 1998 because our subsidiary, OpTech, has recently repurchased $25 million of its 9-7/8% Notes due 2007, thus reducing our level of indebtedness.

(6) ***Income tax.*** Our income-tax benefit of $4.9 million in 1997 included only state income tax, as we were in a net operating loss carryforward position through the fiscal year for federal-income-tax purposes. We expect that we will be paying federal income taxes for 1998 at an overall rate of 43%.

(B) **Comparison of 1996 and 1995.**

(1) ***Net sales.*** Our net sales increased 11.7% in 1996, from $472.9 million to $528 million. At the end of 1996 we operated 950 optical retail locations, versus 925 locations at the end of 1995. The increase in net sales was due to the additional optical retail locations opened during 1995 and 1996. Comparable sales for stores open throughout the two years were flat.

(2) ***Gross margin.*** Our gross margin of 68% in 1996 was the same as our gross margin in 1995.

(3) ***Operating expenses.*** Our operating expenses increased 8.6% in 1996, from $281.2 million to $305.5 million. Our payroll costs increased 30% to $98.1 million, largely because of more stores being open. Our advertising expenses of $27.6 million were about the same as in 1995. Our store-occupancy expense increased 16.3% in 1996, from $86.1 million to $100.9 million, and also increased as a percentage of our sales from 18.2% to 19.1%, in part due to scheduled rent increases of $9.8 million for older stores, as well as $5 million in additional rents for the new stores.

(4) ***Income from operations.*** Our income from operations increased 15.6% in 1996 from $37.2 million to $43 million. This increase was primarily due to the new stores opened during 1995 that became profitable during 1996. It usually takes 13 months for a store to become profitable.

(5) ***Interest expense.*** Our interest expense in 1996 of $23.2 million was comparable to that in 1995.

(6) ***Income tax.*** Our income-tax benefit of $4.9 million in 1996 and 1995 included only state income tax, as we were in a net operating loss carryforward position through the fiscal year for federal-income-tax purposes.

5.3 Liquidity and Capital Resources

(A) **Liquidity—sources of cash.**

(1) ***Funds from subsidiaries.*** Our primary source of cash is funds from subsidiary operations. We also have available a working capital line with commitments of $40 million, which is reduced to the extent that we use letters of credit under the same facility. During 1997 we did not borrow any funds under the working capital line, but we had letters of credit of as much as $13 million outstanding at any one time. The working capital line contains covenants that restrict our subsidiaries' ability to pay dividends or make other restricted payments to us or to our stockholders. The working capital line does allow our subsidiaries — as long as they are not in default to the lender — to pay us the cash we need to pay the consolidated taxes for ourselves and our subsidiaries, and to pay us $3 million for our administrative costs.

(2) ***OpTech's debt securities.*** On January 31, 1998 our subsidiary, OpTech, had outstanding $180 million of 11-1/4% First Mortgage Notes due 2006 and $100 million of 9-7/8% Notes due 2007. The indentures relating to these notes contain covenants that restrict our subsidiaries' ability to pay dividends or make other restricted payments to us or to our stockholders. These restrictions are somewhat looser than those of the working capital line.

(3) ***Debt risk.*** See section 2 for a discussion of the risks associated with our high level of debt.

(4) ***Net cash.*** Our operations generated net cash of $33.1 million in 1995, $34.8 million in 1996, and $82.8 million in 1997. Each year's increases in net cash were the result of the increases in income from operations.

(B) **Capital expenditures.** Our net capital additions were $32.6 million in 1995, $25.1 million in 1996, and $18.1 million in 1997. In addition, during 1997 we spent $4 million in acquiring 107 locations in Ferrier from a competitor. The majority of the net capital additions were for store fixtures for new locations opened during the period, and for remodeling of existing locations. We expect to maintain the same general level of net capital additions in 1998 as we had in 1997, excluding the acquisition of the Ferrier locations. We believe that funds from operations will be adequate to pay for these net capital additions.

5.4 Impact of Accounting Statement Changes

We expect to adopt Financial Accounting Standards Board Statement No. 132 in 1999. We don't expect that adopting this statement will materially affect our financial position or our operations.

6 OUR BUSINESS

6.1 General

We are the largest retailer of eyewear products and optometric services in the United States. We also offer comprehensive eyecare benefits to major employers and healthcare providers through our managed vision-care programs.

6.2 Industry Overview and Competition

(A) **The market.** The domestic optical industry was an estimated $18 billion market in 1997, having grown at an average 10% compound annual rate since 1990, according to *Optical Industries Reports*. Industry sales declined during 1991 to 1993 because of the recession.

(B) **Demographics.** In 1997, according to the same reports, over 60% of the U.S. population used corrective eyewear. As the average age of the U.S. population increases, we believe that the size of the U.S. optical market will continue to grow. The following table, based on 1990 federal census data, shows that more people use corrective eyewear as they grow older:

Age Group	Population (in millions)	Number of Users (in millions)	Percent of Population
13 and under	51.7	7.2	14%
14-24	37.6	15.4	41
25-44	80.9	51.3	63
45-64	46.6	44.5	95
65 and older	29.8	28.6	96
Total	246.6	147.0	60%

(C) **Our competition.** The optical retail industry is highly fragmented, with an estimated 10,000 participants and more than 30,000 retail locations. Although we are the largest optical retailer in the United States, we have a relatively small share (about 6%) of the overall U.S. optical retail market. We compete with many other optical chains and with more than 9,500 independent optometrists and opticians. The second-largest optical chain is estimated to have about a 5% share of the overall U.S. optical retail market.

6.3 Operations

(A) **We operate through licensed departments in host stores.** We operate under the names "Lucid Optical" and "Ferrier Optical." At the end of 1997, we operated 1,000 optical departments in 41 states, including 598 departments inside Lucid, 340 departments inside Ferrier, and 56 freestanding stores operating under the "Lucid Optical" name. We also operated 6 locations inside Stenson's, a small chain of specialty department stores located in southern Ohio. We operate our retail locations under a lease or license arrangement through which the host store collects the sales receipts, retains a percentage of our sales, and remits the remainder to us. We record the amount retained by the host store as rent.

(B) **We carry a broad line of optical products.** Our retail locations offer brand-name and private-label prescription eyeglasses, contact lenses, and accessories. Our eyewear product lines include a broad selection of prescription eyeglasses, contact lenses, and accessories within the price range and categories desired by the middle-market customers who shop at our principal host stores, Lucid and Ferrier. Some of our representative brand names include Tom Baldwin, Cameron Roberts, Marco Venetti, and Julie Duchamp. Our proprietary private label names include Earhart, Lindbergh, and Viator.

(C) **How we operate.** Almost all of our 1,000 locations are full-service retail eyecare stores that also feature an on-site optometrist who performs complete eye exams and prescribes eyeglasses and contact lenses. Most of these optometrists are independent contractors who sublease space from us; we are prohibited by licensing laws in most states from employing optometrists. Because each of our optical departments is computer-linked to our five centralized manufacturing labs, we can provide next-day delivery on most eyewear. Our centralized manufacturing labs provide us with competitive advantages:

(1) We believe we can manufacture products of a more consistent quality, at a lower per-unit cost, and with lower capital and inventory investments, than our competitors that operate optical superstores with in-store labs.

(2) We believe that only a small percentage of customers place a high value on the "one-hour service" feature offered by competitors that use in-store labs.

(3) Many sophisticated lenses and some desirable coatings cannot be made in in-store labs, so our competitors must also operate some centralized facilities.

(D) **Our operating strategy.**

(1) We try to be a leader in the optical industry through superior customer service and technologically innovative products. Our goal is to provide exceptional patient care and value to our customers, combining the personal service associated with private optometrists with the broad selection and cost benefits of a large optical chain. We do this by:

(a) adhering to high professional-service standards;

(b) encouraging the development of professional relationships with the patient, the optometrist, and the opticians;

(c) educating the patient on the importance of proper eyecare; and

(d) combining a program that identifies a patient's eyecare needs with a comprehensive follow-up system.

(2) We also try to increase customer satisfaction by offering a wide selection of technologically innovative optical products and services. For example, we were one of the first optical retailers to offer:

(a) scratch-resistant coatings on eyeglass lenses;

(b) lightweight, almost unbreakable polycarbonate lenses;

(c) no-line bifocal lenses;

(d) disposable contact lenses; and

(e) colored contact lenses.

6.4 Growth Strategies

We plan to take advantage of growth opportunities in the vision-care industry by developing the following areas of our business:

(A) We plan to open more freestanding optical stores. We opened 9 freestanding "Lucid Optical" stores during 1997 in markets where we already had existing in-store Lucid optical departments and where Lucid has a large credit-card customer base. These factors provide advertising support for our expansion. We expect to have some 35 freestanding stores open by the end of 1998. About 400 more potential locations meet our criteria for freestanding Lucid stores. Our freestanding stores are generally located in strip retail malls that are a few miles away from the larger retail malls where Lucid has its major department stores. We also expect to open freestanding stores inside some retail malls where Lucid has a smaller-than-usual store that doesn't have the size or customer volume that fits the profile for an in-store optical department.

(B) We plan to expand our managed vision-care program. We began our managed vision-care programs in 1989. We market our program, which we call "Eyes One," directly to employers, other employee-benefit-plan sponsors, and insurance companies. Here are some highlights:

(1) We believe that our established national network of retail locations, along with our proven ability to administer a national managed vision-care program, makes our program particularly attractive to corporate and other benefit-plan sponsors.

(2) We're the exclusive provider of vision-care benefits to over 42 million members plus their dependents. Direct-employer accounts include more than 250 companies, more than 80 of which have over 10,000 employees. We provide coverage to more than 3 million employees plus their dependents.

(3) We're the exclusive provider of managed vision-care benefits through 4 insurance companies to over 20 associations covering some 5 million members plus their dependents.

(4) We believe that rising healthcare costs are leading benefit-plan sponsors to seek relatively low-cost benefits, such as vision care, to partially offset reductions or limitations placed on traditional health and hospitalization coverages. Our managed vision-care program, which we administer and charge transaction fees for, gives participants access to a nationwide network of optical locations, which typically include our own retail locations and those of several other optical chains, as well as some

independent optometrists and ophthalmologists who operate in locations not reached by chains.

(C) **We plan expansion within existing and into new host stores.** We believe that there are opportunities for opening additional optical departments within our existing host stores. These opportunities include opening new licensed departments in newly opened host stores, opening optical departments in host stores that expand to a size sufficient to support an optical location, and acquiring existing locations within our existing and new host stores previously operated by others. For example, in 1997 we acquired 107 optical locations in Ferrier stores previously operated by others. Lucid has traditionally offered us the opportunity to open an optical department in every new Lucid department store. Also, we have opened optical departments on a test basis in two new host stores, Westview and Park Ridge. We believe these will allow us to expand our customer base beyond the traditional Lucid and Ferrier customer.

(D) **We will try new retailing concepts.** We have continually tried new retailing concepts. During the 1980s, we operated some of the earliest optical superstores, which we sold to a competitor in 1989 for $142 million after concluding that our centralized manufacturing labs were more profitable. In 1993, we acquired a business that sells contact lenses by mail, which contributed $21 million in sales last year. In 1997, we opened five fashion-sunglass boutiques called "Sunshine" within Lucid stores, targeting the rapidly growing premium-sunglass market. These locations, which occupy about 80 square feet in high-traffic areas, are designed to combine our expertise in the eyewear industry and in operating leased departments with the rapidly growing sunglass market. The nonprescription-sunglass market has grown from an estimated $2 billion in 1980 to $6.1 billion in 1996. We will focus on the premium, or above-$30, segment of the market, which has grown at even a faster pace, averaging 15% annual growth over the same period. We plan to expand our test of this concept at selected locations in 1998 and 1999. In earlier years we have operated other licensed business within Lucid, including a specialty gift boutique concept. From time to time, Lucid and Ferrier have asked us to expand our healthcare-related offerings beyond vision products, such as into hearing aids and dental care. Although we haven't yet accepted those opportunities, we may do so in the future.

6.5 Store Operations

Our optical departments usually occupy 1,000 square feet in the host store. We typically staff our locations with a doctor of optometry, a department manager, and from one to seven opticians, depending on the store's sales volume. We also have about 25 locations that carry and dispense a full line of products but that, because of state regulations, don't have an on-site optometrist. Almost all the optometrists are independent contractors, with the rest being our employees. The independent optometrists sublease space and equipment from us where permitted by law, or from the host, and retain their examination fees. We believe that our relations with our independent optometrists are excellent.

6.6 Manufacturing and Distribution

Our five centralized laboratory operations are located in Memphis, Tennessee; Akron, Ohio; Aurora, Illinois; Wheeling, West Virginia; and Ogden, Utah. These operations manufacture and distribute all of our prescription eyeglasses. Orders are electronically transmitted from our retail locations to the our central computer system, and then assigned by the computer to the appropriate lab for that product or service. Orders can generally be manufactured and shipped to the store by overnight delivery for next-day customer pickup.

Many standard prescriptions can be manufactured by cutting and edging a prefinished lens to fit the frame selected by the customer. More complex prescriptions require a highly technical process that grinds the lens to fit the prescription. We use state-of-the-art computerized systems that not only reduce production time but also enhance the accuracy of the manufacturing process and reduce production waste. We believe that this system is year-2000 compliant (see section 2.3(B)).

6.7 Marketing

We conduct a variety of marketing and promotional efforts to build and maintain our customer base. We use television, radio, newspaper, direct-mail, and yellow-pages advertising. We also depend on host advertising, which includes promotional material in sales circulars and in credit-card bills sent by the host store.

We use many promotional techniques, including paid-for examinations and free frames with an eyeglass order. One of our most popular programs includes an offer to pay for the patient's eye examination if the patient buys eyeglasses from us. We believe that this program builds awareness of our on-site optometrists and creates long-term professional relationships that bring customers back to our stores.

6.8 Employees

As of January 31, 1998, we had 3,000 full-time and 1,000 part-time employees. None of our employees are unionized.

6.9 Legal Matters

We are subject to pending or threatened lawsuits that are ordinary to our business. We are also subject to a variety of federal and state laws and regulations, especially those governing the regulation of the optical business. Optical regulations affect our advertising and our ability to employ or maintain on-site doctors of optometry.

7 OUR MANAGEMENT

7.1 Our Directors and Executive Officers

Our board of directors includes nine members, two of whom are executive officers of OSR Inc. The board is divided into three classes, with each class serving staggered terms of a maximum of three years.

Name	Position	Biographical Information
(A) *Class of 1999*		
William Armand	Chairman, Chief Executive Officer, and Director	Mr. Armand, who is 52, has been our Chairman and Chief Executive Officer since 1990, and our employee since 1979. Mr. Armand is also a Director. His sister, Debra Jenkins, is our Chief Financial Officer. Mr. Armand also serves as a director of Quazar Inc.
Tabitha Barnes	Director	Ms. Barnes, 57, is Chairman and Chief Executive Officer of FastCo Inc., a leading software developer. She has been a Director since 1992. She also serves as a director of Mullins Corp.
Seymour Creswell	Director	Mr. Creswell, 48, is Chairman and Chief Executive Officer of Alpine Inc., a leading manufacturer of advanced plastics for industrial and consumer use.
(B) *Class of 2000*		
Kenneth Dalton	Director	Mr. Dalton, 61, is President of Playtime Inc., a company that manufactures innovative play structures for day-care centers and schools throughout the nation.
Stephen Eckhardt	President, Chief Operating Officer, and Director	Mr. Eckhardt, 39, is Chairman and Chief Executive Officer of Central Networks Inc., a leading consulting firm in the office-computing industry.

Charles Foster	Director	Mr. Foster, 38, is the Publisher and Editor of *Industry News*, the most widely read newsletter in the consumer-products industry.

(C) *Class of 2001*

Harold Greaney	Director	Mr. Greaney, 57, is the Executive Vice President and Chief Financial Officer of KLR Venture Corporation, a leading investment firm. Mr. Greaney is also a director of National Management Systems Inc.
Walter Harris	Director	Mr. Harris, 52, is the Chairman and Chief Executive Officer of Kenneco Inc., an industry leader in the production of glass and glass-related products.
Jeffrey Irving	Director	Mr. Irving, 43, is the President of CBD Inc., a leading producer of pediatric medical products.

Our other senior managers include three more executive officers, who are elected annually by the board and report directly to it.

Name	Position	Biographical Information
Debra Jenkins	Chief Financial Officer	Ms. Jenkins, 52, has been our Chief Financial Officer since 1995. She served as our Treasurer from 1984 to 1995. She has been our employee since 1982. She is the sister of Mr. Armand.
Alexander Kerr	Vice President – Manufacturing	Mr. Kerr, 49, is Chief Executive Officer of Municorp Inc., an investment firm specializing in municipal-bond offerings. He is also a director of Miller Hart Investments Inc.
Sidney Liman	Senior Vice President, Secretary, and General Counsel	Mr. Liman, 66, is retired from the position of Chairman and Chief Executive Officer of Charter Bank and Trust Company.

7.2 Committees of Our Board of Directors

(A) Audit Committee. The Audit Committee, consisting of Ms. Barnes, Mr. Creswell, and Mr. Foster, performs the following functions:

(1) recommends to the board — subject to your ratification — the selection of our independent public accountants;

(2) reviews the scope and results of the audit with our independent public accountants;

(3) reviews our annual operating results with management and with our independent public accountants; and

(4) considers the adequacy of our internal accounting procedures and the effect of those procedures on the accountants' independence.

(B) Compensation Committee. The Compensation Committee, consisting of Mr. Dalton, Mr. Foster, and Mr. Greaney, performs the following functions:

(1) reviews and fixes the compensation arrangements for officers and key employees;

(2) grants stock options and makes restricted stock awards to eligible participants under our 1998 Management Equity Plan; and

(3) administers our compensation and incentive plan.

7.3 Compensation Committee Interlocks and Insider Participation

Deliberations over compensation for 1997 generally involved the Compensation Committee and the full board of directors, including Mr. Armand and Mr. Eckhardt, who are our employees.

We lease our headquarters office space in a building that is owned by a partnership in which Mr. Armand has a 25% limited-partnership interest. We believe that the lease terms, at the time we signed the lease, were equivalent to those that we could have obtained in an arms-length transaction from an unaffiliated party.

7.4 Director Compensation

We pay each director who is not our employee $10,000 per year plus $500 for each meeting of the board of directors or of any committee on which the director serves. Mr. Armand and Mr. Eckhardt, as employees, were not paid any extra compensation for their service as directors.

7.5 Executive Compensation

(A) Summary compensation table. The following table summarizes the compensation paid during 1997 to our five executive officers:

				Long-Term Compensation			
	Salary	Other Annual Bonus	Restricted Stock Compensation	Securities Underlying Options/ Awards	LTIP SARS(#)	All Other Payouts	Compensation[1]
William Armand, Chairman and Chief Executive Officer	$668,942	$283,500	—	—	None	—	$82,444
Stephen Eckhardt, President and Chief Operating Officer	510,289	220,500	—	124,344	180,000	—	47,102
Debra Jenkins, Chief Financial Officer	250,000	150,000	10,000	—	90,000	—	25,100
Alexander Kerr, Vice President – Manufacturing	225,000	125,000	—	—	50,000	10,000	22,107
Sidney Liman, Senior Vice President, Secretary, and General Counsel	225,000	125,000	—	—	50,000	10,000	22,007

1 Represents matching payments under our 401(k) Plan.

(B) 1998 management equity plan. Our 1998 Management Equity Plan provides for the granting of stock options for up to 800,000 shares of our common stock to our officers or key employees, including key employees of our subsidiaries. Our shareholders approved this plan. The stock-option grants under the plan provide for vesting over five years, with early vesting of all or part of the unvested options upon certain events, including a public offering of our common stock, a sale of all or most of our assets, certain change-in-control transactions, certain mergers, or the voluntary dissolution of OSR Inc. Grants for 9,000 shares of common stock were made in 1997, none of which were made to our directors or executive officers. As of September 30, 1998, 791,000 shares of common stock remain available for new option grants under this plan. The following table contains information about unexercised stock options held at January 31, 1998. There were no shares acquired on exercise of options during 1997.

Fiscal Year End Option Value

	Number of Shares Underlying Unexercised Options at FY-End Exercisable/Unexercisable	Value of Unexercised Options at FY-End Exercisable/Unexercisable
William Armand Chairman and Chief Executive Officer	92,604/224,053	$2,003,754/$4,982,524
Stephen Eckhardt President and Chief Operating Officer	113,089/197,733	$2,448,066/$4,391,843
Debra Jenkins Chief Financial Officer	75,000/125,000	$1,222,222/$2,225,800
Alexander Kerr Vice President – Manufacturing	75,000/125,000	$1,222,222/$2,225,800
Sidney Liman Senior Vice President, Secretary, and General Counsel	75,000/125,000	$1,222,222/$2,225,800

8 PRINCIPAL STOCKHOLDERS

The following table contains information, computed as of August 15, 1998, about stockholders who are beneficial owners of more than 5% of our common stock, or who are our directors or executive officers. This information was given to us by the stockholders, and the numbers used are based on the definitions of the Securities and Exchange Commission, found in Rules 13d-3 and 13d-5 under the Securities Exchange Act of 1934. Therefore, the number of shares listed in the table represent "beneficial ownership" only for purposes of the reports required by the Commission.

Name of Beneficial Owner	Number of Shares	Percent of Class
Carl Greco	3,500,000	70.00
Mutual Corp.[1] 123 First Street Boston, Massachusetts 02100	374,500	7.49
William Armand	159,067	2.95[2]
Tabitha Barnes	5,000	*
Seymour Creswell	10,000	*
Kenneth Dalton	7,500	*
Stephen Eckhardt	120,000	2.22[2]
Charles Foster	7,500	*
Harold Greaney	7,500	*
Walter Harris	7,500	*
Jeffrey Irving	5,000	*
Debra Jenkins	85,000	1.58[2]
Alexander Kerr	95,000	1.77[2]
Sidney Liman	75,000	1.35[2]
All directors and executive officers as a group	1,125,500	22.51

* Less than 1%.

[1] Stock ownership is based on a Schedule 13D dated February 14, 1997. Mutual Corp. Research, Inc., a wholly owned subsidiary of MutualCorp and an investment adviser registered under the Investment Advisers Act of 1940, is the beneficial owner of the indicated shares as a result of acting as an investment adviser to several companies registered under the Investment Company Act of 1940.

[2] Includes options for the designated individuals that are exercisable within 60 days of August 15, 1998, as follows:

William Armand	92,604
Stephen Eckhardt	113,089
Debra Jenkins	75,000
Alexander Kerr	75,000
Sidney Liman	75,000

Under SEC rules, we calculate the percentage ownership of each person who owns exercisable options by adding (1) the number of exercisable options *for that person only* to (2) the number of total shares outstanding, and dividing that result into (3) the total number of shares and exercisable options owned by that person.

9 DESCRIPTION OF OUR CAPITAL STOCK

9.1 In General

Our articles of incorporation provide that we may issue up to 45,000,000 shares of common stock and 5,000,000 shares of preferred stock. As of September 28, 1998, we had 32 shareholders of record with a total of 5,000,000 shares of common stock outstanding. We do not have any shares of preferred stock outstanding.

9.2 Common Stock

Each outstanding share of common stock is entitled to one vote on all matters to be submitted to a vote of the shareholders. Holders do not have preemptive rights, so we may issue additional shares that may reduce each holder's voting and financial interest in our company. Cumulative voting does not apply in the election of our directors, so holders of a simple majority of the shares voted at a meeting at which a quorum is present can elect all of the directors to be elected at that meeting. The right of holders of our common stock to receive dividends may be restricted by the terms of any shares of our preferred stock issued in the future. If we were to liquidate, dissolve, or wind up our affairs, holders of common stock would share proportionally in our assets that remain after payment of all of our debts and obligations and after any liquidation payments with respect to preferred stock.

9.3 Preferred Stock

We can issue shares of preferred stock in series with such preferences and designations as our board of directors may determine. Our board can, without shareholder approval, issue preferred stock with voting, dividend, liquidation, and conversion rights. This could dilute the voting strength of the holders of the common stock and may help our management impede a takeover or attempted change in control.

9.4 Certain Provisions of Our Articles of Incorporation and Code of Regulations and of Ohio Law

(A) **Articles of incorporation and code of regulations.** Our articles of incorporation provide for a classified board of directors. Other than those who may be expressly elected by virtue of the terms of any preferred stock designation, the directors are divided into three classes. Our directors are elected for terms that are staggered so that the terms of one-third of the directors expire each year. Except as may be provided by the terms of any preferred stock, our code of regulations does not permit our shareholders to remove a director. These provisions of our articles of incorporation and code of regulations may have certain antitakeover effects. These provisions, in addition to the provisions of Ohio law described below and the possible issuance of preferred stock described above, may make it more difficult for other persons, without the approval of our Board of Directors, to make a tender offer or acquisition of substantial amounts of our common stock or to launch other takeover attempts that you might consider to be in your best interest.

(B) **Ohio law.** We are subject to several antitakeover provisions of Ohio law that may make it more difficult for other persons, without the approval of our board of directors, to make a tender offer or acquisition of substantial amounts of our common stock or to launch other takeover attempts that you might consider to be in your best interest.

(1) ***Ohio Control Share Acquisition Act.***

(a) Ohio's Control Share Acquisition Act requires that any "control share acquisition" of our common stock can be made only with the prior authorization of our shareholders. A "control share acquisition" is the acquisition, directly or indirectly, by any person of our shares that, when added to all other of our shares owned by that person, entitles the person, directly or indirectly, to exercise voting power in the election of our directors within any of three ranges: more than 20%, more than 33%, and more than 50%. Thus, a person who owns less than 20% of our shares must receive approval to go above 20%, 33%, or 50%.

(b) The act requires a special meeting of our shareholders and two levels of shareholder approval for any proposed control share acquisition. The acquiring person may only complete the control share acquisition if it is preapproved by:

- a majority vote of the shares represented in person or by proxy at a special meeting where at least a majority of our shares are represented; and
- a majority of the shares represented in person or by proxy at the special meeting, excluding those shares deemed to be "interested shares" for purposes of the act.

(c) The latter requirement makes shareholder approval more difficult to obtain in at least some circumstances, as shares held by certain short term investors, especially arbitragers, may not be eligible to vote. "Interested shares" include shares in respect of which the voting power is controlled by any of the following persons:

- the acquiring person;
- any of our officers; and
- any of our employees who is also a member of our board of directors.

(d) "Interested shares" also would include any of our shares acquired by a person after the date of the first public disclosure of the proposed control share acquisition and before the record date for the special meeting called to authorize the acquisition, if either:

- the aggregate consideration paid by the person or any person with whom that person is acting in concert, for those shares exceeds $250,000; or
- the number of shares acquired by the person or any person with whom that person is working in concert exceeds 1.5% of the outstanding shares of the corporation.

(e) In addition, "interested shares" would include any shares acquired after the record date for the special meeting accompanied by the voting power for the special meeting.

(2) ***Ohio Merger Moratorium Act.*** We are also subject to Ohio's Merger Moratorium Act. This act generally prohibits a wide range of business combinations and other transactions (including mergers, consolidations, asset sales, loans, disproportionate distributions of property, and disproportionate issuances or transfers of shares or rights to acquire shares) between us and any "interested shareholder" — anyone who beneficially owns, alone or with other related parties, shares representing at least 10% of the our voting power — for a period of three years after the person becomes an interested shareholder. But there's an exception: before the person becomes an interested shareholder, our board of directors may approve either the transaction or the acquisition of our shares that results in the person's becoming an interested shareholder. After the three-year moratorium, we could engage in transactions with an interested shareholder only if, among other things:

(a) the transaction receives the approval of the holders of two-thirds of all our voting shares and the approval of the holders of a majority of our voting shares held by persons other than an interested shareholder; or

(b) the remaining shareholders receive an amount for their shares equal to the higher of the highest amount paid in the past by the interested shareholder for our shares or the amount that would be due the shareholders if we were to dissolve.

(3) ***Ohio Control Bid Statute.*** We are also subject to Ohio's Control Bid Statute. This statute would apply to the purchase of or an offer to purchase of our shares from any Ohio resident if, after the purchase, the offeror would directly or indirectly be the beneficial owner of more than 10% of our shares. Under the statute, no one can make a "control bid" for our shares in accordance with a tender offer or a request or invitation for tenders unless, on the day the offeror starts the control bid, it files with the Ohio Division of Securities and with us certain information about the offeror, their ownership of our shares, and their plans for us (including any plans to terminate employee-benefits plans, close any plant or facility, or reduce the workforce). If the Ohio Division of Securities determines that the offeror's disclosures are inadequate, the Division must act within 5 calendar days from the date of the offeror's filing to issue a suspension order. If a bid is suspended, a hearing must be held within 10 calendar days from the date of the Division's suspension order. The hearing procedure must be completed no later than 14 calendar days after the date when the suspension was imposed.

(4) ***Fiduciary Duty Statute.*** Ohio law also provides for the right of our board of directors, in discharging their duties in determining what is in our shareholders' best interests, to consider the interests of various constituencies, including our employees, customers, suppliers, and creditors, as well as the communities where we are located.

9.5 Limitation of Director Liability and Indemnification

(A) **Director liability.** Under Ohio law, our directors won't be found to have violated their fiduciary duties unless there is proof by clear and convincing evidence that they have not acted in good faith, in a manner they reasonably believe to be in or not opposed to our best interests, or with the care that an ordinarily prudent person in a similar position would use under similar circumstances. Generally, a director is liable for monetary damages for any act or omission only if it was undertaken either with deliberate intent to cause injury to us or with reckless disregard for our best interests.

(B) **Director indemnification.** Ohio law requires us to indemnify our directors, as well as our employees and agents, against expenses when that person is successful in defense of a legal proceeding (including derivative suits). We may indemnify a person if the person has acted in good faith and in a manner that the person believes to be in or not opposed to our best interests. In the case of a criminal proceeding, the person must also have no reasonable cause to believe that his or her conduct was unlawful. Indemnification may be made only if ordered by a court or if authorized in a specific case upon a determination that the applicable standard of conduct has been met. Such a determination may be made by a majority of our disinterested directors, by independent legal counsel, or by our shareholders. To obtain reimbursement for expenses in advance of the final disposition of any action, the person must agree to repay the amount if it is ultimately determined that the person is not entitled to be indemnified.

(C) **Legal expenses.** We're required to pay all expenses, including attorney's fees, incurred by a director in defending any legal proceeding as they are incurred in advance of final disposition if the director agrees to repay those amounts if it is proved by clear and convincing evidence that the director's action or omission was undertaken with deliberate intent to cause us injury or with reckless disregard for our best interests and if the director reasonably cooperates with the corporation during the proceeding.

(D) **Code of regulations.** Our code of regulations provides for indemnification, which is coextensive with that permitted under Ohio law. The code of regulations authorizes us to enter into indemnification agreements with each present and future director and with the officers, employees, or agents specified in the code.

The code of regulations also authorizes us to enter into agreements to indemnify those persons to the maximum extent permitted by applicable law. We have done so with each of our current directors and executive officers.

9.6 Transfer Agent and Registrar

The transfer agent and registrar for our common stock is Bering Bank in Cleveland, Ohio.

10 SHARES ELIGIBLE FOR FUTURE SALE

10.1 In General

Once the offering is complete, we will have a total of 10,000,000 shares of common stock outstanding, assuming no exercise of the underwriters' overallotment option and no exercise of outstanding options or warrants to purchase shares of common stock. Of these shares of common stock, the 5,000,000 shares from the offering will be freely tradable without restriction or further registration under the Securities Act, except that any shares held by our "affiliates," as that term is defined in Rule 144 of the Act, may generally be sold only in compliance with the limitations of Rule 144 described below.

10.2 Sales of Restricted Shares

(A) In general. The remaining 5,000,000 shares of common stock are "restricted securities" as defined in Rule 144. Restricted securities may be sold in the public market only if they are registered or if they qualify for an exemption from registration under the Securities Act. Subject to the lockup agreements described below, additional shares of common stock will be available for sale in the public market (subject in the case of shares held by affiliates to compliance with certain volume restrictions) as follows:

(1) 500,000 shares will be available for immediate sale in the public market on the date of this prospectus;

(2) 500,000 shares will be eligible for sale 90 days after the date of this prospectus;

(3) 3,750,000 shares will be eligible for sale upon the expiration of the lockup agreements 180 days after the date of this prospectus; and

(4) 250,000 shares will be eligible for sale under Rule 144 upon the expiration of the applicable one-year holding period.

(B) Who can sell.

(1) ***In general.*** Under Rule 144 a person (or persons whose shares are aggregated), including an affiliate, who has beneficially owned shares for at least one year can sell, within any three-month period beginning 90 days after the date of this prospectus, a number of shares of common stock that does not exceed the greater of:

(a) 1% of the then outstanding shares of common stock (about 100,000 shares immediately after the offering); or

(b) the average weekly trading volume in the common stock during the four calendar weeks before notice of the Rule 144 sale is filed, subject to certain restrictions.

(2) ***No volume limits.*** In addition, any person not deemed to have been our affiliate at any time during the 90 days before a sale and who has beneficially owned the shares proposed to be sold for at least two years may sell those shares under Rule 144(k) without regard to the volume limits described above.

(C) Resale. Any of our employees, officers, directors, or consultants who purchased shares under a written compensatory plan or contract is entitled to rely on the resale provisions of Rule 701 under the Securities Act, which permits nonaffiliates to sell their Rule 701 shares without having to comply with the public-information, holding-period, volume-limitation, or notice provisions of Rule 144 and permits affiliates to sell their Rule 701 shares without having to comply with Rule 144's holding-period restrictions, in each case beginning 90 days after the date of this prospectus.

10.3 Effect of Sales of Shares

Before the offering, there has been no public market for the common stock, and no precise prediction can be made about any effect that market sales of common stock or the availability for sale of common stock will have on the market price of the common stock. Nevertheless, sale of substantial amounts of common stock in the public market could adversely affect prevailing market prices and could impair our future ability to raise capital through the sale of our equity securities.

11 UNDERWRITING

11.1 In General

Subject to certain terms and conditions, the underwriters — whose representatives are Lapin Brothers Incorporated and Gruenewald Securities Corporation — will purchase from us the number of shares of common stock shown below.

	Number of Shares
Lapin Brothers Incorporated	
Gruenewald Securities Corporation	
Total	5,000,000

If the underwriters buy any of the shares, they must buy all of the shares, other than those covered by the overallotment option described below.

The underwriters initially will offer part of the shares to the public at the initial public offering price shown on the cover page of this prospectus, and part of the shares to certain dealers (including the underwriters) at that price minus a concession not more than $_____ per share. The underwriters may allow, and the dealers may reallow to certain other dealers, a concession not more than $_____ per share. After the initial offering of the common stock, the public offering price and other selling terms may be changed by the underwriters' representatives at any time without notice. The underwriters do not intend to confirm sales to any accounts over which they exercise discretionary authority.

11.2 Overallotment Option

We have granted the underwriters an option to buy up to 750,000 additional shares of common stock at the initial public offering price less underwriting discounts and commissions. The underwriters may buy some or all of these additional shares during the 30 days after the date of this prospectus, solely to cover any overallotments made in connection with the offering. Each underwriter generally would purchase its pro rata portion of the additional shares based on the underwriter's proportionate commitment shown in the preceding table.

11.3 Indemnification

We have agreed to indemnify the underwriters against certain liabilities, including liabilities under the Securities Act, or to contribute to payments that the underwriters may be required to make in respect of those liabilities.

11.4 Lockup Agreements

We and each of our executive officers and directors and some of our shareholders, holding a total of 3,750,000 shares of common stock, have agreed, subject to certain exceptions, not to (i) transfer or dispose of any shares of common stock or any securities convertible into or exercisable or exchangeable for common stock, or (ii) enter into any swap or other arrangement that transfers all or portion of the economic consequences associated with the ownership of any common stock for a period of 180 days after the date of this prospectus without the written consent of Lapin Brothers Incorporated. In addition, during that period we have also agreed not to file any registration statement with respect to any shares of common stock or any securities convertible into or exercisable or exchangeable for common stock without the written consent of Lapin Brothers Incorporated.

11.5 Absence of Established Trading Market

Before the offering, there has been no established trading market for the common stock. The initial public offering price for the shares of common stock offered by this prospectus will be determined by negotiation among us and the underwriters' representatives. The factors to be considered in determining the initial public offering price include the history of and the prospects for the industry in which we compete, our prospects for future earnings, the recent market prices of securities of generally comparable companies, and the general condition of the securities markets at the time of the offering.

11.6 Warning About Foreign Restrictions on Public Offering

Neither we nor the underwriters have taken any actions required to permit a public offering of the shares of common stock offered by this prospectus outside the United States. The shares of common stock offered by this prospectus may not be offered or sold, directly or indirectly, nor may this prospectus or any other offering material or advertisements in connection with the offer and sale of the common stock be distributed or published in any jurisdiction, except in compliance with the applicable rules and regulations of that jurisdiction. This prospectus does not constitute an offer to sell or a solicitation of an offer to buy any shares of common stock in any jurisdiction where an offer or a solicitation is unlawful.

If you are outside of the United States, or are dealing with anyone outside the United States, you must observe any applicable restrictions relating to the offering and the distribution of this prospectus.

11.7 Underwriters May Overallot and Engage in Stabilizing Transactions

In this offering, the underwriters may engage in transactions that stabilize, maintain, or otherwise affect the price of the common stock. Specifically, the underwriters may overallot the offering, creating a short position for the underwriting syndicate. The underwriters may bid for and purchase shares of common stock in the open market to cover a syndicate short position or to stabilize the price of the common stock. In addition, the underwriting syndicate may reclaim selling concessions from syndicate members and selected dealers if they repurchase previously distributed common stock in syndicate-covering transactions, in stabilizing transactions, or otherwise. These activities may stabilize or maintain the market price of the common stock above independent market levels. The underwriters are not required to engage in these activities, and may end any of these activities at any time.

12 LEGAL MATTERS

We are being advised on the legality of the issuance of the shares offered by this prospectus by Roswell, Krantz & Skingle, LLP. The underwriters are being advised on legal matters by Sullivan & Oppenheimer, P.C.

13 EXPERTS

Our financial statements and the related schedule as of February 3, 1995, February 1, 1996, and January 31, 1998, and for each of the years in the three-year period ended January 31, 1998 included in this prospectus and elsewhere in the registration statement, have been included in reliance on the report of Bingham & Wallings, our independent certified public accountants, appearing on page F-2, and on the authority of that firm as experts in accounting and auditing.

14 ADDITIONAL INFORMATION

We have filed our Form S-1 registration statement with the SEC. This prospectus does not contain all the information set forth in the registration statement. You'll find additional information about us and our common stock in the registration statement. For example, in this prospectus we've summarized or referred to some contracts, agreements, and other documents that have been filed as exhibits to the registration statement. The registration statement, including its exhibits and schedules, may be inspected without charge at the SEC's principal office at 450 Fifth Street, N.W., Washington, D.C. 20549, and copies may be obtained from that office, upon payment of the applicable fees. The registration statement, including its exhibits and schedules, are also available on the SEC's website at www.sec.gov.

We are subject to the information requirements of the Securities Exchange Act of 1934, and accordingly will file reports, proxy statements, and other information with the SEC. These materials can be inspected and copied at the public reference facilities maintained by the SEC at 450 Fifth Street, N.W., Washington, D.C. 20549, or at its regional offices at 500 West Madison Street, Suite 1400, Chicago, Illinois 60661, and 7 World Trade Center, Suite 1300, New York, New York 10048. And copies of these materials can be obtained from the SEC's Public Reference Section at 450 Fifth Street, N.W., Washington, D.C. 20549 at prescribed rates. Some information about us is also available on the SEC's website at www.sec.gov.

Our common stock will be listed on the New York Stock Exchange, and our reports, proxy materials, and other information can likewise be inspected at their offices at 20 Broad Street, New York, New York 10005.

Prospective investors may rely only on the information contained in this prospectus. Neither OSR Inc. nor any underwriter has authorized anyone to provide any other information. This prospectus isn't an offer to sell to — nor is it seeking an offer to buy these securities from — any person in any jurisdiction in which it is illegal to make an offer or solicitation. The information here is correct only on the date of this prospectus, regardless of the time of the delivery of this prospectus or any sale of these securities.

No action is being take in any jurisdiction outside the United States to permit a public offering of the common stock or possession or distribution of this prospectus. Persons who come into possession of this prospectus in jurisdictions outside the United States must inform themselves about and observe any restrictions on this offering and on the distribution of this prospectus in that jurisdiction.

Until November ___, 1998 (25 days after the date of this prospectus), all dealers effecting transactions in the shares offered by this prospectus — whether or not participating in the offering — may be required to deliver a copy of this prospectus. Dealers may also be required to deliver a copy of this prospectus when acting as underwriters and for their unsold allotments or subscriptions.

OSR Inc.

5,000,000 Shares
Common Stock

P R O S P E C T U S

Lapin Brothers Incorporated

Gruenewald Securities Corporation

October 1, 1998

Notice of Annual Meeting of Shareholders

Drafter:	Richard A. Boehmer O'Melveny & Myers LLP 400 South Hope Street Los Angeles, California 90071-2899
Editorial Consultants:	LawProse, Inc. 5949 Sherry Lane, Suite 1280 Dallas, Texas 75225-8008

THOMPSON STORES, INC.

450 South Hope Street
Los Angeles, California 90071

NOTICE OF ANNUAL MEETING OF SHAREHOLDERS

Date: Wednesday, July 15, 1998
Time: 9:30 a.m.
Place: 450 South Hope Street
Los Angeles, California

Matters to be voted on:

1. Election of eight directors.
2. Approval of our 1998 Employee Stock Option Plan.
3. Ratification of the appointment of KPMG Peat Marwick LLP as our independent accountants for 1998.
4. Any other matters properly brought before the shareholders at the meeting.

By orders of the Board of Directors,

John Thompson
Secretary

June 10, 1998

Contents

PROXY STATEMENT

Your vote at the annual meeting is important to us. Please vote your shares of common stock by completing the enclosed proxy card and returning it to us in the enclosed envelope. This proxy statement has information about the annual meeting and was prepared by the Company's management for the board of directors. This proxy statement was first mailed to shareholders on June 11, 1998.

General Information About Voting

Who can vote?

You can vote your shares of common stock if our records show that you owned the shares on May 28, 1998. A total of 4,497,584 shares of common stock can vote at the annual meeting. You get one vote for each share of common stock, unless cumulative voting is in effect. Cumulative voting is described on page 5. The enclosed proxy card shows the number of shares you can vote.

How do I vote by proxy?

Follow the instructions on the enclosed proxy card to vote on each proposal to be considered at the annual meeting. Sign and date the proxy card and mail it back to us in the enclosed envelope. The proxyholders named on the proxy card will vote your shares as you instruct. If you sign and return the proxy card but do not vote on a proposal, the proxyholders will vote for you on that proposal. Unless you instruct otherwise, the proxyholders will vote for each of the eight director nominees and for each of the other proposals to be considered at the meeting.

What if other matters come up at the annual meeting?

The matters described in this proxy statement are the only matters we know will be voted on at the annual meeting. If other matters are properly presented at the meeting, the proxyholders will vote your shares as they see fit.

Can I change my vote after I return my proxy card?

Yes. At any time before the vote on a proposal, you can change your vote either by giving the Company's secretary a written notice revoking your proxy card or by signing, dating, and returning to us a new proxy card. We will honor the proxy card with the latest date.

Can I vote in person at the annual meeting rather than by completing the proxy card?

Although we encourage you to complete and return the proxy card to ensure that your vote is counted, you can attend the annual meeting and vote your shares in person.

What do I do if my shares are held in "street name"?

If your shares are held in the name of your broker, a bank, or other nominee, that party should give you instructions for voting your shares.

How are votes counted?

We will hold the annual meeting if holders of a majority of the shares of common stock entitled to vote either sign and return their proxy cards or attend the meeting. If you sign and return your proxy card, your shares will be counted to determine whether we have a quorum even if you abstain or fail to vote on any of the proposals listed on the proxy card.

If your shares are held in the name of a nominee, and you do not tell the nominee by July 5, 1998 how to vote your shares (so-called "broker nonvotes"), the nominee can vote them as it sees fit only on matters that the New York Stock Exchange determines to be routine, and not on any other proposal. Broker nonvotes will be counted as present to determine if a quorum exists but will not be counted as present and entitled to vote on any nonroutine proposal.

Who pays for this proxy solicitation?

We do. In addition to sending you these materials, some of our employees may contact you by telephone, by mail, or in person. None of these employees will receive any extra compensation for doing this. We have retained Richardson & Co. to assist us in soliciting your proxy for a fee of $15,000 plus reasonable out-of-pocket expenses.

Stock Ownership

The following table shows the number of shares of common stock beneficially owned (as of December 31, 1997) by:

- each person who we know beneficially owns more than 5% of the common stock;
- each director;
- each executive officer named in the Summary Compensation Table on page 8; and
- the directors and executive officers as a group.

Beneficial Ownership

Name[1]	Number of Shares Beneficially Owned	Percent of Shares Outstanding
Heartland Investors, Inc.[2]	274,350	6.1
Anthony Fuller	364,300	8.1
Susan Gold[3]	5,000	*
Marvin Gray[3]	5,000	*
William Harrison[4]	58,460	1.3
Daniel Ozuna[5]	7,500	*
Frank Taylor[3]	5,000	*
Fred Thompson[6]	886,025	19.7
John Thompson	238,375	5.3
Bernard Dovbish[7]	40,000	*
Lawrence Flores	30,000	*
All directors and executive officers as a group (10 persons)	1,639,660	35.7

* Less than 1%

1 The address of Heartland Investors, Inc. is 20530 Lake View Drive, Fresno, California 93706. The address of each other shareholder is 450 South Hope Street, Los Angeles, California 90071.

2 Based on filings by Heartland Investors, Inc. with the SEC.

3 Represents the number of shares that the person could purchase by exercising an outstanding option.

4 Includes 40,000 shares Mr. Harrison could purchase by exercising outstanding options on December 31, 1997 or before March 1, 1998.

5 Includes 5,000 shares Mr. Ozuna could purchase by exercising an outstanding option.

6 Fred Thompson disclaims beneficial ownership of the shares held by his son, John Thompson. These shares are not included in this total.

7 The number of shares the individual could purchase by exercising outstanding options at December 31, 1997 or before March 1, 1998.

PROPOSAL NO. 1
Election of Directors

An entire board of directors, consisting of eight members, will be elected at the annual meeting. The directors elected will hold office until their successors are elected, which should occur at the next annual meeting.

Vote Required. The eight nominees receiving the highest number of votes will be elected. Votes withheld for a nominee will not be counted. You get one vote for each of your shares of common stock, unless cumulative voting is in effect.

For cumulative voting to be in effect, at least one shareholder must notify the Chair of the annual meeting, before the vote on directors, of his or her intent to cumulate votes. If this notice is given, all shareholders may cumulate votes.

If cumulative voting is in effect, you will be entitled to a number of votes in the election of directors equal to eight (the total number of directors to be elected) multiplied by the number of shares you are entitled to vote. For example, if you have 100 shares, you will have 800 votes. You can give all your votes to one nominee or distribute your votes among as many nominees as you want. Proxyholders can cumulate the shares they are entitled to vote as they see fit.

Nominations. At the annual meeting, we will nominate the persons named in this proxy statement as directors. Although we don't know of any reason why one of these nominees might not be able to serve, the board of directors will propose a substitute nominee if any nominee is not available for election.

Shareholders also can nominate persons to be directors. If you want to nominate a person, you must follow the procedures in the Company's bylaws. You must deliver a notice to the Company's secretary at the Company's principal executive offices between April 17, 1998 and May 17, 1998. That notice must contain the information required by the bylaws about you and you nominees. Unless you have complied with these bylaw provisions, your nominee won't be accepted and can't be voted on by the shareholders.

General Information About the Nominees. All of the nominees are currently directors of the Company. Each has agreed to be named in this proxy statement and to serve as a director if elected. The ages listed for the nominees are as of June 1, 1998.

Anthony Fuller Director since 1995

Anthony Fuller, 48, is a private investor and was a principal of International Securities, Inc., a registered broker-dealer, from 1988 through 1993.

Susan Gold Director since 1996

Susan Gold, 43, founded Indigo Services, a supplier of automobile parts, in 1993 and has been President since then. She is also a director of Carter Stores, Inc.

Melvin Gray Director since 1995

Melvin Gray, 54, has been the Chairman of the Board and Chief Executive Officer of Fabrics, Inc., a clothing retailer, since 1992. He is also a director of ICE Corporation.

William Harrison Director since 1991
William Harrison, 47, has been the Vice President of Marketing of the Company since 1991.

Daniel Ozuna Director since 1995
Daniel Ozuna, 42, is a partner in the law firm of Campos and Ozuna LLP.

Frank Taylor Director since 1995
Frank Taylor, 50, has been a Vice President of Hometown Bank since 1990.

Fred Thompson Director since 1980
Fred Thompson, 60, founded the Company in 1980 and has served as its Chairman of the Board and Chief Executive Officer since that time.

John Thompson Director since 1995
John Thompson, 37, has been the Chief Financial Officer and Secretary of the Company since June 1995. Between 1985 and June 1995, he was with the accounting firm of Taylor and Young. He is the son of Fred Thompson.

Committees of the Board. The board of directors has two principal committees. The following chart describes the function and membership of each committee and the number of times it met in 1997:

Audit Committee—5 Meetings

Function	Members
• Review internal financial information	Susan Gold (Chair)
• Review audit program	Melvin Gray
• Review the results of audits with the independent auditors	Frank Taylor
• Oversee quarterly reporting	

Compensation Committee—2 Meetings

Function	Members
• Review and approve compensation and benefit programs	Anthony Fuller (Chair)
• Approve compensation of senior executives	Daniel Ozuna
• Administer Stock Option Plan	Frank Taylor

The board of directors had four meetings during 1997. Each director attended all of the meetings of the board and of each committee that he or she belongs to.

Executive Compensation

The following report and the performance graph on page 9 do not constitute soliciting materials and are not considered filed or incorporated by reference into any other Company filing under the Securities Act of 1993 or the Securities Exchange Act of 1934, unless we state otherwise.

Report of the Compensation Committee

General Philosophy on Executive Compensation

The Committee's goals are to:

- provide compensation competitive with other similar companies;
- reward executives consistent with the performance of the Company;
- recognize individual performance;
- retain and attract qualified executives; and
- encourage executives to increase shareholder value.

To achieve these goals, the Committee has put in place an executive-compensation program with three basic elements: base salary, annual cash bonus, and stock options.

Base Salary. The Committee determines the base salary of each executive officer other than the CEO. The Committee considers competitive industry salaries, the nature of the officer's position, the officer's contribution and experience, and the officer's length of service.

Annual Cash Bonus. Before the beginning of each year, the Committee sets specific annual performance targets for each executive officer. The performance targets are tailored to the officer's position. They can be based on net income, return on equity, customer satisfaction, and other factors. The Committee sets each annual bonus based on the officer's success in meeting or exceeding the performance targets.

Stock Options. The Committee grants options to an executive officer when the officer is hired, when the officer is promoted, and when the officer's existing options have fully vested. The Committee determines the number of options to be granted to an officer based on the officer's level of responsibility. Options vest over a four-year period. The Committee believes that the use of stock options ties a significant portion of an officer's compensation to increases in the price of the Company's stock realized by all of the Company's shareholders.

Compensation of Chief Executive Officer

The Company and Fred Thompson, the CEO, have entered into an employment agreement that extends to December 31, 1999. Under this agreement, Mr. Thompson receives a base salary of $250,000 and is entitled to an annual bonus if he achieves certain performance targets based on net income and return on equity. Mr. Thompson's maximum annual bonus is 125% of his base salary.

Internal Revenue Code Limits

Section 162(a) of the Internal Revenue Code disallows a tax deduction to public corporations for compensation over $1,000,000 paid for any fiscal year to the corporation's chief executive officer or to any of the four other most highly compensated executive officers. The statute exempts qualifying performance-based compensation from the deduction limit if certain requirements are met. The Committee currently intends to structure its executive-compensation packages to meet these requirements.

Compensation Committee Interlocks and Insider Participation

None of the Compensation Committee members is or has been a Company officer or employee. No Company executive officer currently serves on the Compensation Committee or any similar committee of another public company.

Summary Compensation Table

Name and Principal Position	Year	Annual Compensation		Long-Term Compensation Awards
		Salary	Bonus	Number of Stock Options Granted
Fred Thompson	1997	$250,000	$275,000	—
Chief Executive Officer	1996	250,000	200,000	—
	1995	200,000	200,000	—
John Thompson				
Chief Financial Officer	1997	$200,000	$100,000	5,000
Secretary	1996	200,000	50,000	—
	1995	175,000	75,000	5,000
William Harrison				
Vice President—Marketing	1997	$178,000	$100,000	2,500
	1996	178,000	68,000	—
	1995	150,000	75,000	2,500
Michael Murphy	1997	$178,000	$75,000	2,500
Vice President—Sales	1996	178,000	90,000	—
	1995	150,000	60,000	2,500
Kenneth Taylor	1997	$150,000	$25,000	1,000
General Counsel	1996	150,000	25,000	—
	1995	100,000	50,000	1,000

Options Granted in 1997

Name	Number of Securities Underlying Options Granted	Percent of Total Options Granted to All Employees 1997	Exercise Price (Per Share)	Expiration Date	Grant Date Present Value[1]
Fred Thompson	—	—	—	—	—
John Thompson	5,000	33%	$8.00	9/30/07	
William Harrison	2,500	17	8.00	9/30/07	
Michael Murphy	2,500	17	8.00	9/30/07	
Kenneth Taylor	1,000	7	8.00	9/30/07	

[1] The following assumptions were used under the Black-Scholes method: dividend yield 0%; expected volatility 32.3%; risk-free rate of return 6.6%; and expected lives of five years.

Option Exercises and Year-End Value Table

Name	Number of Shares Acquired on Exercise	Value Realized	Number of Securities Underlying Unexercised Options at December 31, 1997		Value of Unexercised In-the-Money Options as of December 31, 1997[1]	
			Exercisable	Unexercisable	Exercisable	Unexercisable
Fred Thompson	—	—	—	—	—	—
John Thompson	—	—	5,000	5,000	$21,250	$1,250
William Harrison	—	—	2,500	2,500	10,625	625
Michael Murphy	—	—	2,500	2,500	10,625	625
Kenneth Taylor	1,000	$4,000	—	2,500	—	250

[1] Value based on $10.25 closing price per share of common stock on December 31, 1997.

Performance Graph

The graph below shows the cumulative total return to Company stockholders during the five years ended December 31, 1997 in comparison to the cumulative return on Standard & Poor's 500 Index and the S&P SmallCap 600 Index. The results assume that $100 was invested on December 31, 1992 and that dividends were reinvested.

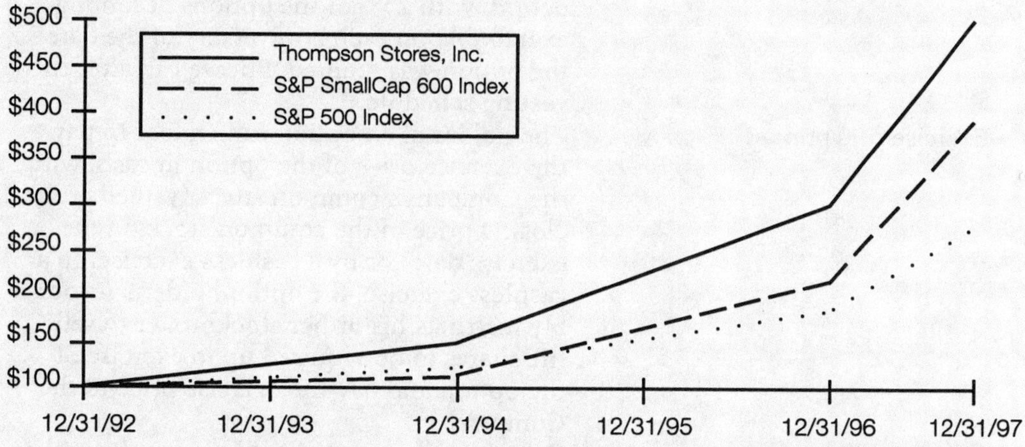

Section 16(a) Beneficial Ownership Reporting Requirement

Our directors and executive officers must file reports with the Securities and Exchange Commission indicating the number of shares of the Company's common stock they beneficially own and any changes in their beneficial ownership. Copies of these reports must be provided to us. Based on our review of these reports and written representations from the persons required to file them, we believe each of our directors and executive officers filed all the required reports during 1997.

PROPOSAL NO. 2
Approval of Employee Stock Option Plan

At the annual meeting, you will be asked to vote to approve the Company's 1998 Stock Option Plan. We recommend that you vote for it.

Vote Required. If a majority of the shares of common stock entitled to vote at the meeting are voted for the Company's 1998 Employee Stock Option Plan, the Plan will be approved.

Summary of the Plan. Here is a summary of the significant terms of the Plan approved by us on February 4, 1998:

Total Number of Shares Covered	500,000
Administration	The board of directors administers the Plan.
Eligible Persons	Officers and other key employees of the Company.
Exercise Price	Generally the closing price of the Company's common stock on the date we grant the option, but could be lower.
Term of Options	Generally 10 years, but could be a shorter period.
Vesting of Options	Options will generally vest over a four-year period, with 25% of the options becoming exercisable on each anniversary of the date the option was granted. But we can alter this vesting schedule.
Exercise of Options...........	The holder of an option can choose to pay the exercise price of the option in cash, with the Company's common stock (valued at the closing price of the common stock on the exercise date) or by a cashless exercise. In a cashless exercise, the optionholder irrevocably instructs his or her stockbroker to sell the shares to be acquired upon exercise of the option and pay the exercise price to the Company.
Transferability...............	Options are not transferable except by will or by intestate succession.
Acceleration of Vesting of Options	If a Change in Control Event (as defined in the Plan) occurs, the options will vest immediately and become exercisable in full unless we determine otherwise before the event.
Term of Plan	The Plan will expire on February 4, 2008, unless we terminate it earlier.

Federal Income Tax Consequences to Option-Holders. All options granted under the Plan will be nonstatutory options. An option-holder will not recognize any taxable income when the option is granted. But when the option is exercised, the option-holder will recognize ordinary income for tax purposes measured by the excess of the then fair market value of the shares over the exercise price. In certain circumstances, where the shares are subject to a substantial risk of forfeiture when acquired, the date of taxation may be deferred unless the option-holder files an election with the Internal Revenue Service under Section 83(b) of the Internal Revenue Code within 30 days after the exercise. The income recognized by an option-holder who is also a Company employee will be subject to tax withholding by the Company by payment of cash or out of the current earnings paid to the option-holder. When shares are resold by the option-holder, any difference between the sale price and the exercise price, to the extent not recognized as ordinary income as provided above, will be treated as capital gain or loss. The Company will be entitled to a deduction in the same amount as the ordinary income recognized by the option-holder.

This is only a summary of the federal income tax consequences of the grant and exercise of options under the Plan. It is not a complete statement of all tax consequences. In particular, we have not discussed the income tax laws of any municipality, state, or foreign country where an optionee resides.

PROPOSAL NO. 3
Appointment of Independent Accountants

We recommend that you vote for ratification of the appointment of KPMG Peat Marwick LLP.

We have appointed the accounting firm of KPMG Peat Marwick LLP as our independent accountants to examine the Company's financial statements for the year ending December 31, 1998. A resolution to ratify the appointment will be presented at the annual meeting. A majority of the votes cast must vote in favor to ratify the appointment. If the shareholders do not ratify the appointment, we will reconsider our selection of KPMG Peat Marwick LLP.

KPMG Peat Marwick LLP examined the Company's financial statements for 1997. A representative of KPMG Peat Marwick LLP will be at the meeting and available to answer questions.

Shareholder Proposals for 1999 Annual Meeting

If you want to include a shareholder proposal in the proxy statement for the 1999 annual meeting, it must be delivered to the Company's secretary at the Company's executive offices before February 11, 1999.

Other Matters

At the date of mailing of this proxy statement, we are not aware of any business to be presented at the annual meeting other than the proposals discussed above. If other proposals are properly brought before the meeting, any proxies returned to us will be voted as the proxyholders see fit.

You can obtain a copy of the Company's Annual Report on Form 10-K for the year ended December 31, 1997 at no charge by writing to the Company at 450 South Hope Street, Los Angeles, California 90071, attention Shareholder Relations.

By order of the Board of Directors,

John Thompson
Secretary

June 10, 1998

PART THREE

APPENDIXES

INTRODUCTION TO SEC MATERIALS

The Securities and Exchange Commission recently amended Securities Act Rules 421 and 481 to require companies to apply plain-English principles to the front parts of prospectuses filed after October 1, 1998. The SEC has also adopted new Rule 498 (effective June 1, 1998), which permits mutual funds to provide a new disclosure document—a "profile"—that summarizes key information about the fund. It too must reflect plain-English principles.

The new rules, the accompanying releases, and the SEC's *Plain English Handbook* are reproduced starting on page 191.

The Plain-English Rules: An Overview

A new prospectus's cover page, summary, and risk-factors section must be written in plain English. "Plain English" means short sentences, active voice, and concrete, everyday language. It means avoiding legal jargon and multiple negatives. And it means using tables, bullet lists, pictures, and other design features to make complex information easier to understand.

A prospectus shouldn't depend on a glossary of defined terms to explain its content. Companies should limit glossaries to terms that can't be understood from the context or from a concise explanation. A glossary need not, for example, define commonly understood abbreviations or acronyms such as SEC and NASDAQ. Except for brand names or trade names, companies shouldn't create vocabularies unique to their prospectuses.

For highly technical prospectuses, the SEC prefers a brief general description of the business at the outset. Concrete examples of technical matters are encouraged.

Liability Concerns

Some securities-industry professionals have worried that the plain-English rules will force them to omit important information from prospectuses. But plain English doesn't mean omitting important information—it means writing in words that investors can understand, and using a format that invites reading. So the SEC doesn't believe that a safe harbor from liability is necessary. The SEC also warns against including language to create a safe harbor for the plain-English front sections of a prospectus.

The SEC believes that the courts will continue to view the summary section merely as a highlight of important information. A summary isn't supposed to disclose everything, and courts should consider a document in its entirety before deciding whether a company has made a full disclosure. And failure to include everything in the summary shouldn't trigger application of the "buried facts" doctrine, under which a court would consider disclosure to be false and misleading if its overall significance is obscured because material information is buried in, for example, footnotes or appendixes.

SEC Staff Review

The SEC staff will review prospectuses to see whether they are clear and readable and whether they disclose material information. The staff won't correct grammatical mistakes. The staff recognizes that a document can still be clear despite the occasional long sentence or use of passive voice. But the staff also recognizes that a document is clearer when it's in plain English.

Companies shouldn't focus on making the disclosure brief at the expense of completeness or accuracy. The SEC staff understands that writing in plain English can sometimes make certain parts of the document longer.

The SEC may conduct random plain-English reviews, or "monitors," of selected registration statements. The number of monitors conducted will depend on several factors, including the staff's workload. The staff member assigned to review a registration will be responsible for the plain-English review. Any comments on plain English will appear in the regular comment letter.

Plain-English Rule

Final Rule:

Plain English Disclosure

SECURITIES AND EXCHANGE COMMISSION

17 CFR Parts 228, 229, 230, 239, and 274

Release Nos. 33-7497; 34-39593; IC-23011

International Series No. 1113; File No. S7-3-97

RIN 3235-AG88

Plain English Disclosure

AGENCY: Securities and Exchange Commission

ACTION: Final Rules

SUMMARY: We are adopting the plain English rule with some changes based on the comments we received and the lessons we learned from the plain English pilot participants. The rule requires issuers to write the cover page, summary, and risk factors section of prospectuses in plain English. We are changing the existing requirements for these sections to the extent they conflict with the plain English rule. We are also giving issuers more specific guidance on how to make the entire prospectus clear, concise, and understandable. We believe that using plain English in prospectuses will lead to a better informed securities market—a market in which investors can more easily understand the disclosure required by the federal securities laws.

DATES: Effective Date: October 1, 1998. Compliance Date: October 1, 1998. When we act on the amendments to the mutual fund disclosure requirements that we proposed in February 1997, we may change the date by which mutual funds must comply with these amendments.

FOR FURTHER INFORMATION CONTACT: Ann D. Wallace or Carolyn A. Miller at (202) 942-2980 or David Maltz at (202) 942-1921 in the Division of Corporation Finance. If your questions involve mutual funds, call Kathleen K. Clarke at (202) 942-0724 or Markian Melnyk at (202) 942-0592 in the Division of Investment Management. Direct your questions on the staff's plain English handbook to Nancy M. Smith at (202) 942-7040.

SUPPLEMENTARY INFORMATION: We are adopting amendments to Rules 421,[1] 461,[2] and 481[3] of Regulation C[4] and Items 101,[5] 501,[6] 502,[7] 503,[8] and 508[9] of Regulations S-K[10] and S-B.[11] We are also adopting minor amendments to Forms S-2,[12] S-3,[13] S-4,[14] S-20,[15] F-2,[16] F-3,[17] F-4,[18] and N-2.[19]

Our Office of Investor Education and Assistance will, within the next six weeks, issue a final version of *A Plain English Handbook: How to Create Clear SEC Disclosure Documents*. The handbook will give techniques and tips on how to create plain English disclosure documents. We suggest you order a hard copy by calling 800-SEC-0330. Some of the handbook's graphic elements will not be available on the web version. A draft version is available now on our Internet site (http://www.sec.gov).

TABLE OF CONTENTS

I. EXECUTIVE SUMMARY

Full and fair disclosure is one of the cornerstones of investor protection under the federal securities laws. If a prospectus fails to communicate information clearly, investors do not receive that basic protection. Yet, prospectuses today often use complex, legalistic language that is foreign to all but financial or legal experts. The proliferation of complex transactions and securities magnifies this problem. A major challenge facing the securities industry and its regulators is assuring that financial and business information reaches investors in a form they can read and understand.

In response to this challenge, we undertake today a sweeping revision of how issuers must disclose information to investors. This new package of rules will change the face of every prospectus used in registered public offerings of securities.[20] Prospectuses will be simpler, clearer, more useful, and we hope, more widely read.

First, the new rules require issuers to write and design the cover page, summary, and risk factors section of their prospectuses in plain English. Specifically, in these sections, issuers will have to use: short sentences; definite, concrete, everyday language; active voice; tabular presentation of complex information; no legal or business jargon; and no multiple negatives. Issuers will also have to design these sections to make them inviting to the reader. In response to comments, the new rules will not require issuers to limit the length of the summary, limit the number of risk factors, or prioritize risk factors.

Second, we are giving guidance to issuers on how to comply with the current rule that requires the entire prospectus to be clear, concise, and understandable. Our goal is to purge the entire document of legalese and repetition that blur important information investors need to know.

Also, our Office of Investor Education and Assistance is finalizing a handbook with practical tips on how to prepare plain English documents. This handbook explains how to apply plain English principles to disclosure documents.

To ensure a smooth transition, the plain English rule and the other changes adopted today will apply beginning October 1, 1998. We encourage all participants in securities offerings to start following these plain English principles now when writing their prospectuses. Our staff will continue its efforts to assist companies in drafting prospectuses in plain English.

II. LESSONS FROM THE PLAIN ENGLISH PILOT PROGRAM

To test plain English in disclosure documents, the Division of Corporation Finance started a pilot program in 1996 for public companies willing to file plain English documents under either the Securities Act of 1933[21] or the Securities Exchange Act of 1934.[22] More than 75 companies have volunteered to participate in the pilot program. Many participants have prepared disclosure documents that will not be subject to the plain English rule, including proxy statements, footnotes to financial statements,[23] and management's discussion and analysis of financial condition and results of operations.[24]

We have included in Appendix B a list of pilot participants that filed plain English documents. These pilot participants produced examples of disclosure that is clear, well-written, and designed to increase investors' understanding.

Our experience with the pilot participants affirms our belief that preparing documents in plain English increases investors' understanding and helps them make informed investment decisions. The package of rules we are adopting, as well as the handbook, will enable issuers to improve dramatically the clarity of their disclosure documents.

III. RULES ON HOW TO PREPARE PROSPECTUSES

A. Plain English Rule—Rule 421(d)

Rule 421(d), the plain English rule, requires you to prepare the front portion of the prospectus in plain English. You must use plain English principles in the organization, language, and design of the front and back cover pages, the summary, and the risk factors section. Also, when drafting the language in these front parts of the prospectus, you must comply substantially with six basic principles:

- Short sentences;
- Definite, concrete, everyday language;
- Active voice;
- Tabular presentation or bullet lists for complex material, whenever possible;
- No legal jargon or highly technical business terms; and
- No multiple negatives.

A number of comment letters noted that our rule dictates how to write the front of the prospectus. They are correct. We have seen marked improvement in the clarity of disclosure when pilot participants have used these widely recognized, basic principles of clear writing. We believe the benefits to investors support mandating the use of these writing principles for the front of the prospectus.

In addition, you must design the cover page, summary, and risk factors section to make them easy to read. You must format the text and design the document to highlight important information for investors. The rule permits you to use pictures, charts, graphics, and other design features to make the prospectus easier to understand.

B. Clear, Concise, and Understandable Prospectuses—Rule 421(b)

Rule 421(b) currently requires that the entire prospectus be clear, concise, and understandable. This requirement is in addition to the plain English rule we are adopting, which applies only to the front of the prospectus.

We are adopting, as proposed, amendments to Rule 421(b). These amendments provide guidance on how to prepare a prospectus that is clear, concise, and understandable. The amendments set out four general writing techniques that you must follow and list four conventions to avoid when drafting the prospectus. As several comment letters noted, these amendments codify our earlier interpretive advice.[25]

Amended Rule 421(b) requires you to use the following techniques when writing the entire prospectus:

- Present information in clear, concise sections, paragraphs, and sentences. Whenever possible, use short explanatory sentences and bullet lists;
- Use descriptive headings and subheadings;
- Avoid frequent reliance on glossaries or defined terms as the primary means of explaining information in the prospectus. Define terms in a glossary or other section of the document only if the meaning is unclear from the context. Use a glossary only if it facilitates understanding of the disclosure; and
- Avoid legal and highly technical business terminology.

The new note to Rule 421(b) provides guidance on how to comply with the rule's general requirements. The note lists the following drafting conventions to avoid because they make your document harder to read:

- Legalistic or overly complex presentations that make the substance of the disclosure difficult to understand;
- Vague boilerplate explanations that are readily subject to differing interpretations;
- Complex information copied directly from legal documents without any clear and concise explanation of the provision(s); and
- Repetitive disclosure that increases the size of the document, but does not enhance the quality of the information.

C. Comments on Proposed Amendments to Rule 421(b) and Rule 421(d)

Several comment letters stated that we should permit public companies to use legal and technical business terminology. The letters noted, for example, that high technology companies must use technical terms to distinguish their products or services from others in the industry. We recognize that certain business terms may be necessary to describe your operations properly. But, you should avoid using excessive technical jargon that only your competitors or an industry specialist can understand.

You should write the disclosure in your prospectus for investors. When you use many highly technical terms, the investor must learn your dictionary of terms to understand your disclosure. If technical terms are unavoidable, you should make every effort to explain their meaning the first time you use them.

Several comment letters noted that some investors, particularly institutional investors, want to read the specific terms of contracts or the securities offered. For example, an investor may want to read the specific language of a loan agreement's financial covenants or an indenture's default provisions.

Our current rule permits you to summarize an exhibit's key provisions in your prospectus.[26] Moreover, we require you to file material contracts and any instruments that define the rights of security holders. We believe this approach generally serves the needs of all investors in the market. If you cannot adequately summarize the language from an exhibit in the prospectus, then you should include that language. However, you must present it clearly and explain what it means to investors.

IV. REVISIONS TO REGULATIONS S-K AND S-B

We are adopting these revisions largely as we proposed them. However, based on the comment letters and our belief that communicating clearly should be the focus of disclosure to investors, we are not adopting any requirements that would require you to:

- limit the length of the summary;
- limit the number of risk factors; or
- prioritize risk factors.

A. Item 501—Forepart of Registration Statement and Outside Front Cover Page of Prospectus[27]

As proposed, we are eliminating the formal design requirements for the prospectus cover page. We are, however, requiring you to limit the front cover of the prospectus to one page. We believe these revisions will allow you to design and write a cover page that will focus investors on key information about the offering and encourage them to read the important information in the prospectus. Also, we intend for these amendments to give you the flexibility you need to design a cover page tailored to your company and the offering.

Under the revised disclosure item, you are free to use pictures, graphs, charts, and other designs that accurately depict your company, business products, and financial condition. The staff will object to design features and font types that make the disclosure hard to read or understand.

We are amending the formalized requirements on how you present the mandatory legends on the cover page. We are not placing any restrictions on how you present these legends, except:

- you must make the legends prominent; and
- you must make the print type easy to read.

Using all capitalized letters for the legends does not give them proper prominence. Rather, it makes them hard to read. A well-designed cover page that does not crowd the legends with other text can give them the prominence they need.

We have amended Item 501 to give you two plain English examples of the legend that states the Commission has not approved the offering.[28] The item also gives you a plain English example of the legend that states the prospectus is not yet complete, commonly called the "red herring" legend.

We are revising the requirements on information that you must always include on the prospectus cover page. Our goal is to have the cover page focus on key information about the offering. You should avoid moving information to the cover page unnecessarily.

We had proposed to eliminate the requirement that the cover page include a cross-reference to the risk factors section in the prospectus. In response to comment letters emphasizing the importance of this information, we are keeping this requirement. The cover page must reference the risk factors section and state the page number on which the risk factors begin.

The following table shows the current requirements for the prospectus cover page and the changes we are adopting.

Regulation S-K—Item 501

Current	Final
Cover page of registration statement	Same
Company name	Same
Title, amount, and description of securities offered	Same
Selling security holders offering	Same
Cross reference to risk factors	Same, except cross-reference must include page number. No print type specified
Formatted distribution table showing price, underwriting commission, and proceeds of offering	Delete distribution table. Use bullet list or other design that highlights the information
Show bona fide estimate of range of maximum offering price and number of securities	Same
If price not set, show how price will be determined	Same
Formatted best efforts disclosure and distribution table	Delete distribution table. Use bullet list or other design that highlights the information
Commission legend	Retain in plain English. Include reference to state securities commissions. No print type specified
State-required legends	Same
Underwriters' over-allotment option, expenses of offering commissions paid by others, and other non-cash consideration and finders' fees	Identify existence of the option and the number of shares. Move all other information to the plan of distribution section
No requirement to identify market for securities, trading symbol, underwriters, or type of underwriting arrangements	Identify market for securities, trading symbol, underwriters, and type of underwriting arrangements
Date of prospectus	Same
Prospectus "Subject to Completion" legend	Retain in plain English
No page limit	Must limit cover to one page

In our proposing release, we asked whether we should require specific information on the prospectus cover page for certain types of offerings, such as mergers, exchange offers, or limited partnership offerings. Several comment letters suggested that the plain English rule and the revised disclosure requirements should replace our earlier interpretive advice on cover page disclosure for limited partnership offerings.[29]

We believe that the plain English rule and the revised disclosure requirements are consistent with our earlier advice on limited partnership offering prospectuses and similar offerings, with one significant exception. Under our advice, the cover page must list the offering's key risks, resulting in repetitious disclosure of those risks. However, we believe the unique nature of these offerings and the risks they present to investors warrant requiring the issuer to highlight these risks on the cover page. Of course, the cover page, summary, and risk factors section must otherwise comply with the plain English rule and the revised disclosure requirements we are adopting.

We are not adopting special requirements for any other type of offering. We have had a number of merger prospectuses in the pilot program that provide excellent guidance on how to apply plain English to these offerings.

B. Item 502—Inside Front and Outside Back Cover Pages of Prospectus[30]

We are amending the requirements for the inside front cover page and outside back cover page of the prospectus to limit significantly the information you are required to include on these pages. We believe this will give you further freedom to arrange the information in the prospectus from investors' viewpoints. The table at the end of this section shows the current requirements for these pages and the changes we are adopting.[31]

Although we prefer that the required table of contents immediately follow the cover page, we believe you should continue to have the flexibility to include it on either the inside front or outside back cover page of the prospectus. However, if you deliver a prospectus to investors electronically, you must include the table of contents immediately after the cover page. This placement will benefit investors because they will not have to scroll to the end of the prospectus to see how it is organized.

Although some comment letters recommended that we eliminate the requirement to disclose the dealer's prospectus delivery obligations, we have decided to retain this disclosure on the outside back cover page. We believe this disclosure is helpful to dealers in meeting their legal obligation to deliver the prospectus.

Regulation S-K—Item 502

Current	Final
Availability of Exchange Act reports generally	Move to description of business section or, for short-form registration statements, to the incorporation by reference disclosure
Identify market for securities	Move to cover page
Availability of annual reports to shareholders with financial statements for foreign issuers and others not subject to proxy rules	Move to description of business section
Availability of Exchange Act reports incorporated by reference in short-form registration statements	Move to incorporation by reference disclosure
Stabilization legend	Move to plan of distribution section
Passive market making activities legend	Delete. Disclosure remained in plan of distribution section
Dealer prospectus delivery	Retain on outside back cover page
Enforceability of civil liability provisions of federal securities laws against foreign persons	Move to description of business section
Table of contents	Same. If prospectus delivered electronically, must immediately follow cover page

C. Item 503—Summary Information, Risk Factors, and Ratio of Earnings to Fixed Charges[32]

1. Summary Information

If you include a summary, it must be brief and in plain English. Further, if you include a summary description of the company's business operations or financial condition, you must write this information in plain English even if you do not caption it a "summary."

Although we have not limited the length of the summary, we believe this section should highlight the most important features of the offering. For example, the summary should not include a lengthy description of the company's business and business strategy. This detailed information is better suited to the disclosure in the body of the prospectus.

Several comment letters suggested that we require a summary section. We decided against this because a summary may not be helpful in all prospectuses. For example, you may not need to summarize the prospectus in a short-form registration statement.

Several comment letters suggested that we specify the information that must be in a summary. Because we believe you need flexibility to write a summary that is appropriate to your offering, we are not adopting specific disclosure items for the summary. However, because the financial statements are an important part of the disclosures made by public companies, we believe you should continue to highlight financial information in the summary. You should present this financial information in a manner that allows investors to understand it easily.

2. Risk Factors

If you include a risk factors section in your prospectus, you must write the risk factors in plain English and avoid "boilerplate" risk factors. We believe a discussion of risk in purely generic terms does not tell investors how the risk may affect their investment in a specific company. You should place any risk factor in context so investors can understand the specific risk as it applies to your company and its operations.

3. Ratio of Earnings to Fixed Charges

When you offer debt or preferred equity, you must disclose a ratio of earnings to fixed charges. Where you include a prospectus summary, amended Item 503 requires you to show the ratio of earnings to fixed charges as part of the summarized financial data.

V. PLAIN ENGLISH FOR INVESTMENT COMPANIES

The plain English rule applies to prospectuses of investment companies and will complement our disclosure initiatives for these companies.[33] Also, the amendments we are adopting to Rule 481 require these companies to write and design the front parts of their prospectuses in plain English.

As part of our commitment to improve mutual fund disclosure, in February 1997, we proposed significant changes to the disclosure requirements for mutual fund prospectuses and new summary disclosure documents called "profiles."[34] These proposals would require a standardized risk/return summary in mutual fund prospectuses and profiles. The risk/return summary would include a concise narrative discussion of fund risks and a bar chart showing a fund's annual returns for the past ten years. We expect to consider these and other changes to mutual fund prospectuses shortly. The plain English rule will apply to the cover page and the risk/return summary in prospectuses and the new fund profiles.[35]

Investment companies must comply with the plain English rule and the revised disclosure requirements for new registration statements filed on or after October 1, 1998. When we act on the changes to the mutual fund disclosure requirements, we may change the compliance date for mutual funds so they may comply with these new requirements with one filing.[36]

VI. PHASE-IN OF THE PLAIN ENGLISH RULE AND OTHER REQUIREMENTS FOR ISSUERS OTHER THAN INVESTMENT COMPANIES

To ease the transition to plain English and to avoid delaying your access to the capital markets, we will phase in the plain English rule and the other changes as follows:

- If you first file a registration statement on or after October 1, 1998, you must comply with the new requirements.[37] If you file a registration statement before October 1, 1998, but it is not yet effective on that date, you do not have to amend it to comply with the new requirements before it is effective.
- On or after October 1, 1998, any supplement you file to a prospectus in an effective registration statement that relies on Rule 415(a)(1)(x) must comply with the new requirements.
- If you file a post-effective amendment on or after October 1, 1998, either to include the company's latest audited financial statements in the registration statement or to update the prospectus under Section 10(a)(3),[38] you must comply with the new requirements.

If you elect to comply immediately with any of the plain English requirements, we believe you should comply with all of them to make the document more readable. For example, you should not have a plain English cover page and a legalistic summary or risk factors section.

During the phase-in period, we will hold workshops to help issuers, underwriters, and their counsel comply with the plain English rule. Until October 1, 1998, the staff will continue the plain English pilot program, but because of limited resources and because we expect high demand by issuers to participate in the pilot, the staff will no longer offer expedited review. We encourage issuers to participate in the pilot program with both Securities Act and Exchange Act documents.

VII. COMMENTS ON THE PLAIN ENGLISH PROPOSALS

We received 45 comment letters on the plain English proposals.[39] Generally, the comment letters favored requiring plain English for the front of prospectuses—he cover page, summary, and risk factors section. The American Society of Corporate Secretaries and the American Corporate Counsel Association, as well as several public companies, supported the plain English requirements. They believe that requiring plain English will focus all parties involved in the offering process—issuers, underwriters, trustees, and counsel—on clear and readable disclosure. Investor groups, such as the American Association of Retired Persons and the Consumer Federation of America, supported adopting the plain English rule to ensure that investors receive clear information.

Other comment letters raised the following general concerns about the plain English rule:

- Will the plain English rule increase a registrant's liability?
- How will the staff review and comment on plain English filings?
- Will the Commission deny acceleration of a filing if it does not comply with the plain English rule?

We address these concerns in the following three sections.

A. Liability Concerns

Several comment letters, including those of the American Bar Association and the Securities Industry Association, recommended a voluntary rather than a mandatory approach to improving the readability of prospectuses. These comment letters argued against mandating plain English primarily because of liability concerns. These comment letters expressed concern that issuers may omit material information in the course of simplifying the language. The comment letters urged us to adopt a safe harbor rule from legal liability to cover the sections of the prospectus that must be in plain English.

Other letters from groups representing public companies and the mutual fund industry stated they believe plain English will not increase their liability. They stated that plain English disclosure should reduce potentialliability because it decreases the likelihood that an investor will misunderstand the prospectus.[40]

Using plain English does not mean omitting important information. These rules only require you to disclose information in words investors can understand and in a format that invites them to read the document. For these reasons, we do not believe that a safe harbor rule is necessary or appropriate. We also believe it is inappropriate for you to include language that attempts to create a safe harbor for these sections.

The letters raising liability concerns also questioned whether it is possible to summarize in plain English complex matters covered in the body of the document. We believe the courts will continue to view the summary section, as its caption indicates, as a highlight of important information in the prospectus. A summary, by its very nature, cannot disclose everything. In determining whether a company has made full disclosure, courts should look at the disclosure in the entire document.

Moreover, a company's failure to include everything in the summary should not trigger automatically the application of the "buried facts" doctrine. Under the buried facts doctrine, a court would consider disclosure to be false and misleading only if its overall significance is obscured because material information is "buried," for example, in footnotes or appendices.[41]

The package of rules we are adopting should lead to clearer documents that are easier for investors to understand. We believe that compliance with these requirements will not increase the risk of litigation.

B. Staff Plain English Review and Comment Process

Several comment letters questioned whether the staff's time would be well spent giving comments on grammar. The letters also stated that the staff's past comments have caused many immaterial disclosures and much of the repetition in current prospectuses.

Our staff will focus on whether you disclose material information and whether that disclosure is clear and readable. The staff will not correct grammatical mistakes.

We recognize that a document can still be clear despite the occasional long sentence or use of passive voice. But we have learned from the plain English pilot program that a document becomes clearer and easier to read when its writer uses plain English.

The staff will issue their comments in plain English and avoid requesting repetitive information in the document. If the staff selects your registration statement for a legal and accounting review, the same people who review your document will issue any plain English comments.

Because the format and design of your document play a large part in its readability, we will request paper copies of the plain English sections that you plan to deliver to investors. We are working to upgrade our Electronic Data Gathering Analysis and Retrieval system, EDGAR, to permit the filing of an exact duplicate of the paper copy sent to investors but this may not occur for some time.

C. Requests for Acceleration

Rule 461 currently requires the Commission staff, when presented with a request for acceleration, to consider the accuracy and adequacy of the prospectus that you circulated.[42] The rule also requires the staff to consider whether you have made a bona fide effort to make the prospectus reasonably concise and understandable. We are amending Rule 461 to require the staff to consider also whether you have made a bona fide effort to satisfy the plain English rule in drafting the front part of the prospectus. Because compliance with the plain English rule will facilitate investors' understanding of the prospectus information, we believe it is important that the preliminary prospectus that you circulate to investors complies with the plain English rule.

Comment letters expressed concern that the amendment to Rule 461 could frequently delay the effective date of registration statements. We believe that these concerns are unfounded. The procedures for addressing deficiencies and for granting or denying acceleration requests have worked very well for many years. We believe the continued use of these procedures will work in implementing the plain English rule. If we select your registration statement for review, the staff will give you comments on how to comply with the plain English rule as well as other requirements. You will have the same opportunity you have now to work with the staff to resolve all comments on your document, consistent with your financing schedule.

VIII. COST-BENEFIT ANALYSIS

The plain English rule and amendments should improve communications between public companies and investors and promote investor protection. Specifically, we anticipate, and many public comment letters concur, that adopting the plain English rule will:

- allow investors to make better-informed assessments of the risk and rewards of investment opportunities;
- reduce the likelihood that investors make investment mistakes because of incomprehensible disclosure documents;
- reduce investors' costs of investing by lowering the time required to read and understand information;
- increase consumers' interest in investing by giving them greater confidence in their understanding of investments;
- reduce the number of costly legal disputes because investors are more likely to better understand disclosure documents; and
- lower offering costs because investors will ask issuers fewer questions about the offering.

Several comment letters suggested that writing documents in plain English would impose substantial costs on public companies.[43] While there may be some additional costs initially, we expect them to be modest and to diminish over time as firms learn to prepare documents using plain English principles. After a short phase-in period, public companies should incur little, if any, additional cost from this rule or these amendments. In some instances, we anticipate that companies will save on printing and mailing costs because plain English tends to reduce document length. Some firms may also save time answering investors' questions. We believe the substantial benefits to investors and the public markets more than justify the phase-in costs.

We base these conclusions, in part, on companies' experiences in the plain English pilot program. To help assess the benefits and costs, we asked nine randomly selected plain English pilot participants, one of which prepared an initial public offering prospectus, about their experiences preparing plain English documents. Six of the nine participants responded, including the initial public offering issuer. All of the participants agreed that investors benefit from clearer, more readable, less redundant disclosure. Specifically, several predicted that investor misunderstandings and mistakes would decline. They did not generally believe, however, that writing their disclosures in plain English would reduce their liability for disclosures. The consensus was that investors file lawsuits on the basis of disclosure materiality, not brevity or wording. Several participants found, however, that they spent less time answering investors' questions when they wrote their documents in plain English.[44]

In terms of the costs of writing documents in plain English, all of the responding participants spent more time writing their documents in plain English than they otherwise would have if they used conventional language.[45] Pilot participants found that legal and technical writing costs rose for plain English filings by approximately 15 percent.[46] Because legal and technical writing comprises approximately 48 percent of the total burden hours necessary to complete a registration statement (with accounting comprising the other 52 percent),[47] we estimate that total burden hours will rise by approximately seven percent in the first year.

The table below shows the current and estimated burden hours per filing, the estimated change in burden hours per filing, and the number of forms filed in 1997 by form type.[48] The information in the table indicates that we estimate public companies will require on average 60 additional hours per filing to comply with the plain English requirements in the first year. At $120 per hour,[49] this translates to an added cost in the first year of approximately $7,200 per filing.[50] Based on pilot program participants' experiences,[51] we expect the number of hours and cost to fall in the following year to the current level as firms gain experience with the plain English principles. We anticipate the cost to repeat filers to fall even sooner.

Form	Estimated Burden Hours/ Filing Before Plain English Rule	Estimated Burden Hours/ Filing After Plain English Rule	Change in Estimated Burden Hours/ Filing	Filings/ Year[52]	Change in Estimated Burden Hours by Filings Type After Plain English Rule
S-1	1,267	1,358	91	1,067	97,097
S-2	470	504	34	145	4,930
S-3	398	427	29	3,137	90,973
S-4	1,233	1,322	89	2,044	181,916
F-1/S-20	1,868	2,002	134	162	21,708
F-2	559	599	40	3	120
F-3	166	178	12	220	2,640
F-4	1,308	1,402	94	243	22,842
S-11	147	158	11	68	748
SB-1	710	761	51	8	408
SB-2	876	939	63	434	27,342
Total				7,531	450,724

We believe the estimate of seven-percent higher cost in the first year is somewhat overstated because it is based on the experiences of pilot participants who did not have models to follow. The time required for future registrants to comply with the requirements should be lower. To help reduce compliance time, the staff is including a list of filings by pilot participants and the information issuers need to locate filings. The staff is also issuing a handbook on how to prepare plain English documents and will hold workshops to help public companies, their counsel, and underwriters comply with the rules. We also anticipate that public companies' legal counsel, who will gain experience from all their clients' transactions, will help to speed the transition to plain English. Finally, some firms filed multiple registration statements in 1997 and we applied the same burden hour increase to all filings. We believe that required compliance time for firms' later filings should be lower than earlier filings as companies gain experience writing in plain English.

These results are consistent with those found by the American Society of Corporate Secretaries, which surveyed the 57 member companies represented on its Securities Law Committee. The twelve members who had prepared at least one plain English document predicted no "material change in annual burden reporting or hours."[53] Similarly, Baltimore Gas and Electric Company incurred no additional cost once the company learned the process.[54]

One benefit generally found by pilot program participants was that document length was shortened on average by 11 percent.[55] Given that the average length of an S-1 prospectus is approximately 116 pages, this decline would result in a 13-page reduction. For an S-3 prospectus, whose average length is 52 pages, the decline would save 6 pages. And the length of an S-4 prospectus, which averages 219 pages, would fall by 24 pages.[56] Where plain English shortened documents, several responding participants estimated lower printing and distribution costs. Even if costs dropped by only five percent, firms would save approximately $3,160 per filing. In aggregate, firms would save approximately $24 million per year—savings that could continue for as long as firms comply with the plain English requirements.[57]

In summary, while all of the participants that answered our questions incurred some additional document preparation costs, the majority estimated them to be low and predicted that they would fall over time. The participants anticipated little added, and perhaps even lower, overall cost. Some even predicted they might save money on printing and distribution costs and time answering investors' questions. Based on the experiences of pilot program participants, we believe that the substantial benefits to investors of plain English and the on-going cost savings to issuers justify the short-term cost to public companies of learning to prepare documents in plain English.

IX. FINAL REGULATORY FLEXIBILITY ANALYSIS

The staff has prepared this Final Regulatory Flexibility Analysis in accordance with Section 603 of the Regulatory Flexibility Act (5 U.S.C. 603). This analysis relates to revisions of Rules 421, 461, and 481 of Regulation C and Items 101, 501, 502, 503, and 508 of Regulations S-K and S-B to implement the Commission's plain English initiative. The Commission is also adopting minor amendments to Forms

S-2, S-3, S-4, S-20, F-2, F-3, and F-4 under the Securities Act and Form N-2 under the Investment Company Act.

Need for and Objectives of Plain English Rules

In August 1995, Chairman Arthur Levitt organized the Task Force on Disclosure Simplification to find ways to simplify the disclosure process and increase the effectiveness and efficiency of capital formation where consistent with investor protection. In its final report to the Commission, the Task Force suggested that the Commission require public companies to write certain parts of prospectuses in plain English.[58] The Commission responded in January 1997 by proposing a rule and several amendments that required public companies to write the front of prospectuses using plain English principles.[59] The amendments revised current rules and forms to eliminate certain language requirements in the front of prospectuses and relocate highly technical language within the prospectus. The Commission proposed these rules to enhance the clarity and conciseness of prospectuses.

The Commission received 45 comment letters from 43 entities in response to the proposing release.[60] The commentators generally expressed strong support for the plain English proposals, although several expressed concerns with specific provisions and some suggested alternative approaches for addressing particular issues. The Commission is adopting the plain English proposals with minor modifications that clarify provisions and reflect the suggestions of some comment letters and the plain English pilot program participants. These rules will make prospectuses simpler, clearer, more useful, and, we hope, more widely read.

The amendments will be adopted pursuant to Sections 6, 7, 8, 10, and 19(a) of the Securities Act, Sections 12, 13, 15(d), 16(a), and 23(a) of the Exchange Act, and Sections 8, 24, 30, 31, and 38 of the Investment Company Act of 1940.

Small Entities Subject to the Rules

For the purposes of the Regulatory Flexibility Act, the term "small business," as used in reference to a public company other than an investment company, is defined by Rule 157 under the Securities Act as an issuer whose total assets on the last day of its most recent fiscal year were $5 million or less and is engaged or proposing to engage in small business financing.[61] An issuer is considered to be engaged in small business financing if it is conducting or proposes to conduct an offering of securities that does not exceed $5 million. The Securities Exchange Act defines a "small business" issuer, other than an investment company, to be an issuer that, on the last day of its most recent fiscal year, had total assets of $5 million or less. When used with respect to an issuer that is an investment company, the term is defined as an investment company with net assets of $50 million or less as of the end of its most recent fiscal year.[62]

The Commission estimates that approximately 1,100 of approximately 12,700 Exchange Act reporting companies and 800 investment companies of approximately 3,700 active registered investment companies currently satisfy the definition of "small business," all of which will be subject to the plain English requirements. We have no reliable way, however, to determine how many businesses may become subject to Commission reporting obligations in the future, or may otherwise be impacted by the plain English requirements.

Significant Issues Raised by Public Comment

The Commission received no requests for the Initial Regulatory Flexibility Analysis and received no comments specifically in response to its request for information about the impact of the rule and amendments on small businesses. Nine comment letters, however, discussed the costs and benefits to public companies in general. Six believed that costs would generally be low and temporary as firms learn to write in plain English. Three believed that the costs would be more significant. These costs are discussed in greater detail in the next subsection. The Commission's efforts to minimize the compliance costs to all reporting companies, both large and small, are discussed in the final subsection of this Final Regulatory Flexibility Analysis.

Projected Reporting, Recordkeeping, and Other Compliance Requirements

The plain English rules and amendments do not affect the substance of the disclosures that public companies must make. They do not impose any new recordkeeping requirements or require reporting of additional information. We anticipate, however, that there will be a temporary increase in cost that will diminish over time as firms learn to prepare documents using plain English principles. Thus, after a short phase-in period, public companies should incur little, if any, additional cost from this rule or these amendments. In some instances, we anticipate that companies will save on printing and mailing costs because plain English tends to reduce document length. Some firms may also save time answering investors' questions.

We base these conclusions, in part, on companies' experiences in the plain English pilot program. We solicited information about firms' experiences by questioning a group of pilot participants. Based on their responses, discussed in detail in Section VIII, we anticipate a temporary increase in cost that will diminish over time as firms learn to prepare documents using plain English principles. While none of the pilot participants specifically qualified as a "small business," the company that wrote its initial public offering prospectus in plain English had a favorable experience.

In addition, we requested information about the impact of the plain English requirements on small businesses in the proposing release. While no one commented specifically on the burden to small firms, several letters indicated that the additional cost of writing in plain English would be low and would diminish after the initial effort of learning to write in plain English. Some commentators even predicted savings. This evidence contrasts, however, with three letters expressing concern that writing in plain English would increase document preparation costs and lengthen documents. While we considered these concerns, experience from the pilot program suggests that phase-in costs will be low and that documents will be shorter and easier to read and understand.

Agency Action to Minimize Effect on Small Businesses

The Regulatory Flexibility Act directs the Commission to consider significant alternatives that would accomplish the stated objectives, while minimizing any significant adverse impact on small issuers. In connection with the plain English rules and amendments, we considered several alternatives, including (a) establishing different compliance and reporting requirements for small businesses; and (b) using performance rather than design standards, and (c) exempting small businesses from all or part of the requirements. We do not believe, however, that these alternatives are appropriate. First, these alternatives would be inconsistent with our statutory mandate to require prospectuses to disclose fully and fairly all material information to investors. Second, these alternatives would significantly dilute or negate the important benefits of plain English disclosure to investors. For these reasons, we also believe there would be no benefit in providing separate requirements for small issuers based on the use of performance rather than design standards.

We have tried before, through interpretive advice and other means, to address the problems with current prospectus disclosure, which too often includes arcane, needlessly complex, and incomprehensible language. These earlier measures have not resulted in widespread improvement in prospectus readability. Therefore, we believe the plain English requirements are necessary to improve communication between public companies and investors, particularly given the relatively low compliance burden. In addition, we believe the rules and amendments should apply equally to all entities required to disclose information under the Securities Act to enhance protection of all investors.

The plain English principles are generally broad statements that provide registrants flexibility in how to disclose information. Thus, there are a variety of ways in which registrants, including small businesses, can use the principles and guidance in making their disclosures. Modifications of the plain English proposals by the Commission will reduce the short-term cost to small issuers. Based on suggestions in several comment letters, the Commission is not adopting limitations on the length of summaries, limitations on the number of risk factors or the requirement that companies prioritize risk factors. To provide compliance assistance to both small and large issuers, the release includes a list of filings by pilot participants and the information issuers need to locate those filings. The staff is also issuing a handbook on how to prepare plain English documents and will hold workshops to help small and large issuers, their counsels, underwriters, and others comply with the rules. Finally, the Commission is minimizing the impact by delaying the effective date of the rules until October 1, 1998.

X. PAPERWORK REDUCTION ACT

The plain English rule and amendments affect several regulations and forms that contain "collection of information requirements" within the meaning of the Paperwork Reduction Act of 1995.[63] In the proposing release, the Commission stated its belief that the plain English rule and amendments would not result in a substantive or material change to the affected collections of information. Nevertheless, the Commission solicited comment on whether the rule and amendments would materially affect the burden on public companies and mutual funds that prepare prospectuses. Because several comment letters indicated that the burden would increase, at least in the short term, the Commission has determined to submit the rule and amendments to the Office of Management and Budget for review in accordance with 44 U.S.C. 3507(d). The Commission is amending Rules 421, 461, and 481 of Regulation C and Items 101, 501, 502, 503, and 508 of Regulations S-K and S-B. The Commission is also adopting minor amendments to Forms S-2, S-3, S-4, S-20, F-2, F-3, and F-4 under the Securities Act and Form N-2 under the Investment Company Act as a part of the plain English initiative.[64]

The rule and amendments require public companies to write information included in the front of prospectuses—the cover page, summary, and risk factors section—in everyday language that investors can understand. The changes also codify existing Commission interpretive advice and eliminate requirements no longer deemed useful. The requirements do not affect the substance of the disclosures that registrants must make. They do not impose any new record keeping requirements or require reporting of additional information.

As discussed in detail in Section VII, we anticipate that there will be a temporary increase in burden that will diminish over time as firms learn to prepare documents using plain English principles. As indicated in the Cost/Benefit Analysis table, we estimate that public companies will require on average 60 additional burden hours per filing or 450,724 hours in total to comply with the plain English requirements in the first year. We then expect burden hours to fall to their current level. Thus, after a short phase-in period, public companies should incur little, if any, additional cost from this rule or these amendments. In some instances, we anticipate that companies will save on printing and mailing costs because plain English tends to reduce document length. Some firms may also save time answering investors' questions. The added burden will be reflected in the estimated burden hours for Regulation C.[65]

The information collection requirements imposed by the forms and regulations are mandatory to the extent that a company elects to do a registered offering. The information is made publicly available. An agency may not conduct or sponsor, and a person is not required to respond to, a collection of information unless it displays a currently valid OMB control number.

In accordance with 44 U.S.C. 3506(c)(2)(B), the Commission solicits comment on the following:

- whether the changes in the collection of information are necessary for the proper performance of the function of the agency;
- the accuracy of the Commission's estimate of the burden of the changes to the collection of information;
- the quality, utility, and clarity of the information to be collected; and
- whether there are ways to minimize the burden of the collection of information on those who are to respond, including through the use of automated collection techniques or other forms of information technology.

Anyone desiring to submit comments on the collection of information requirements should direct them to the Office of Management and Budget, Attention: Desk Officer for the Securities and Exchange Commission, Office of Information and Regulatory Affairs, Washington, D.C. 20503, and should also send a copy of their comments to Jonathan G. Katz, Secretary, Securities and Exchange Commission, 450 Fifth Street, N.W., Washington, D.C. 20549, with reference to File No. S7-3-97. The Office of Management and Budget is required to make a decision concerning the collection of information between 30 and 60 days after publication, so a comment to OMB is best assured of having its full effect if OMB receives it within 30 days of publication.

XI. STATUTORY AUTHORITY

The rule amendments are proposed under Sections 6, 7, 8, 10 and 19(a) of the Securities Act, Sections 12, 13, 15(d), 16(a) and 23(a) of the Exchange Act, and Sections 8, 24, 30, 31 and 38 of the Investment Company Act of 1940.

List of Subjects in 17 CFR Parts 228, 229, 230, 239, and 274

Reporting and recordkeeping requirements, Securities, and Investment companies.

TEXT OF THE AMENDMENTS

For the reasons discussed in the preamble, the Securities and Exchange Commission amends Title 17, Chapter 11 of the Code of Federal Regulations as follows:

PART 228—INTEGRATED DISCLOSURE SYSTEM FOR SMALL BUSINESS ISSUERS

1. The authority citation for Part 228 continues to read as follows:

Authority: 15 U.S.C. 77e, 77f, 77g, 77h, 77j, 77k, 77s, 77z- 2, 77aa(25), 77aa(26), 77ddd, 77eee, 77ggg, 77hhh, 77jjj, 77nnn, 77sss, 78l, 78m, 78n, 78o, 78u-5, 78w, 78ll, 80a-8, 80a-29, 80a-30, 80a-37, 80b-11, unless otherwise noted.

2. By amending 228.101 to add paragraphs (c) and (d) to read as follows:

228.101 (Item 101) Description of Business.

* * * * *

(c) **Reports to security holders.** Disclose the following in any registration statement you file under the Securities Act of 1933:

(1) If you are not required to deliver an annual report to security holders, whether you will voluntarily send an annual report and whether the report will include audited financial statements;

(2) Whether you file reports with the Securities and Exchange Commission. If you are a reporting company, identify the reports and other information you file with the SEC; and

(3) That the public may read and copy any materials you file with the SEC at the SEC's Public Reference Room at 450 Fifth Street, N.W., Washington, D.C. 20549.

State that the public may obtain information on the operation of the Public Reference Room by calling the SEC at 1-800-SEC-0330. If you are an electronic filer, state that the SEC maintains an Internet site that contains reports, proxy and information statements, and other information regarding issuers that file electronically with the SEC and state the address of that site (http://www.sec.gov). You are encouraged to give your Internet address, if available;

(d) **Canadian Issuers.** Provide the information required by Items 101(f)(2) and 101(g) of Regulation S-K (229.101(f)(2) and (g)).

3. Section 228.501 is revised to read as follows:

228.501 (Item 501) Front of Registration Statement and Front Cover of Prospectus.

The small business issuer must furnish the following information in plain English. See 230.421(d) of Regulation C of this chapter.

(a) Limit the outside front cover page of the prospectus to one page and include the following information:

(1) The registrant's name. A foreign registrant also must give the English translation of its name;

(2) The title, amount, and description of securities offered. If the underwriter has any arrangement with the issuer, such as an over-allotment option, under which the underwriter may purchase additional shares in connection with the offering, indicate that this arrangement exists and state the amount of additional shares that the underwriter may purchase under the arrangement;

(3) If there are selling security holders, a statement to that effect;

(4) Whether any national securities exchange or the Nasdaq Stock Market lists the securities offered, naming the particular market(s), and identifying the trading symbol(s) for those securities;

(5) A cross-reference to the risk factors section, including the page number where it appears in the prospectus. Highlight this cross-reference by prominent type or in another manner;

(6) Any legend or statement required by the law of any state in which the securities are offered;

(7) A legend that indicates that neither the Securities and Exchange Commission nor any state securities commission has approved or disapproved of the securities or passed on the adequacy or accuracy of the disclosures in the prospectus. Also make clear that any representation to the contrary is a criminal offense. You may use one of the following or other clear, plain language:

Example A: Neither the Securities and Exchange Commission nor any state securities commission has approved or disapproved of these securities or passed upon the adequacy or accuracy of the prospectus. Any representation to the contrary is a criminal offense.

Example B: Neither the Securities and Exchange Commission nor any state securities commission has approved or disapproved of these securities or determined if this prospectus is truthful or complete. Any representation to the contrary is a criminal offense.

(8) If you are not a reporting company and the preliminary prospectus will be circulated, as applicable:

(i) A bona fide estimate of the range of the maximum offering price and maximum number of shares or units offered; or

(ii) A bona fide estimate of the principal amount of debt securities offered;

(9)(i) Name(s) of the lead or managing underwriter(s) and an identification of the nature of the underwriting arrangements;

(ii) If the offering is not made on a firm commitment basis, a brief description of the underwriting arrangements;

(iii) If you offer the securities on a best efforts or best efforts minimum/maximum basis, the date the offering will end, any minimum purchase requirements, and whether or not there are any arrangements to place the funds in an escrow, trust, or similar account; and

(iv) If you offer the securities for cash, the price to the public for the securities, the underwriting discounts and commissions, and proceeds to the registrant or other persons. Show the information on both a per share or unit basis and for the total amount of the offering. If you make the offering on a minimum/maximum basis, show this information based on the total minimum and total maximum amount of the offering. You may present the information in a table, term sheet format, or other clear presentation. You may present the information in any format that fits the design of the cover page so long as the information can be easily read and is not misleading;

(10) If the prospectus will be used before the effective date of the registration statement, a prominent statement that:

(i) The information in the prospectus will be amended or completed;

(ii) A registration statement relating to these securities has been filed with the Securities and Exchange Commission;

(iii) The securities may not be sold until the registration statement becomes effective; and

(iv) The prospectus is not an offer to sell the securities and it is not soliciting an offer to buy the securities in any state where offers or sales are not permitted. You may use the following or other clear, plain language:

The information in this prospectus is not complete and may be changed. We may not sell these securities until the registration statement filed with the Securities and Exchange Commission is effective. The prospectus is not an offer to sell these securities and it is not soliciting an offer to buy these securities in any state where the offer or sale is not permitted.

(11) If you use 230.430A of this chapter to omit pricing information and the prospectus is used before you determine the public offering price, the information in paragraph (a)(10) of this section; and

(12) The date of the prospectus.

(b) [Reserved]

4. Section 228.502 is revised to read as follows:

228.502 (Item 502) Inside Front and Outside Back Cover Pages of Prospectus.

The small business issuer must furnish the following information in plain English. See 230.421(d) of Regulation C of this chapter.

(a) **Table of Contents.** On either the inside front or outside back cover page of the prospectus, provide a reasonably detailed table of contents. It must show the page number of the various sections or subdivisions of the prospectus. Include a specific listing of the risk factors section required by Item 503 of this Regulation S-B (17 CFR 228.503). You must include the table of contents immediately following the cover page in any prospectus you deliver electronically;

(b) **Dealer Prospectus Delivery Obligation.** If applicable to your offering, on the outside back cover page of the prospectus, advise dealers of their prospectus delivery obligation, including the expiration date specified by Section 4(3) of the Securities Act (15 U.S.C. 77d(3)) and 230.174 of this chapter. You may use the following or other clear, plain language:

Dealer Prospectus Delivery Obligation

Until (insert date), all dealers that effect transactions in these securities, whether or not participating in this offering, may be required to deliver a prospectus. This is in addition to the dealers' obligation to deliver a prospectus when acting as underwriters and with respect to their unsold allotments or subscriptions.

5. By revising 228.503 to read as follows:

228.503 (Item 503) Summary Information and Risk Factors.

The small business issuer must furnish the following information in plain English. See 230.421(d) of Regulation C of this chapter.

(a) **Summary.** Provide a summary of the information in the prospectus where the length or complexity of the prospectus makes a summary useful. The summary should be brief. The summary should not contain, and is not required to contain, all of the detailed information in the prospectus. If you provide summary business or financial information, even if you do not caption it as a summary, you still must provide that information in plain English.

Instruction to paragraph 503(a)

The summary should not merely repeat the text of the prospectus but should provide a brief overview of the key aspects of the offering. Carefully consider and identify those aspects of the offering that are the most significant and determine how best to highlight those points in clear, plain language.

(b) **Address and phone number.** Include, either on the cover page or in the summary section of the prospectus, the complete mailing address and telephone number of your principal executive offices.

(c) **Risk factors.** (1) Discuss in a section captioned "Risk Factors" any factors that make the offering speculative or risky. The factors may include, among other things, the following:

(i) Your lack of an operating history;

(ii) Your lack of recent profits from operations;

(iii) Your poor financial position;

(iv) Your business or proposed business; or

(v) The lack of a market for your common equity securities.

(2) The risk factor discussion must immediately follow the summary section. If you do not include a summary section, the risk factor discussion must immediately follow the cover page or the pricing information that immediately follows the cover page. Pricing information means price and price-related information that you may omit from the prospectus in an effective registration statement based on 230.430A(a) of this chapter.

6. Section 228.508 is amended to revise the heading of paragraph (a), add two sentences to the end of paragraph (a) and revise paragraph (j) to read as follows:

228.508 (Item 508) Plan of Distribution.

(a) **Underwriters and underwriting obligations.** * * * The small business issuer must disclose the offering expenses specified in Item 511 of this Regulation S-B (17 CFR 228.511). If there is an arrangement under which the underwriter may purchase additional shares in connection with the offering, such as an over-allotment option, describe that arrangement and disclose information on the total offering price, underwriting discounts and commissions, and total proceeds assuming the underwriter purchases all of the shares subject to that arrangement.

* * * * *

(j) **Stabilization and other transactions.** (1) Briefly describe any transaction that the underwriter intends to conduct during the offering that stabilizes, maintains, or otherwise affects the market price of the offered securities. Include information on stabilizing transactions, syndicate short covering transactions, penalty bids, or any other transaction that affects the offered security's price. Describe the nature of the transactions clearly and explain how the transactions affect the offered security's price. Identify the exchange or other market on which these transactions may occur. If true, disclose that the underwriter may discontinue these transactions at any time;

(2) If the stabilizing began before the effective date of the registration statement, disclose the amount of securities bought, the prices at which they were bought, and the period within which they were bought. If you use 230.430A of this chapter, the final prospectus must contain information on the stabilizing transactions that took place before the public offering price was set; and

(3) If you are making a warrant or rights offering of securities to existing security holders and the securities not purchased by existing security holders are to be reoffered to the public, disclose the following information in the reoffer prospectus:

(i) The amount of securities bought in stabilization activities during the offering period and the price or range of prices at which the securities were bought;

(ii) The amount of the offered securities subscribed for during the offering period;

(iii) The amount of the offered securities purchased by the underwriter during the offering period;

(iv) The amount of the offered securities sold by the underwriter during the offering period and the price or range of prices at which the securities were sold; and

(v) The amount of the offered securities that will be reoffered to the public and the offering price.

PART 229—STANDARD INSTRUCTIONS FOR FILING FORMS UNDER SECURITIES ACT OF 1933, SECURITIES EXCHANGE ACT OF 1934 AND ENERGY POLICY AND CONSERVATION ACT OF 1975—REGULATION S-K

7. The authority citation for Part 229 continues to read as follows:

Authority: 15 U.S.C. 77e, 77f, 77g, 77h, 77j, 77k, 77s, 77z- 2, 77aa(25), 77aa(26), 77ddd, 77eee, 77ggg, 77hhh, 77iii, 77jjj, 77nnn, 77sss, 78c, 78i, 78j, 78l, 78m, 78n, 78o, 78u-5, 78w, 78ll(d), 79e, 79n, 79t, 80a-8, 80a-29, 80a-30, 80a-37, 80b-11, unless otherwise noted.

* * * * *

8. By amending 229.101 to add paragraphs (e), (f), and (g) before "Instructions to Item 101" to read as follows:

229.101 (Item 101) Description of business.

* * * * *

(e) **Available Information.** Disclose the following in any registration statement you file under the Securities Act of 1933:

(1) Whether you file reports with the Securities and Exchange Commission. If you are a reporting company, identify the reports and other information you file with the SEC.

(2) That the public may read and copy any materials you file with the SEC at the SEC's Public Reference Room at 450 Fifth Street, N.W., Washington, D.C. 20549. State that the public may obtain information on the operation of the Public Reference Room by calling the SEC at 1-800-SEC-0330. If you are an electronic filer, state that the SEC maintains an Internet site that contains reports, proxy and information statements, and other information regarding issuers that file electronically with the SEC and state the address of that site (http://www.sec.gov). You are encouraged to give your Internet address, if available;

(f) **Reports to Security Holders.** Disclose the following information in any registration statement you file under the Securities Act:

(1) If the SEC's proxy rules or regulations, or stock exchange requirements, do not require you to send an annual report to security holders or to holders of American depository receipts, describe briefly the nature and frequency of reports that you will give to security holders. Specify whether the reports that you give will contain financial information that has been examined and reported on, with an opinion expressed "by" an independent public or certified public accountant.

(2) For a foreign private issuer, if the report will not contain financial information prepared in accordance with U.S. generally accepted accounting principles, you must state whether the report will include a reconciliation of this information with U.S. generally accepted accounting principles.

(g) **Enforceability of Civil Liabilities Against Foreign Persons.** Disclose the following if you are a foreign private issuer filing a registration statement under the Securities Act:

(1) Whether or not investors may bring actions under the civil liability provisions of the U.S. federal securities laws against the foreign private issuer, any of its officers and directors who are residents of a foreign country, any underwriters or experts named in the registration statement that are residents of a foreign country, and whether investors may enforce these civil liability provisions when the assets of the issuer or these other persons are located outside of the United States. The disclosure must address the following matters:

(i) The investor's ability to effect service of process within the United States on the foreign private issuer or any person;

(ii) The investor's ability to enforce judgments obtained in U.S. courts against foreign persons based upon the civil liability provisions of the U.S. federal securities laws;

(iii) The investor's ability to enforce, in an appropriate foreign court, judgments of U.S. courts based upon the civil liability provisions of the U.S. federal securities laws; and

(iv) The investor's ability to bring an original action in an appropriate foreign court to enforce liabilities against the foreign private issuer or any person based upon the U.S. federal securities laws.

(2) If you provide this disclosure based on an opinion of counsel, name counsel in the prospectus and file as an exhibit to the registration statement a signed consent of counsel to the use of its name and opinion.

* * * * *

9. By revising 229.501 to read as follows:

229.501 (Item 501) Forepart of Registration Statement and Outside Front Cover Page of Prospectus.

The registrant must furnish the following information in plain English. See 230.421(d) of Regulation C of this chapter.

(a) **Front Cover Page of the Registration Statement.** Where appropriate, include the delaying amendment legend from 230.473 of Regulation C of this chapter.

(b) **Outside Front Cover Page of the Prospectus.** Limit the outside cover page to one page. If the following information applies to your offering, disclose it on the outside cover page of the prospectus.

(1) **Name.** The registrant's name. A foreign registrant must give the English translation of its name.

Instruction to paragraph 501(b)(1).

If your name is the same as that of a company that is well known, include information to eliminate any possible confusion with the other company. If your name indicates a line of business in which you are not engaged or you are engaged only to a limited extent, include information to eliminate any misleading inference as to your business. In some circumstances, disclosure may not be sufficient and you may be required to change your name. You will not be required to change your name if you are an established company, the character of your business has changed, and the investing public is generally aware of the change and the character of your current business.

(2) **Title and amount of securities.** The title and amount of securities offered. Separately state the amount of securities offered by selling security holders, if any. If the underwriter has any arrangement with the issuer, such as an over-allotment option, under which the underwriter may purchase additional shares in connection with the offering, indicate that this arrangement exists and state the amount of additional shares that the underwriter may purchase under the arrangement. Give a brief description of the securities except where the information is clear from the title of the security. For example, you are not required to describe common stock that has full voting, dividend and liquidation rights usually associated with common stock.

(3) **Offering price of the securities.** Where you offer securities for cash, the price to the public of the securities, the underwriter's discounts and commissions, the net proceeds you receive, and any selling shareholder's net proceeds. Show this information on both a per share or unit basis and for the total amount of the offering. If you make the offering on a minimum/maximum basis, show this information based on the total minimum and total maximum amount of the offering. You may present the information in a table, term sheet format, or other clear presentation. You may present the information in any format that fits the design of the cover page so long as the information can be easily read and is not misleading;

Instructions to paragraph 501(b)(3)

1. If a preliminary prospectus is circulated and you are not subject to the reporting requirements of Section 13(a) or 15 (d) of the Exchange Act, provide, as applicable:

(A) A bona fide estimate of the range of the maximum offering price and the maximum number of securities offered; or

(B) A bona fide estimate of the principal amount of the debt securities offered.

2. If it is impracticable to state the price to the public, explain the method by which the price is to be determined. If the securities are to be offered at the market price, or if the offering price is to be determined by a formula related to the market price, indicate the market and market price of the securities as of the latest practicable date.

3. If you file a registration statement on Form S-8, you are not required to comply with this paragraph (b)(3).

(4) **Market for the Securities.** Whether any national securities exchange or the Nasdaq Stock Market lists the securities offered, naming the particular market(s), and identifying the trading symbol(s) for those securities;

(5) **Risk Factors.** A cross-reference to the risk factors section, including the page number where it appears in the prospectus. Highlight this cross-reference by prominent type or in another manner;

(6) **State Legend.** Any legend or statement required by the law of any state in which the securities are to be offered. You may combine this with any legend required by the SEC, if appropriate;

(7) **Commission Legend.** A legend that indicates that neither the Securities and Exchange Commission nor any state securities commission has approved or disapproved of the securities or passed upon the accuracy or adequacy of the disclosures in the prospectus and that any contrary representation is a criminal offense. You may use one of the following or other clear, plain language:

Example A: Neither the Securities and Exchange Commission nor any state securities commission has approved or disapproved of these securities or passed upon the adequacy or accuracy of this prospectus. Any representation to the contrary is a criminal offense.

Example B: Neither the Securities and Exchange Commission nor any state securities commission has approved or disapproved of these securities or determined if this prospectus is truthful or complete. Any representation to the contrary is a criminal offense.

(8) **Underwriting.** (i) Name(s) of the lead or managing underwriter(s) and an identification of the nature of the underwriting arrangements;

(ii) If the offering is not made on a firm commitment basis, a brief description of the underwriting arrangements. You may use any clear, concise, and accurate description of the underwriting arrangements. You may use the following descriptions of underwriting arrangements where appropriate:

Example A: Best efforts offering. The underwriters are not required to sell any specific number or dollar amount of securities but will use their best efforts to sell the securities offered.

Example B: Best efforts, minimum-maximum offering. The underwriters must sell the minimum number of securities offered (insert number) if any are sold. The underwriters are required to use only their best efforts to sell the maximum number of securities offered (insert number).

(iii) If you offer the securities on a best efforts or best efforts minimum/maximum basis, the date the offering will end, any minimum purchase requirements, and any arrangements to place the funds in an escrow, trust, or similar account. If you have not made any of these arrangements, state this fact and describe the effect on investors;

(9) **Date of Prospectus.** The date of the prospectus;

(10) **Prospectus "Subject to Completion" Legend.** If you use the prospectus before the effective date of the registration statement, a prominent statement that:

(i) The information in the prospectus will be amended or completed;

(ii) A registration statement relating to these securities has been filed with the Securities and Exchange Commission;

(iii) The securities may not be sold until the registration statement becomes effective; and

(iv) The prospectus is not an offer to sell the securities and it is not soliciting an offer to buy the securities in any state where offers or sales are not permitted. The legend may be in the following or other clear, plain language:

The information in this prospectus is not complete and may be changed. We may not sell these securities until the registration statement filed with the Securities and Exchange Commission is effective. This prospectus is not an offer to sell these securities and it is not soliciting an offer to buy these securities in any state where the offer or sale is not permitted.

(11) If you use 230.430A of this chapter to omit pricing information and the prospectus is used before you determine the public offering price, the information and legend in paragraph (b)(10) of this section.

10. By revising 229.502 to read as follows:

229.502 (Item 502) Inside Front and Outside Back Cover Pages of Prospectus.

The registrant must furnish this information in plain English. See 230.421(d) of Regulation C of this chapter.

(a) **Table of Contents.** On either the inside front or outside back cover page of the prospectus, provide a reasonably detailed table of contents. It must show the page number of the various sections or subdivisions of the prospectus. Include a specific listing of the risk factors section required by Item 503 of this Regulation S-K (17 CFR 229.503). You must include the table of contents immediately following the cover page in any prospectus you deliver electronically.

(b) **Dealer Prospectus Delivery Obligation.** On the outside back cover page of the prospectus, advise dealers of their prospectus delivery obligation, including the expiration date specified by Section 4(3) of the Securities Act (15 U.S.C. 77d(3)) and 230.174 of this chapter. If you do not know the expiration date on the effective date of the registration statement, include the expiration date in the copy of the prospectus you file under 230.424(b) of this chapter. You do not have to include this information if dealers are not required to deliver a prospectus under 230.174 of this chapter or Section 24(d) of the Investment Company Act (15 U.S.C. 80a-24). You may use the following or other clear, plain language:

Dealer Prospectus Delivery Obligation Until (insert date), all dealers that effect transactions in these securities, whether or not participating in this offering, may be required to deliver a prospectus. This is in addition to the dealers' obligation to deliver a prospectus when acting as underwriters and with respect to their unsold allotments or subscriptions.

11. By revising 229.503 to read as follows:

229.503 (Item 503) Prospectus Summary, Risk Factors, and Ratio of Earnings to Fixed Charges.

The registrant must furnish this information in plain English. See 230.421(d) of Regulation C of this chapter.

(a) **Prospectus Summary.** Provide a summary of the information in the prospectus where the length or complexity of the prospectus makes a summary useful. The summary should be brief. The summary should not contain, and is not required to contain, all of the detailed information in the prospectus. If you provide summary business or financial information, even if you do not caption it as a summary, you still must provide that information in plain English.

Instruction to paragraph 503(a).

The summary should not merely repeat the text of the prospectus but should provide a brief overview of the key aspects of the offering. Carefully consider and identify those aspects of the offering that are the most significant and determine how best to highlight those points in clear, plain language.

(b) **Address and Telephone Number.** Include, either on the cover page or in the summary section of the prospectus, the complete mailing address and telephone number of your principal executive offices.

(c) **Risk Factors.** Where appropriate, provide under the caption "Risk Factors" a discussion of the most significant factors that make the offering speculative or risky. This discussion must be concise and organized logically. Do not present risks that could apply to any issuer or any offering. Explain how the risk affects the issuer or the securities being offered. Set forth each risk factor under a subcaption that adequately describes the risk. The risk factor discussion must immediately follow the summary section. If you do not include a summary section, the risk factor section must immediately follow the cover page of the prospectus or the pricing information section that immediately follows the cover page. Pricing information means price and price-related information that you may omit from the prospectus in an effective registration statement based on 230.430A(a) of this chapter. The risk factors may include, among other things, the following:

(1) Your lack of an operating history;

(2) Your lack of profitable operations in recent periods;

(3) Your financial position;

(4) Your business or proposed business; or

(5) The lack of a market for your common equity securities or securities convertible into or exercisable for common equity securities.

(d) **Ratio of Earnings to Fixed Charges.** If you register debt securities, show a ratio of earnings to fixed charges. If you register preference equity securities, show the ratio of combined fixed charges and preference dividends to earnings. Present the ratio for each of the last five fiscal years and the latest interim period for which financial statements are presented in the document. If you will use the proceeds from the sale of debt or preference securities to repay any of your outstanding debt or to retire other securities and the change in the ratio would be ten percent or greater, you must include a ratio showing the application of the proceeds, commonly referred to as the pro forma ratio.

Instructions to paragraph 503(d)

1. **Definitions.** In calculating the ratio of earnings to fixed charges, you must use the following definitions:

(A) **Fixed charges.** The term "fixed charges" means the sum of the following: (a) interest expensed and capitalized, (b) amortized premiums, discounts and capitalized expenses related to indebtedness, (c) an estimate of the interest within rental expense, and (d) preference security dividend requirements of consolidated subsidiaries.

(B) **Preference security dividend.** The term "preference security dividend" is the amount of pre-tax earnings that is required to pay the dividends on outstanding preference securities. The dividend requirement must be computed as the amount of the dividend divided by (1 minus the effective income tax rate applicable to continuing operations).

(C) **Earnings.** The term "earnings" is the amount resulting from adding and subtracting the following items. Add the following: (a) pretax income from continuing operations before adjustment for minority interests in consolidated subsidiaries or income or loss from equity investees, (b) fixed charges, (c) amortization of capitalized interest, (d) distributed income of equity investees, and (e) your share of pre-tax losses of equity investees for which charges arising from guarantees are included in fixed charges. From the total of the added items, subtract the following: (a) interest capitalized, (b) preference security dividend requirements of consolidated subsidiaries, and (c) the minority interest in pre-tax income of subsidiaries that have not incurred fixed charges. Equity investees are investments that you account for using the equity method of accounting. Public utilities following SFAS 71 should not add amortization of capitalized interest in determining earnings, nor reduce fixed charges by any allowance for funds used during construction.

2. **Disclosure.** Disclose the following information when showing the ratio of earnings to fixed charges:

(A) **Deficiency.** If a ratio indicates less than one-to-one coverage, disclose the dollar amount of the deficiency.

(B) **Pro forma ratio.** You may show the pro forma ratio only for the most recent fiscal year and the latest interim period. Use the net change in interest or dividends from the refinancing to calculate the pro forma ratio.

(C) **Foreign private issuers.** A foreign private issuer must show the ratio based on the figures in the primary financial statement. A foreign private issuer must show the ratio based on the figures resulting from the reconciliation to U.S. generally accepted accounting principles if this ratio is materially different.

(D) **Summary Section.** If you provide a summary or similar section in the prospectus, show the ratios in that section.

3. **Exhibit.** File an exhibit to the registration statement to show the figures used to calculate the ratios. See paragraph (b)(12) of Item 601 of Regulation S-K (17 CFR 229.601(b)(12)).

12. By amending 229.508 by revising paragraphs (e) and (l) to read as follows:

229.508 (Item 508) Plan of distribution.

* * * * *

(e) **Underwriter's compensation.** Provide a table that sets out the nature of the compensation and the amount of discounts and commissions to be paid to the underwriter for each security and in total. The table must show the separate amounts to be paid by the company and the selling shareholders. In addition, include in the table all other items considered by the National Association of Securities Dealers to be underwriting compensation for purposes of that Association's Rules of Fair Practice.

Instructions to paragraph 508(e)

1. The term "commissions" is defined in paragraph (17) of Schedule A of the Securities Act. Show separately in the table the cash commissions paid by the registrant and selling security holders. Also show in the table commissions paid by other persons. Disclose any finder's fee or similar payments in the table.

2. Disclose the offering expenses specified in Item 511 of Regulation S-K (17 CFR 229.511).

3. If the underwriter has any arrangement with the issuer, such as an over-allotment option, under which the underwriter may purchase additional shares in connection with the offering, indicate that this arrangement exists and state the amount of additional shares that the underwriter may purchase under the arrangement. Where the underwriter has such an arrangement, present maximum-minimum information in a separate column to the table, based on the purchase of all or none of the shares subject to the arrangement. Describe the key terms of the arrangement in the narrative.

* * * * *

(l) **Stabilization and other transactions.** (1) Briefly describe any transaction that the underwriter intends to conduct during the offering that stabilizes, maintains, or otherwise affects the market price of the offered securities. Include information on stabilizing transactions, syndicate short covering transactions, penalty bids, or any other transaction that affects the offered security's price. Describe the nature of the transactions clearly and explain how the transactions affect the offered security's price. Identify the exchange or other market on which these transactions may occur. If true, disclose that the underwriter may discontinue these transactions at any time;

(2) If the stabilizing began before the effective date of the registration statement, disclose the amount of securities bought, the prices at which they were bought and the period within which they were bought. If you use 230.430A of this chapter, the prospectus you file under 230.424(b) of this chapter or include in a post-effective amendment must contain information on the stabilizing transactions that took place before the determination of the public offering price; and

(3) If you are making a warrants or rights offering of securities to existing security holders and any securities not purchased by existing security holders are to be reoffered to the public, disclose in a supplement to the prospectus or in the prospectus used in connection with the reoffering:

(i) The amount of securities bought in stabilization activities during the offering period and the price or range of prices at which the securities were bought;

(ii) The amount of the offered securities subscribed for during the offering period;

(iii) The amount of the offered securities subscribed for by the underwriter during the offering period;

(iv) The amount of the offered securities sold during the offering period by the underwriter and the price or price ranges at which the securities were sold; and

(v) The amount of the offered securities that will be reoffered to the public and the public offering price.

PART 230—GENERAL RULES AND REGULATIONS, SECURITIES ACT OF 1933

13. The general authority citation for Part 230 is revised to read as follows:

Authority: 15 U.S.C. 77b, 77f, 77g, 77h, 77j, 77s, 77sss, 78c, 78d, 78l, 78m, 78n, 78o, 78w, 78ll(d), 79t, 80a-8, 80a-24, 80a-29, 80a-30, and 80a-37, unless otherwise noted.

* * * * *

14. By amending 230.421 by revising paragraph (b) and adding paragraph (d) to read as follows:

230.421 Presentation of information in prospectuses.

* * * * *

(b) You must present the information in a prospectus in a clear, concise and understandable manner. You must prepare the prospectus using the following standards:

(1) Present information in clear, concise sections, paragraphs, and sentences. Whenever possible, use short, explanatory sentences and bullet lists;

(2) Use descriptive headings and subheadings;

(3) Avoid frequent reliance on glossaries or defined terms as the primary means of explaining information in the prospectus. Define terms in a glossary or other section of the document only if the meaning is unclear from the context. Use a glossary only if it facilitates understanding of the disclosure; and

(4) Avoid legal and highly technical business terminology.

Note to 230.421(b):

In drafting the disclosure to comply with this section, you should avoid the following:

1. Legalistic or overly complex presentations that make the substance of the disclosure difficult to understand;

2. Vague "boilerplate" explanations that are imprecise and readily subject to different interpretations;

3. Complex information copied directly from legal documents without any clear and concise explanation of the provision(s); and

4. Disclosure repeated in different sections of the document that increases the size of the document but does not enhance the quality of the information.

* * * * *

(d)(1) To enhance the readability of the prospectus, you must use plain English principles in the organization, language, and design of the front and back cover pages, the summary, and the risk factors section.

(2) You must draft the language in these sections so that at a minimum it substantially complies with each of the following plain English writing principles:

(i) Short sentences;

(ii) Definite, concrete, everyday words;

(iii) Active voice;

(iv) Tabular presentation or bullet lists for complex material, whenever possible;

(v) No legal jargon or highly technical business terms; and

(vi) No multiple negatives.

(3) In designing these sections or other sections of the prospectus, you may include pictures, logos, charts, graphs, or other design elements so long as the design is not misleading and the required information is clear. You are encouraged to use tables, schedules, charts and graphic illustrations of the results of operations, balance sheet, or other financial data that present the data in an understandable manner. Any presentation must be consistent with the financial statements and non-financial information in the prospectus. You must draw the graphs and charts to scale. Any information you provide must not be misleading.

Instruction to 230.421

You should read Securities Act Release No. 33-7497 (January 28, 1998) for information on plain English principles.

15. By revising paragraph (b)(1) of 230.461 to read as follows.

230.461 Acceleration of effective date.

* * * * *

(b) * * *

(1) Where there has not been a bona fide effort to make the prospectus reasonably concise, readable, and in compliance with the plain English requirements of Rule 421(d) of Regulation C (17 CFR 230.421(d)) in order to facilitate an understanding of the information in the prospectus.

* * * * *

16. Revise 230.481 to read as follows:

230.481 Information required in prospectuses.

Disclose the following in registration statements prepared on a form available solely to investment companies registered under the Investment Company Act of 1940 or in registration statements filed under the Act for a company that has elected to be regulated as a business development company under Sections 55 through 65 of the Investment Company Act (15 U.S.C. 80a-54–80a-64):

(a) **Facing Page.** Indicate the approximate date of the proposed sale of the securities to the public.

(b) **Outside Front Cover Page.** If applicable, include the following in plain English as required by 230.421(d):

(1) **Commission Legend.** Provide a legend that indicates that the Securities and Exchange Commission has not approved or disapproved of the securities or passed upon the accuracy or adequacy of the disclosure in the prospectus and that any contrary representation is a criminal offense. The legend may be in one of the following or other clear and concise language:

Example A: The Securities and Exchange Commission has not approved or disapproved these securities or passed upon the adequacy of this prospectus. Any representation to the contrary is a criminal offense.

Example B: The Securities and Exchange Commission has not approved or disapproved these securities or determined if this prospectus is truthful or complete. Any representation to the contrary is a criminal offense.

(2) **"Subject to Completion" Legend.** (i) If a prospectus or Statement of Additional Information will be used before the effective date of the registration statement, include on the outside front cover page of the prospectus or Statement of Additional Information, a prominent statement that:

(A) The information in the prospectus or Statement of Additional Information will be amended or completed;

(B) A registration statement relating to these securities has been filed with the Securities and Exchange Commission;

(C) The securities may not be sold until the registration statement becomes effective; and

(D) In a prospectus, that the prospectus is not an offer to sell the securities and it is not soliciting an offer to buy the securities in any state where offers or sales are not permitted, or in a Statement of Additional Information, that the Statement of Additional Information is not a prospectus.

(ii) The legend may be in the following language or other clear and understandable language:

The information in this prospectus (or Statement of Additional Information) is not complete and may be changed. We may not sell these securities until the registration statement filed with the Securities and Exchange Commission is effective. This prospectus (or Statement of Additional Information) is not an offer to sell these securities and is not soliciting an offer to buy these securities in any state where the offer or sale is not permitted.

(iii) In the case of a prospectus that omits pricing information under 230.430A, provide the information and legend in paragraph (b)(2) of this section if the prospectus or Statement of Additional Information is used before the initial public offering price is determined.

(c) **Table of Contents.** Include on either the outside front, inside front, or outside back cover page of the prospectus, a reasonably detailed table of contents. It must show the page number of the various sections or subdivisions of the prospectus. Include this table of contents immediately following the cover page in any prospectus delivered electronically.

(d) **Stabilization and Other Transactions.** (1) Indicate on the front cover page of the prospectus if the underwriter has any arrangement with the issuer, such as an over-allotment option, under which the underwriter may purchase additional shares in connection with the offering, and state the amount of additional shares the underwriter may purchase under the arrangement. Provide disclosure in the prospectus that briefly describes any transaction that the underwriter intends to conduct during the offering that stabilizes, maintains, or otherwise affects the market price of the offered securities. Include information on stabilizing transactions, syndicate short covering transactions, penalty bids, or any other transactions that affect the offered security's price. Describe the nature of the transactions clearly and explain how the transactions affect the offered security's price. Identify the exchange or other market on which these transactions may occur. If true, disclose that the underwriter may discontinue these transactions at any time;

(2) If the stabilizing began before the effective date of the registration statement, disclose in the prospectus the amount of securities bought, the prices at which they were bought and the period within which they were bought. In the event that 230.430A of this chapter is used, the prospectus filed under 230.497(h) or included in a post-effective amendment must contain information on the stabilizing transactions that took place before the determination of the public offering price shown in the prospectus; and

(3) If you are making a warrant or rights offering of securities to existing security holders and the securities not purchased by existing security holders are to be reoffered to the public, disclose in the prospectus used in connection with the reoffering:

(i) The amount of securities bought in stabilization activities during the offering period and the price or range of prices at which the securities were bought;

(ii) The amount of the offered securities subscribed for during the offering period;

(iii) The amount of the offered securities subscribed for by the underwriters during the offering period;

(iv) The amount of the offered securities sold during the offering period by the underwriters and the price or range of prices at which the securities were sold; and

(v) The amount of the offered securities to be reoffered to the public and the public offering price.

(e) **Dealer Prospectus Delivery Obligations.** On the outside back cover page of the prospectus, advise dealers of their prospectus delivery obligation, including the expiration date specified by Section 4(3) of the Act (15 U.S.C. 77d(3)) and 230.174. If the expiration date is not known on the effective date of the registration statement, include the expiration date in the copy of the prospectus filed under 230.497. This information need not be included if dealers are not required to deliver a prospectus under 230.174 or Section 24(d) of the Investment Company Act of 1940 (15 U.S.C. 80a-24). Use the following or other clear, plain language:

Dealer Prospectus Delivery Obligation

Until (insert date), all dealers that effect transactions in these securities, whether or not participating in this offering, may be required to deliver a prospectus. This is in addition to the dealers' obligation to deliver a prospectus when acting as underwriters and with respect to their unsold allotments or subscriptions.

(f) **Electronic Distribution.** Where a prospectus is distributed through an electronic medium, issuers may satisfy legibility requirements applicable to printed documents, such as paper size, type size and font, bold-face type, italics and red ink, by presenting all required information in a format readily communicated to investors, and where indicated, in a manner reasonably calculated to draw investor attention to specific information.

PART 239—FORMS PRESCRIBED UNDER THE SECURITIES ACT OF 1933

17. The authority citation for Part 239 continues to read in part as follows:

Authority: 15 U.S.C. 77f, 77g, 77h, 77j, 77s, 77z-2, 77sss, 78c, 78l, 78m, 78n, 78o(d), 78u-5, 78w(a), 78ll(d), 79e, 79f, 79g, 79j, 79l, 79m, 79n, 79q, 79t, 80a-8, 80a-29, 80a-30 and 80a-37, unless otherwise noted.

* * * * *

18. By amending Form S-2 (referenced in 239.12), Item 12 to add paragraph (d) to read as follows:

[Note: The text of Form S-2 does not, and this amendment will not, appear in the Code of Federal Regulations]

FORM S-2

REGISTRATION STATEMENT UNDER THE SECURITIES ACT OF 1933

* * * * *

Item 12. Incorporation of Certain Information by Reference.

* * * * *

(d)(1) You must state (i) that you will provide to each person, including any beneficial owner, to whom a prospectus is delivered, a copy of any or all of the information that has been incorporated by reference in the prospectus but not delivered with the prospectus;

(ii) that you will provide this information upon written or oral request;

(iii) that you will provide this information at no cost to the requester; and (iv) the name, address, and telephone number to which the request for this information must be made.

Note to Item 12(d)

(1) If you send any of the information that is incorporated by reference in the prospectus to security holders, you also must send any exhibits that are specifically incorporated by reference in that information.

(2) You must (i) identify the reports and other information that you file with the SEC; and

(ii) state that the public may read and copy any materials you file with the SEC at the SEC's Public Reference Room at 450 Fifth Street, N.W., Washington, D.C. 20549. State that the public may obtain information on the operation of the Public Reference Room by calling the SEC at 1-800-SEC-0330. If you are an electronic filer, state that the SEC maintains an Internet site that contains reports, proxy and information statements, and other information regarding issuers that file electronically with the SEC and state the address of that site (http://www.sec.gov). You are encouraged to give your Internet address, if available.

* * * * *

19. By amending Form S-3 (referenced in 239.13) Item 12 to add paragraph (c) before the instruction to read as follows:

[Note: The text of Form S-3 does not, and this amendment will not, appear in the Code of Federal Regulations]

FORM S-3

REGISTRATION STATEMENT UNDER THE SECURITIES ACT OF 1933

* * * * *

Item 12. Incorporation of Certain Information by Reference.

* * * * *

(c)(1) You must state (i) that you will provide to each person, including any beneficial owner, to whom a prospectus is delivered, a copy of any or all of the information that has been incorporated by reference in the prospectus but not delivered with the prospectus;

(ii) that you will provide this information upon written or oral request;

(iii) that you will provide this information at no cost to the requester; and

(iv) the name, address, and telephone number to which the request for this information must be made.

Note to Item 12(c)(1)

If you send any of the information that is incorporated by reference in the prospectus to security holders, you also must send any exhibits that are specifically incorporated by reference in that information.

(2) You must (i) identify the reports and other information that you file with the SEC; and (ii) state that the public may read and copy any materials you file with the SEC at the SEC's Public Reference Room at 450 Fifth Street, N.W., Washington, D.C. 20549. State that the public may obtain information on the operation of the Public Reference Room by calling the SEC at 1-800-SEC-0330. If you are an electronic filer, state that the SEC maintains an Internet site that contains reports, proxy and information statements, and other information regarding issuers that file electronically with the SEC and state the address of that site (http://www.sec.gov). You are encouraged to give your Internet address, if available.

* * * * *

20. By amending Form S-20 (referenced in 239.20) to revise the reference in Item 1 "Item 502(f) of Regulation S-K [229.502(f) of this chapter]" to read "Item 101(g) of Regulation S-K [229.101(g) of this chapter]."

[Note: The text of Form S-20 does not, and this amendment will not, appear in the Code of Federal Regulations]

21. By amending Form S-4 (referenced in 239.25) to revise Item 2 and adding paragraph (c) to Item 11 and paragraph (d) to Item 13 to read as follows:

[Note: The text of Form S-4 does not, and this amendment will not, appear in the Code of Federal Regulations]

FORM S-4

REGISTRATION STATEMENT UNDER THE SECURITIES ACT OF 1933

* * * * *

Item 2. Inside Front and Outside Back Cover Pages of Prospectus.

Provide the information required by Item 502 of Regulation S-K. In addition, on the inside front cover page, you must state (1) that the prospectus incorporates important business and financial information about the company that is not included in or delivered with the document; and

(2) that this information is available without charge to security holders upon written or oral request. Give the name, address, and telephone number to which security holders must make this request. In addition, you must state that to obtain timely delivery, security holders must request the information no later than five business days before the date they must make their investment decision. Specify the date by which security holders must request this information. You must highlight this statement by print type or otherwise.

Note to Item 2.

If you send any of the information that is incorporated by reference in the prospectus to security holders, you also must send any exhibits that are specifically incorporated by reference in that information.

* * * * *

Item 11. Incorporation of Certain Information by Reference.

* * * * *

(c) You must (1) identify the reports and other information that you file with the SEC; and

(2) state that the public may read and copy any materials you file with the SEC at the SEC's Public Reference Room at 450 Fifth Street, N.W., Washington, D.C. 20549. State that the public may obtain information on the operation of the Public Reference Room by calling the SEC at 1-800-SEC-0330. If you are an electronic filer, state that the SEC maintains an Internet site that contains reports, proxy and information statements, and other information regarding issuers that file electronically with the SEC and state the address of that site (http://www.sec.gov). You are encouraged to give your Internet address, if available.

* * * * *

Item 13. Incorporation of Certain Information by Reference.

* * * * *

(d) You must (1) identify the reports and other information that you file with the SEC; and

(2) state that the public may read and copy any materials you file with the SEC at the SEC's Public Reference Room at 450 Fifth Street, N.W., Washington, D.C. 20549. State that the public may obtain information on the operation of the Public Reference Room by calling the SEC at 1-800-SEC-0330. If you are an electronic filer, state that the SEC maintains an Internet site that contains reports, proxy and information statements, and other information regarding issuers that file electronically with the SEC and state the address of that site (http://www.sec.gov). You are encouraged to give your Internet address, if available.

* * * * *

22. By amending Form F-2 (referenced in 239.32) to revise Item 12 to read as follows:

[Note: The text of Form F-2 does not, and this amendment will not, appear in the Code of Federal Regulations]

FORM F-2

REGISTRATION STATEMENT UNDER THE SECURITIES ACT OF 1933

* * * * *

Item 12. Information with respect to the Registrant.

(a) You must state (1) that you will provide to each person, including any beneficial owner, to whom a prospectus is delivered, a copy of any or all of the information that has been incorporated by reference in the prospectus but not delivered with the prospectus;

(2) that you will provide this information upon written or oral request;

(3) that you will provide this information at no cost to the requester; and

(4) the name, address, and telephone number to which the request for this information must be made.

Note to Item 12(a)

If you send any of the information that is incorporated by reference in the prospectus to security holders, you also must send any exhibits that are specifically incorporated by reference in that information.

(b) You must (1) identify the reports and other information that you file with the SEC; and

(2) state that the public may read and copy any materials you file with the SEC at the SEC's Public Reference Room at 450 Fifth Street, N.W., Washington, D.C. 20549. State that the public may obtain information on the operation of the Public Reference Room by calling the SEC at 1-800-SEC-0330. If you are an electronic filer, state that the SEC maintains an Internet site that contains reports, proxy and information statements, and other information regarding issuers that file electronically with the SEC and state the address of that site (http://www.sec.gov). You are encouraged to give your Internet address, if available.

* * * * *

23. By amending Form F-3 (referenced in 239.33) by adding paragraphs (d) and (e) to Item 12 before the instruction to read as follows:

[Note: The text of Form F-3 does not, and this amendment will not, appear in the Code of Federal Regulations]

FORM F-3

REGISTRATION STATEMENT UNDER THE SECURITIES ACT OF 1933

* * * * *

Item 12. Incorporation of Certain Information by Reference.

* * * * *

(d) You must state (1) that you will provide to each person, including any beneficial owner, to whom a prospectus is delivered, a copy of any or all of the information that has been incorporated by reference in the prospectus but not delivered with the prospectus;

(2) that you will provide this information upon written or oral request;

(3) that you will provide this information at no cost to the requester; and

(4) the name, address, and telephone number to which the request for this information must be made.

Note to Item 12(d)

If you send any of the information that is incorporated by reference in the prospectus to security holders, you also must send any exhibits that are specifically incorporated by reference in that information.

(e) You must (1) identify the reports and other information that you file with the SEC; and

(2) state that the public may read and copy any materials you file with the SEC at the SEC's Public Reference Room at 450 Fifth Street, N.W., Washington, D.C. 20549. State that the public may obtain information on the operation of the Public Reference Room by calling the SEC at 1-800-SEC-0330. If you are an electronic filer, state that the SEC maintains an Internet site that contains reports, proxy and information statements, and other information regarding issuers that file electronically with the SEC and state the address of that site (http://www.sec.gov). You are encouraged to give your Internet address, if available.

* * * * *

24. By amending Form F-4 (referenced in 239.34) to revise Item 2 and add paragraph (b) to Item 11 and paragraph (c) to Item 13 to read as follows:

[Note: The text of Form F-4 does not, and this amendment will not, appear in the Code of Federal Regulations]

FORM F-4

REGISTRATION STATEMENT UNDER THE SECURITIES ACT OF 1933

* * * * *

Item 2. Inside Front and Outside Back Cover Pages of Prospectus.

Provide the information required by Item 502 of Regulation S-K. In addition, on the inside front cover page, you must state (1) that the prospectus incorporates important business and financial information about the company that is not included in or delivered with the document; and

(2) that this information is available without charge to security holders upon written or oral request. Give the name, address, and telephone number to which security holders must make this request. In addition, you must state that to obtain timely delivery, security holders must request the information no later than five business days before the date they must make their investment decision. Specify the date by which security holders must request this information. You must highlight this statement by print type or otherwise.

Note to Item 2.

If you send any of the information that is incorporated by reference in the prospectus to security holders, you also must send any exhibits that are specifically incorporated by reference in that information.

* * * * *

Item 11. Incorporation of Certain Information by Reference.

* * * * *

(b) You must (1) identify the reports and other information that you file with the SEC; and

(2) state that the public may read and copy any materials you file with the SEC at the SEC's Public Reference Room at 450 Fifth Street, N.W., Washington, D.C. 20549. State that the public may obtain information on the operation of the Public Reference Room by calling the SEC at 1-800-SEC-0330. If you are an electronic

filer, state that the SEC maintains an Internet site that contains reports, proxy and information statements, and other information regarding issuers that file electronically with the SEC and state the address of that site (http://www.sec.gov). You are encouraged to give your Internet address, if available.

* * * * *

Item 13. Incorporation of Certain Information by Reference.

(c) You must (1) identify the reports and other information that you file with the SEC; and

(2) state that the public may read and copy any materials you file with the SEC at the SEC's Public Reference Room at 450 Fifth Street, N.W., Washington, D.C. 20549. State that the public may obtain information on the operation of the Public Reference Room by calling the SEC at 1-800-SEC-0330. If you are an electronic filer, state that the SEC maintains an Internet site that contains reports, proxy and information statements, and other information regarding issuers that file electronically with the SEC and state the address of that site (http://www.sec.gov). You are encouraged to give your Internet address, if available.

* * * * *

PART 274—FORMS PRESCRIBED UNDER THE INVESTMENT COMPANY ACT OF 1940

25. The authority citation for Part 274 continues to read as follows:

Authority: 15 U.S.C. 77f, 77g, 77h, 77j, 77s, 78c(b), 78l, 78m, 78n, 78o(d), 80a-8, 80a-24, and 80a-29, unless otherwise noted.

26. Amend Form N-2 (referenced in 274.11a-1) to revise Item 2, Item 3, and Item 14 to read as follows:

[Note: The text of Form N-2 does not, and this amendment will not, appear in the Code of Federal Regulations.]

FORM N-2

* * * * *

Item 2. Cover Pages; Other Offering Information

1. Disclose whether any national securities exchange or the Nasdaq Stock Market lists the securities offered, naming the particular market(s), and identify the trading symbol(s) for those securities, on the inside front or outside back cover page of the prospectus unless the information appears on the front cover page.

2. Provide the information required by paragraph (d) of Rule 481 under the Securities Act [17 CFR 230.481(d)] in an appropriate place in the prospectus.

3. Provide the information required by paragraph (e) of Rule 481 under the Securities Act [17 CFR 230, 481(d)] on the outside back cover page of the prospectus.

Item 3. Fee Table and Synopsis

* * * * *

3. In the case of a business development company, include the information required by Item 101(e) of Regulation S-K [17 CFR 229.101(e)] (concerning reports and other information filed with the SEC).

* * * * *

Item 14. Cover Page

1. The outside cover page must contain the following information:

(e) the statement required by paragraph (b)(2) of Rule 481 under the Securities Act [17 CFR 230.481(b)(2)].

* * * * *

By the Commission.

Jonathan G. Katz

Secretary

January 28, 1998 ______________________________

endnotes

[1] 17 CFR 230.421.

[2] 17 CFR 230.461.

[3] 17 CFR 230.481.

[4] 17 CFR 230.400 et seq.

[5] 17 CFR 229.101.

[6] 17 CFR 229.501.

[7] 17 CFR 229.502.

[8] 17 CFR 229.503.

[9] 17 CFR 229.508.

[10] 17 CFR 229.10 et seq.

[11] 17 CFR 228.10 et seq.

[12] 17 CFR 239.12.

[13] 17 CFR 239.13.

[14] 17 CFR 239.25.

[15] 17 CFR 239.20.

[16] 17 CFR 239.32.

[17] 17 CFR 239.33.

[18] 17 CFR 239.34.

[19] 17 CFR 239.14.

[20] We proposed this package of rules in January 1997. See Release No. 33-7380 (January 14, 1997), 62 FR 3512 (January 21, 1997).

[21] 15 U.S.C. 77a et seq.

[22] 15 U.S.C. 78a et seq.

[23] See the Forms 10-Q of Pfizer, Inc. (File No. 1-3619) for fiscal 1997.

[24] See the 1996 Form 10-K filed by Baltimore Gas and Electric Company (File No. 1-1910) and the Boddie-Noell Properties, Inc. registration statement filed December 2, 1997 (File No. 333-39803).

[25] See Securities Act Release No. 6900 (June 17, 1991).

[26] Rule 421(c), 17 CFR 230.421(c).

[27] Item 501 of Regulation S-K, 17 CFR 229.501, and Item 501 of Regulation S-B, 17 CFR 228.501.

[28] The North American Securities Administrators Association, Inc.'s Disclosure Reform Task Force recommended that the suggested legend include a reference to the state securities commissions. We have changed the legend to reflect this suggestion.

[29] See Securities Act Release No. 6900 for our interpretive advice on limited partnership offerings.

[30] Item 502 of Regulation S-K, 17 CFR 229.502, and Item 502 of Regulation S-B, 17 CFR 228.502.

[31] We are also amending Forms S-2, S-3, S-4, F-2, F-3, and F-4. Along with the list of reports incorporated by reference, you will include information on (1) how investors may obtain a copy of these reports, and (2) how they may obtain copies of the other reports you file with the SEC.

[32] Item 503 of Regulation S-K, 17 CFR 229.503, and Item 503 of Regulation S-B, 17 CFR 228.503.

[33] See the amendments to Rule 481 under Regulation C, 17 CFR 230.481.

[34] The proposed amendments to Form N-1A are included in Investment Company Act Release No. 22528 (February 27, 1997) and the proposed profile rule is in Investment Company Act Release No. 22529 (February 27, 1997).

[35] We are also adopting amendments to Rule 481 to require plain English legends in fund prospectuses.

[36] The Commission proposed to allow mutual funds a transition period of six months after the effective date of the proposed rules before they would need to comply with the new prospectus disclosure requirements. See Investment Company Act Release Nos. 22528 and 22529 (February 27, 1997).

[37] If you file a registration statement under Rule 462(b), you must comply with new requirements only if they applied to the earlier offering.

[38] 15 U.S.C. 77j(a)(3).

[39] You may read and copy the comment letters and the staff's summary of these letters in our Public Reference Room at 450 Fifth Street, N.W., Washington, D.C. 20549. Ask for File No. S7-3-97.

[40] For example, see the Investment Company Institute's comment letter, dated March 24, 1997.

[41] See Gould v. American Hawaiian Steamship Company, 331 F. Supp. 981 (D. Del. 1971); Kohn v. American Metal Climax, Inc., 322 F. Supp. 1331 (E.D. Pa. 1970), modified, 458 F.2d 255 (3d Cir. 1972).

[42] See Rule 461 of Regulation C, 17 CFR 230.461.

[43] PSA The Bond Market Trade Association, in their comment letter dated March 24, 1997, for example, estimated that costs "could increase by up to 50 percent."

[44] For example, one participant indicated that they spent 12 percent less time answering investors' questions, while another spent 20 percent less time.

[45] Four of the six participants spent 10 percent longer; the initial public offering issuer spent 15 percent longer; and one participant took "significantly longer." For the participant that took significantly longer, we received two estimates—one from the company of 75 percent longer and one from the firm's legal counsel of 200 percent longer.

[46] This estimate is based on responses to a survey of nine plain English pilot program participants and on a summary of the results of an informal survey of pilot participants conducted by the American Society of Corporate Secretaries. See Public Comment letter dated March 24, 1997.

[47] The Division of Corporation Finance collected Item 511 of Regulation S-K expense information from approximately 1500 registration statements filed between January 1 and December 31, 1995. Assuming legal costs averaged $150/hour and accounting costs averaged $75/hour, the survey indicates that approximately 48 percent of burden hours are for legal and technical writing, while 52 percent are accounting-related. Because the rule and amendments apply predominately to legal and technical writing, we apply the increased burden to those hours.

[48] We do not anticipate that the plain English requirements will change the burden hours or cost for preparing Form N-2. Consequently, we do not include Form N-2 in the table.

[49] We anticipate that some firms will comply, in part, with the plain English requirements using in-house counsel, which will lower hourly costs.

[50] In 1997, registrants filed 7,531 filings. At $7,200 per filing, the total increase in cost would be approximately $54 million.

[51] Four of the six participants believed that once they developed plain English formats, it would take them less time to write a document in plain English than in the conventional language. One participant predicted that writing documents in plain English would require no additional time after the initial effort. The other participant did not comment directly.

[52] These estimates are based on the number of such filings made in calendar year 1997.

[53] See American Society of Corporate Secretaries Public Comment letter dated March 24, 1997.

[54] See Baltimore Gas and Electric Company Public Comment letter dated March 26, 1997.

[55] One of the six participants indicated that writing in plain English shortened their document by 5 percent; one by 10 to 15 percent; one by 15 percent; and one by 35 percent. Interestingly, the pilot participant who spent 75 percent more time on its plain English prospectus shortened its prospectus the largest amount—35 percent. One found no appreciable difference, and one estimated that plain English increased document length by one percent.

[56] The staff randomly selected prospectuses filed in 1997 to estimate document length.

[57] The Division of Corporation Finance collected Item 511 of Regulation S-K expense information from approximately 1500 registration statements filed between January 1 and December 31, 1995. Printing expenses averaged $63,200 per filing. Assuming five-percent cost savings, public companies would save $3,160 per filing or a total of about $24 million in printing and mailing costs on 7,531 filings per year.

[58] See Report of the Task Force on Disclosure Simplification (March 1996).

[59] Securities Act Release No. 33-7380.

[60] A summary of comments is available, along with the comment letters, in Public File No. S7-3-97. The file is available for inspection and copying in the Commission's Public Reference Room, 450 Fifth Street N.W., Washington, D.C. 20549.

[61] 17 CFR 230.157.

[62] 17 CFR 240.0-10.

[63] 44 U.S.C. 3501 et seq.

[64] Regulations S-K, S-B, and C do not impose reporting burdens directly on public companies. For administrative convenience, each of these regulations is currently assigned one burden hour. The burden hours imposed by the disclosure regulations are currently included in the estimates for the forms that refer to the regulations.

[65] Regulations S-K and S-B will continue to show an estimated burden hour of one.

APPENDIX A—Charts on Amendments to Small Business Issuer Rules

Chart 1: Regulation S-B—Item 501

Current	Final
Small business issuer name	Same
Title, amount, and description of securities offered	Same
Selling security holders offering	Same
Cross-reference to risk factors	Same, except cross-reference must include page number. No print type specified
Formatted distribution table showing price, underwriting commission, and proceeds of offering	Delete distribution table. Use bullet list or other design that highlights the information
Show bona fide estimate of range of maximum offering price and number of shares	Same
Formatted best efforts disclosure and distribution table	Delete distribution table. Use bullet list or other design that highlights the information
Prospectus "Subject to Completion" legend	Retain in plain English
Commission legend	Retain in plain English. Include reference to state securities commissions. No print type specified
State-required legends	Same
Underwriters' over-allotment option, expenses of offering, commissions paid by others, and other non-cash consideration and finders fees	Identify existence of the option and the number of shares. Move all other information to the plan of distribution section
Date of prospectus	Same
Expenses of offering	Move to plan of distribution section

No requirement to identify market for securities	Identify market for securities, trading symbol, underwriters, and type of underwriting
No page limit	Must limit cover to one page

Chart 2: Regulation S-B—Item 502

Current	Final
Availability of Exchange Act Reports	Move to description of business section or, for short-form registration statements, include with incorporation by reference disclosure
Identify market for securities	Move to cover page
Availability of reports with audited financial statements	Move to description of business section
Availability of reports incorporated by reference	Move to incorporation by reference disclosure
Stabilization legend	Move to plan of distribution section
Passive market making activities legend	Delete. Disclosure retained in plan of distribution section
Dealer prospectus delivery obligation	Retain an outside back page of prospectus
Canadian issuers' disclosure on enforceability of civil liability against foreign person	Move to description of business section
Table of contents	Same. If prospectus delivered electronically, must immediately follow cover page

Chart 3: Regulation S-B—Item 503

Current	Final
Summary	Retain in plain English
Address and telephone number	Retain. Permit on cover page or in summary
Risk factors	Retain in plain English

Disclosure Option for Mutual Funds (Profile Rule)

Final Rule:

New Disclosure Option for Open-End Management Investment Companies

SECURITIES AND EXCHANGE COMMISSION

17 CFR Parts 230 and 270

Release Nos. 33-7513; IC-23065; File No. S7-18-96

RIN 3235-AH03

New Disclosure Option for Open-End Management Investment Companies

AGENCY: Securities and Exchange Commission

ACTION: Final rule

SUMMARY: The Securities and Exchange Commission is adopting a new rule that would permit a mutual fund to offer investors a new disclosure document called a "profile," which summarizes key information about the fund, including the fund's investment strategies, risks, performance, and fees, in a concise, standardized format. A fund that offers a profile will be able to give investors a choice of the amount of information that they wish to consider before making a decision about investing in the fund; investors will have the option of purchasing the fund's shares after reviewing the information in the profile or after requesting and reviewing the fund's prospectus (and other information). An investor deciding to purchase fund shares based on the information in a profile will receive the fund's prospectus with the confirmation of purchase.

DATES: Effective on June 1, 1998.

FOR FURTHER INFORMATION CONTACT: Kathleen K. Clarke, Assistant Director, George J. Zornada, Team Leader, or Laura J. Riegel, Attorney, (202) 942-0721, Office of Disclosure Regulation, Division of Investment Management, Securities and Exchange Commission, 450 Fifth Street, N.W., Mail Stop 5-6, Washington, D.C. 20549-6009. Contact the Office of Chief Counsel, Division of Investment Management, Securities and Exchange Commission, at (202) 942-0659 or 450 Fifth Street, N.W., Mail Stop 5-6, Washington, D.C. 20549-6009 for additional information, including interpretive guidance, relating to this release or the profile.

SUPPLEMENTARY INFORMATION: The Securities and Exchange Commission (the "Commission") today is adopting new rule 498 (17 CFR 230.498) under the Securities Act of 1933 (15 U.S.C. 77a, *et seq.*) ("Securities Act") and the Investment Company Act of 1940 (15 U.S.C. 80a-1, *et seq.*) ("Investment Company Act"). Rule 498 permits an open-end management investment company that registers on Form N-1A (17 CFR 274.11A) (a "fund") to provide to investors a disclosure document called a "profile," which summarizes key information about the fund and gives investors the option of purchasing the fund's shares based on the information in the profile. The Commission also is adopting amendments to rule 497 under the Securities Act (17 CFR 230.497) to require a fund to file a profile with the Commission at least 30 days prior to the profile's first use. In a companion release, the Commission is adopting revisions to the prospectus disclosure requirements in Form N-1A, the registration statement used by funds.[1] These revisions seek to minimize prospectus disclosure about technical, legal, and operational matters that generally are common to all funds and to focus prospectus disclosure on essential information about a particular fund that would assist an investor in making a decision about investing in that fund.

TABLE OF CONTENTS

I. INTRODUCTION AND BACKGROUND

Over the last decade, the fund industry has grown tremendously. Over 6,000 funds are now available to investors and close to 40 million American households own funds.[2] Today, fund assets exceed the deposits of commercial banks.[3]

As more investors turn to funds for professional management of current and retirement savings, funds have introduced new investment options and shareholder services to meet the needs of investors. While benefiting from these developments, investors also face an increasingly difficult task in choosing among different fund investments. The Commission, fund investors, and others have recognized the need to improve fund disclosure documents to help investors evaluate and compare funds.[4] In the Commission's view, the growth of the fund industry and the diversity of fund investors warrant a new approach to fund disclosure that will offer more choices in the format and amount of information available about fund investments.[5]

In seeking to meet this goal, the Commission proposed, on February 27, 1997, new rule 498, which would permit a fund to provide investors with a profile (the "Proposed Profile").[6] The Proposed Profile would summarize key information about a fund, including the fund's investment objectives, strategies, risks, performance, fees, investment adviser and portfolio manager, purchase and redemption procedures, distributions, and the services available to the fund's investors. The Proposed Profile was designed to provide summary information about a fund that would assist an investor in deciding whether to invest in a fund or to request additional information about the fund before deciding whether to buy shares in that fund. Proposed rule 498 would require a fund to mail the prospectus and other information to the requesting investor within 3 business days of a request. An investor deciding to purchase fund shares based on the Proposed Profile would receive the fund's prospectus with the purchase confirmation.

On the same day that it proposed rule 498 for comment, the Commission published a release in which it proposed major changes to the prospectus disclosure requirements in Form N-1A ("Form N-1A Proposing Release").[7] The proposed amendments to Form N-1A were designed to focus prospectus disclosure on essential information about a particular fund that would assist an investor in making a decision about investing in that fund. The proposed amendments reflected the Commission's strongly-held belief that a prospectus, as the primary disclosure document contemplated under the federal securities laws, should present clear, concise, and understandable information about an investment in a fund.

The Proposed Profile was based on a number of initiatives undertaken by the Commission to assess options for improving fund disclosure documents. One of these initiatives was a pilot program conducted by the Commission, with participation by the Investment Company Institute ("ICI") and several large fund groups, in which the funds used profile-like summaries ("Pilot Profiles") with their prospectuses.[8] The Pilot Profiles, like the profile adopted today, summarized important information about funds. The purpose of the pilot program was to assess whether investors found the Pilot Profiles helpful in making investment decisions. Focus groups conducted on the Commission's behalf ("Focus Groups") responded positively to the profile concept, indicating that a disclosure document such as the Pilot Profile would assist them in making investment decisions. Fund investors participating in a survey sponsored by the ICI also strongly supported the Pilot Profiles.[9]

The Commission received 256 comment letters on the Proposed Profile, a large percentage of which were from individual investors (226 letters or 88%).[10] Commenters expressed strong support for the Proposed Profile.[11] Many commenters cited the advantages of a document that is less technical and easier to read. Commenters believed that the Proposed Profile would assist investors in selecting a fund in which to invest. Many of those commenting on the Proposed Profile, particularly individual investors, endorsed the Proposed Profile's goal of providing standardized, summary information about a fund.[12]

The Commission is adopting rule 498 with modifications that reflect the Commission's consideration of commenters' suggestions. Rule 498 permits a fund to provide investors with a new disclosure option in the form of a profile that summarizes key information about the fund.[13] A fund that makes a profile available will be able to offer an investor the option of purchasing the fund's shares after reviewing the information in the profile or of requesting and reviewing the fund's prospectus (and other information) before making an investment decision. An investor deciding to purchase fund shares based on the profile will receive the fund's prospectus with the purchase confirmation.

Under rule 498, as adopted, the profile will include:

- *Standardized Fund Summaries.* The profile includes concise disclosure of 9 items of key information about a fund in a specific sequence.
- *Improved Risk Disclosure.* A risk/return summary (also required at the beginning of a fund's prospectus) provides information about a fund's investment objectives, principal strategies, risks, performance, and fees.
- *Graphic Disclosure of Variability of Returns.* The risk/return summary provides a bar chart of a fund's annual returns over a 10-year period that illustrates the variability of those returns and gives investors some idea of the risks of an investment in the fund. To help investors evaluate a fund's risks and returns relative to "the market," a table accompanying the bar chart compares the fund's average annual returns for 1-, 5-, and 10-year periods to that of a broad-based securities market index.
- *Other Fund Information.* The profile includes information on the fund's investment adviser and portfolio manager, purchase and redemption procedures, tax considerations, and shareholder services.
- *Plain English Disclosure.* The Commission's recently adopted plain English disclosure requirements, which are designed to give investors understandable disclosure documents, will apply to the profile.[14] The Commission's plain English rule requires the use of plain English writing principles, including short sentences, everyday language, active voice, tabular presentation of complex material, no legal or business jargon, and no multiple negatives.[15]

Rule 498, as adopted, also permits a fund that serves as an investment option for a participant-directed defined contribution plan (or for certain other tax-deferred arrangements) to provide investors with a profile that includes disclosure that is tailored for the plan (or other arrangement). Profiles tailored for such use can exclude information relating to the purchase and sale of fund shares, fund distributions, tax consequences, and fund services otherwise required in a profile.

The Commission has determined to adopt rule 498 and permit funds to use summary disclosure documents in accordance with the rule under the authority of section 10(b) of the Securities Act[16] and other provisions of the federal securities laws.[17] Section 10(b) gives the Commission the authority to adopt rules allowing the use of a summary prospectus if the Commission determines that doing so is "necessary or appropriate in the public interest and for the protection of investors."[18] In making this determination about profiles, the Commission considered, among other things: an extensive analysis of fund disclosure issues it recently conducted; its assessment of funds' use of Pilot Profiles; its assessment of certain other disclosure initiatives; and its substantial experience gained in administering the two-part disclosure format adopted in 1983 permitting a fund to provide investors with a simplified prospectus containing essential information about the fund and to place more detailed information about the fund in a Statement of Additional Information ("SAI"), which investors can obtain upon request.[19] The Commission believes, and the broad support for the Proposed Profile confirms its belief, that rule 498 will benefit investors and promote effective communication of information about funds.

Today, the Commission also is adopting the proposed amendments to Form N-1A.[20] As they did with the Proposed Profile, commenters strongly supported the revised prospectus disclosure requirements. Taken together, these two disclosure initiatives are intended to allow funds flexibility to respond to the diverse information needs of investors and to improve fund disclosure.[21]

II. DISCUSSION

A. General

1. Overview of Comments

The vast majority of commenters on the Proposed Profile expressed strong support for the profile and specifically supported the concept of giving investors the option of purchasing shares of a fund on the basis of information contained in a summary disclosure document.[22] A small number of commenters, however, questioned whether providing investors with this option was in the best interests of fund investors. These commenters asserted that investors may not appreciate the significance of an investment in a fund if they purchase its shares based on a summary document rather than the prospectus. These commenters also were concerned that widespread use of a profile could cause fewer investors to read the prospectus and asserted that the Commission would be better advised to direct its efforts to improving the prospectus.

Implicit in these comments would seem to be the view that all investors should use a longer document—the prospectus—rather than a shorter document—the profile—in making a decision about investing in a fund. Such a view appears to be inconsistent with the sentiments of fund investors. The Commission and others, in seeking to identify ways to improve the disclosure of information about mutual funds to investors, have collected data about investors. This data demonstrates that different investors desire and use different types and amounts of materials in determining whether to invest in funds.[23] The Commission believes that the data supports its conclusion to allow funds the option of offering their shares through the profile with delivery of a prospectus with the confirmation of purchase.

The Commission's strongly held belief is that the principal goal of fund disclosure, whether it takes the form of a long or short document, should be to provide investors with useful and relevant information. Each of the disclosure initiatives that the Commission is adopting today has this goal, which the Commission believes complements the themes underlying the recently adopted plain English rule.[24] To further this goal, the Commission encourages all funds that decide to use profiles to take the steps necessary to ensure that their prospectuses effectively communicate information to investors. The Commission believes that funds need to take this action if the initiatives adopted today are to achieve their objectives.

2. Liability

In its release proposing new rule 498 ("the Profile Proposing Release"), the Commission discussed the protections afforded investors under the federal securities laws for false and misleading statements in a profile.[25] These protections include the provisions of sections 12(a)(2) and 17(a) of the Securities Act, which impose civil and criminal liability upon any person who offers or sells securities using an untrue statement of material fact or who omits to state a material fact necessary in order to make a statement, in light of the circumstances under which it was made, not misleading.[26] Investor protections applicable to a profile also include the antifraud provisions of section 10(b) of the Securities Exchange Act of 1934 and rule 10b-5 under that Act.[27]

When it gave the Commission the authority to permit the use of a summary prospectus under section 10(b) of the Securities Act, Congress provided a specific exception from strict liability for misleading statements and omissions imposed under section 11 of the Securities Act[28] for these type of disclosure documents. The purpose of the exception was to encourage the use of a summary prospectus while maintaining investor protection by requiring delivery of a section 10(a) prospectus at or before the time that the investor receives the confirmation of the purchase of the security described in the summary prospectus.[29]

The Commission believes that the profile fits squarely within the statutory framework contemplated by Congress for the offering and sale of securities under the federal securities laws. The profile of a fund will be a summary prospectus under section 10(b) of the Securities Act, but the fund's section 10(a) prospectus will remain the primary disclosure document under the federal securities laws. To inform investors about the availability of the prospectus, a profile includes a legend on the cover page (or at the beginning of the profile) explaining that the profile is a summary document and stating that more information about the fund is available in the prospectus.[30]

While most commenters strongly favored the profile, several commenters expressed concern that a fund using a profile could face increased liability under the federal securities laws. These commenters argued in particular that a fund's use of a profile could result in claims under section 12(a)(2) of the Securities Act alleging that the profile is misleading because it omits information disclosed in the fund's prospectus.[31]

To address this concern, several commenters urged the Commission to permit funds to incorporate by reference the prospectus into the profile to provide funds with a defense against unwarranted claims that a profile omits material information. As stated in the Profile Proposing Release, however, the Commission believes that allowing funds to incorporate by reference the prospectus into the profile would be inconsistent with the purpose of the profile and not in the public interest.[32] The profile is designed to provide summary information about a fund in a self-contained format that will assist an investor in deciding to invest in, or in deciding to request additional information about, the fund. Permitting a fund to incorporate by reference the prospectus into the profile would result in the prospectus being considered a part of the profile and would be inconsistent with the profile being a self-contained document.[33]

On the basis of, among other things, its prior experience with summary documents, such as advertisements designed to meet the requirements of rule 482 under the Securities Act,[34] the Commission does not agree with commenters' claims that the use of profiles will lead to significant potential liabilities under the federal securities laws. In the Commission's view, a fund using a profile generally should not face liability for omitting information included in the fund's prospectus if the profile includes the information required or permitted by rule 498; potential liability would arise only if a profile contains a material misstatement or omits a statement necessary to make the disclosure in the profile not materially misleading. The mere omission of information from the profile that is required or permitted in the prospectus should not, in the Commission's view, give rise to liability under the federal securities laws.[35]

The Commission believes that the intended purpose of a profile as a summary disclosure document supports the view that a fund using a profile should not be subject to liability under the federal securities laws for omitting information from the profile that is included in the fund's prospectus. Rule 498 specifies the information that can or must be included in a fund's profile and requires the fund to state that the profile contains a summary of certain information in the fund's prospectus. The Commission's goal in adopting rule 498, which is to facilitate the use of a short, summary disclosure document that investors can use to evaluate and compare funds, would not be met unless rule 498 is read as limiting the information required to be included in the profile.

Commenters on the Proposed Profile requested that the Commenters on the Proposed Profile requested that the Commission provide guidance about the applicability of section 19(a) of the Securities Act to a fund that uses a profile under new rule 498. By its terms, section 19(a) protects a defendant from liability for actions taken in good faith in conformity with any rule of the Commission.[36] The Commission believes that a fund that provides investors with a profile in good faith compliance with rule 498 would be able to rely on section 19(a) against a claim that its profile did not include information that is disclosed in the fund's prospectus.

3. Plain English Disclosure

In seeking to encourage all issuers, including funds, to provide disclosure materials required under the federal securities laws that are simpler, clearer, and more useful to investors, the Commission recently adopted initiatives that would require the use of plain English in drafting those materials.[37] These initiatives contemplate disclosure documents using plain English writing principles including short sentences, everyday language, active voice, tabular presentation of complex material, no legal or business jargon, and no multiple negatives. The Commission strongly believes that, by drafting profiles in strict compliance with plain English principles, funds can provide improved disclosure to investors. Rule 498, as adopted, reflects this belief. The rule requires that funds disclose the information in the profile using the plain English writing principles set out in the Commission's plain English rule.[38]

4. Use of the Profile by Other Types of Investment Companies

The Commission proposed to permit funds to use profiles, but did not propose to permit other types of investment companies, such as closed-end investment companies, unit investment trusts, and separate accounts that offer variable annuities, to rely on rule 498. Several commenters disagreed with the Commission's decision and urged the Commission to allow other types of investment companies to use profiles. The Commission is not persuaded at this time by these commenters, and rule 498, as adopted, is available only to funds. Although it recognizes that a short, summary disclosure document such as the profile could potentially benefit investors in other types of investment companies, the Commission has concluded that it should assess the use of profiles by funds over a period of time before considering a rule that would allow other types of investment companies to use similar summary documents. As the Commission gains experience with funds' use of the profile and analyzes the results of other pilot profile programs that are underway,[39] it will consider expanding use of the concept to other types of investment companies.[40]

5. Standardized Format

The Proposed Profile required disclosure of 9 items of key information presented in a specific sequence following a question-and-answer format. The purpose of standardizing the order of the items was to help investors locate similar information in the profiles of different funds and compare the funds. The proposed question-and-answer format, frequently used by many funds in their prospectuses, was intended to help communicate the required information effectively. Most commenters supported a standardized presentation in profiles, but several commenters criticized the prescribed question-and-answer format, suggesting that funds should be able to choose other formats to set out the information required in a profile. The Commission is adopting the standardized presentation requirement as proposed because it believes that requiring the profile items in a specific sequence will substantially assist investors in locating information and comparing funds. Consistent with the goal of allowing funds to design effective disclosure documents, however, rule 498 does not limit the presentation of the required information to a question-and-answer format.[41] Any fund that chose to do so could use a question-and-answer format in its profile.

6. Additional Disclosure Items

Several commenters suggested that additional disclosure items would be useful in a profile, including:

- a fund's top ten portfolio holdings;
- an investment style box;
- additional measures of risk; and
- financial highlights.

The Commission acknowledges that the disclosure suggested by the commenters could be useful to some fund investors and could generally enhance the information available about funds. Nonetheless, the Commission has concluded that none of these items should be required by rule 498 at this time.

In considering fund disclosure requirements, the Commission must balance many factors, including, among other things, the amount of information that is consistent with the purpose of a particular disclosure document. The purpose of the profile is to provide investors with a short, standardized disclosure document containing summary information about a fund. In the Commission's view, the additional items suggested by commenters could be of interest to some fund investors but are not necessarily essential information for the average or typical investor. The Commission believes that some of the types of information cited by commenters may be more helpful in connection with a fund's discussion of its current investment activities that is presently included in fund shareholder reports.[42] The Commission has directed the Division of Investment Management ("Division") to begin work on a comprehensive assessment of the Commission's existing rules specifying the disclosure to be included in fund reports to shareholders to assess whether other types of information should be added to those reports.[43]

7. Eligibility

In the Profile Proposing Release, the Commission suggested that certain funds might not be eligible to use a profile. In particular, the Commission stated that, if material information about a fund exists but is not addressed by the 9 items of disclosure required to be in a profile, the fund might not appropriately use a profile.[44] Several commenters strongly objected to this assertion. They argued that it is inconsistent with the premise underlying the profile initiative that a typical fund investor would have enough information to make an investment decision about a fund using a summary disclosure document containing the 9 required items accompanied by a statement about the availability of additional information in the fund's prospectus and other documents. One commenter suggested that the Commission address the eligibility issue by requiring the profile to provide additional summary information about other items of disclosure that are required in prospectuses. Another commenter suggested that, as an alternative, the Commission provide for a tenth item in the profile in response to which a fund could include at its option any other information that the fund believed was material to an investor's consideration of an investment in the fund. Several other commenters, however, argued that such an item was not consistent with the

Commission's purpose in developing the Proposed Profile as a short, standardized, self-contained disclosure document.

After consideration of these comments, the Commission has determined to adopt rule 498 to require funds to include only the information specified by the 9 items in the rule and to delete any suggestion that certain funds may be ineligible to use profiles.[45] The Commission has selected these items because it believes that they fulfill the goal of providing investors with a short, summary disclosure document on the basis of which investors can make decisions about investing in a fund. Under rule 498, as adopted, an investor who believes that he or she needs more information before making such a decision has the option of obtaining additional information by requesting the fund's prospectus or other disclosure materials.[46]

8. Number of Funds Described in a Profile

Rule 498, as proposed, would permit a profile to describe more than one fund. As discussed in the Profile Proposing Release, the Commission concluded, on the basis of the Pilot Program and Focus Group responses, that a profile that describes more than one fund can be consistent with the goal of a summary disclosure document that assists investors in evaluating and comparing funds. Describing more than one fund or class in a profile, for example, could be a useful means of providing investors with information about related investment alternatives offered by a fund group (e.g., a range of tax-exempt funds or different types of money market funds) or about the classes of a multiple class fund.

Recognizing that too much information could make the profile lengthy, complex, and difficult to understand, the Commission requested comment whether use of a profile should be limited to one fund or to some other number of funds. Most commenters supported the proposal to allow a profile to describe more than one fund. One commenter expressed concerns about the proposal and suggested that funds instead be allowed to bind separate profiles together.

The Commission believes that the ability to describe different investment options in one summary document will enable funds to develop profiles that help investors compare investment alternatives offered by a fund group. Therefore, the Commission is adopting rule 498, as proposed, with no express limitation on the number of funds that can be described in a profile. Information about multiple funds in a single profile, however, would need to be set out in a concise and summary manner in a format designed to communicate the information effectively.[47]

B. Profile Disclosure

1. Cover Page

Proposed rule 498 would require the cover page of a fund's profile to include certain basic information about the fund and to disclose that the profile is a summary disclosure document. As proposed, the cover page would identify the disclosure document as a "profile," would include a legend explaining the profile's purpose, and would include the fund's name. A fund also could describe its investment objectives or its type or category (e.g., that the fund is a growth fund or invests its assets in a particular country). Proposed rule 498 also would require the cover page to state the approximate date of the profile's first use and, if applicable, the date of the most recent updated performance information included in the profile.

The Commission is adopting the proposed cover page requirements with modifications to reflect the suggestions of various commenters.[48] Some commenters questioned the proposed requirement to state on a profile's cover page the date of the most recent performance information included in the profile, asserting that this requirement would necessitate a fund's reprinting its profile frequently to reflect updated performance information. These commenters suggested that, as an alternative, the Commission permit the date of the most recent performance information to accompany that information in the body of the profile. The Commission has concluded that the date of performance information included in a profile can be communicated to investors effectively if the date accompanies the disclosure of performance information. Rule 498, as adopted, reflects this conclusion.[49]

Proposed rule 498 would require funds to identify the document on the cover page as a "profile" without using the term "prospectus."[50] Several commenters asserted that funds should be able to refer to the profile as a prospectus because a profile is a summary prospectus under the federal securities laws. [51] When proposing the profile as an optional disclosure document, the Commission made it clear that the profile was not intended to supersede the section 10(a) prospectus as the primary disclosure document for funds under the federal securities laws.[52] In restricting funds from referring to the profile as a prospectus, the Commission intended to avoid investor confusion by distinguishing between the two documents. The Commission believes that, if a profile is labeled a prospectus, investors may not understand the difference between the two documents. In the Commission's view, the technical legal status of the profile as a summary prospectus should not be determinative of the appropriate label for the document. The Commission believes that investors will benefit from clear identification of the disclosure documents and is adopting rule 498, as proposed, with the restriction on the use of the term "prospectus."[53]

The Commission proposed that the cover page of the profile include a legend designed to alert an investor to the summary nature of a fund's profile and to inform the investor that he or she can obtain the fund's prospectus and other disclosure materials of the fund before making a decision about investing in the fund. In considering an appropriate profile legend, the Commission sought a concise, clear statement that minimized technical or legal jargon; provided investors with a description of a fund's profile; and informed them about the availability of other information about the fund. The Profile Proposing Release set out two alternative legends about which a number of commenters expressed strong views.[54]

The primary difference between the two legends proposed by the Commission was the reference to information in the prospectus. The first legend, which was similar to that used in the Pilot Profile, stated that the profile summarizes key information in the prospectus.[55] The second legend added a statement that the prospectus includes additional material information about the fund.[56]

No commenters expressed support for the first proposed legend, and the comments on the second were mixed. Many commenters believed that the second legend would clearly inform investors that the profile contains summary disclosure of key information about a fund and that additional important information about the fund is available in the prospectus. Several of these commenters, however, strongly urged the Commission to delete the word material from the legend. They asserted that the use of that term would imply incorrectly that a fund's profile may be legally deficient simply because it did not contain all of the information contained in the fund's prospectus. Several commenters suggested that both of the proposed legends were insufficient and should be strengthened to alert investors more clearly about the summary nature of the profile and the availability of additional information in the prospectus.

The Commission believes that the profile legend serves an important purpose and that the numerous comments that it received on the proposed legends clearly indicate that commenters share this belief. To ensure that the legend sufficiently serves its purpose of informing investors of the summary nature of the profile, the Commission has determined to strengthen the legend and include specific language offered by commenters. As adopted, rule 498 requires the following legend on the cover page, or at the beginning, of a profile:

This profile summarizes key information about a Fund that is included in the Fund's prospectus. The Fund's prospectus includes additional information about the Fund, including a more detailed description of the risks associated with investing in the Fund that you may want to consider before you invest. You may obtain the prospectus and other information about the Fund at no cost by calling ____________.[57]

To ensure that fund investors who, after reviewing a profile, request other information about a fund receive that information promptly, the Commission proposed to require a fund to send its prospectus to the requesting investors within 3 business days of a request. Those commenters addressing this requirement generally supported it, although one commenter maintained that revising the requirement to state that mailings need to be made "reasonably promptly," which the commenter stated should normally be deemed to be within 3 business days of a request, would protect funds against claims that they failed to meet the requirements as a result of unforeseen circumstances. The Commission continues to believe, as discussed in the Profile Proposing Release, that prompt mailing of the prospectus to investors who request it is an essential component of the profile initiative and the goal of promoting effective communication of information about funds.[58] Therefore, the Commission is adopting the 3-business day mailing requirement as proposed.[59]

Some commenters requested clarification from the Commission about the procedure that a fund should follow in responding to requests for additional information when its shares are sold through financial intermediaries, such as broker-dealers or banks. Commenters recommended that the Commission revise rule 498 to permit the legend to state that additional information in such a case may be obtained from financial intermediaries. The Commission acknowledges that many funds use intermediaries in distributing or servicing their shares and that investors may look to these intermediaries for information about the funds. Thus, rule 498, as adopted, allows funds to state that additional information about a fund is available from a financial intermediary.[60] A fund whose information is available through another entity, however, retains the obligation to ensure that information is sent to investors within 3 business days of an investor's request. The Commission expects that funds will fulfill this obligation through contractual arrangements with broker-dealers, banks, or other financial intermediaries.

2. Risk/Return Summary

The Commission proposed that the first 4 items of the profile elicit information that would be substantially identical to the proposed risk/return summary at the beginning of every prospectus. Most commenters supported the risk/return summary in the profile, and the Commission is adopting it generally as proposed. The Form N-1A Release discusses in detail the prospectus risk/return summary.[61] The risk/return summary required in the profile by rule 498, as adopted, will incorporate substantially all of the requirements for the summary in Form N-1A, as amended. The following discussion summarizes the main features of the risk/return summary required by Form N-1A and discusses specific disclosure required in the profile.

• Fund Investment Objectives/Goals

To assist investors in identifying funds that meet their general investment needs, the proposed risk/return summary would require a fund to disclose its investment objectives or goals. The Commission is adopting this disclosure requirement in rule 498 as proposed.[62]

• Principal Investment Strategies

The proposed risk/return summary would require a fund to summarize, based on the information provided in its prospectus, how the fund intends to achieve its investment objectives. The purpose of the proposed disclosure was to provide a summary of the fund's principal investment strategies, including the specific types of securities in which the fund invests or will invest principally, and any policy of the fund to concentrate its investments in an industry or group of industries. The Commission is adopting this requirement in rule 498 as proposed.[63]

In seeking to supplement the information about a fund's principal investment strategies set out in a profile, the Commission proposed to require that a fund's risk summary inform investors about the availability in the fund's shareholder reports of additional information about the fund's investments.[64] Some commenters questioned the proposed placement of this disclosure, arguing that the disclosure should appear together with the legend on the cover page of the profile, while other commenters supported requiring the disclosure in the profile's risk/return summary. The Commission believes that requiring this disclosure on the cover page of the profile would result in too much information on the cover page. Therefore, the Commission is adopting the proposal requiring a fund's profile to indicate in its risk summary that additional information about a fund's investments is available in its shareholder reports.[65]

• Principal Risks of Investing in the Fund

Summary Risk Disclosure. The proposed risk/return summary would require a fund to summarize the information contained in the fund's prospectus about the principal risks of investing in the fund. Reflecting the Commission's proposed new approach to risk disclosure described in the Form N-1A Proposing Release, the profile disclosure was intended to summarize the risks of a fund's anticipated portfolio holdings as a whole, and the circumstances reasonably likely to affect adversely the fund's net asset value, yield, and total return.[66] Commenters generally supported the summary risk disclosure contemplated by proposed rule 498, agreeing that it would be focused and brief and would assist investors in identifying the principal risks of investing in a particular fund. The Commission is adopting this disclosure requirement with modifications to reflect certain commenters' suggestions.[67]

The Commission proposed to require that the risk summary identify the types of investors for whom the fund may be an appropriate or inappropriate investment. Commenters either opposed or raised significant concerns about this provision, arguing that it could be viewed as requiring a fund to determine whether its shares, among other things, are an investment suitable for a particular investor.[68] Commenters also stated that the disclosure would tend to be generic and not meaningful or useful for investors.

The Commission is persuaded by commenters that disclosure about the appropriateness of funds for particular investors should not be required in all profiles and has deleted this requirement from the risk summary. The Commission believes, however, that disclosure indicating whether a fund is appropriate for specific types of investors or is consistent with certain investment goals, even if generic in nature, may be useful for some investors and may provide a means for the fund to distinguish itself from other investment alternatives. Therefore, the risk summary requirement, as adopted, will give a fund the option to include disclosure in its profile about the types of investors for whom the fund is intended and the types of investment goals that may be consistent with an investment in the fund.[69]

Under the proposed risk/return summary, a fund could at its option discuss the potential rewards of investing in the fund in the risk summary as long as the discussion provided a balanced presentation of the fund's risks and rewards. One commenter strongly questioned this provision of the proposal, asserting that it would detract from a clear presentation of risks in the summary. The Commission has reconsidered this disclosure in light of the intended standardized and summary nature of the risk summary and has concluded that the disclosure there should focus solely on the risks of investing in the fund. Thus, the Commission has determined to eliminate the option to describe the rewards of investing in a fund in the risk summary.[70]

Special Risk Disclosure Requirements. The Commission proposed to require special disclosure in the risk summary for money market funds[71] and for funds advised by or sold through banks. Commenters supported the proposed disclosure requirements, and the Commission is adopting them substantially as proposed.[72]

The Commission proposed to require a tax-exempt money market fund that concentrates its investments in a particular state (a "single state money market fund") to include specific disclosure in its profile risk summary describing certain risks associated with an investment in such a fund.[73] In the Form N-1A Proposing Release, the Commission asked, however, whether it should continue to require this disclosure in prospectuses.[74] The Commission noted that this disclosure may exaggerate the risk of investing in single state money market funds. As the Form N-1A Proposing Release pointed out, although these funds are subject to less stringent issuer diversification provisions under Commission rules than other money market funds, they are subject to credit quality and maturity investment restrictions that are comparable to other money market funds.

In response to the Commission's question regarding single state money market funds, commenters indicated that the special disclosure now required in fund prospectuses overstates the risks of investing in single state money market funds, particularly in view of the minimal risk that commenters asserted is associated with these funds. The Commission is persuaded by these commenters and has determined not to require the disclosure in either the profile or the prospectus.[75]

Risk/Return Bar Chart and Table. The proposed risk/return summary would require a fund's profile to include a bar chart showing the fund's annual returns for each of the last 10 calendar years and a table comparing the fund's average annual returns for the last 1-, 5-, and 10-fiscal years to those of a broad-based securities market index. The bar chart reflects the Commission's determination that investors need improved disclosure about the risks of investing in a fund. The bar chart is intended to illustrate graphically the variability of a fund's returns (*e.g.*, whether a fund's annual returns for a 10-year period have varied significantly from year to year or were relatively even over the period). Presenting return information in this format was designed to give investors some indication of the variability of a fund's annual returns and thus some idea of the risk of an investment in the fund. The average annual return information in the table would assist investors in evaluating a fund's performance and risks relative to "the market." Commenters generally supported the proposed bar chart and performance table, and the Commission is adopting these requirements with modifications to reflect suggestions of commenters.[76]

In the Form N-1A Proposing Release, the Commission requested comment about alternative presentations that could improve fund risk disclosure.[77] In particular, the Commission expressed interest in disclosure that would show a fund's highest and lowest returns (or "range" of returns) for annual or other periods as an alternative, or in addition, to the bar chart. The Commission suggested that this information could be presented in a separate table or included in the performance table.

In response to the Commission's request, some commenters suggested including in a fund's bar chart one or more indexes or other benchmarks (such as 3-month Treasury returns or the rate of inflation) to help investors evaluate the fund's returns by comparisons to other measures of market performance or economic factors.[78] Most commenters, however, opposed requiring additional information in the bar chart, asserting that it could complicate and reduce the effectiveness of the bar chart.

Several commenters supported the inclusion of annual return information in the bar chart on a quarterly or semi-annual rather than an annual basis. They argued that this change to the bar chart would respond to concerns that fund investors may not sufficiently appreciate that an investment in a fund may be subject to the risk of a short-term decline in value. This risk, commenters asserted, may not be apparent from the annual returns proposed to be shown in the bar chart.

The Commission acknowledges that a fund's returns may vary significantly and could decrease in value over short periods and that the annual returns in the bar chart, as proposed, would not necessarily reflect this pattern. On the other hand, the Commission is concerned that requiring quarterly returns over a 10-year period would make the bar chart more complex and less useful in communicating information to investors. In balancing the desire to make typical fund investors aware that fund shares may experience price fluctuations over shorter periods with its underlying goal that fund documents communicate information in as straightforward and uncomplicated a manner as possible, the Commission has determined to require a fund to disclose, in addition to the bar chart, its best and worst returns for a quarter during the 10-year (or other) period reflected in the bar chart.[79] The Commission believes that this information will assist investors in understanding the variability of a fund's returns and the risks of investing in the fund by illustrating, without adding unwarranted complexity to the bar chart, that the fund's shares may be subject to short-term price fluctuations.

Presentation of Return Information. The proposed risk/return summary would require a fund to include the bar chart and table under a separate sub-heading that referred to both risk and performance. Several commenters argued that the separate sub-heading requirement was unnecessary and suggested that a fund should be able to choose whether to include any sub-heading. Consistent with the objective of encouraging funds to develop disclosure formats that are most helpful to investors, the profile risk/return summary, as adopted, does not require the sub-heading included in the proposed risk/return summary. To help investors use the information in the bar chart and table, the profile risk/return summary, as adopted, however, does require a fund to provide a brief narrative explanation of how the information illustrates the variability of the fund's returns.[80]

Bar Chart Return Information. The Commission proposed to require that a fund's bar chart show the fund's annual returns for the last 10-calendar years of the fund's existence. The purpose of the calendar-year requirement was to facilitate the comparison of the annual returns among funds, which typically have fiscal periods that do not correspond to the calendar year.[81] Unlike the proposed bar chart, the proposed performance table required disclosure of a fund's returns for fiscal year periods. In requiring this disclosure to be made for fiscal year periods, the proposal was consistent with existing disclosure requirements for the presentation of other financial information included in a fund's prospectus.

Several commenters argued that using different time periods for the proposed bar chart and performance table would confuse investors and urged the Commission to minimize potential investor confusion by adopting consistent time periods for this information. The Commission is persuaded by these comments and believes that requiring both the bar chart and the performance table to be based on calendar periods will promote understandable information in the profile. Therefore, the risk/return summary, as adopted, requires calendar-year periods for both the bar chart and table.[82] Under rule 498, as adopted, the average annual return information in the table in a fund's profile risk/return summary must be as of the most recent calendar quarter and updated quarterly.[83]

The proposed bar chart would not reflect sales loads assessed upon the sale of a fund's shares, although the average annual return information for the fund in the table would reflect the payment of any sales loads. Commenters generally supported this presentation of annual return information. The Commission believes that, in light of the different types of sales loads that may be charged on fund shares, it would be difficult for funds to compute annual returns for the purpose of the bar chart and to communicate the information effectively to investors.[84] In addition, the Commission has concluded that more precise return information is not necessary for the bar chart to serve the purposes of graphically showing a fund's annual returns and illustrating the variability of an investment in the fund over a 10-year period. Therefore, the bar chart, as adopted, is not required to show returns adjusted for sales loads.

Bar Chart Presentation. Consistent with the bar chart as proposed, the bar chart, as adopted, may include return information for more than one fund.[85] In contrast, the risk/return summary, as adopted, would require a fund offering more than one class of shares in a profile to include annual return information in its bar chart for only one class.[86] Unlike individual funds, classes of funds represent interests in the same portfolio of securities and the returns of each class differ only to the extent that the classes do not have the same expenses. The Commission believes that including return information for all classes offered through a fund's profile is not necessary to provide an indication of the risks of investing in the fund. In addition, the table accompanying such a fund's bar chart would provide return information for each class offered in the profile so that investors will be able to identify and compare the performance of each class.[87]

The proposed risk/return summary would require the bar chart of a fund offering more than one class of shares through a profile to reflect annual return information for the class offered in the profile that had the longest performance history over the last 10 years. Most commenters considering the issue suggested that the Commission instead permit such a fund to include the performance of any existing class in the bar chart, maintaining that the effect of expenses on the returns for different classes of shares is not significant.[88] The Commission is persuaded that allowing a multiple class fund in such a case to choose the class reflected in the fund's bar chart will simplify compliance with the bar chart requirement and provide investors with sufficient information to evaluate the variability of returns for any class of the fund. Therefore, the profile risk/return summary, as adopted, permits a fund to choose the class to be reflected in the bar chart, subject to certain limitations.[89]

• Fees and Expenses of the Fund

The proposed risk/return summary would require a table accompanying a fund's bar chart showing the fund's fees and expenses, including any sales loads charged in connection with an investment in the fund. Including the fee table in both the profile and the prospectus reflects the Commission's strongly held belief in the importance of fees and expenses in a typical investor's decision to invest in a fund. The fee table is designed to help investors understand the costs of investing in a fund and to compare those costs with the costs of other funds. The Commission is adopting the requirement for a fee table with modifications incorporating suggestions from commenters.[90]

3. Other Disclosure Requirements

The Commission proposed to require the profile of a fund to include not only the risk/return summary, but also disclosure about other key aspects of investing in the fund. Commenters generally supported these disclosure requirements, which are summarized below, and the Commission is adopting them substantially as proposed.

- **Investment Adviser and Portfolio Manager of the Fund**

Proposed rule 498 would generally require a fund to identify in its profile its investment adviser and the person or persons primarily responsible for the day-to-day management of the fund's portfolio ("portfolio manager"). The proposed disclosure in the profile about portfolio managers also would require a fund to indicate the length of time that a portfolio manager has managed the fund and to summarize the portfolio manager's business experience for the last 5 years. Proposed rule 498 contemplated that a fund for which a committee or other group shared day-to-day management of its portfolio would disclose that it was managed in this fashion and not identify any individual portfolio manager. Commenters supported all of these proposed requirements, which the Commission has determined to adopt.[91]

In seeking to meet its goal that profile disclosure be clear, concise, and summary in nature, the Commission proposed that, subject to one exception, a fund having 3 or more portfolio managers, each with responsibility over a portion of the fund's portfolio, could choose to disclose the number, and not the names, of its portfolio managers. Under the proposed exception, a fund would be required to disclose the identity of a portfolio manager who was responsible for managing 40% or more of its portfolio.[92] One commenter questioned the operation of these provisions and suggested that the Commission instead adopt a requirement that a fund disclose the name and experience of only those portfolio managers having responsibility over the day-to-day management of a significant portion of the fund's investments. The commenter suggested further that 30 to 40% of a fund's portfolio should be deemed significant for this purpose.

The Commission believes that the commenter's suggestions are consistent with the goal underlying the profile and could result in better disclosure than that contemplated by the Commission's proposal. Thus, under rule 498, as adopted, a fund with 3 or more portfolio managers need not identify each of the managers, except that the fund must identify any manager who is (or is reasonably expected to be) responsible for the management of a significant portion of the fund's assets.[93] Under rule 498, as adopted, a portfolio manager of 30% or more of a fund's net assets generally would be deemed to be responsible for the management of a significant portion of the fund's net assets.[94]

Proposed rule 498 generally would require a fund to identify in its profile any person or entity serving as a sub-adviser of the fund.[95] Under the proposal, a fund would not need to identify a sub-adviser whose sole responsibility for the fund is limited to managing the fund's cash positions on a day-to-day basis.[96] Commenters supported, and the Commission has adopted, this provision, with a clarification that recognizes that responsibility for cash management generally is incidental to a fund's investment objectives and unlikely to affect the fund's overall portfolio management and risks.[97]

Under rule 498, as proposed, a fund with 3 or more sub-advisers, each of which manages a portion of the fund's portfolio, could choose to disclose the number, and not the identity, of its sub-advisers, subject to one exception. Under the exception, a fund would be required to identify any sub-adviser that manages 40% or more of its net assets. Consistent with the modification to the disclosure requirement for portfolio managers, rule 498, as adopted, requires a fund to identify any sub-adviser that is (or is reasonably expected to be) responsible for the management of a significant portion of the fund's net assets. The rule defines a significant portion of the fund's net assets for this purpose generally to be 30% or more of the fund's net assets.[98]

- **Purchase and Sale of Fund Shares**

The Commission proposed to require a fund to describe in its profile how to purchase its shares under one caption and how to redeem its shares under another caption. Proposed rule 498 would require, under the purchase caption, information about the fund's minimum investment requirements (*e.g.*, initial and minimum account balances) and, when applicable, any breakpoints in or waivers of sales loads.

Several commenters criticized the generic nature of the information on purchases and sales of fund shares contemplated by proposed rule 498. They argued that without some guidance as to the specific kinds of information relating to purchases and sales of fund shares that the Commission believes is of importance to investors, funds would include an excessive amount of information in their profiles. The Commission believes that such a result would be inconsistent with the profile's intended purpose as a summary disclosure document and has revised rule 498 to specify in greater detail the information about a fund's purchase and sale procedures that funds must include in a profile. Under rule 498, as adopted, a fund must disclose the minimum initial or subsequent investment requirements, the initial sales load (or other loads), and, if applicable, the initial sales load breakpoints or waivers.[99] Rule 498 also requires a fund to state that its shares are redeemable, to identify the procedures for redeeming shares (*e.g.*, on any business day by written request, telephone, or wire transfer), and to identify any charges or sales loads that may be assessed upon redemption (including, if applicable, the existence of waivers of these charges).[100]

- **Fund Distributions and Tax Information**

The Commission is adopting the proposed requirement that a fund disclose information in its profile about the terms and conditions under which it makes distributions, as well as the expected tax treatment of those distributions.[101] Rule 498, as adopted, requires a fund's profile to describe how frequently the fund intends to make distributions and what reinvestment options for distributions (if any) are available to investors in the fund. Rule 498 also requires a fund to disclose whether its distributions to shareholders may be taxed as ordinary income or capital gains and that the rates shareholders pay on capital gains will depend on the length of time that the fund holds its assets.[102] Rule 498 requires a tax-exempt fund to state that it intends to distribute tax-exempt income and to disclose, as applicable, that a portion of its distributions may be taxable.

- **Other Services Provided By the Fund**

Recognizing that funds often seek to distinguish themselves by the services that they offer investors and that investors often select funds for the services that they provide, the Commission proposed to require a fund to summarize or list in its profile the services available to its investors, including, for example, any exchange privileges or automated information services. One commenter expressed concern about the open-ended nature of this item and suggested that the Commission clarify that a fund need not respond to the item by disclosing all of its services available to all investors. This clarification, according to the commenter, would ensure that the profile serves its intended purpose as a summary document that includes information of use to a typical fund investor. The Commission agrees, and as adopted, rule 498 requires only that a fund's profile provide a summary of services available to typical investors in the fund.[103]

4. Application to Purchase Shares

The Commission proposed to permit a fund to include in its profile an application to purchase its shares.[104] To ensure that investors are informed of the availability of a fund's prospectus, which can be reviewed by an investor before investing in the fund, proposed rule 498 would require the application to note with equal prominence that an investor has the option of purchasing shares of the fund after reviewing the information in the profile or after requesting and reviewing the fund's prospectus (and other information).

Commenters generally supported permitting a fund to include an application in its profile, and the Commission is adopting rule 498 as proposed. One commenter questioned why an application needed to be included within a profile and suggested that it should be sufficient for an application to accompany the profile. The Commission recognizes that allowing funds to separate purchase applications from profiles may facilitate the printing and distribution of profiles and make it easier for funds to administer and process investors' applications. The Commission is concerned, however, that separating the application from the profile may cause investors to overlook the information provided in the profile. Balancing these concerns with a desire to ease the administrative burden on funds, the Commission has revised rule 498 to permit a fund to provide an application for purchase of fund shares either in the profile, or together with the profile in a manner reasonably designed to alert investors that the application is to be considered along with the information about the fund disclosed in the profile.[105]

C. Filing Requirements

The Commission proposed to require a fund to file its profile with the Commission at least 30 days before its first use.[106] Proposed rule 498 would require a fund to file any profile containing substantive changes to a previously filed profile 30 days before use. The proposed rule would not require a fund to re-file a previously filed profile that has been revised only to update return information about the fund's past performance included in the risk/return summary. Commenters generally supported the proposed filing requirement, although some commenters suggested that it was unnecessary to require the subsequent re-filing of a profile with substantive changes 30 days before use. Commenters recommended that, if the Commission believes that such a filing requirement is necessary, the period before an amended profile can be used should be shortened to 5 days. Other commenters requested clarification about the kinds of changes made to a profile in use that would trigger a second filing requirement.

The Commission has determined to adopt the proposed filing requirements with modifications to address commenters' concerns.[107] As discussed in the Profile Proposing Release, requiring profiles to be filed prior to their first use will allow the Commission's staff to monitor the document's compliance with the provisions of rule 498 and other provisions under the federal securities laws.[108] The Commission believes that the 30-day filing requirement for a new profile will provide the staff with sufficient time to review the profile.[109] The subsequent filing of an amended profile was intended to enable the Commission to continue to monitor and assess the use of profiles by funds. Because substantive changes to the profile, particularly the risk/return summary, will be reflected in amended prospectuses filed with the Commission that can be reviewed by the Division, the Commission believes that a subsequent filing of amendments to a profile before its use is not necessary. Therefore, the Commission has revised the procedures under which profiles are filed to require that a fund file its amended profile within 5-business days after its use.[110]

Funds would be required to submit profiles electronically on the Commission's electronic data gathering analysis and retrieval ("EDGAR") system.[111] Because filings on the EDGAR system currently are text-only, do not reflect formatting, and do not reproduce graphic images (such as the bar chart required to be in the profile), the Commission proposed to require a fund to submit 2 copies of the profile in the primary form intended to be distributed to investors (*e.g.*, paper or electronic media) with its electronically-filed profile. The purpose of this requirement was to allow the Commission to assess how funds present information in the profile.[112] Pointing out that all funds are now required to file their disclosure documents required under the federal securities laws electronically and are no longer permitted to file paper copies, one commenter argued that it would be burdensome to require an additional paper submission of a profile and that the paper filing was not necessary to review the content of the profile. The commenter suggested that, if the Commission determines that a paper (or other distributed form of) filing is necessary, the Commission should require that the first filing of the profile be in its primary format and allow subsequent filings to be made electronically on EDGAR only. The Commission believes that review of profiles in the form in which they will be distributed to investors will allow its staff to evaluate the effectiveness of the profile and will be helpful in assessing whether the Commission should permit other types of investment companies to use a form of profile.[113] To avoid unnecessary administrative burdens on funds, which file most forms required by the Commission electronically, however, the Commission is revising the additional profile filing requirement. Under these revisions, the first profile filing must be accompanied by the submission of a profile in the format in which it will be distributed to investors.[114] Subsequent filings will not require the additional formatted profile.

D. Dissemination of Profiles

The Commission believes, on the basis of its own research and studies undertaken by others, that the profile has the potential to be used by a significant number of fund investors. To facilitate use of the profile, the Commission proposed to permit profiles to be distributed to investors through any form of media.[115] Commenters generally supported this approach, although one commenter urged the Commission to limit distribution of the profile to mass print media, arguing that the use of electronic media or direct mail to distribute a profile could promote fraud. The Commission believes that the profile's filing requirements and its staff's periodic regular review of fund operations through its inspections program provide important safeguards against the fraudulent use of the profile. In addition, the Commission has determined that it is in the interest of fund investors to provide them with different means to access sources of information about funds. Therefore, the Commission has decided not to restrict the means that funds may use to distribute profiles.

Notwithstanding its decision to permit funds to use all media to distribute profiles, the Commission acknowledges that some media may have limitations that make communicating information in a profile difficult or that raise issues about whether investors have adequate opportunity to consider the information conveyed by that form of media.[116] Regardless of how it is distributed (*e.g.*, through electronic means or in paper format), a profile must contain all of the information contemplated by rule 498.[117] In addition, while a fund's profile may be delivered without the fund's prospectus, the profile, if accompanied by supplemental sales literature, cannot be delivered without the prospectus.[118]

As discussed in the Profile Proposing Release, electronic media, such as the Internet, may be particularly well suited for the delivery of the profile to investors.[119] Including the profile together with the prospectus (and other information) on a fund's Internet web site may be an efficient method for the fund to disseminate, and for investors to receive, disclosure documents. Electronic availability of both the profile and prospectus would allow investors to access the fund's prospectus for more information contemporaneously with deciding to make an investment in the fund.[120]

Several commenters pointed out that funds could decide to send profiles to prospective investors with cover letters designed to be "omitting prospectuses" within the meaning of rule 482 under the Securities Act.[121] Noting that rule 482 materials are designed for a purpose different from that of the profile and are required to contain a legend that is inconsistent with the legend in the profile, the commenters requested that the Commission clarify the circumstances under which these materials could be used with a profile. The commenters suggested specifically that the statement required by rule 482, that a prospectus is available from a fund and that the investor should read it carefully before investing, could confuse investors who receive rule 482 materials with a profile that contains an application to purchase shares of the fund. To avoid this type of confusion, the Commission is revising rule 482 so that a fund can indicate in a letter or other rule 482 material accompanying the fund's profile that information about the fund, and the procedures for investing in the fund, are available in the accompanying profile.[122] The

Commission also is revising rule 482 to provide that a profile containing, or accompanied by, an application can be used with rule 482 materials.[123]

E. Modified Profiles for Certain Funds

The Commission proposed to permit a fund to tailor a profile for use by investors in participant–directed defined contribution plans ("plans"). The Commission believes that plan participants may find a profile helpful in evaluating and comparing the funds offered as investment alternatives in a plan.[124] In proposing rule 498, the Commission recognized that certain information of importance to typical fund investors is of little importance to participants in plans. Thus, proposed rule 498 would permit a fund offered through a plan to omit information relating to the purchase and sale of fund shares, fund distributions, and tax consequences.[125]

Commenters generally supported allowing funds to develop profiles containing disclosure of particular relevance for plan participants who invest in funds. The Commission is adopting the special provisions for profiles used for plans as proposed with modifications to reflect suggestions of the commenters.[126]

Under rule 498, as adopted, funds can tailor disclosure for profiles to be used for investments in defined contribution plans qualified under the Internal Revenue Code.[127] One commenter suggested that the Commission also permit funds that serve as investment options for variable insurance contracts to modify profiles to take into account specialized purchase and sale procedures and tax consequences applicable to these funds.[128] In response to the commenter's suggestions, the Commission is revising rule 498 to permit the profile to be tailored for funds offered through variable insurance contracts. The Commission believes that this revision will help to ensure that profiles contain information that investors will find meaningful and useful. Rule 498, as adopted, permits a profile for a fund offered as an investment option for a plan to include, or be accompanied by, an enrollment form for the plan.[129] An application or enrollment form for a variable insurance contract may accompany the profile for the funds that serve as investment options, however, only if the form also is accompanied by a full prospectus for the contract.[130]

Some commenters suggested that rule 498 permit other modifications to the disclosure in fund profiles used in connection with plans, such as including information about purchases and sales of the fund's shares, taxation, or transfer of participant accounts under the plan or describing from whom this information can be obtained. Commenters also suggested that rule 498 permit such a fund to alter the legend in its profile used by plans to distinguish clearly that profile from another profile of the same fund. Consistent with the goal of providing meaningful and useful information that is effectively communicated to investors, rule 498, as adopted, permits funds to modify the legend and other disclosure in profiles intended for use in connection with defined contribution plans, other tax-deferred arrangements described in the rule, and variable insurance contracts.

III. EFFECTIVE DATE

The Commission proposed a transition period after the effective date of revised Form N-1A to give funds sufficient time to prepare their registration statements under the proposed amendments.[131] One commenter suggested that, in light of the significant overlap of information in fund prospectuses and profiles, funds would revise their prospectuses and develop profiles concurrently, and requested that the transition period be the same for both rule 498 and Form N-1A, as amended. The commenter also requested that the Commission continue to permit funds to use Pilot Profiles during the transition period.[132] The Commission expects that the practical result of the adoption of rule 498 and revisions to prospectus disclosure requirements may be that funds begin using both documents at the same time. In light of the profile's purpose to provide investors with a new source of clear, concise information about funds, the Commission believes that funds should have the option to use the profile as soon as possible and is making rule 498 effective on June 1, 1998.[133] The amendments to Form N-1A will become effective on the same date.[134] Although existing funds will have until December 1, 1999 to comply with the Form N-1A amendments, a fund may, at its option, prepare documents in accordance with the requirements of the amended Form at any time after the effective date of the amendments.

IV. COST/BENEFIT ANALYSIS AND EFFECTS ON COMPETITION, EFFICIENCY, AND CAPITAL FORMATION

Section 2(b) of the Securities Act provides that whenever the Commission engages in rulemaking requiring it to consider whether its action is in the public interest, the Commission also must consider whether the action will promote efficiency, competition, and capital formation.[135] For the reasons stated in the cost/benefit analysis below, as well as the reasons discussed elsewhere in this adopting release, the Commission has concluded that rule 498 will protect investors and will promote efficiency, competition, and capital formation.

Evaluating and comparing funds has become an increasingly difficult task for investors as the number of funds has grown. The Commission has designed the profile to allow funds to use different offering documents to meet the diverse information needs of investors. The Commission believes that rule 498 allows funds to provide investors with a profile that conveys information to investors efficiently, to the benefit of investors and funds. For example, funds may include profiles in various media, such as magazines, and may use profiles specifically tailored for investors in defined contribution plans, certain other tax-deferred arrangements, and variable insurance contracts. The profile, by providing investors with a concise, standardized information option, also may enable investors to use information efficiently by making it easier to compare funds before investing. This result will promote competition among funds and better enable investors to select an investment that is appropriate and consistent with their investment goals.

The Commission did not receive any comments addressing specifically the costs associated with rule 498. Acknowledging that it is difficult to quantify costs and benefits related to the use of a profile, the Commission notes that commenters strongly favored the proposal. A fund's use of a profile under rule 498 is voluntary and not every fund will choose to prepare a profile. Developing a profile consistent with rule 498, however, would not be burdensome, because a fund that chooses to use a profile is likely to have developed much of the information required to appear in a profile as a part of its registration statement on Form N-1A. As discussed in the Commission's Paperwork Reduction Act submission in conjunction with the Profile Proposing Release, the Commission estimated that approximately 2,500 funds, or one third of eligible funds, will prepare profiles, and that the average profile will describe 2 funds. The Commission estimated that the annual cost to the industry of preparing and filing updated profiles would be approximately $5,600,000.[136]

The Commission anticipates that the use of profiles may cause funds to restructure their expenditures on advertising. It is difficult, however, to determine how the use of profiles will affect aggregate expenditures on advertising. Expenditures on profiles may be offset by reductions in other advertising costs, resulting in no net cost increase.

The Commission has taken steps to minimize the costs associated with the use of a profile, such as designing the required risk/return summary to allow funds to update return information without necessitating the reprinting of the entire profile. The ability to provide better information to investors and encourage investments in a fund may offset any additional costs to funds created by the development of a profile. Profiles also may lead to lower printing and distribution costs for funds that mail fewer prospectuses. On balance, the Commission believes that rule 498 fosters efficiency and tends to promote competition and capital formation without imposing significant costs on funds.

V. PAPERWORK REDUCTION ACT

As set forth in the Profile Proposing Release, this rulemaking contains "collection of information" requirements within the meaning of the Paperwork Reduction Act of 1995 ("PRA").[137] The collection of information requirements in the Profile Proposing Release were submitted to the Office of Management and Budget ("OMB") for review under section 3507(d) of the PRA. OMB approved the collection of information under the title "Profiles for Open-End Management Investment Companies" and assigned it control number 3235-0488. The collection of information contained in the Profile Proposing Release is in accordance with the clearance requirements of 44 U.S.C. 3507. An agency may not conduct or sponsor, and a person is not required to respond to, a collection of information unless an agency displays a valid OMB control number.

Rule 498 permits funds to provide investors with a profile that contains a summary of key information about a fund. A fund that chooses to make a profile available would give investors the option of purchasing the fund's shares after reviewing the information contained in the profile or after requesting and reviewing the fund's prospectus (and other information about the fund). Under rule 498, use of the profile by a fund is voluntary, but compliance with the rule is mandatory for any fund that decides to use a profile. Responses to the collection of information will not be confidential.

The Profile Proposing Release solicited public comment on the collection of information requirements contained in that release. The Commission received no comments on the PRA portion of the release. The estimated total reporting burden, purpose, use and necessity of the collection of information, as detailed in the Profile Proposing Release, remains the same.

VI. SUMMARY OF FINAL REGULATORY FLEXIBILITY ANALYSIS

A summary of the Initial Regulatory Flexibility Analysis ("Analysis"), which was prepared in accordance with the Regulatory Flexibility Act, 5 U.S.C. 603, was published in the Profile Proposing Release. The Commission received no comments on the Analysis. The Commission has prepared a Final Regulatory Flexibility Analysis ("FRFA") in accordance with 5 U.S.C. 604. The FRFA explains that a profile would include a summary of key information about a fund in a concise, standardized format designed to help investors evaluate and compare funds. The FRFA also explains that, if a fund makes a profile available, investors will have the option to purchase the fund's shares after reviewing the information in the profile or after requesting and reviewing the fund's prospectus (and other information about the fund). An investor deciding to purchase fund shares based on the information in the profile would receive the fund's prospectus no later than with the confirmation of the purchase.

The FRFA discusses the effect of rule 498 on small entity investment companies, which are defined, for the purposes of the Securities Act and Investment Company Act, as investment companies with net assets of $50 million or less as of the end of the most recent fiscal year (17 CFR 230.157(b) and 270.0-10). The Commission estimates that there are approximately 620 small entity investment companies and that approximately one-third (207) could choose to use proposed rule 498. As explained in more detail in the FRFA, the Commission estimates that the total hour burden on small entities to prepare, file, and update the profile annually would be approximately 2,420 hours. While the profile would include a summary of key information about the fund that is included in the prospectus, the disclosure requirements for the profile and the prospectus are designed for different purposes.

The FRFA explains that rule 498 would not be significantly burdensome for small entity investment companies because use of the profile is optional, and the information to be included in a fund's profile will typically be drawn from information required to be disclosed in the fund's prospectus. In addition, some investors may use profiles instead of prospectuses to narrow their choices among funds, which would reduce a fund's printing and distribution costs. Lower printing and distribution costs could benefit small entities as much as or more than it could for large funds.

As stated in the FRFA, the Commission considered several alternatives to rule 498, including establishing different compliance or reporting requirements for small entity investment companies or exempting them from all or part of the rule.

Because use of the profile would be optional, and, if used, profiles of all funds would be subject to the same disclosure requirements, the Commission believes that the rule would not impose additional burdens on small entity investment companies. Separate treatment for small entity investment companies would be inconsistent with the protection of investors.

A copy of the Final Regulatory Flexibility Analysis may be obtained by contacting George J. Zornada, Team Leader, Office of Disclosure Regulation, Division of Investment Management, Securities and Exchange Commission, 450 Fifth Street, N.W., Mail Stop 5-6, Washington, D.C. 20549-6009.

VII. STATUTORY AUTHORITY

The Commission is adopting rule 498 under sections 5, 7, 8, 10, and 19(a) of the Securities Act (15 U.S.C. 77e, 77g, 77h, 77j, and 77s(a)) and sections 8, 22, 24(g), 30, and 38 of the Investment Company Act (15 U.S.C. 80a-8, 80a-22, 80a-24(g), 80a-29, and 80a-37). The authority citations for the rule precede the text of the amendments.

List of Subjects in 17 CFR Parts 230 and 270

Investment companies, Reporting and recordkeeping requirement, Securities.

TEXT OF RULE

For the reasons set out in the preamble, the Commission amends Chapter II, Title 17 of the Code of Federal Regulations as follows:

PART 230—GENERAL RULES AND REGULATIONS, SECURITIES ACT OF 1933

1. The general authority citation for Part 230 is revised to read, in part, as follows:

Authority: 15 U.S.C. 77b, 77f, 77g, 77h, 77j, 77r, 77s, 77sss, 78c, 78d, 78l, 78m, 78n, 78o, 78w, 78ll(d), 79t, 80a-8, 80a-24, 80a-28, 80a-29, 80a-30, and 80a-37, unless otherwise noted.

* * * * *

2. Amend § 230.431 to revise the introductory text of paragraph (a) to read as follows:

§ 230.431 Summary prospectuses.

(a) A summary prospectus prepared and filed (except a summary prospectus filed by an open-end management investment company registered under the Investment Company Act of 1940) as part of a registration statement in accordance with this section shall be deemed to be a prospectus permitted under section 10(b) of the Act (15 U.S.C. 77j(b)) for the purposes of section 5(b)(1) of the Act (15 U.S.C. 77e(b)(1)) if the form used for registration of the securities to be offered provides for the use of a summary prospectus and the following conditions are met:

* * * * *

3. Amend § 230.482 to revise the introductory text of paragraph (a), paragraphs (a)(3), (a)(5), and (a)(7), and in paragraph (d) remove the period at the end of paragraph (d)(1)(ii) and add in its place "; or" and add paragraph (d)(1)(iii) to read as follows:

§ 230.482 Advertising by an investment company as satisfying requirements of section 10.

(a) An advertisement or other sales material that is not a prospectus, or an advertisement or sales material excluded from the definition of prospectus by section 2(10) of the Act (15 U.S.C. 77b(10)) and related § 230.134, will be deemed to be a prospectus under section 10(b) of the Act (15 U.S.C. 77j(b)) for the purpose of section 5(b)(1) of the Act (15 U.S.C. 77e(b)(1)), if:

(1) * * *

(3) It includes a conspicuous statement that:

(i) Identifies a source from which an investor may obtain a prospectus containing more complete information about the investment company, which should be read carefully before investing; or

(ii) If used with a profile under § 230.498 ("Profile"), indicates that information is available in the Profile about the investment company, the procedures for investing in the investment company, and the availability of the investment company's prospectus.

NOTE to paragraph (a)(3).—The fact that the statements included in the advertisement are included in the section 10(a) prospectus does not relieve the issuer, underwriter, or dealer of the obligation to ensure that the advertisement is not false or misleading.

(4) * * *

(5) It does not contain and is not accompanied by any application by which a prospective investor may invest in the investment company, except that:

(i) A prospectus meeting the requirements of section 10(a) of the Act (15 U.S.C. 77j(a)) by which a unit investment trust offers periodic payment plan certificates may contain a contract application although the prospectus includes another prospectus that, pursuant to this section, omits certain information required by section 10(a) of the Act, regarding investment companies in which the unit investment trusts invests; and

(ii) It may be used with a Profile that includes, or is accompanied by, an application to purchase shares of the investment company as permitted under § 230.498.

(6) * * *

(7)(i) In the case of an investment company that holds itself out to be a money market fund, it includes the following statement:

An investment in the Fund is not insured or guaranteed by the Federal Deposit Insurance Corporation or any other government agency. Although the Fund seeks to preserve the value of your investment at $1.00 per share, it is possible to lose money by investing in the Fund.

(ii) A money market fund that does not hold itself out as maintaining a stable net asset value may omit the second sentence of the statement in (a)(7)(i) of this section.

(d) * * *

(1) * * *

(iii) A quotation or quotations of tax equivalent yield or tax equivalent effective yield if it appears in the same advertisement as a quotation of current yield and each quotation relates to the same base period as the quotation of current yield, is presented with equal prominence, and states the income tax rate used in the calculation.

* * * * *

4. Amend § 230.497 to revise paragraph (a) and to add paragraph (k) to read as follows:

§ 230.497 Filing of investment company prospectuses—number of copies.

(a) Five copies of every form of prospectus sent or given to any person prior to the effective date of the registration statement that varies from the form or forms of prospectus included in the registration statement filed pursuant to § 230.402(a) shall be filed as part of the registration statement not later than the date that form of prospectus is first sent or given to any person, except that:

(1) An investment company advertisement under § 230.482 shall be filed under this paragraph (but not as part of the registration statement) unless filed under paragraph (i) of this section; and

(2) A profile under § 230.498 shall be filed in accordance with paragraph (k) of this section and not as part of the registration statement.

* * * * *

(k)(1) *Profile Filing Requirements.* A form of profile under § 230.498 shall not be used unless:

(i) The form of profile that has not been previously filed with the Commission is filed at least 30 days before the date that it is first sent or given to any person.

(A) No additional filing is required during the 30-day period for changes (material or otherwise) to a form of profile filed under this paragraph if the changes are included in the definitive profile that is filed with the Commission under paragraph (k)(2)(ii) of this section.

(B) The form of profile filed under paragraph (k)(1)(i) can be used on the later of 30 days after the date of filing or, if the profile is filed in connection with an initial registration statement or a post-effective amendment that adds a series of an investment company to a registration statement, or reflects changes to a prospectus included in a post-effective amendment filed to update a registration statement under § 230.485, the date that the registration statement or post-effective amendment becomes effective.

(ii) A definitive form of a profile filed under paragraph (k)(1)(i) of this section is filed with the Commission no later than the fifth business day after the date that it is used.

(iii) A form of profile that differs from any definitive form of profile that was filed under this paragraph (k) is filed with the Commission in definitive form no later than the fifth business day after the date that it is first used. This filing shall be made under one of the following sub-paragraphs according to the character of the change contained in the form of profile:

(A) A form of profile that contains a material change to the information disclosed under paragraph (c)(2)(i)–(iii) of § 230.498; and

(B) A form of profile that does not contain a material change to the information under paragraphs (c)(2)(i)–(iii) of § 230.498.

(2) *Filing Procedures.* (i) Designate, at the top of the first page of any form of profile that is filed under this paragraph (k), the paragraph and sub-paragraph under which the profile is filed.

(ii) Send two additional copies of the first definitive form of profile filed electronically under paragraph (k)(1)(ii) of this section to the Commission, in the primary form intended to be used for distribution to investors (*e.g.*, paper, electronic media), by mail or other means reasonably calculated to result in receipt by the Commission, no later than the fifth business day after the date the profile is first sent or given to any person. Send copies to the following address: Office of Disclosure and Review, Division of Investment Management, U.S. Securities and Exchange Commission, 450 Fifth St., N.W., Mail Stop 5-6, Washington, D.C. 20549-6009. Note prominently that the submission is made in accordance with § 230.497(k)(2) of Regulation C under the Securities Act. If the profile is distributed primarily on the Internet, supply, in lieu of copies, the electronic address ("URL") of the profile page(s) in an exhibit to the electronic filing under this paragraph (k). This additional requirement will expire on June 1, 2000.

5. Add § 230.498 to read as follows:

§ 230.498 Profiles for certain open-end management investment companies.

(a) *Definitions.*

(1) A *Fund* means an open-end management investment company, or any series of such a company, that has, or is included in, an effective registration statement on Form N-1A (§§ 274.11A and 239.15A of this chapter) and that has a current prospectus under section 10(a) of the Act (15 U.S.C. 77j(a)).

(2) A *Profile* means a summary prospectus that is authorized under section 10(b) of the Act (15 U.S.C. 77j(b)) and section 24(g) of the Investment Company Act (15 U.S.C. 80a-24(g)) for the purpose of section 5(b)(1) of the Act (15 U.S.C. 77e(b)(1)).

(b) *General requirements.* A Fund may provide a Profile to investors, which may include, or be accompanied by, an application that investors may use to purchase the Fund's shares, if the Profile contains the information required or not precluded by paragraph (c) of this section and does not incorporate any information by reference to another document.

Instructions to paragraph (b).

1. The Profile is intended to be a standardized summary of key information in the Fund's prospectus under section 10(b) of the Act. Additional information is available in the Fund's prospectus under section 10(a) of the Act, in the Fund's Statement of Additional Information under Form N-1A, and in the Fund's annual and semi-annual shareholder reports prepared in accordance with § 270.30d-1. Funds may not use cross-references in the Profile to other Fund disclosure documents unless required or permitted by this rule. Funds should minimize cross-references and the use of footnotes within the Profile; cross-references and footnotes should generally be used only to promote a better understanding of the information about the Fund contained in the Profile.

2. Provide clear and concise information in the Profile in a format designed to communicate the information effectively. Avoid excessive detail, technical or legal terms, and long sentences and paragraphs. Provide the information in the Profile using the plain English writing principles in § 230.421(d).

3. A Fund may use document design techniques intended to promote effective communication of the information in the Profile unless inconsistent with the requirements of this section.

4. A Profile may describe more than one Fund or class of a Fund. A Profile that offers the securities of more than one Fund or class of a Fund does not need to repeat information that is the same for each Fund or class of Fund described in the Profile.

5. File the Profile with the Commission as required by § 230.497(k).

(c) *Specific requirements.*

(1) Include on the cover page of the Profile or at the beginning of the Profile:

(i) The Fund's name and, at the Fund's option, the Fund's investment objective or the type of fund or class offered, or both;

(ii) A statement identifying the document as a "Profile," without using the term "prospectus";

(iii) The approximate date of the Profile's first use;

(iv) The following legend:

This Profile summarizes key information about the Fund that is included in the Fund's prospectus. The Fund's prospectus includes additional information about the Fund, including a more detailed description of the risks associated with investing in the Fund that you may want to consider before you invest. You may obtain the prospectus and other information about the Fund at no cost by calling ____________.

(v) Provide a toll-free (or collect) telephone number that investors can use to obtain the prospectus and other information. The Fund may indicate, as applicable, that the prospectus and other information is available on the Fund's Internet site or by E-mail request. The Fund also may indicate, if applicable, that the prospectus and other information is available from a financial intermediary (such as a broker-dealer or bank) through which shares of the Fund may be purchased or sold.

Instruction to paragraph (c)(1)(v). When the Fund (or financial intermediary through which shares of the Fund may be purchased or sold) receives a request for the Fund's prospectus, the Fund's Statement of Additional Information, or the Fund's annual or semi-annual report, the Fund (or financial intermediary) must send the requested document within three business days of receipt of the request, by first-class mail or other means designed to ensure equally prompt delivery. Funds are encouraged to send other information requested by shareholders within the same period.

(2) Provide the information required by paragraphs (c)(2)(i) through (ix) of this section in the order indicated:

(i) *Fund objectives/goals.*

Provide the information about the Fund's investment objectives or goals required by Item 2(a) of Form N-1A.

(ii) *Principal investment strategies of the Fund.*

Provide the information about the Fund's principal investment strategies required by Item 2(b) of Form N-1A. In addition, a Fund (other than a Fund that has not yet been required to deliver a semi-annual or annual report under § 270.30d-1 of this chapter) must provide disclosure to the following effect:

Additional information about the Fund's investments is available in the Fund's annual and semi-annual reports to shareholders. In the Fund's annual report you will find a discussion of the market conditions and investment strategies that significantly affected the Fund's performance during the last fiscal year. You may obtain either or both of these reports at no cost by calling ______________.

(iii) *Principal risks of investing in the Fund.*

Provide the narrative disclosure, bar chart, and table required by Item 2(c) of Form N-1A. Provide in the table the Fund's average annual total returns and, if applicable, yield as of the end of the most recent calendar quarter prior to the Profile's first use. Update the return information as of the end of each succeeding calendar quarter as soon as practicable after the completion of the quarter. Disclose the date of the return information adjacent to the table.

Instruction to paragraph (c)(2)(iii). A Fund may reflect the updated performance information in this section of the profile by affixing a label or sticker, or by other reasonable means.

(iv) *Fees and expenses of the Fund.*

Include the fee table required by Item 3 of Form N-1A.

(v) *Investment adviser, sub-adviser(s) and portfolio manager(s) of the Fund.*

(A) Identify the Fund's investment adviser.

(B) Identify the Fund's sub-adviser(s) (if any) except that:

(1) A Fund need not identify a sub-adviser(s) whose sole responsibility for the Fund is limited to day-to-day management of the Fund's holdings of cash and cash

equivalent instruments, unless the Fund is a money market fund or other Fund with a principal investment strategy of regularly holding cash and cash equivalent instruments.

(2) A Fund having three or more sub-advisers, each of which manages a portion of the Fund's portfolio, need not identify each such sub-adviser, except that the Fund must identify any sub-adviser that is (or is reasonably expected to be) responsible for the management of a significant portion of the Fund's net assets. For purposes of this paragraph, a significant portion of a Fund's net assets generally will be deemed to be 30% or more of the Fund's net assets.

(C) State the name and length of service of the person or persons employed by or associated with the Fund's investment adviser (or the Fund) who are primarily responsible for the day-to-day management of the Fund's portfolio and summarize each person's business experience for the last five years in accordance with the Instructions to Item 6(a)(2) of Form N-1A. A Fund with three or more such persons, each of whom is (or is reasonably expected to be) responsible for the management of a portion of the Fund's portfolio, need not identify each person, except that a Fund must identify and summarize the business experience for the last five years of each person who is (or is reasonably expected to be) responsible for the management of a significant portion of the Fund's net assets. For purposes of this paragraph, a significant portion of a Fund's net assets generally will be deemed to be 30% or more of the Fund's net assets.

(vi) *Purchase of Fund shares.*

Disclose the Fund's minimum initial or subsequent investment requirements, the initial sales load (or other loads) to which the Fund's shares are subject, and, if applicable, the initial sales load breakpoints or waivers.

(vii) *Sale of Fund shares.*

Disclose that the Fund's shares are redeemable, identify the procedures for redeeming shares (*e.g.*, on any business day by written request, telephone, or wire transfer), and identify any charges or sales loads that may be assessed upon redemption (including, if applicable, the existence of waivers of these charges).

(viii) *Fund distributions and tax information.*

Describe how frequently the Fund intends to make distributions and what options for reinvestment of distributions (if any) are available to investors. State, as applicable, that the Fund intends to make distributions that may be taxed as ordinary income or capital gains (which may be taxable at different rates depending on the length of time that the Fund holds its assets) or that the Fund intends to distribute tax-exempt income. If a Fund expects that its distributions, as a result of its investment objectives or strategies, primarily will consist of ordinary income or capital gains, provide disclosure to that effect. For a Fund that holds itself out as investing in securities generating tax-exempt income, provide, as applicable, a general statement to the effect that a portion of the Fund's distributions may be subject to federal income tax.

(ix) *Other services are available from the Fund.*

Provide a brief summary of services available to the Fund's shareholders (*e.g.*, any exchange privileges or automated information services), unless otherwise disclosed in response to paragraphs (c)(2)(vi) through (viii) of this section.

Instruction to paragraph (c)(2)(ix). A Fund should disclose only those services that generally are available to typical investors in the Fund.

(3) The Profile may include an application that a prospective investor can use to purchase the Fund's shares as long as the application explains with equal prominence that an investor has the option of purchasing shares of the Fund after reviewing the information in the Profile or after requesting and reviewing the Fund's prospectus (and other information) before making a decision about investing in the Fund.

Instruction to paragraph (c)(3). A Fund may include the application in a Profile or otherwise provide an application together with a Profile in any manner reasonably designed to alert investors that the application is to be considered along with the information about the Fund disclosed in the Profile.

(d) *Modified Profile for Certain Funds*

(1) A Fund may modify or omit the information required by paragraphs (c)(2)(vi) through (ix) of this section for a Profile to be used for a Fund that is offered as an investment option for:

(i) A defined contribution plan that meets the requirements for qualification under section 401(k) of the Internal Revenue Code (26 U.S.C. 401(k));

(ii) A tax-deferred arrangement under sections 403(b) or 457 of the Internal Revenue Code (26 U.S.C. 403(b) and 457); and

(iii) Variable contracts as defined in section 817(d) of the Internal Revenue Code (26 U.S.C. 817(d)).

(2) A Fund that uses a Profile permitted under paragraph (d)(1) of this section may:

(i) Alter the legend required by paragraph (c)(1)(iv) of this section to include a statement to the effect that the Profile is intended for use in connection with a defined contribution plan, another tax-deferred arrangement, or a variable contract, as applicable, and is not intended for use by other investors; and

(ii) Modify other disclosure in a Profile consistent with offering the Fund as a specific investment option for a defined contribution plan, tax-deferred arrangement, or variable contract.

(3) A Profile used under paragraph (d)(1)(i) or (ii), but not paragraph (d)(1)(iii), of this section may include, or be accompanied by, an enrollment form for the plan or arrangement. The enrollment form does not need to be filed with the Profile under § 230.497.

PART 270—RULES AND REGULATIONS, INVESTMENT COMPANY ACT OF 1940

6. The general authority citation for Part 270 is revised to read, in part, as follows:

Authority: 15 U.S.C. 80a-1 *et seq.*, 80a-34(d), 80a-37, 80a-39 unless otherwise noted;

* * * * *

7. Amend § 270.34b-1 to revise paragraph (b)(1)(ii)(B) to read as follows:

§ 270.34b-1 Sales literature deemed to be misleading.

* * * * *

(b)(1) * * *

(ii) * * *

(B) Accompany any quotation of the money market fund's tax equivalent yield or tax equivalent effective yield with a quotation of current yield as specified in paragraph (d)(1)(iii) of § 230.482 of this chapter; and

* * * * *

By the Commission.

Jonathan G. Katz

Secretary

Dated: March 13, 1998

endnotes

1 Investment Company Act Release No. 23064 (Mar. 13, 1998) ("Form N-1A Release").

2 See Investment Company Institute ("ICI"), Trends in Mutual Fund Investing: September 1997 at 3 (Oct. 30, 1997) (ICI News No. 97-93) ("ICI Trends") (as of Sept. 1997, there were 6,666 funds) and ICI, Mutual Fund Ownership in the U.S., fundamentals, Dec. 1996, at 1 (approximately 36.8 million households owned mutual funds either directly or through a retirement plan as of April 1996).

3 Compare ICI Trends at 1 (fund net assets exceeded $4.4 trillion as of Sept. 1997) with Federal Reserve Bank Statistical Release H.8: Assets and Liabilities of Commercial Banks in the United States (Nov. 7, 1997) (commercial bank deposits were approximately $3.0 trillion as of Oct. 1997).

4 See, e.g., "Fulfilling the Promise of Disclosure," Remarks by Arthur Levitt, Chairman, SEC, before the American Savings Education Council, New York, NY (July 23, 1997); Remarks by Steven M.H. Wallman, Commissioner, SEC, before the ICI's 1995 Investment Company Directors Conference and New Directors Workshop, Wash., D.C. (Sept. 22, 1995); "Mutual Funds and the International Marketplace: A Regulatory Challenge," Remarks by Isaac C. Hunt, Jr., Commissioner, SEC, before the Sixth Annual Conference on International Issues, The University of Tulsa, Tulsa, Okla. (Mar. 6, 1997). See also McTague, Simply Beautiful: Shorn of Legalese, Even Prospectuses Make Sense, Barron's, Oct. 7, 1996, at F10 (concerning the recent efforts of the John Hancock funds and other fund groups to simplify their prospectuses).

5 The Commission has demonstrated an on-going commitment to improve the information provided in fund disclosure documents to meet changes in the fund industry and investors' needs. The Commission has taken a number of steps in recent years to meet this goal. See Investment Company Act Release No. 20974 (Mar. 29, 1995) (60 FR 17172) (requesting comment on ways to improve risk disclosure and comparability of fund risk levels) ("Risk Concept Release"); Investment Company Act Release No. 19382 (Apr. 6, 1993) (58 FR 19050) (simplifying financial highlights information and requiring management's discussion of fund performance ("MDFP")); Investment Company Act Release No. 16245 (Feb. 2, 1988) (53 FR 3868) ("Fund Performance Release") (adopting a uniform formula for calculating fund performance); Investment Company Act Release No. 16244 (Feb. 1, 1988) (53 FR 3182) (adopting a uniform fee table in fund prospectuses). See also SEC, Report of the Advisory Committee on the Capital Formation and Regulatory Processes (July 24, 1996); SEC, Report of the Task Force on Disclosure Simplification (1996) (recommending specific improvements in the disclosure provided by corporate issuers).

6 Investment Company Act Release No. 22529 (Feb. 27, 1997) (62 FR 10943), correction (62 FR 24160) ("Profile Proposing Release").

7 Investment Company Act Release No. 22528 (Feb. 27, 1997) (62 FR 10898), correction (62 FR 24160) ("Form N-1A Proposing Release").

8 See Investment Company Institute (pub. avail. July 31, 1995) ("1995 Profile Letter"); Investment Company Institute (pub. avail. July 29, 1996) ("1996 Profile Letter"). The Division of Investment Management ("Division") has permitted the pilot program to continue until adoption of proposed rule 498. See Investment Company Institute (pub. avail. July 16, 1997) ("1997 Profile Letter").

9 Letter from Paul Schott Stevens, Senior Vice President and General Counsel, ICI, to Barry P. Barbash, Director, Division of Investment Management, SEC, at 5–6 (May 20, 1996) ("ICI Survey Letter") (enclosing Investment Company Institute, The Profile Prospectus: An Assessment by Mutual Fund Shareholders (1996) (survey of over 1,000 fund investors) ("ICI Profile Survey")).

10 In addition to the comment letters from individuals, the Commission received comment letters from 6 broker-dealers and investment advisers, 8 funds, 3 law firms, 1 rating agency, 4 trade associations, and 8 other interested organizations. The comment letters, as well as a comment summary prepared by the Commission's staff, are available for public inspection and copying at the Commission's public reference room in File No. S7-18-96.

11 Of the comment letters received by the Commission, 88% supported the Proposed Profile.

12 See also Middleton, Cure on the Way for ... Prospectusphobia, Mutual Funds Magazine, June 1997, at 58; Fosback, Profiles—A Valuable New Tool for Investors, Mutual Funds Magazine, May 1997, at 10; Profile Prospectuses: An Idea Whose Time Has Come, Mutual Funds Magazine, Aug. 1996, at 11.

13 The ICI recently conducted a survey to assess information that investors considered before making a fund purchase. The results indicated that investors considered fund risk levels, total returns, and investment goals most frequently (listed respectively as first, second, and fourth). ICI, Understanding shareholders' use of information and advisers at 4 (1997) ("ICI Shareholder Survey").

[14] See Securities Act Release No. 7497 (Jan. 28, 1998) (63 FR 6370) ("Plain English Release") (adopting amendments to rule 421 under the Securities Act (17 CFR 230.421) requiring the use of plain English disclosure principles).

[15] Rule 421(d).

[16] 15 U.S.C. 77j(b). Section 10(b) of the Securities Act of 1933 ("Securities Act") permits the use of a summary prospectus (which provides information the substance of which is included in the prospectus) to communicate information for purposes of an offer under section 5(b)(1) of the Securities Act (15 U.S.C. 77e(b)(1)). Section 5(b)(2) of the Securities Act (15 U.S.C. 77e(b)(2)) requires, as a condition of selling a security, the delivery to investors of a prospectus that meets the requirements of section 10(a) of the Securities Act (15 U.S.C. 77j(a)).

[17] Congress recently confirmed the authority of the Commission to permit the use of a summary prospectus by adding new section 24(g) to the Investment Company Act (15 U.S.C. 80a-24(g)). National Securities Markets Improvement Act of 1996, Pub. L. No. 104-290 (1996) ("Improvements Act"), section 204 (amending section 24 to add new paragraph (g)). While the profile, as adopted, will include a summary of information that is required in the prospectus, the Commission may adopt other rules under section 24(g) allowing a fund to use a summary prospectus that includes information the substance of which is not included in the prospectus.

[18] See supra note 16.

[19] Investment Company Act Release No. 13436 (Aug. 12, 1983) (48 FR 37928) ("1983 Form N-1A Adopting Release"). See also supra note 5.

[20] See Form N-1A Release, supra note 1.

[21] The Commission also proposed as part of these disclosure initiatives a new rule to address investment company names that are likely to mislead investors about the investments and risks of an investment company. Investment Company Act Release No. 22530 (Feb. 27, 1997) (62 FR 10955), correction (62 FR 24161). The proposed rule would require, among other things, funds and other registered investment companies with names suggesting a specific investment emphasis to invest at least 80% of their assets in the type of investment suggested by their name. The Commission received a number of substantive comments on the proposed rule, many of which asserted that the proposal had flaws that the Commission should address. The Division is analyzing the comments and expects to recommend a final rule for Commission consideration in the near future.

[22] The Commission has long encouraged summary prospectuses under section 10(b) of the Securities Act to provide investors with a condensed statement of important information included in the prospectus. In 1956, the Commission adopted a rule permitting the use of a summary prospectus under section 10(b), which was extended to investment companies in 1972. See Securities Act Release No. 3722 (Nov. 23, 1956) (adopting rule 434A (17 CFR 230.434A) to permit the use of a summary prospectus); Securities Act Release No. 5248 (May 9, 1972) (37 FR 10071) (extending rule 434A to investment companies); Securities Act Release No. 6383 (Mar. 3, 1982) (47 FR 11380) (renumbering rule 434A as rule 431) (17 CFR 230.431). The profile permitted by rule 498 is intended to replace the summary prospectuses that funds are currently permitted to use by rule 431 under the Securities Act, and the Commission is amending rule 431 to clarify that the rule no longer applies to funds. The Commission also is eliminating the "Instructions as to Summary Prospectuses" that now accompany Form N-1A. See Form N-1A Release, supra note 1.

[23] As noted above, Focus Groups responded very positively to the profile option. A number of individual investors also have written to the Commission and expressed strong support for the profile. See Profile Proposing Release, supra note 6, at 10944. See also ICI Profile Survey, supra note 9, at 22, 26; ICI Shareholder Survey, supra note 13, at 4.

[24] See Plain English Release, supra note 14.

[25] See Profile Proposing Release, supra note 6, at 10950.

[26] 15 U.S.C. 77l(a)(2); 15 U.S.C. 77q(a).

[27] 15 U.S.C. 78j(b); 17 CFR 240.10b-5. In addition, the Commission has the authority under section 10(b) of the Securities Act to suspend the use of a profile, as a summary prospectus, if the profile includes a false or misleading statement or omits to state a material fact necessary in order to make the statements, in light of the circumstances under which they were made, not misleading. This authority supplements the Commission's authority under section 8(b) of the Securities Act (15 U.S.C. 77h(b)) to issue an order to stop the sale of securities by means of a materially inaccurate or incomplete section 10(a) prospectus.

[28] 15 U.S.C. 77k.

29 See I Loss & Seligman, Securities Regulation 480 and n.214 (3d ed. 1989) (citing S. Rep. 1036, 83d Cong., 2d Sess. 17–18 (1954) and H.R. Rep. 1542, 83d Cong., 2d Sess. 26 (1954)). Although section 11 liability would not apply to the profile, section 11 liability would apply to the sale of a fund's securities if a misleading statement is included in both the profile and the prospectus.

30 The legend also indicates that other information about the fund is available in addition to the prospectus. See infra Section ... for a discussion of the profile legend.

31 Section 12(a)(2) imposes liability for material misstatements or omissions when the seller cannot demonstrate the exercise of "reasonable care." An action under section 12(a)(2) does not require proof of scienter (i.e., intent to mislead investors), e.g., Wigand v. Flo-Tek, Inc., 609 F.2d 1028, 1034 (2d Cir. 1979), or investor reliance on a misleading statement or omission, e.g., MidAmerica Fed. S. & L. Assoc. v. Shearson/American Express, Inc., 886 F.2d 1249, 1256 (10th Cir. 1989); Sanders v. John Nuveen & Co., 619 F.2d 1222, 1225 (7th Cir. 1980), cert. denied , 450 U.S. 1005 (1981). In contrast, claims by private plaintiffs under the antifraud provisions of section 10(b) of the Securities Exchange Act of 1934 ("Securities Exchange Act") require proof of scienter and investor reliance. Under either type of claim, however, it must be established that the misrepresentation or omission was "material," which generally means that a substantial likelihood exists that a reasonable investor would consider the information important in making an investment decision. TSC Industries, Inc. v. Northway, Inc., 426 U.S. 438, 449 (1976); Basic, Inc. v. Levinson, 485 U.S. 224, 231–32 (1988). Commenters cited several cases as examples of the claims funds may face under section 12(a)(2) for alleged nondisclosures in profiles. See, e.g., In re TCW/DW North Am. Gov. Income Trust Secs. Litigation, 941 F. Supp. 326, 337–38 (S.D.N.Y. 1996) (dismissing certain allegations that fund misstated and omitted information regarding risks of international investing on the basis that a reasonable investor would not have been misled); In Re Alliance North Am. Gov. Income Trust, Inc. Secs. Litigation, 1996 U.S. Dist. LEXIS 14209 (S.D.N.Y. 1996) (same); Tabankin v. Kemper Short-Term Global Income Fund, 1994 U.S. Dist. LEXIS 965 (N.D.Ill. 1994) (dismissing allegations that fund failed to disclose adequately the risks of investment).

32 Profile Proposing Release, supra note 6, at 10950. One commenter suggested as an alternative to incorporation by reference that the Commission create a liability "safe harbor" for funds using profiles. Under such a provision, a fund using a profile meeting the requirements of rule 498 would be deemed to have disclosed all material information about a fund for purposes of the profile if the fund's prospectus contained all material information. Such a provision, in effect, would amount to incorporation by reference and, in the Commission's view, would be inconsistent with the purpose of the profile.

33 See White v. Melton , 757 F. Supp. 267, 271–72 (S.D.N.Y. 1991). See also 1983 Form N-1A Adopting Release, supra note 19, at 37930.

34 In 1979, the Commission adopted rule 434d under the Securities Act (17 CFR 230.434d), subsequently redesignated rule 482 (17 CFR 230.482), which permits investment companies to use advertisements that are designed to be omitting prospectuses of the type contemplated by section 10(b) of the Securities Act. Securities Act Release No. 6116 (Aug. 31, 1979) (44 FR 52816).

35 Like those commenting on the Proposed Profile, commenters on proposed rule 434d argued that a fund using an advertisement under the rule would be subject to potential liability under section 12(a)(2) if the advertisement did not contain all of the information included in the fund's prospectus. In adopting rule 434d, the Commission stated its belief that a fund should not be liable under section 12(a)(2) merely because information included in the fund's section 10(a) prospectus was not included in the advertisement. 44 FR at 52817. The Commission is not aware of any lawsuits brought since the adoption of rule 434d in which a fund was found liable for an advertisement meeting the requirements of the rule on the basis that the advertisement failed to include information contained in the fund's prospectus.

36 15 U.S.C. 77s(a). See also section 38(c) of the Investment Company Act (15 U.S.C. 80a-37(c)).

37 See Plain English Release, supra note 14. As part of the plain English initiatives, the Commission plans to issue A Handbook on Plain English: How to Create Clear SEC Disclosure Documents, prepared by the Commission's Office of Investor Education and Assistance.

38 Instruction 2 to rule 498(b) (requiring funds to use the plain English writing principles set out in rule 421(d) in drafting the disclosure in the profile). See supra note 14 and accompanying text.

39 See National Association for Variable Annuities (pub. avail. June 4, 1996) (staff no-action letter allowing pilot program for variable annuity profiles). The Division has permitted this program to continue pending its taking any further action with respect to variable annuity profiles. National Association for Variable Annuities (pub. avail. May 30, 1997) (staff no-action letter).

40 The Proposed Profile refined the prototype profile used in the pilot program, which allowed the Commission to evaluate use of the profile concept for funds. See supra note 8 and accompanying text. The Commission

believes that further initiatives to adapt the profile concept for other types of investment companies should follow a similar approach that includes a review of existing prospectus disclosure requirements and an assessment of investor responses to a different disclosure format.

41 The profile is, however, subject to certain other format requirements. Under rule 498, as adopted, profiles must meet requirements with respect to font size and legibility set out in rule 420 under the Securities Act (17 CFR 230.420). Rule 420 requires, among other things, that prospectuses be in roman type at least as large and as legible as 10-point modern type.

42 See section 30(d) of the Investment Company Act (15 U.S.C. 80a-29(d)) and rule 30d-1 (17 CFR 270.30d-1) (requiring funds to provide investors with semi-annual reports about a fund's current operations).

43 See Form N-1A Release, supra note 1. In proposing changes to improve the disclosure in fund prospectuses, the Commission recognized that revisions to shareholder report requirements could enhance the disclosure provided to investors. See Form N-1A Proposing Release, supra note 7, at 10912. Recent legislation gives the Commission greater authority to specify the content of annual reports and to require additional disclosure in annual and semi-annual reports as necessary or appropriate in the public interest or for the protection of investors. Improvements Act, supra note 16, section 206(f) (amending section 30 of the Investment Company Act (15 U.S.C. 80a-29) to add new paragraph (f)). The Commission notes its preliminary view that an "integrated" approach to registration and reporting requirements applicable to funds could improve the overall information about funds available to investors. See Form N-1A Release, supra note 1.

44 See Profile Proposing Release, supra note 6, at 10945.

45 Rule 498(b). The profile generally will provide a summary of certain items in the prospectus, while the prospectus will provide a fuller description of each of these items. The prospectus, for example, discloses the amount of any rule 12b-1 fees charged by a fund in the fee table and includes a narrative discussion about the fund's rule 12b-1 fees. In contrast, the profile as a summary disclosure document discloses the amount of the fund's rule 12b-1 fees as part of the fee table disclosure. Similarly, a prospectus identifies each investment adviser of a fund, including a sub-adviser of the fund, while, in certain cases, a profile could disclose the number of sub-advisers managing the fund's portfolio without identifying each sub-adviser. See Form N-1A Release, supra note 1, and infra notes 90 and 93–94 and accompanying text.

46 Proposed rule 498 provided that a fund could not use footnotes or include cross-references within the profile or to information appearing in another of the fund's disclosure documents, unless specifically required or permitted in the rule. See Profile Proposing Release, supra note 6, at 10945 n.22. The Commission believes that footnotes and cross-references should generally be unnecessary in a summary document such as a profile. The Commission acknowledges, however, that circumstances may exist under which footnotes or cross-references within the profile may result in better disclosure. Thus, the Commission is revising rule 498 to discourage, but not to preclude, the use of footnotes or cross-references within a profile; under the rule, a fund may use footnotes or cross-references within a profile if their use promotes a better understanding of the information about the fund contained in the profile. Instruction 1 to rule 498(b). Rule 498, as adopted, continues to preclude use of cross-references to information appearing in another of the fund's disclosure documents. Such cross-references would be inconsistent with the purpose that the profile be a self-contained document. For purposes of the profile only, a hyperlink to a fund's prospectus from the fund's profile when both documents are available electronically would not be deemed a cross-reference. See infra note 120 (describing and explaining the use of hyperlinks in a profile).

47 Instruction 2 to rule 498(b). A fund must use plain English writing principles in drafting disclosure in the profile. See supra note 37. In response to a comment, the Commission is modifying rule 498 to clarify that information that is common to all funds or classes described in a profile need be stated only once and not repeated for each fund or class. Instruction 4 to rule 498(b). Rule 498, as adopted, does not preclude binding separate profiles for different funds together in one document.

48 One commenter requested clarification whether a profile must include a separate cover page. Rule 498, as adopted, clarifies that a profile need not have a separate cover page so long as the specified cover page disclosure is included as introductory information at the beginning of the profile. The proposed cover page requirements were intended to identify introductory information that should appear at the beginning of a profile.

49 Rule 498(c)(2)(iii). Rule 498 permits a fund to reflect updated performance information in a "sticker" or similar means to avoid requiring frequent reprinting of the profile to change this section of the profile. Instruction to rule 498(c)(2)(iii).

50 Proposed rule 498(c)(1)(ii).

51 See supra note 16.

52 See Profile Proposing Release, supra note 6, at 10950. See also supra Section ...

53 Rule 498(c)(1)(ii).

54 See Profile Proposing Release, supra note 6, at 10946.

55 See id . The first proposed legend read as follows: This Profile summarizes key information about the Fund that is included in the Fund's prospectus. If you would like more information before you invest, you may obtain the Fund's prospectus and other information about the Fund at no cost by calling ____________.

56 See id . The second proposed legend read as follows: This Profile summarizes key information about the Fund that is included in the Fund's prospectus. The prospectus includes additional material information about the Fund that you may want to consider before you invest. You may obtain the Fund's prospectus and other information about the Fund at no cost by calling ____________.

57 Rule 498(c)(1)(iv). A fund will be required to provide a toll-free or collect telephone number for investors to request the prospectus or other information. A fund also may, if applicable, indicate that the prospectus is available on its Internet web site or by E-mail. Rule 498(c)(1)(v). Rule 498 requires that an application to purchase shares of a fund that accompanies the fund's profile present with equal prominence the option to invest in the fund based on the information included in the profile or to request the prospectus and other information before making an investment decision. Rule 498(c)(3). See infra note 104 and accompanying text.

58 See Profile Proposing Release, supra note 6, at 10946.

59 Instruction to rule 498(c)(1)(v). The Commission's Office of Compliance Inspections and Examinations will, as a part of its routine periodic inspections of a fund's operations, examine a fund's compliance with the 3-business day mailing requirement. In addition to the 3-business day mailing requirement for prospectuses, rule 498 requires a fund to send within 3 business days of a request its annual or semi-annual shareholder report and Statement of Additional Information ("SAI"). Id. The Commission staff also will examine a fund's compliance with this requirement. Failure to comply with either requirement could result in action by the Commission to ensure compliance, including an enforcement action in an appropriate case.

60 Instruction to Rule 498(c)(1)(v).

61 See Form N-1A Release, supra note 1.

62 Rule 498(c)(2)(i).

63 Rule 498(c)(2)(ii).

64 A fund's annual report to its shareholders typically contains a MDFP. The Commission believes that the information in a fund's MDFP, including the discussion of the fund's performance during its most recent fiscal year, could be useful to some investors considering an investment in the fund.

65 Rule 498(c)(2)(ii). This provision requires a fund (other than a new fund) to include disclosure in the risk/return summary to the following effect: Additional information about the fund's investments is available in the fund's annual and semi-annual reports to shareholders. In the fund's annual report you will find a discussion of the market conditions and investment strategies that significantly affected the fund's performance during the last fiscal year. You may obtain either or both of these reports at no cost by calling ______________.
Unlike rule 498, as adopted, Form N-1A, as amended, requires that the statement about the availability of a fund's shareholder reports appear together with disclosure about the availability of the fund's SAI and other information about the fund on the back cover page of the fund's prospectus. Item 1(b)(1) of Form N-1A.

66 See Form N-1A Proposing Release, supra note 7 (regarding fund risk disclosure required in the prospectus).

67 Rule 498(c)(2)(iii) (incorporating Item 2(c)(1)(i) of Form N-1A).

68 As several commenters pointed out, applicable regulatory rules for brokers and other investment professionals require that these determinations be made on the basis of a review of information about the unique circumstances of an individual investor. See, e.g ., rule 2310(a) of the National Association of Securities Dealers, Inc. ("NASD") Conduct Rules, NASD Manual (CCH) ¶ 4261 (suitability of recommendations); rule 405 of the New York Stock Exchange, 2 N.Y.S.E. Guide (CCH) ¶ 2403 (the "know your customer rule").

69 Rule 498(c)(2)(iii) (incorporating Item 2(c)(1)(i) of Form N-1A).

70 In keeping with the disclosure flexibility provided to funds under Form N-1A, as amended, a fund could discuss the potential rewards of investing in the fund elsewhere in its prospectus as long as the information is not incomplete, inaccurate, or misleading. See Form N-1A Release, supra note 1.

71 For these purposes, a money market fund is a fund that holds itself out to investors as a money market fund and meets the conditions of paragraphs (c)(2), (c)(3), and (c)(4) of rule 2a-7 under the Investment Company Act (17 CFR 270.2a-7).

72 Rule 498(c)(2)(iii) (incorporating Item 2(c)(1)(ii) of Form N-1A). This provision, as adopted, requires the following disclosure by a money market fund in the risk summary of its profile: An investment in the Fund is not insured or guaranteed by the Federal Deposit Insurance Corporation or any other government agency. Although the Fund seeks to preserve the value of your investment at $1.00 per share, it is possible to lose money by investing in the Fund. A fund advised by or sold though a bank would disclose in the risk summary of its profile: An investment in the Fund is not a deposit of the bank and is not insured or guaranteed by the Federal Deposit Insurance Corporation or any other government agency. Some commenters asserted that the proposed disclosure was inconsistent with that required by bank regulators in the Interagency Statement on Retail Sales of Nondeposit Investment Products. See Board of Governors of the Federal Reserve System, FDIC, Office of the Comptroller of the Currency, and Office of Thrift Supervision, Interagency Statement on Retail Sales of Nondeposit Products, 6 Fed. Banking L. Rep. (CCH) ¶ 70,113, at 82,598 (Feb. 15, 1994) ("Interagency Statement") (requiring disclosure that the fund is not a deposit or other obligation of the bank). The Commission has confirmed with these bank regulators that no such inconsistency exists, because the disclosure required by the Interagency Statement applies to sales material and not to fund prospectuses. In response to suggestions from bank regulators, the Commission has revised the required disclosure to add language indicating that an investment in a fund advised by or sold through a bank is not a deposit of the bank. The requirement, as amended in this way, is consistent with the requirement now in effect. The Commission is making conforming amendments to the disclosure requirement contained in rule 482(a)(7) for advertisements by money market funds. The Commission also is amending rule 482(d) under the Securities Act and rule 34b-1 under the Investment Company Act (17 CFR 270.34b-1) to conform to changes made in Item 21 of Form N-1A, as amended. See Form N-1A Release, supra note 1.

73 Proposed rule 498 would require a single state money market fund to make disclosure similar to that Form N-1A currently requires such a fund to disclose in its prospectus. Existing Form N-1A requires a single state money market fund to disclose that it may invest a significant percentage of its assets in a single issuer and that investing in it may be riskier than investing in other types of money market funds. See Form N-1A Proposing Release, supra note 7, at 10903.

74 See Form N-1A Proposing Release, supra note 7, at 10904.

75 See Form N-1A Release, supra note 1.

76 Rule 498(c)(2)(iii) (incorporating Item 2(c)(2) of Form N-1A). This provision requires a fund to have at least one calendar year of returns before including the bar chart and requires a fund whose profile does not include a bar chart because the fund does not have annual returns for a full calendar year to modify the narrative explanation to refer only to information presented in the table. The provision also requires the bar chart of a fund in operation for fewer than 10 years to include annual returns for the life of the fund. In adopting the bar chart requirement, the Commission does not mean to suggest that all, or even a significant portion of all fund investors equate the variation in a fund's returns to the risk of investing in the fund. As it indicated in the Form N-1A Release, the Commission acknowledges that investors have a wide range of ideas of what "risk" means. See Form N-1A Release, supra note 1.

77 See Form N-1A Proposing Release, supra note 7, at 10907.

78 Rule 498, as adopted, in incorporating the requirements of Form N-1A, as amended, permits a fund to use other indexes in the presentation of the average annual return information in the table accompanying the bar chart. Rule 498(c)(2)(iii) (incorporating Instruction 2(b) to Item 2(c)(2) of Form N-1A).

79 Rule 498(c)(2)(iii) (incorporating Item 2(c)(2)(ii) of Form N-1A).

80 Rule 498(c)(2)(iii) (incorporating Item 2(c)(2)(i) of Form N-1A).

81 The Commission understands that funds increasingly organize themselves as series companies and tend to stagger the financial periods of their series to spread audits and financial reporting periods over an entire calendar year.

82 Rule 498(c)(2)(iii) (incorporating Item 2(c)(2) of Form N-1A).

83 Rule 498(c)(2)(iii). Unlike rule 498, as adopted, Form N-1A, as amended, requires the fund's prospectus risk/return summary to reflect average annual return information as of the end of a fund's most recent calendar year. Item 2(c)(2) of Form N-1A, as amended. A fund would update the information in the prospectus in connection with the filing of an annual post-effective amendment to update a fund's registration statement.

84 In contrast, sales loads can be accurately and fairly reflected in return information of the type contained in the table by deducting sales loads at the beginning (or end) of particular periods from a hypothetical initial fund investment.

85 While rule 498 does not limit the number of funds whose return information may be included in a bar chart, the presentation of the bar chart is subject to the general requirement that disclosure should be presented in a format designed to communicate information effectively. Instruction 2 to rule 498(b).

86 Rule 498(c)(2)(iii) (incorporating Instruction 3(a) to Item 2(c)(2) of form N-1A).

87 Rule 498(c)(2)(iii) (incorporating Instruction 3(b) to Item 2(c)(2) of form N-1A).

88 In making this argument, commenters cited rule 18f-3 under the Investment Company Act (17 CFR 270.18f-3), which provides that a class of shares may have different expenses for shareholder services, distribution fees, or other expenses actually incurred in a different amount by the class. The rule does not permit expenses for advisory or custodial fees, or other management fees, to vary among classes.

89 Rule 498(c)(2)(iii) (incorporating Instruction 3(a) to Item 2(c)(2) of Form N-1A). The bar chart must reflect the performance of any class that has returns for at least 10 years (e.g. , a fund could not present a class in the bar chart with 2 years of returns when another class has returns for at least 10 years). In addition, if two or more classes offered in the profile have returns for less than 10 years, the bar chart must reflect returns for the class that has returns for the longest period.

90 Rule 498(c)(2)(iv) (incorporating Item 3 of Form N-1A). The modifications adopted by the Commission are discussed in the Form N-1A Release, supra note 1.

91 Rule 498(c)(2)(v). Item 6(a)(2) of Form N-1A sets out the disclosure requirements for Form N-1A covering this information. As discussed in the Form N-1A Release, the Commission has provided additional guidance in Form N-1A regarding the prospectus disclosure obligations of a fund for which day-to-day management responsibilities are shared. See Form N-1A Release, supra note 1 (Instructions to Item 6(a)(2)).

92 Under the 1996 Profile Letter, supra note 8, at 3, a fund could disclose that 3 or more persons managed the fund's portfolio, without regard to the percentage of the portfolio managed by any one person.

93 Rule 498(c)(2)(v)(C). In tying this disclosure to the portion of a fund's net assets over which a person has day-to-day responsibility, the Commission intends to provide funds with a standard way of determining whether a person has responsibility over a significant portion of a fund's portfolio. Like Form N-1A, as amended, rule 498, as adopted, does not require disclosure about the portfolio manager of a money market fund or an index fund.

94 Rule 498, as adopted, requires disclosure about a portfolio manager of a fund who is, or who is reasonably expected to be, responsible for the management rather than one who "manages" a significant portion of the fund's portfolio. The revised language recognizes that the portion of a fund's portfolio over which a manager has responsibility may change from time to time.

95 See section 2(a)(20) of the Investment Company Act (15 U.S.C. 80a-2(a)(20)) (defining "investment adviser" broadly so as to include a sub-adviser).

96 In contrast, the 1996 Profile Letter, supra note 8, at 3, required disclosure about a sub-adviser only if it managed a material portion of a fund's portfolio.

97 Rule 498(c)(2)(v). As adopted, this exception does not apply to any sub-adviser for a money market fund because the primary investment objective for such a fund can be viewed as cash management. The exception also does not apply to any other type of fund with a principal strategy of regularly holding cash or cash equivalent instruments. A fund, for example, with a principal strategy of allocating its assets among cash equivalents, equity securities, and income securities, and which employed different sub-advisers to manage each of these asset categories, would need to identify all of the sub-advisers.

98 Rule 498(c)(2)(v)(B)(2).

99 Rule 498(c)(2)(vi).

100 Rule 498(c)(2)(vii).

101 Rule 498(c)(2)(viii).

102 If a fund expects that its distributions, as a result of its investment objectives or strategies, primarily will consist of ordinary income or capital gains, the fund must provide disclosure to that effect in responding to rule 498(c)(2)(viii). Funds subject to this requirement would include, for example, those often described as "tax-managed," "tax-sensitive," or "tax-advantaged," which have investment strategies to maximize long-term capital gains and minimize ordinary income. To the extent that a fund has a principal investment objective or strategy to achieve tax-managed results (e.g., to maximize long-term gains and minimize ordinary income),

the fund would be required under rule 498 to provide disclosure to that effect in the discussion of its investment objectives. Rule 498(c)(2)(ii).

[103] Rule 498(c)(2)(ix).

[104] Proposed rule 498(c)(3). Rule 482 under the Securities Act prohibits a fund from including an application to purchase its shares in an advertisement. This prohibition was based on concerns that an application would be inconsistent with the purpose of rule 482, which was to provide a limited amount of information about a fund and a means of requesting a fund's prospectus. See Fund Performance Release, supra note 5. In 1993, the Commission proposed to amend rule 482 to permit a fund to include in an advertisement a purchase application if the advertisement included certain information about a fund. Investment Company Act Release No. 19342 (Mar. 5, 1993) (58 FR 16141). In lieu of adopting the proposed revisions to rule 482, the Commission is adopting rule 498. The Commission is amending rule 482 in a number of respects to reflect the adoption of rule 498. In addition, the Commission is adopting revisions to rule 482 to permit letters or other materials permitted under the rule to accompany a profile. See infra note 123 and accompanying text.

[105] Instruction to rule 498(c)(3).

[106] Proposed rule 498 would require a fund to file the profile under rule 497, which sets out general filing requirements for fund prospectuses. The Commission proposed to include the profile filing requirement in new paragraph (k) to rule 497.

[107] The Commission has determined that it is not necessary or appropriate in the public interest or for the protection of investors to require that a fund's profile be filed as part of the fund's registration statement on Form N-1A. Filing the profile as part of a registration statement would not add to the Commission's ability to monitor the disclosure in the profile, would provide no additional protection to investors, and would impose unnecessary administrative burdens on funds.

[108] See Profile Proposing Release, supra note 6, at 10950. Under rule 498, as adopted, a profile can be used by a fund only with an effective registration statement and a current prospectus.

[109] Rule 497, as amended, requires a fund to file a definitive form of any profile required to be filed with the Commission within 5 days after it is used.

[110] Rule 497(k)(1)(ii). Rule 497(k) separates filings of amended profiles into those that contain a material change to the investment objectives/goals, strategies, or risks of investing in the fund (changes to the information in, respectively, paragraphs (c)(2)(i)–(iii) of rule 498) and those that do not. Rule 497(k)(1)(iii)(A) and (B). As with any profile filing, rule 497 requires that a fund filing an amended profile designate under which paragraph and sub-paragraph of rule 497 the fund is filing the amended profile. Rule 497(k)(2)(i). This requirement will assist the staff of the Division in determining whether an amended profile contains substantive changes to the information in the risk/return summary.

[111] The Commission requires most other filings to be made in the same manner. Rule 101(a)(1)(i) of Regulation S-T (17 CFR 232.101(a)(1)(i)), for example, requires prospectuses filed pursuant to the Securities Act to be submitted in electronic format.

[112] See Profile Proposing Release, supra note 6, at 10951 nn. 86–88 and accompanying text.

[113] See supra Section ... (discussion of use of profile by other investment companies).

[114] Rule 497(k)(2)(ii). If a fund intends to disseminate its profile electronically, the supplemental submission need only include the Internet web site electronic address ("URL").

[115] For example, a fund could make a profile available through direct mail and mass print (e.g., magazines and newspapers), broadcast, and electronic media, such as electronic bulletin boards, E-mail, facsimiles, Internet web sites, audiotapes, and videotapes. See, e.g. , Investment Company Act Release No. 21399 (Oct. 6, 1995) (60 FR 53458, 53458 n.9) ("Electronic Distribution Release"). A fund may find that posting both its profile and its prospectus (and other information) on its Internet web site may disseminate disclosure documents to investors more efficiently than other ways. The Commission has encouraged the electronic dissemination of information by allowing funds and other types of companies significant choice in selecting and using distribution media. See, e.g., id. at 53460 n.20 (providing guidance on the electronic delivery of documents including prospectuses, shareholder reports, and proxies, under the Securities Act, the Securities Exchange Act, and the Investment Company Act); Investment Company Act Release No. 21945 (May 9, 1996) (61 FR 24644) (addressing the use of electronic media by broker-dealers, transfer agents, and investment advisers); Investment Company Act Release No. 21946 (May 9, 1996) (61 FR 24652) ("Release 21946") (adopting technical amendments to rules premised on the delivery of paper documents).

[116] The Commission noted the same point generally in the Electronic Distribution Release, supra note 115, at 53460 & n.20. For example, broadcast media may be more difficult to use for disseminating the profile because they may not communicate the profile information effectively (e.g., the bar chart may not be

effectively conveyed by a radio broadcast) or provide a meaningful opportunity for retaining the information (e.g., a short television commercial).

[117] Release 21946, supra note 115, at 24653. The Commission has taken the position generally that any document contemplated by the federal securities laws, whether delivered electronically or on paper, must contain all required information and, if the order of information has been specified by the Commission, must present the information in substantially the prescribed order. Electronic Distribution Release, supra note 115, at 53460 n.20.

[118] Profiles may be accompanied by material deemed to be an omitting prospectus within the meaning of rule 482 under the Securities Act. The conclusion that a profile accompanied by supplemental sales literature cannot be delivered to investors without the prospectus is based on section 2(a)(10) of the Securities Act (15 U.S.C. 77b(a)(10)), which excludes sales literature from the definition of a "prospectus" (and from the filing requirements under the Securities Act) if a section 10(a) prospectus (but not a summary prospectus under section 10(b)) precedes or accompanies the sales literature. For a discussion of the use of a profile with rule 482 materials, see infra notes 121 and 122 and accompanying text. See also Electronic Distribution Release, supra note 115, at 53463 and 53465 (examples 15 and 35).

[119] See Profile Proposing Release, supra note 6, at 10951.

[120] A fund could provide a hyperlink to its prospectus from its profile. A hyperlink in a document (which, for example, may be an underlined word or phrase) permits a viewer to move to another document (or part of the same document) with a computer command. The words "investment strategies" in the profile, for example, could be set up as a hyperlink to the discussion of investment strategies in the prospectus. Using hyperlinks could facilitate the profile's serving as a means through which fund investors can obtain additional information in the prospectus and other documents. An investor's use of an electronic profile application contemplated by rule 498 would create the inference of delivery of the prospectus if both the profile and the prospectus are available at the same electronic site. Cf. Electronic Distribution Release, supra note 115, at 53465–66 (example (39)) ("If the fund can identify the application form as coming from the electronic system that contains both the application and the prospectus, electronic delivery of the prospectus can be inferred."). A fund that does not electronically disseminate the profile and prospectus together could not rely on this presumption and generally would be required to provide a copy of the prospectus with the purchase confirmation.

[121] See supra note 104.

[122] Rule 482(a)(3).

[123] Rule 482(a)(5).

[124] The Division has taken the view that certain informational materials about a fund offered as an investment option in a defined contribution plan can be deemed an omitting prospectus within the meaning of rule 482. Fidelity Institutional Retirement Services Company, Inc. (pub. avail. Apr. 5, 1995) (staff no-action letter). None of the initiatives being adopted by the Commission today is intended to supersede this position of the Division.

[125] Proposed rule 498(c)(4). The proposed rule also would permit funds to exclude information about some fund services (e.g., exchange privileges) that may not apply to plan participants. In addition, the proposed rule acknowledged that a plan typically effects purchases and sales of a fund's shares on behalf of plan participants and would permit the fund's profile to include the plan's enrollment form in lieu of the application form.

[126] Rule 498(d). General Instruction C.3.(d) of Form N-1A includes similar provisions enabling funds to omit certain information from their prospectuses that are used in connection with plans. Form N-1A Release, supra note 1.

[127] In addition to plans under rule 401(k) of the Internal Revenue Code (26 U.S.C. 401(k)), these plans include those under section 403(b) (26 U.S.C. 403(b)) (available to employees of certain tax-exempt organizations and public educational systems) and section 457 (26 U.S.C. 457) (available to employees of state and local governments and other tax-exempt employers).

[128] The prospectus for a variable insurance contract discloses the purchase and sale procedures and tax consequences of investing in the contract and is provided to investors in addition to prospectuses for one or more funds that are offered as investment options under the contract. Use of a profile for the available investment options could make it easier for investors in variable contracts to compare and select from the investment alternatives available under the contract.

[129] Rule 498(d)(3).

[130] The Commission is currently considering whether it should extend the profile to variable annuity contracts. See supra note 39 and accompanying text. The staff of the Division has indicated that, for variable annuity contracts used to fund employee retirement plans, summaries of the contract and fund prospectuses,

accompanied by payroll deduction and allocation forms, could be treated as satisfying the requirements of rule 482 under certain circumstances. See Aetna Life Insurance and Annuity Co. (pub. avail. Jan. 6, 1997) (staff no-action letter). A profile could be used as a summary of a fund prospectus for these purposes.

131 See Form N-1A Proposing Release, supra note 7, at 10921.

132 In the 1997 Profile Letter, supra note 8, the Division stated that the Commission would address the transition from use of a Pilot Profile in connection with the adoption of proposed rule 498.

133 After the effective date of rule 498, funds could continue to use a Pilot Profile as supplemental sales literature.

134 To simplify compliance with rule 498 and the revised prospectus disclosure requirements, the Commission is specifying the same effective date for both as June 1, 1998. All new registration statements or post-effective amendments that are annual updates to effective registration statements filed after December 1, 1998 must comply with the amendments to Form N-1A. The final compliance date for filing amendments to effective registration statements to conform with the new Form N-1A requirements is December 1, 1999. See Form N-1A Release, supra note 1.

135 15 U.S.C. 77b(b). See also section 2(c) of the Investment Company Act (15 U.S.C. 80a-2(c)).

136 Profile Proposing Release, supra note 6.

137 44 U.S.C. 3501, et seq.

A Plain English Handbook

How to create clear SEC disclosure documents

By the Office of Investor Education and Assistance
U.S. Securities and Exchange Commission
450 5th Street, N.W.
Washington, DC 20549
August 1998

This handbook shows how you can use well-established techniques for writing in plain English to create clearer and more informative disclosure documents. We are publishing this handbook only for your general information. Of course, when drafting a document for filing with the SEC, you must make sure it meets all legal requirements.

Acknowledgments

Nancy M. Smith
Director, Office of Investor Education and Assistance

This handbook reflects the work, ideas, and generosity of many individuals and organizations at the SEC and in the private sector.

At the SEC, staff in the Divisions of Corporation Finance and Investment Management, the Offices of Public Affairs and General Counsel, and the Chairman's Office provided insightful comments. In particular, Commissioner Isaac C. Hunt Jr., Nick Balamaci, Barry Barbash, Gregg Corso, Brian Lane, Diane Sanger, Jennifer Scardino, Michael Schlein, Heidi Stam, and Tony Vertuno offered invaluable advice and guidance.

Corporate officials and lawyers enthusiastically helped us to breathe life into our plain English initiatives and this handbook. The Society of Corporate Secretaries, the American Bar Association, and The Bond Market Association invited us to conduct workshops where we tested much of the information in the handbook. Kathleen Gibson, Peggy Foran, Susan Wolf, Bruce Bennett, Jim McKenzie, Jeff Klauder, Fred Green, Mark Howard, Pierre de Saint Phalle, Richard M. Phillips, and Alan J. Davis contributed mightily to our efforts.

Special thanks to Warren Buffett for his support and preface, to Ken Morris of Lightbulb Press, and to the talented staff at Siegel & Gale. I am especially grateful to the staff of my office for giving me the time and support I needed to work on the handbook.

Three people poured their hearts and minds into this handbook from the start: Ann Wallace, from the Division of Corporation Finance; Carolyn Miller, formerly of Siegel & Gale and now with the SEC; and William Lutz, author and Professor of English at Rutgers University. All of the credit and none of the blame goes to them.

And finally, many thanks to Chairman Arthur Levitt, who made it all possible by putting plain English at the top of his agenda so that investors might better understand their investments. •

Table of Contents

Preface

by Warren E. Buffett

This handbook, and Chairman Levitt's whole drive to encourage "plain English" in disclosure documents, are good news for me. For more than forty years, I've studied the documents that public companies file. Too often, I've been unable to decipher just what is being said or, worse yet, had to conclude that nothing was being said. If corporate lawyers and their clients follow the advice in this handbook, my life is going to become much easier.

There are several possible explanations as to why I and others sometimes stumble over an accounting note or indenture description. Maybe we simply don't have the technical knowledge to grasp what the writer wishes to convey. Or perhaps the writer doesn't understand what he or she is talking about. In some cases, moreover, I suspect that a less-than-scrupulous issuer doesn't want us to understand a subject it feels legally obligated to touch upon.

Perhaps the most common problem, however, is that a well-intentioned and informed writer simply fails to get the message across to an intelligent, interested reader. In that case, stilted jargon and complex constructions are usually the villains.

This handbook tells you how to free yourself of those impediments to effective communication. Write as this handbook instructs you and you will be amazed at how much smarter your readers will think you have become.

One unoriginal but useful tip: Write with a specific person in mind. When writing Berkshire Hathaway's annual report, I pretend that I'm talking to my sisters. I have no trouble picturing them: Though highly intelligent, they are not experts in accounting or finance. They will understand plain English, but jargon may puzzle them. My goal is simply to give them the information I would wish them to supply me if our positions were reversed. To succeed, I don't need to be Shakespeare; I must, though, have a sincere desire to inform.

No siblings to write to? Borrow mine: Just begin with "Dear Doris and Bertie." •

Introduction

by Arthur Levitt
Chairman, U.S. Securities and Exchange Commission

Investors need to read and understand disclosure documents to benefit fully from the protections offered by our federal securities laws. Because many investors are neither lawyers, accountants, nor investment bankers, we need to start writing disclosure documents in a language investors can understand: plain English.

The shift to plain English requires a new style of thinking and writing, whether you work at a company, a law firm, or the U.S. Securities and Exchange Commission. We must question whether the documents we are used to writing highlight the important information investors need to make informed decisions. The legalese and jargon of the past must give way to everyday words that communicate complex information clearly.

The good news is that more and more companies and lawyers are using plain English and filing documents with the SEC that others can study, use, and improve upon. With the SEC's plain English rules in place, every prospectus will have its cover page, summary, and risk factors in plain English.

The benefits of plain English abound. Investors will be more likely to understand what they are buying and to make informed judgments about whether they should hold or sell their investments. Brokers and investment advisers can make better recommendations to their clients if they can read and understand these documents quickly and easily.

Companies that communicate successfully with their investors form stronger relationships with them. These companies save the costs of explaining legalese and dealing with confused and sometimes angry investors. Lawyers reviewing plain English documents catch and correct mistakes more easily. Many companies have switched to plain English because it's a good business decision. They see the value of communicating with their investors rather than sending them impenetrable documents. And as we depend more and more on the Internet and electronic delivery of documents, plain English versions will be easier to read electronically than legalese.

The SEC's staff has created this handbook to help speed and smooth the transition to plain English. It includes proven tips from those in the private sector who have already created plain English disclosure documents. This handbook reflects their substantial contributions and those of highly regarded experts in the field who were our consultants on this project, Dr. William Lutz at Rutgers University and the firm of Siegel & Gale in New York City.

But I hasten to add that the SEC has not cornered the market on plain English advice. Our rules and communications need as strong a dose of plain English as any disclosure document. This handbook gives you some ideas on what has worked for others, but use whatever works for you.

No matter what route you take to plain English, we want you to produce documents that fulfill the promise of our securities laws. I urge you —in long and short documents, in prospectuses and shareholder reports—to speak to investors in words they can understand. Tell them plainly what they need to know to make intelligent investment decisions. •

1

What Is a "Plain English" Document?

We'll start by dispelling a common misconception about plain English writing. It does not mean deleting complex information to make the document easier to understand. For investors to make informed decisions, disclosure documents must impart complex information. Using plain English assures the orderly and clear presentation of complex information so that investors have the best possible chance of understanding it.

Plain English means analyzing and deciding what information investors need to make informed decisions, before words, sentences, or paragraphs are considered. A plain English document uses words economically and at a level the audience can understand. Its sentence structure is tight. Its tone is welcoming and direct. Its design is visually appealing. A plain English document is easy to read and looks like it's meant to be read.

This handbook's purpose

This handbook gives you practical tips on how to create plain English documents. All of these were born of experience. They come from experts and those who have already written or rewritten their documents in plain English.

As with all the advice in this handbook, feel free to tailor these tips to your schedule, your document, and your budget. Not all of the tips will apply to everyone or to every document. Pick and choose the ones that make sense for you.

Some of our tips cover very basic mechanical issues, like how to photocopy your working draft. We've included them because they were learned the hard way and have saved people time, money, and aggravation. You'll see them listed in Chapter 8, titled "Time-Saving Tips."

This handbook is by no means the last word on plain English. We expect to change it and add more tips as we learn more about writing securities documents in plain English. So please keep notes on your experiences and copies of your original and rewritten language. We want to hear from you and include your tips and rewrites in the next edition.

Finally, we encourage you to give this handbook out freely. It is not copyrighted, so you can photocopy it without fear of penalty. •

2

Getting Started

Assemble the team or move ahead on your own

As with a lot of things in life, it's the preparation that often determines the success or failure of an effort to write documents in plain English. Many of you routinely select a team to think and talk about how to write a document from scratch or rewrite an existing document. Or you may do it on your own. In that case, rest assured that one person can do it alone.

The list below describes the types of people who have participated in successful plain English teams. *We're not suggesting that you need to select everyone listed.* Some will not apply to your company or your situation. The people you select, and the point at which you involve them in your plain English project, will depend on your document, your schedule, and your budget.

- **A team leader** who has the authority to make decisions that keep the project moving forward and bring it to a successful conclusion. (More than one plain English project has faltered because the team leader has not had this level of authority.) The team leader may be a company's or an underwriter's lawyer.
- **A lead writer** who ensures the document uses a logical structure and simple, clear language. If more than one person is drafting sections of the document, the lead writer makes sure the final draft has a consistent tone and the individual parts form a coherent whole.
- **Lawyers for the company or the underwriter** who know what information must be included and why.

- **An investor relations expert** who knows firsthand the financial sophistication of your investors. Investor relations people know which questions investors typically ask and where past disclosure documents have failed to make information clear.

- **A compliance officer** who can lend guidance to the writer and who knows, along with your lawyers, what information must be included.

- **A production and operations person** who understands the mechanics and costs of printing and mailing your document, so that your improved document doesn't get ahead of your in-house capabilities or budget.

- **A marketing person** who may have market survey research or polls on your investors. Also, the marketing department is usually attuned to the terminology that your investors can readily understand.

- **An information designer** who is a graphic designer trained to work closely with the writers and to think about how to present complex information visually.

Select documents

You may want to consider these issues as you start writing in plain English:

- How long is the document?
- Will you write all of it, or only sections of it, in plain English?
- How much time do you have before you need to file your document?

You will also want to gather and distribute other documents that your company has written for investors. It's likely that your company has already used plain English in its glossy annual reports and other communications prepared especially for investors. These documents may save you time by showing you the type of language your company is already comfortable using. •

3

Knowing Your Audience

Knowing your audience is the most important step in assuring that your document is understandable to your current or prospective investors. To write understandable documents, you need to gauge the financial sophistication of your investors.

Through polls and other market survey research tools, some companies know the demographics of their investors well. Other companies rely on their investor relations staff or their underwriters to describe who has bought, or is likely to buy, their securities.

Using whatever information is available, you can create a profile of your investors or prospective investors based on the following questions:

- What are their demographics—age, income, level of education, and job experience?
- How familiar are they with investments and financial terminology?
- What investment concepts can you safely assume they understand?
- How will they read the document for the first time? Will they read it straight through or skip around to the sections that interest them?
- Will they read your document and your competitors' side by side?
- How will they use the document while they own the security? What information will they be looking for later, and is it easy to find?

Your investors or prospective investors may include individuals and institutions with varying degrees of financial sophistication. While your audience will include analysts and other industry experts, you may want to keep in mind that your least sophisticated investors have the greatest need for a disclosure document they can understand. Some companies have faced the differing needs of their investors and other audiences by making basic educational information visually distinctive from the rest of the text so that sophisticated investors can easily recognize and scan it.

Once you've drawn a profile of your investors, keep it constantly in mind. Some writers keep a photo of a typical investor to make sure they don't lose sight of their readers.

After analyzing who your investors are, you can turn to the document you want to write or rewrite. •

4

Knowing the Information You Need to Disclose

The steps outlined in this section have been used successfully by others who have written disclosure documents in plain English. As we said earlier, feel free to tailor these steps to your own schedule and team. This is one approach if you are rewriting an existing document, but others may work equally well.

Read and outline the current document

Read the entire document once without making any notes or comments on the text. This should give you a general understanding of the information covered in the document and make your next read more productive.

When you read it the second time, make notes on what information is covered and any questions you have. Your notes will also help you to assess if information flows through your document in a logical order.

As you read, consider the following:

- Will the investors understand the language?
- Does the document highlight information that is important to investors?
- Is any important information missing?
- Does the document include information that is not legally required and will not help investors make informed decisions?

Meet to resolve questions

Meet with the authors of the original document or others who understand it and any members of the team who can help to answer the questions you wrote in the margins. Besides the obvious reason for the meeting, another more important goal is

to question the need for everything that appears in the document.

"Because it's always been there" is not reason enough to keep it in your draft. Since much of the language in these documents is recycled from older (or another company's) documents, often no one knows who initially wrote it or why it is needed now. If you've done your legal research and no one knows why the information is important or required, consider taking it out.

Eliminate redundant information

Question the need for repeating any information. Reading the same material two or three times can bore and even trouble readers. Most readers skip over paragraphs if they think they've read them before. If you cut down on repetitious paragraphs or sentences, you'll not only earn the gratitude of your reader, you'll reduce printing and mailing costs.

Discuss the cover page and the summary

A cover page should be an introduction, an inviting entryway into your document, giving investors some key facts about your offering, but not telling everything all at once. If it looks dense and overgrown with thorny details, no one will want to pick it up and start reading. If it looks like a legal document written *by* lawyers and *for* lawyers, many investors will not even attempt to read it.

To create an inviting cover page, you'll need to strip away much of what is conventionally placed there, but which is not required.

As you review your cover page, question why each item of information is there. It may be important, but does it have to be on the cover page? You usually have a substantial document following the cover page—let some of those other pages carry the information load in logical order.

What would be helpful for investors to see on this page? Look through your investors' eyes and you'll make better decisions about where to place information.

The same goes for the summary. A summary should orient the reader, highlighting the most important points that are presented in greater detail in the prospectus. Many summaries now seem as long as the document itself and consist merely of paragraphs copied straight from the body of the document.

Use defined terms sparingly

Although customary, introducing defined terms on the cover page and in the summary discourages many readers from getting beyond the first pages. Overwhelmed with memorizing a new and unnatural vocabulary, and bothered by constantly having to flip back and hunt for the first time a defined term's definition appears, many an investor will not stick with the document. One plain English expert has advised, don't let a shortcut for the writer become a roadblock for the reader. •

5

Reorganizing the Document

A few principles of good organization apply universally.

First, present the big picture before the details. Prospectuses routinely start with a detailed description of the securities. You may read pages before you find out what the company produces, or why it is merging or spinning off a subsidiary. It's hard to absorb the details if you don't know why they are being given to you. Imagine trying to put together a complicated jigsaw puzzle without first seeing the picture of the completed puzzle. An individual piece of information means more to your readers if they know how it fits into the big picture.

Second, use descriptive headers and subheaders to break your document up into manageable sections. Prospectuses impart a lot of information. If you present the information in bite-sized pieces, it's easier to digest. Make sure your headings tell the reader what the upcoming sections will cover. Headings like "general" or "background" aren't especially helpful.

Third, always group related information together. This helps you identify and eliminate repetitious information.

Fourth, your audience's degree of investment expertise will affect how you organize the document. If you are writing for financially unsophisticated investors, your document's overall organization may take an educational approach. You may need to explain industry terms or concepts where they first appear.

Fifth, review your document by taking a good look at the flow of information from beginning to end. Start making decisions on how the content should be moved around into a new and logical order based on:

- the audience profile
- the notes you made in the margins
- the decisions you've made on your cover page and summary
- the information you've learned in answering your questions

Once you have finished physically reorganizing the document, you may want to write an outline of your new organization. Your outline can later become your table of contents.

You're now ready to start rewriting your document in plain English.

And, speaking of writing... •

6

Writing in Plain English

We thought it would be helpful to list the most common problems we've encountered with disclosure documents.

Common problems

- Long sentences
- Passive voice
- Weak verbs
- Superfluous words
- Legal and financial jargon
- Numerous defined terms
- Abstract words
- Unnecessary details
- Unreadable design and layout

In the following pages we offer some ways to fix these problems.

For example, here's a common sentence found in prospectuses:

> NO PERSON HAS BEEN AUTHORIZED TO GIVE ANY INFORMATION OR MAKE ANY REPRESENTATION OTHER THAN THOSE CONTAINED OR INCORPORATED BY REFERENCE IN THIS JOINT PROXY STATEMENT/PROSPECTUS, AND, IF GIVEN OR MADE, SUCH INFORMATION OR REPRESENTATION MUST NOT BE RELIED UPON AS HAVING BEEN AUTHORIZED.

Here's one possible plain English rewrite:

> You should rely only on the information contained in this document or that we have referred you to. We have not authorized anyone to provide you with information that is different.

The plain English rewrite uses everyday words, short sentences, active voice, regular print, and personal pronouns that speak directly to the reader.

Do you think the rewrite captures the meaning of the original? Would you write it differently?

Throughout this chapter, you'll find "before" examples from disclosure documents with plain English "after" examples to illustrate specific principles of plain English. Since some of the "before" examples contain ambiguities that can be successfully resolved only by studying their context in a particular document, we did not attempt to provide rewrites to cover every interpretation. We encourage you to write your own plain English versions to fit your views and your needs. We don't want to create a new generation of plain English "boilerplate."

Although the principles that follow may sound deceptively simple, if you use them, your writing will improve dramatically.

Use the active voice with strong verbs

The plodding verbosity of most disclosure documents makes readers yearn for clear words and short sentences. The quickest fix lies in using the active voice with strong verbs. Strong verbs are guaranteed to liven up and tighten any sentence, virtually causing information to spring from the page. When you start to rewrite or edit your work, highlighting all the verbs can help. You may be surprised by the number of weak verbs, especially forms of "to be" or "to have" that you'll find.

The time you spend searching for a precise and strong verb is time well spent. When a verb carries more meaning, you can dispense with many of the words used to bolster weak verbs.

Weak verbs keep frequent company with two more grammatical undesirables: passive voice and hidden verbs. In tandem, they add unnecessary length and confusion to a sentence.

The active and passive voices

If you need it, here's a quick refresher on the active and passive voice.

> **active**
> The investor buys the stock.

In the active voice, the subject of the sentence, the investor, performs the action, buying the stock.

> **passive**
> The stock is bought by the investor.

In the passive voice the subject, the stock, is acted upon. The person or the thing doing the action is introduced with "by." But sometimes, the person or thing doing the action is deleted, leading to...

> **passive with agent deleted**
> The stock is bought.

You don't know who bought the stock. You'll find many examples of the "passive with agent deleted" in disclosure documents.

Readers understand sentences in the active voice more quickly and easily because it follows how we think and process information. Many times the passive voice forces readers to take extra mental steps as they convert the passive into the active.

To recognize the passive voice, ask yourself:

Does the sentence use a form of the verb "to be" with:

- another verb in the past tense; and
- a prepositional phrase beginning with "by"?

Remember that it's harder to recognize the passive voice when the object (the phrase introduced with "by") is left out. When you rewrite the sentence in the active voice, use a strong verb. These examples show how strong verbs and the active voice transform sentences, making them shorter and easier to understand.

before
The foregoing Fee Table **is intended** to assist investors in understanding the costs and expenses that a shareholder in the Fund will bear directly or indirectly.

The before example uses the passive with agent deleted. We don't know who "intended" to assist investors. Note how long it took to get to the meat of the sentence—the costs and expenses. Dispensing with the filler words "...to assist investors in understanding..." moves the reader more quickly to the important points.

after
This table describes the fees and expenses that you may pay if you buy and hold shares of the fund.

Here's another example:

before
The proxies solicited hereby for the Heartland Meeting **may be revoked,** subject to the procedures described herein, at any time up to and including the date of the Heartland Meeting.

after
You may revoke your proxy and reclaim your right to vote up to and including the day of the meeting by following the directions on page 10.

The plain English version tells you who may revoke a proxy and where to find the information on how to do it. It replaces the abstract "subject to the procedures described herein" with concrete, everyday words, "by following the directions on page 10." It's not enough merely to translate existing texts—the key is to add useful information.

Don't ban the passive voice, use it sparingly

As with all the advice in this handbook, we are presenting guidelines, not hard and fast rules you must always follow. The passive voice may make sense when the person or thing performing the action is of secondary importance to another subject that should play the starring role in sentence. Use the passive voice only when you have a very good reason for doing so. When in doubt, choose the active voice.

Find hidden verbs

Does the sentence use any form of the verbs "to be," "to have," or another weak verb, with a noun that could be turned into a strong verb? In these sentences, the strong verb lies hidden in a nominalization, a noun derived from a verb that usually ends in-*tion*. Find the noun and try to make it the main verb of the sentence. As you change nouns to verbs, your writing becomes more vigorous and less abstract.

before	after
We made an **application**...	We **applied**...
We made a **determination**...	We **determined**...
We will make a **distribution**...	We will **distribute**...

before

We will provide appropriate **information** to shareholders concerning...

after

We will **inform** shareholders about...

before

We will have no stock **ownership** of the company.

after

We will not **own** the company's stock.

before

There is the possibility of prior Board **approval** of these investments.

after

The Board might **approve** these investments in advance.

Try personal pronouns

No matter how sophisticated your audience is, if you use personal pronouns the clarity of your writing will dramatically improve. Here's why.

First, personal pronouns aid your reader's comprehension because they clarify what applies to your reader and what applies to you.

Second, they allow you to "speak" directly to your reader, creating an appealing tone that will keep your reader reading.

Third, they help you to avoid abstractions and to use more concrete and everyday language.

Fourth, they keep your sentences short.

Fifth, first- and second-person pronouns aren't gender-specific, allowing you to avoid the "he or she" dilemma. The pronouns to use are first-person plural (we, us, our/ours) and second-person singular (you, your/yours).

Observe the difference between these two examples:

before

This Summary does not purport to be complete and is qualified in its entirety by the more detailed information contained in the Proxy Statement and the Appendices hereto, all of which should be carefully reviewed.

after

Because this is a summary, it does not contain all the information that may be important to you. You should read the entire proxy statement and its appendices carefully before you decide how to vote.

Bring abstractions down to earth

Abstractions abound in the financial industry. What pictures form in your mind when you read these phrases: mutual fund, the Dow Jones Industrial Average, zero coupon bond, call option, or foreign currency trading? Most people don't have an image in their minds when they hear abstract words like these. And yet, it's far easier to comprehend a concept or a situation when your mind can form images.

In a study conducted at Carnegie-Mellon University, a cognitive psychologist and an English professor discovered that readers faced with complex written information frequently resorted to creating "scenarios" in an effort to understand the text. That is, they often made an abstract concept understandable by using it in a hypothetical situation in which *people performed actions.*

You can make complex information more understandable by giving your readers an example using one investor. This technique explains why "question and answer" formats often succeed when a narrative, abstract discussion fails.

Here is an example of how this principle can be used to explain an abstract concept—call options:

> For example, you can buy an option from Mr. Smith that gives you the right to buy 100 shares of stock X from him at $25.00 per share anytime between now and six weeks from now. You believe stock X's purchase price will go up between now and then. He believes it will stay the same or go down. If you exercise this option before it expires, Mr. Smith must sell you 100 shares of stock X at $25.00 per share, even if the purchase price has gone up. Either way, whether you exercise your option or not, he keeps the money you paid him for the option.

Although it is impossible to eliminate all abstractions from writing, always use a more concrete term when you can.

Read this list of progressively less abstract terms and consider how you might make abstract concepts you write about more concrete:

> Asset ➡ Investment ➡ Security ➡ Equity ➡ Stock ➡
> ➡ Common stock ➡ One share of IBM common stock

The following examples show how you can replace abstract terms with more concrete ones and increase your reader's comprehension:

> **before**
> Sandyhill Basic Value Fund, Inc. (the "Fund") seeks **capital appreciation** and, secondarily, income by investing in securities, primarily equities, that management of the Fund believes are **undervalued** and therefore represent **basic investment value.**
>
> **after**
> At the Sandyhill Basic Value Fund, we will strive to increase the value of your shares (capital appreciation) and, to a lesser extent, to provide income (dividends). We will invest primarily in undervalued stocks, meaning those selling for low prices given the financial strength of the companies.

> **before**
> No **consideration** or **surrender** of Beco Stock will be required of shareholders of Beco in return for the shares of Unis Common Stock **issued pursuant to the Distribution.**
>
> **after**
> You will not have to turn in your shares of Beco stock or pay any money to receive your shares of Unis common stock from the spin-off.

Omit superfluous words

Words are superfluous when they can be replaced with fewer words that mean the same thing. Sometimes you can use a simpler word for these phrases:

superfluous	**simpler**
in order to	to
in the event that	if
subsequent to	after
prior to	before
despite the fact that	although
because of the fact that	because, since
in light of	because, since
owing to the fact that	because, since

Another source of superfluous words is "shotgunning": letting loose a blast of words hoping at least one conveys your intended meaning. The simplest solution here is to replace your laundry list of adjectives with a single word or phrase that adequately expresses your intended meaning.

Omitting superfluous words is one of the easiest ways to improve your disclosure document because it doesn't require you to revise sentence structure.

before
The following summary **is intended only** to highlight certain information **contained elsewhere** in this Prospectus.

after
This summary highlights some information from this Prospectus.

before
Machine Industries and Great Tools, Inc. **are each subject to the information requirements of the Securities Exchange Act of 1934, as amended (the "Exchange Act"), and in accordance therewith** file reports, proxy statements and other information with the Securities and Exchange Commission (the "Commission").

after
We file annual, quarterly, and special reports, proxy statements, and other information with the Securities and Exchange Commission (SEC).

before

Drakecorp has **filed** with the Internal Revenue Service **a tax ruling request concerning, among other things,** the tax **consequences** of the Distribution to the United States holders of Drakecorp Stock. It is expected **that the Distribution of Beco Common Stock to the shareholders of Drakecorp** will be tax-free **to such shareholders** for federal income tax **purposes,** except **to the extent** that cash is received for fractional share **interests.**

after

While we expect that this transaction will be tax free for U.S. shareholders at the federal level (except for any cash paid for fractional shares), we have asked the Internal Revenue Service to rule that it is.

Write in the "positive"

Positive sentences are shorter and easier to understand than their negative counterparts. For example:

before
Persons other than the primary beneficiary may not receive these dividends.

after
Only the primary beneficiary may receive these dividends.

Also, your sentences will be shorter and easier to understand if you replace a negative phrase with a single word that means the same thing. For example:

negative compound	single word
not able	unable
not accept	reject
not certain	uncertain
not unlike	similar, alike
does not have	lacks
does not include	excludes, omits
not many	few
not often	rarely
not the same	different
not ... unless	only if
not ... except	only if
not ... until	only when

Use short sentences

No one likes to read a sentence that's two pages long. And yet, lengthy, information-packed sentences choke many prospectuses today. To complicate matters further, these sentences are filled with jargon and legalese. The longer and more complex a sentence, the harder it is for readers to understand any single portion of it.

before

The following description encompasses all the material terms and provisions of the Notes offered hereby and supplements, and to the extent inconsistent therewith replaces, the description of the general terms and provisions of the Debt Securities (as defined in the accompanying Prospectus) set forth under the heading "Description of Debt Securities" in the Prospectus, to which description reference is hereby made. The following description will apply to each Note unless otherwise specified in the applicable Pricing Supplement.

If you really want to root out the problem with this paragraph, you need to think of the deeper reasons why it doesn't work. If you look beyond the language used, you'll find that it presents complex information without first providing a context for the reader.

The rewrites that follow show two ways to provide the context, with and without tabulation.

after

We provide information to you about our notes in three separate documents that progressively provide more detail: 1) the prospectus, 2) the prospectus supplement, and 3) the pricing supplement. Since the terms of specific notes may differ from the general information we have provided, in all cases rely on information in the pricing supplement over different information in the prospectus and the prospectus supplement; and rely on this prospectus supplement over different information in the prospectus.

or

We provide information to you about our notes in three separate documents that progressively provide more detail:

1 The Prospectus
General information that may or may not apply to each note.

2 The Prospectus Supplement
More specific than the prospectus, and to the extent information differs from the prospectus, rely on the different information in this document.

3 The Pricing Supplement
Provides final details about a specific note including its price. To the extent information differs from the prospectus or the prospectus supplement, rely on the different information in this document.

Information-packed sentences leave most investors scratching their heads. So many of these sentences have become "boilerplate" that writers cut and paste them into new documents without thinking about how they can be improved. Since these sentences can be a little intimidating, we thought we'd tackle another one:

before

The Drake Capital Corporation (the "Company") may offer from time to time its Global Medium-Term Notes, Series A, Due from 9 months to 60 Years From Date of Issue, which are issuable in one or more series (the "Notes"), in the United States in an aggregate principal amount of up to U.S. $6,428,598,500, or the equivalent thereof in other currencies, including composite currencies such as the European Currency Unit (the "ECU") (provided that, with respect to Original Issue Discount Notes (as defined under "Description of Notes—Original Issue Discount Notes"), the initial offering price of such Notes shall be used in calculating the aggregate principal amount of Notes offered hereunder).

after

The Drake Capital Corporation may offer at various times up to U.S. $6,428,598,500 worth of Global Medium-term notes. These notes will mature from 9 months to 60 years after the date they are purchased. We will offer these notes in series, starting with Series A, and in U.S., foreign, and composite currencies, like the European Currency Unit. If we offer original issue discount notes, we will use their initial offering prices to calculate when we reach $6,428,598,500.

As you can see, one long sentence became four shorter sentences. The paragraph moves from the general to the specific, contains short, common words, and is written in the active voice. You only need to read the paragraph once to understand it.

Replace jargon and legalese with short, common words

Ruthlessly eliminate jargon and legalese. Instead, use short, common words to get your points across. In those instances where there is no plain English alternative, explain what the term means when you first use it.

If you have been in the financial or legal industry for awhile, it may be hard to spot jargon and legalese in your writing. Consider asking someone outside the industry to check your work for incomprehensible words.

Last, don't create new jargon that's unique to your document in the form of acronyms or other words. It's asking too much of your readers to memorize a new vocabulary while they are trying to understand complicated concepts. This holds true for individual and institutional investors. Note the following, which is the first sentence on the cover page of an exchange offer:

> NLR Insured Mortgage Association, Inc., a Delaware corporation ("NLR MAE"), which is an actively managed, infinite life, New York Stock Exchange-listed real estate investment trust ("REIT"), and PAL Liquidating REIT, Inc., a newly formed, finite life, self-liquidating Delaware corporation which intends to qualify as a REIT ("PAL Liquidating REIT"), hereby jointly offer, upon the terms and subject to the conditions set forth herein and in the related Letters of Transmittal (collectively, the "Offer"), to exchange (i) shares of NLR MAE's Common Stock, par value $.01 per share ("NLR MAE Shares"), or, at the option of Unitholders, shares of PAL Liquidating REIT's Common Stock, par value $.01 per share ("PAL Liquidating REIT Shares"), and (ii) the right to receive cash payable 60 days after closing on the first of any Acquisitions (as defined below) but in no event later than 270 days (nine months) following consummation of the Offer (the "Deferred Cash Payment"), for all outstanding Limited Partnership Interests and Depository Units of Limited Partnership Interest (collectively, "Units") in each of PAL Insured Mortgage Investors, a California limited partnership ("PAL 84"), PAL Insured Mortgage Investors - Series 85, A California Limited Partnership, a California limited partnership ("PAL 85"), and PAL Insured Mortgage Investors L.P. - Series 86, a Delaware limited partnership ("PAL 86"). See "THE OFFER."

This sentence suffers from many shortcomings. It's long and laden with defined terms and other data that mask the fundamental information: the two companies are offering to exchange their stock for the investors' limited partnership holdings. Some of the information, such as par value and places of incorporation, can be moved to another part of the document. Much of the language modifies the subjects and the objects: this language, too, can be moved to a separate sentence or another section of the prospectus.

This example shows the hazards of creating unfamiliar acronyms. They provide false economies, especially when they are introduced on the cover page and in the first pages of the prospectus. They may save a few words, but they may also frustrate and force the reader to take more time and effort to understand the document. Where acronyms, such as REIT, are widely understood to the investing public, they can safely be used without creating confusion.

Occasionally, it's necessary to assign a shorter word to a long proper noun and use this word throughout the rest of the document. In these rare instances, try to choose a word that has an intuitive, logical relationship to the one it's replacing. This reduces the number of new words or phrases the reader needs to memorize to understand the document.

Choose the simpler synonym

Surround complex ideas with short, common words. For example, use *end* instead of *terminate, explain* rather than *elucidate,* and *use* instead of *utilize.* When a shorter, simpler synonym exists, use it.

Keep the subject, verb, and object close together

Short, simple sentences enhance the effectiveness of short, common words. We've covered a number of guidelines for writing shorter sentences, but there are a few more you can use to streamline your writing further.

To be clear, sentences must have a sound structure. Here are a few ways to ensure yours do.

The natural word order of English speakers is *subject-verb-object*. Your sentences will be clearer if you follow this order as closely as possible. In disclosure documents, this order is frequently interrupted by modifiers. For example:

before

Holders of the Class A and Class B-1 certificates **will be entitled to receive** on each Payment Date, to the extent monies are available therefor (but not more than the Class A Certificate Balance or Class B-1 Certificate Balance then outstanding), **a distribution.**

after

Class A and Class B-1 certificate **holders will receive a distribution** on each payment date if cash is available on those dates for their class.

before

The following description of the particular terms of the Notes offered hereby (referred to in the accompanying Prospectus as the "Debt Securities") **supplements, and** to the extent inconsistent therewith **replaces, the description** of the general terms and provisions of the Debt Securities set forth **in the Prospectus**, to which description reference is hereby made.

after

This document describes the terms of these notes in greater detail than our prospectus, and may provide information that differs from our prospectus. If the information does differ from our prospectus, please rely on the information in this document.

Write using "if-then" conditionals

Conditional statements are very common in disclosure documents—although they are rarely written that way. When we rewrote the last example as a conditional, we followed the natural English word order very closely. That's why the sentence is easier to read.

Here are four rules of thumb to help you write conditional statements effectively:

- **One "if," one "then"** When there is only one *if* and one *then*, starting with the *if* may spare some of your readers from having to read the rest of the sentence. In these cases, the *if* clause defines who or what the "then" clause applies to.

  If you invested in Class A shares, then...

- **One "if," multiple "thens"** When there is only one *if* and more than one *then*, start with the *if* and tabulate the *thens*.

- **Multiple "ifs," one "then"** When there is only one *then* and more than one *if*, start with the *then* and tabulate the *ifs*.

- **Multiples "ifs" and "thens"** When there is more than one *if* and more than one *then*, you'll probably need to break it down into more than one sentence, taking care to specify which *ifs* apply to which *thens*. If the information is still unclear, consider presenting the information in a table.

Keep your sentence structure parallel

A long sentence often fails without a parallel structure. Parallelism simply means ensuring a list or series of items is presented using parallel parts of speech, such as nouns or verbs. Note the quotation in the margin.

In this section, we've shown each parallel structure we've used in bold.

Here's an example from a mutual fund prospectus that lacks parallel structure:

before

If you want to buy shares in Fund X by mail, **fill out** and **sign** the Account Application form, **making** your check payable to "The X Fund," and **put** your social security or taxpayer identification number on your check.

after

If you want to buy shares in Fund X by mail, **fill out** and **sign** the Account Application form, **make** your check payable to "The X Fund," and **put** your social security or taxpayer identification number on your check.

Here is a more subtle example from another mutual fund prospectus:

before

We invest the Fund's assets in short-term money market securities **to provide** you with **liquidity**, **protection** of your investment, and **high** current income.

This sentence is unparallel because its series is made up of two nouns and an adjective before the third noun. It's also awkward because the verb *provide* is too closely paired with the nominalization *protection*.

One logical revision to the original sentence is to change the noun series to a verb series.

after

We invest in short-term money market securities **to provide** you with liquidity, **to protect** your investment, and **to generate** high current income.

All writers, regardless of their degree of expertise, occasionally write unparallel sentences. The best way to rid your document of them is to read through it once solely to find these mistakes. Reading your document aloud can make unparallel constructions easier to spot.

Steer clear of "respectively"

How easy is it to read the following sentence once and understand what it means?

before

The Senior Notes and the guarantee (the "Guarantee") of the Senior Notes by Island Holdings will constitute unsecured senior obligations of the Issuer and Island Holdings, respectively.

after

The senior notes are an unsecured senior obligation of the issuer, while the guarantee of the senior notes is an unsecured senior obligation of Island Holdings.

Whenever you use "respectively," you force your reader to go back and match up what belongs to what. You may be saving words by using "respectively," but your reader has to use more time and read your words twice to understand what you've written. •

7

Designing the Document

A plain English document reflects thoughtful design choices. The right design choices make a document easier to read and its information easier to understand. The wrong design choices can make even a well-written document fail to communicate.

Some documents suffer because no one knew how basic design decisions, like typeface selection, dramatically determine whether or not a document is easy to read. Other documents suffer because expensive design features give them artistic appeal, but at the cost of obscuring the text. In a plain English document, design serves the goal of communicating the information as clearly as possible.

Beginning the design process

Check with your in-house printing or graphics department—your company may have already dealt with design issues in other documents or may have skilled designers who can help you with your document. If your company or underwriter has a style manual, it typically will define a required "look" that specifies typefaces and layouts.

Since some standards or guidelines in your style manual may have been adopted when plain English was not a concern, review them to ensure they contribute to good design and ease of reading.

If you are using a designer, keep the following in mind:

- Good design requires clear communication between the writer and the designer. Keep the lines of communication open and flowing.
- Take the time to explain the nuances of your document to your designer.
- Don't move into the design phase until your text is final. Once the document is put into page layout software, or once it is at the printer, making text changes can be tedious and expensive.

If you don't have a design professional, fear not. You can apply many of the simple concepts discussed in this chapter to produce a readable, visually appealing document.

While the field of design extends broadly, this chapter covers five basic design elements and how they contribute to creating a plain English document:

- hierarchy or distinguishing levels of information
- typography
- layout
- graphics
- color

Hierarchy

Much like an outline, a document's hierarchy shows how you've organized the information and helps the reader to understand the relationship between different levels of information.

A typical hierarchy in the prospectus might include:

- the document title
- section headings (first level)
- subsection headings (second level)
- paragraph headings (third level)
- general text (fourth level)

Designers use different typefaces in the headings to distinguish these levels for the reader. As a rule of thumb, there should be no more than six levels in the document, excluding the document's title.

You can signal a new level by varying the same typeface or by using a different typeface. Here's a demonstration of how we've used different typefaces to distinguish levels in this handbook:

Section headings

Subsection headings

General text

Example headings

Typography

Although it may seem like a minor decision, your typeface selection will be one of the elements that most strongly defines the design and readability of your document.

Kinds of typefaces

Typefaces come in two varieties: serif and sans serif.

serif	**sans serif**
N	**N**

All serif typefaces have small lines at the beginning or ending strokes of each letter. Virtually all newspapers and many magazines use some form of serif type for their general text because serif fonts are easier to read than sans serif. This handbook uses a serif typeface called Scala for general text. Other popular serif typefaces are: Caslon, Century Schoolbook, Garamond, and Times. Here are some examples:

serif
This is an example of Scala.
This is an example of Caslon.
This is an example of Century Schoolbook.
This is an example of Garamond.
This is an example of Times.

Sans serif typefaces lack those small connective lines. The type used for most headings throughout this document is a sans serif typeface, Scala Sans. Franklin Gothic, Frutiger, Helvetica, and Univers are examples of sans serif typefaces.

sans serif
This is an example of Franklin Gothic.
This is an example of Frutiger.
This is an example of Helvetica.
This is an example of Univers.

Generally, serif typefaces are easier to read in documents like this than sans serif because the small connective lines of serif help to lead your eye more quickly and smoothly over text. It is best to use sans serif typefaces in small quantities—for emphasis or headings, but not for general text. Both serifs and sans serifs work well for headings.

Selecting the right typeface

When choosing a typeface, think carefully about where the typeface will appear in the document. For example, will it be general text, or will it apply to information that needs to be highlighted? Will it introduce a section?

Some typefaces are harder to read than others, and were never intended for text. Typefaces like Bodoni Poster or other bold, italic, or condensed typefaces were designed for headlines or for large display type. These examples show how difficult it is to read text in these typefaces.

Bodoni Poster

Justified text was the style for many years—we grew up on it. But there has been a great deal of research on readability (how easy something is to read) and it shows that those disruptive, inconsistent gaps between the words inhibit the flow of reading. Besides, they look dumb. Keep your eyes open as you look at professionally-printed work... and you'll find there's a very strong trend now to align type on the left and leave the right ragged.

Robin Williams, *The Mac Is Not a Typewriter*

Franklin Gothic Condensed

Justified text was the style for many years—we grew up on it. But there has been a great deal of research on readability (how easy something is to read) and it shows that those disruptive, inconsistent gaps between the words inhibit the flow of reading. Besides, they look dumb. Keep your eyes open as you look at professionally-printed work...and you'll find there's a very strong trend now to align type on the left and leave the right ragged.

Robin Williams, *The Mac Is Not a Typewriter*

You can mix different typefaces, but do so with discretion; not all typefaces work well together. Mixing a serif and sans serif, as we have done in this handbook, can look good and create a clear contrast between your levels. Mixing two serif or two sans serif typefaces can look like a mistake. As a general rule, do not use more than two typefaces in any document, not including the bold or italic versions of a typeface.

Type measurement

All typefaces are measured in points (pts). But don't assume that different typefaces in the same point size are of equal size. For example, here are four typefaces set in 11pt:

This is an example in 11pt. Franklin Gothic
This is an example in 11pt. Century Schoolbook
This is an example in 11pt. Garamond
This is an example in 11pt. Helvetica
This is an example in 11pt. Times

Choose a legible type size

A point size that is too small is difficult for everyone to read. A point size that is too large is also hard to read. Generally, type in 10pt–12pt is most common. But as you can see from the examples above, some typefaces in 11pt will strain some readers. If you have special concerns about legibility, especially for an elderly audience, you should consider using 12pt or larger.

Emphasizing text

It's common in disclosure documents to see blocks of text in bold and uppercase letters. The capitalization and bold type attempt to catch the reader's attention. Unfortunately, those capitals make the text difficult to read. All uppercase sentences usually bring the reader to a standstill because the shapes of words disappear, causing the reader to slow down and study each letter. Ironically, readers tend to skip sentences written in all uppercase.

To highlight information and maintain readability, use a different size or weight of your typeface. Try using extra white space, bold type, shading, rules, boxes, or sidebars in the margins to make information stand out. In this handbook we use dotted rules to highlight the examples. Whatever method you choose to highlight information, use it consistently throughout your document so your readers can recognize how you flag important information.

before

THE SECURITIES AND EXCHANGE COMMISSION HAS NOT APPROVED OR DISAPPROVED THESE SECURITIES OR DETERMINED IF THIS PROSPECTUS IS TRUTHFUL OR COMPLETE. ANY REPRESENTATION TO THE CONTRARY IS A CRIMINAL OFFENSE.

after

The Securities and Exchange Commission has not approved or disapproved these securities or determined if this prospectus is truthful or complete. Any representation to the contrary is a criminal offense.

after

The Securities and Exchange Commission has not approved or disapproved these securities or determined if this prospectus is truthful or complete. Any representation to the contrary is a criminal offense.

Layout

Designers think carefully about white space, column width, linespacing, and paragraph length. These design elements determine whether reading is easy or becomes too much of a physical or mental chore.

Use white space effectively

Generous use of white space on the page enhances readability, helps to emphasize important points, and lightens the overall look of the document. White space especially affects the readers of disclosure documents because these documents usually feature dense blocks of impenetrable text.

You should fight the impulse to fill up the entire page with text or graphics. A wide left or right margin can make the document easier to read. The use of white space between sections or subsections helps readers recognize which information is related.

Use left justified, ragged right text

Research shows that the easiest text to read is left justified, ragged right text. That is, the text is aligned, or flush, on the left with a loose, or ragged, right edge. The text in this handbook is set left justified, ragged right.

Fully justified text means both the right and left edges are flush, or even. When you fully justify text, the spacing between words fluctuates from line to line, causing the eye to stop and constantly readjust to the variable spacing on each line. Currently, most disclosure documents are fully justified. This, coupled with a severe shortage of white space, makes these documents visually unappealing and difficult to read.

Be especially wary of centering text, or using text to form a shape or design. Uneven margins may make a visual impact, but they make reading extremely difficult.

recommended: left justified, ragged right

Justified text was the style for many years—we grew up on it. But there has been a great deal of research on readability (how easy something is to read) and it shows that those disruptive, inconsistent gaps between the words inhibit the flow of reading. Besides, they look dumb. Keep your eyes open as you look at professionally-printed work...and you'll find there's a very strong trend now to align type on the left and leave the right ragged.

not recommended: fully justified text

Justified text was the style for many years—we grew up on it. But there has been a great deal of research on readability (how easy something is to read) and it shows that those disruptive, inconsistent gaps between the words inhibit the flow of reading. Besides, they look dumb. Keep your eyes open as you look at professionally-printed work...and you'll find there's a very strong trend now to align type on the left and leave the right ragged.

not recommended: centered text

Justified text was the style for many years—we grew up on it.
But there has been a great deal of research on readability
(how easy something is to read) and it shows that those
disruptive, inconsistent gaps between the words
inhibit the flow of reading. Besides, they look dumb.
Keep your eyes open as you look at professionally-printed
work...and you'll find there's a very strong trend now to align type
on the left and leave the right ragged.

Use linespacing to lighten the page

Linespacing, or "leading" (rhymes with sledding), refers to the amount of space between lines of text. Leading controls the density and readability of the text. Just as type is measured in points, so is leading. A type description of 12/16 means that 12pt type has been set with 4pts of additional leading between the lines. Generous leading can give a long paragraph a lighter, "airier" feeling and make it easier to read.

Avoid setting type without any additional leading (such as 10/10 or 12/12), sometimes referred to as being "set solid." Typically, you should allow *at least* 2pts of leading between lines of type. You may want to add more leading, depending on the "airiness" you would like the document to have. In this document, for ease of reading, the general text has been set at 11/16, and most examples have been set at 10/12. Review the following examples to see how leading affects readability.

11/11
Justified text was the style for many years—we grew up on it. But there has been a great deal of research on readability (how easy something is to read) and it shows that those disruptive, inconsistent gaps between the words inhibit the flow of reading. Besides, they look dumb. Keep your eyes open as you look at professionally-printed work...and you'll find there's a very strong trend now to align type on the left and leave the right ragged.

11/13
Justified text was the style for many years—we grew up on it. But there has been a great deal of research on readability (how easy something is to read) and it shows that those disruptive, inconsistent gaps between the words inhibit the flow of reading. Besides, they look dumb. Keep your eyes open as you look at professionally-printed work...and you'll find there's a very strong trend now to align type on the left and leave the right ragged.

11/15
Justified text was the style for many years—we grew up on it. But there has been a great deal of research on readability (how easy something is to read) and it shows that those disruptive, inconsistent gaps between the words inhibit the flow of reading. Besides, they look dumb. Keep your eyes open as you look at professionally-printed work...and you'll find there's a very strong trend now to align type on the left and leave the right ragged.

Keep lines to a reasonable length

A comfortable line length for most readers is 32 to 64 characters. Any longer than that, and your readers will lose their place when they read from line to line. A safe rule to follow is: the smaller the type size, the shorter the line length. This is why when you pick up any newspaper, magazine, or large book, you'll rarely see text that goes from one side of the page clear to the other, as you do in disclosure documents.

Columns also help your readers to move quickly and easily through large amounts of text. An average column width can vary from 25–40 characters. Remember to use ample white space between columns, too.

don't

Justified text was the style for many years—we grew up on it. But there has been a great deal of research on readability (how easy something is to read) and it shows that those disruptive, inconsistent gaps between the words inhibit the flow of reading. Besides, they look dumb. Keep your eyes open as you look at professionally-printed work...and you'll find there's a very strong trend now to align type on the left and leave the right ragged.

do

Justified text was the style for many years—we grew up on it. But there has been a great deal of research on readability (how easy something is to read) and it shows that those disruptive, inconsistent gaps between the words inhibit the flow of reading. Besides, they look dumb. Keep your eyes open as you look at professionally-printed work...and you'll find there's a very strong trend now to align type on the left and leave the right ragged.

do

Justified text was the style for many years—we grew up on it. But there has been a great deal of research on readability (how easy something is to read) and it shows that those disruptive, inconsistent gaps between the words inhibit the flow of reading.

Besides, they look dumb. Keep your eyes open as you look at professionally-printed work...and you'll find there's a very strong trend now to align type on the left and leave the right ragged.

Keep paragraph length relatively short

To reduce dense text, keep paragraphs as short as possible. Even though paragraph length is determined by content, here are some design tips that can help to lighten a long paragraph.

Use bullets to list information wherever possible. This makes information easier to absorb in one quick glance, as the following illustrates:

before

The funds invest mainly in the stocks of U.S. and foreign companies that are showing improved earnings and that sell at low prices relative to their cash flows or growth rates. The Fund also invests in debt, both investment grade and junk bonds, and U.S Treasury securities.

after

We invest the fund's assets in:

- stocks of U.S. and foreign companies that
  - show improved earnings, and
  - sell at low prices relative to their cash flows or growth rates;
- debt, both investment grade and junk bonds; and
- U.S. Treasuries.

Use tables to increase clarity

Use tables to increase clarity and cut down text. Tables often convey information more quickly and clearly than text. The information in this table is more easily grasped in a table than in narrative form:

before

Our investment advisory agreements cover the Growth Fund, International Fund, Muni Fund, Bond Fund, and the Money Market Fund. The effective date for agreements for the Growth Fund and the International Fund is June 1, 1993, and for the Muni Fund, Bond Fund and Money Market Fund, June 1, 1994.

after

Our Investment Advisory Agreement covers these funds:

Investment Advisory Agreement effective date	Fund name
June 1, 1993	Growth Fund International Fund
June 1, 1994	Muni Fund Bond Fund Money Market Fund

Graphics

Graphics often illuminate information more clearly and quickly than text. This section introduces some basic guidelines about using graphics in your document. To learn more, books and articles cover the topic in rich and rewarding detail. The best known work, *The Visual Display of Quantitative Information,* by Edward R. Tufte, provides practical advice on creating graphics. In the introduction of his book, he writes about the importance and value of graphics:

> *At their best, graphics are instruments for reasoning about quantitative information. Often the most effective way to describe, explore, and summarize a set of numbers—even a very large set—is to look at pictures of those numbers. Furthermore, of all methods for analyzing and communicating statistical information, well-designed data graphics are usually the simplest and at the same time the most powerful.*

On page 51 of his book, Tufte formulates a number of basic principles to follow in creating excellent graphics. Among them are these:

> *Graphical excellence is that which gives to the viewer the greatest number of ideas in the shortest time with the least ink in the smallest space.*
>
> *And graphical excellence requires telling the truth about data.*

A few experts have studied the use of graphics in securities documents, isolating the areas presenting the most problems. We can boil down their advice to these guidelines.

Keep the design simple

Keep the design of any graphic as simple as possible. Pare away any non-essential design elements so the data stands out. Think of it this way: as much of the ink as possible in a graphic should deal with a data point and not decoration. Some of the worst mistakes occur when design elements interfere with the clear presentation of information, such as needless 3-D effects, drop shadows, patterns, and excessive grid lines. Don't let a design element turn into what Tufte calls "chartjunk."

These examples show how a 3-D bar graph provides initial visual appeal, but is harder to read and understand than a straightforward presentation of the same information. The multiple lines of the 3-D bars confuse some readers because the front of the bars appear to have a lower value than the back of the bars.

before

1997 Quarterly Sales Revenue in millions

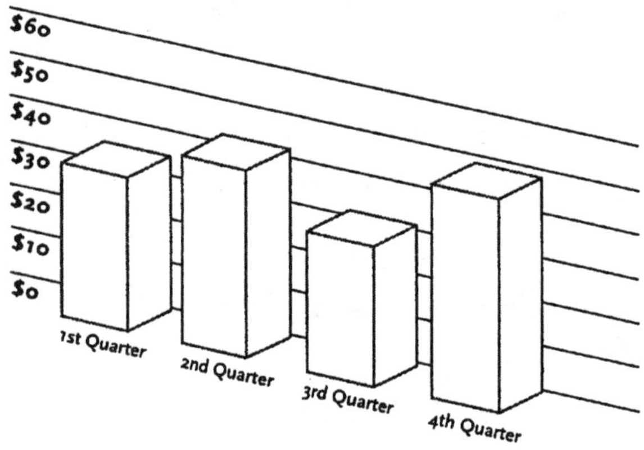

after

1997 Quarterly Sales Revenue in millions

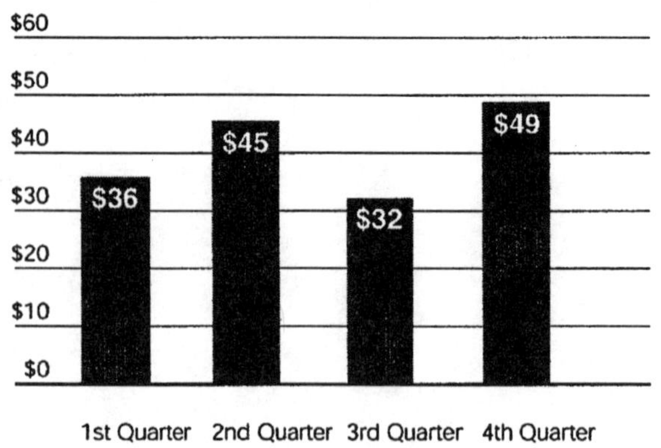

Check proportions of visuals

Generally, you should avoid graphics that start at a non-zero baseline, because they distort differences by destroying correct proportions. Compare these two bar charts to see how the non-zero baseline can mislead the reader as to the magnitude of change from quarter to quarter.

before

1997 Quarterly Sales Revenue in millions

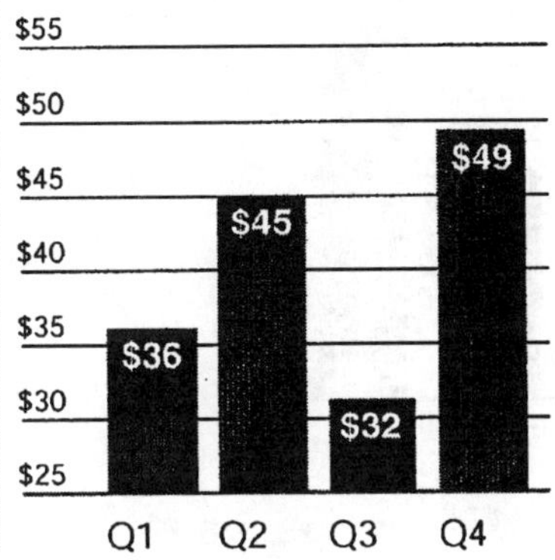

after

1997 Quarterly Sales Revenue in millions

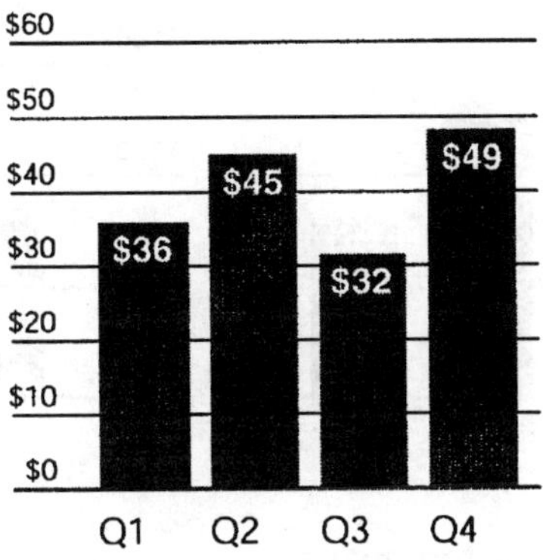

Draw graphics to scale

Any graphic should be proportionately correct or drawn to scale. For example, if you are showing an increase in oil production through a series of oil barrels in ever-increasing sizes, make sure a barrel isn't represented as 50% bigger when production only went up 25% that year.

Be consistent when grouping graphics

If you group graphics side-by-side, avoid changing your scale from one graphic to another, as in the examples above. Also, lining up three graphics that present data in billions, millions, then dollars can mislead the reader.

Don't reverse time

In graphics showing information over time, time should flow forward, not backward. In these examples, even though the first graphic is clearly labeled, it gives a false visual impression that earnings are going down over time rather than up.

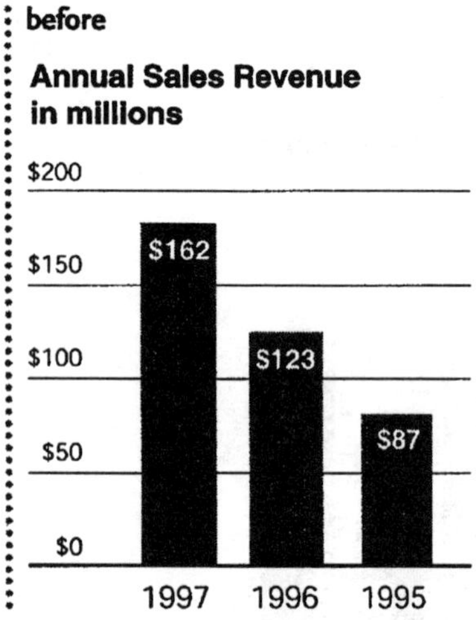

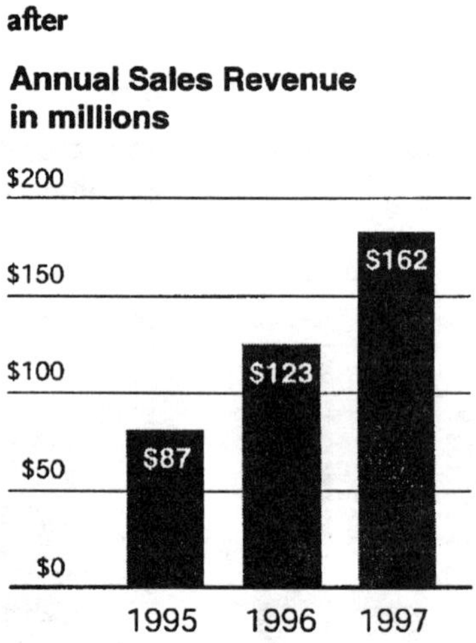

Organize data to hasten insights

Choose an organization that helps the reader grasp information and comparisons quickly. For instance, if you have a list of foreign stock markets showing their returns in one year, list them in descending order by the magnitude of their returns instead of in alphabetical order.

before

1994 Foreign Markets Total Returns in U.S. dollars	
Argentina	−23.6 %
Brazil	+64.3
Greece	+ 0.6
Hong Kong	−28.9
Indonesia	−26.3
Malaysia	−20.2
Mexico	−39.7
Philippines	− 10.1
Singapore	+ 5.8
Turkey	−50.5

after

1994 Foreign Markets Total Returns in U.S. dollars	
Brazil	+64.3 %
Singapore	+ 5.8
Greece	+ 0.6
Philippines	− 10.1
Malaysia	−20.2
Argentina	−23.6
Indonesia	−26.3
Hong Kong	−28.9
Mexico	−39.7
Turkey	−50.5

Integrate text with graphics

A graphic and its text should be together. You don't want to break your reader's concentration by separating the two, forcing your reader on a detour to another page in search of the graphic that goes with the text.

Think twice about pie charts

According to Tufte, "...the only worse design than a pie chart is several of them...." Pie charts can be useful in illustrating parts of a whole, but not when you divide the pie into more than 5 or 6 slices. Most readers find it difficult to draw accurate comparisons between pie slices or between multiple pie charts because the slices form irregular shapes. Showing the same information in a table can often be clearer.

Don't forget your typography

When choosing a typeface for text such as axis labels, consider using a sans serif typeface if the type is small and the text is short in length. If you want to insert a note or explanation directly on the graphic, use a serif font if the text is long. Continue to use upper and lowercase type for increased legibility. The guidelines for good typography we discussed earlier still apply when creating graphics.

Trust your eye

Finally, one guideline rises above all others in importance and rests squarely with you. Cultivate an appreciation of graphics and then trust your eye. If a graphic seems unclear or unhelpful to you, no matter how many "guidelines" it follows, it probably is.

Graphics communicate numbers and concepts visually. You turn to graphics when they stimulate a deeper or quicker understanding and appreciation of a situation than words alone. To create a good graphic, you must study the design critically and assess whether it conveys information honestly, accurately, and efficiently.

Color

Black is a color

The majority of your documents will be produced in black and white. When designing these documents, it's easy to forget that you are using a color: black. Since black is such a powerful color, balancing it on the page can be a tightrope act: too little emphasis can grey-out the page, too much can blacken it.

If you are using only black, your use of type is usually the way you balance the page's color. Some typefaces are heavier or lighter than others, and most type families are available in varying weights. For example:

heavy: Times Extra Bold
less heavy: Times Bold
lighter: Times Semi Bold
lighter still: Times Regular

heavy: Univers Black
less heavy: Univers Bold
lighter: Univers Regular
lighter still: Univers Light

Choosing the proper combinations of type weights will help to make your document look more inviting.

Some additional ways to introduce visual appeal to a one-color document are through:

- shading
- graphics
- rules or lines
- colored paper stocks

Again, your use of these elements should not overwhelm or distract from the legibility of your text. •

8

Time-Saving Tips

Following are some tips that have saved time for those who routinely rewrite documents in plain English:

Photocopy the document, single sided, on 11" x 17" paper (ledger paper) to 120% of its original size. This gives you room to make notes in the margins and helps to save your eyesight. Keep your original document handy. You'll use it again later.

Read through the ledger-sized copy and take notes. In the margin of each paragraph, jot down the main and supporting points. (We suggest using a pencil unless you're one of those people who does crossword puzzles in ink.) If you can't find these points too easily, it may mean the paragraph is a hodgepodge of unrelated topics.

This stage of the process can be "space-consuming." In your workspace or in a conference room, tape or tack the pages of your document to the wall. If it's too long, you may want to spread out just your outline and summary.

Then, thinking of your investors, physically move the pages into the order that makes the most sense. If only parts of pages need to be moved, cut them out and move just the parts. Remember to group like information together.

When you start to reorder your document by moving pages or parts of pages, write on the page or section:

- where it appeared in the original document (the page number and paragraph, if applicable); and
- a number or letter to indicate its place in the new draft.

It's a good idea to keep the notes and questions you wrote in the margins distinct from your cross-reference marks by writing them in a different color. Use colored pencils, since it's likely you'll move sections around more than once.

Once you have finished physically reorganizing the document, you may want to outline the new organization. On a separate piece of paper, write the names for the new sections you created. Under each section name, write down its major elements. This is the outline of your plain English draft and, with some revisions, will become your table of contents.

Keep in mind that the most effective outlines are more like sketches—just detailed enough to set priorities and create logical relationships.

Next to each entry on your outline, be sure to note where this information appeared in the original document. This is very important. Cross-referencing accurately now may save you hours of backtracking later.

Tape your reordered sections on blank pieces of ledger size paper and photocopy them. This will be the master document from which you'll rewrite. As you rewrite, each time you complete a sentence or paragraph, draw a line through it in pencil. This way you'll be sure to account for all the original content in your rewrite. •

9

Using Readability Formulas and Style Checkers

Readability formulas determine how difficult a piece of writing is to read. However, you should be aware of a major flaw in every readability formula.

No formula takes into account the content of the document being evaluated. In other words, no formula can tell you if you have conveyed the information clearly. For the most part, they count the numbers of syllables and words in a sentence and the number of sentences in the sample. Of course, if you applied a readability formula to a traditional disclosure document, it would fail miserably. But keep in mind that by some formulas' calculations, Einstein's theory of relativity reads at a 5th grade level.

Some computerized style checkers analyze your grammar and identify the passive voice. They may suggest ways to make your writing more "readable." Take their suggestions as just that—suggestions. The final test of whether any piece of writing meets its goal of communicating information comes when humans read it. •

10

Evaluating the Document

You can evaluate your document by testing it with a focus group. Experts call this "audience-centered" testing because it focuses on the interaction between a particular document and a representative sample of its readers. While the results are reliable, focus groups require time and money.

Focus group testing tends to work better with shorter documents or portions of longer ones. You can also test the portions of your document that you plan to use repeatedly. At the very least, you'll have helpful feedback on the sections that investors are most likely to read and on the language that appears most frequently in your disclosure documents. Based on the test results, you can isolate the parts that cause the most confusion and fix them.

If you don't have the budget to test your document formally through focus groups, improvise. Ask individuals in your office who most closely resemble your investors to read your draft document and listen closely to their reactions. Ask others who have some distance from the project to read it. A fresh pair of eyes often picks up the "obvious" problems that those who have worked with the document miss. •

11

Reading List

If you want more information on how to write in plain English, we've listed just a few of the many resources available, including those from the SEC. You may want to visit your local library to review these books or a broader selection. Goldstein and Lieberman's book, *The Lawyer's Guide to Writing Well,* includes a comprehensive list of books about legal writing. We are not endorsing any of these books, but have included them as a resource for your convenience.

Claire Kehrwald Cook, *Line by Line*
(Houghton Mifflin, 1985).

Alan J. Davis, *Graphs and Doublespeak, Quarterly Review of Doublespeak,*
Volume XVIII, Number 4, July 1992.

Bryan A. Garner, *The Elements of Legal Style*
(Oxford University Press, 1991).

_______, *A Dictionary of Modern Legal Usage*
(Oxford University Press, 2nd ed., 1995).

Tom Goldstein and Jethro K. Lieberman, *The Lawyer's Guide to Writing Well*
(University of California Press, 1989).

Karen Elizabeth Gordon, *The Transitive Vampire: A Handbook of Grammar for the Innocent, the Eager, and the Doomed*
(Times Books, 1984).

_______, *The New Well-Tempered Sentence, A Punctuation Handbook for the Innocent, the Eager, and the Doomed*
(Ticknor & Fields, 1993).

William Lutz, *The New Doublespeak: Why No One Knows What Anyone's Saying Anymore*
(HarperCollins, 1996).

David Mellinkoff, *Legal Writing: Sense & Nonsense*
(West Publishing Company, 1982).

William Strunk, Jr., and E.B. White, *Elements of Style*
(Macmillan, 3rd rev. ed., 1981).

Edward R. Tufte, *The Visual Display of Quantitative Information*
(Graphics Press, 1983).

Robin Williams, *The Mac Is Not a Typewriter*
(Peachpit Press, 1990).

Richard C. Wydick, *Plain English for Lawyers*
(Carolina Academic Press, 2nd ed., 1985).

William Zinsser, *On Writing Well*
(Harper & Row, 4th ed., 1988).

SEC publications

Before & After Plain English Examples and Sample Analyses
(SEC Division of Corporation Finance, April 4, 1998).

Plain English Pilot Program: Selected Plain English Samples
(SEC Division of Corporation Finance, January 28, 1998).

Securities Act Release No. 33-7380, Plain English Disclosure, proposing release, (January 14, 1997) 62 FR 3512 (January 21, 1997).

Securities Act Release No. 33-7497, Plain English Disclosure, adopting release, (January 28, 1998) 63 FR 6370 (February 6, 1998). •

12

Keeping in Touch with Us

We hope that this handbook will prove useful to you in drafting and creating plain English documents. Although we have drawn the suggestions in the handbook from those who have written plain English documents and from experts in the field, we realize that much more will be learned along the way that can benefit all of us.

We would appreciate receiving your suggestions on how we can improve this handbook. We would also like to collect as many examples of "befores" and their plain English "afters" as possible, as well as any tips that helped you save time and energy.

Please forward your suggestions and "before" and "after" examples to:

Nancy M. Smith
Director
Office of Investor Education and Assistance
SEC
450 5th Street, N.W.
Washington, D.C. 20549 •

Plain English at a Glance

Appendix A

Plain English means creating a document that is

- visually inviting,
- logically organized, and
- understandable on the first reading.

You create a plain English document by

- knowing your readers, and
- presenting information your readers need in an order they'll understand.

Summary of the plain English rules

Rule 421(b)

Entire Prospectus

Clear, concise, and understandable

- short sentences whenever possible
- bullet lists whenever possible
- descriptive headers and sub-headers
- avoid relying on glossaries and defined terms
- avoid legal and highly technical business terms

Note

Avoid:

- legalistic, overly complex presentations
- vague boilerplate
- excerpts from legal documents
- repetition

This is a summary, so please read the entire rule to make sure you comply with every aspect of it.

Rule 421(d)

Cover and Back Pages, Summary, and Risk Factors

Use plain English principles in the organization, language, and design of documents

Substantially use:

- short sentences
- definite, concrete, everyday words
- active voice
- tables and bullet lists
- no legal jargon, highly technical business terms
- no multiple negatives

Entire Prospectus—Design

In designing the entire prospectus:

- may use pictures, logos, charts, graphs, or other design elements
- encouraged to use tables, schedules, charts, and graphics for financial data
- must draw graphs and charts to scale
- cannot use misleading design and information

§230.421
Presentation of information in prospectuses

• • • • •

(b) You must present the information in a prospectus in a clear, concise and understandable manner. You must prepare the prospectus using the following standards:

(1) Present information in clear, concise sections, paragraphs, and sentences. Whenever possible, use short, explanatory sentences and bullet lists;

(2) Use descriptive headings and subheadings;

(3) Avoid frequent reliance on glossaries or defined terms as the primary means of explaining information in the prospectus. Define terms in a glossary or other section of the document only if the meaning is unclear from the context. Use a glossary only if it facilitates understanding of the disclosure; and

(4) Avoid legal and highly technical business terminology.

Note to §230.421(b):

In drafting the disclosure to comply with this section, you should avoid the following:

1. Legalistic or overly complex presentations that make the substance of the disclosure difficult to understand;

2. Vague "boilerplate" explanations that are imprecise and readily subject to different interpretations;

3. Complex information copied directly from legal documents without any clear and concise explanation of the provision(s); and

4. Disclosure repeated in different sections of the document that increases the size of the document but does not enhance the quality of the information.

• • • • •

(d) (1) To enhance the readability of the prospectus, you must use plain English principles in the organization, language, and design of the front and back cover pages, the summary, and the risk factors section.

(2) You must draft the language in these sections so that at a minimum it substantially complies with each of the following plain English writing principles:

(i) Short sentences;
(ii) Definite, concrete, everyday words;
(iii) Active voice;
(iv) Tabular presentation or bullet lists for complex material, whenever possible;
(v) No legal jargon or highly technical business terms; and
(vi) No multiple negatives.

(3) In designing these sections or other sections of the prospectus, you may include pictures, logos, charts, graphs, or other design elements so long as the design is not misleading and the required information is clear. You are encouraged to use tables, schedules, charts and graphic illustrations of the results of operations, balance sheet, or other financial data that present the data in an understandable manner. Any presentation must be consistent with the financial statements and non-financial information in the prospectus. You must draw the graphs and charts to scale. Any information you provide must not be misleading.

Instruction to §230.421

You should read Securities Act Release No. 33-7497 (January 28, 1998) for information on plain English principles. •

Plain English Examples

Appendix B

This appendix contains "before" and "after" examples from participants in the Division of Corporation Finance's plain English pilot. The Division's staff added marginal notes to show how aspects of the plain English rules apply to specific documents.

These annotated examples are excerpted from the booklet, *Before & After Plain English Examples and Sample Analyses,* prepared by the Division of Corporation Finance. Although we revised the presentation and wording of the marginal notes in this appendix, the filings remain identical to those from the booklet. To get a complete copy of the booklet, please call the SEC's public reference room at (202) 942-8090.

Differences between the proposed and final amendments to Item 501

When the issuers prepared these documents, they relied on staff interpretations for filings in the plain English pilot and the proposed amendments to Item 501.

The following information was not required under Item 501 as *proposed,* but this information is required under Item 501 as *adopted:*

- the market(s) and the trading symbol;
- the underwriter's over-allotment or similar option, if applicable;
- a prominent cross-reference to the risk factors section including the page number;
- the following on a total and per share basis, if applicable:
  - the price to the public;
  - the underwriter's discounts and commissions; and
  - the net proceeds the issuer and selling shareholders receive.

Examples for illustration purposes only

We are providing these examples and marginal notes only to illustrate the principles of plain English. We have not made any determination as to whether the filings are accurate or complete. You are responsible for the substance in your plain English filings. To understand the plain English rules fully, you must read the proposing and adopting releases:

- the proposing release—Release no. 33-7380; and
- the adopting release—Release no. 33-7497.

Both releases are available from the SEC's Public Reference Room and our web site at www.sec.gov.

We collected many filings from the Division's plain English pilot in one book. You can get a photocopy of this 756-page book, *Plain English Pilot Program: Selected Plain English Samples,* from the SEC's Public Reference Room or a printed copy from Bowne Publishing in New York City. (The SEC does not endorse Bowne, nor do we have a business relationship with them.)

Before

MBNA cover page, core prospectus

Note: When MBNA filed this disclosure document, they relied on the SEC rules that were in effect at that time.

Fully-justified text and lengthy paragraphs give page a dense, block-like appearance.

Abstract terms and legal jargon prevalent

A lot of passive voice, adding to sentence length

Eliminate defined terms from the cover page.

Long sentence–60+ words

Why capitalize these common terms?

Long sentence–50+ words

Many long sentences–40+ words

Centered text and all capital letters are hard to read.

Legends are in legalese.

Legalistic tone–does Item 501 require all this information?

All information is presented the same way: What does this page focus my attention on?

Sans serif font is hard to read.

Text runs in long lines across the page.

PROSPECTUS

MBNA Master Credit Card Trust II

Asset Backed Certificates

MBNA America Bank, National Association

Seller and Servicer

The Asset Backed Certificates (collectively, the "Certificates") described herein may be sold from time to time in one or more series (each, a "Series") in amounts, at prices and on terms to be determined at the time of sale and to be set forth in a supplement to this Prospectus (a "Prospectus Supplement"). The Certificates of each Series will represent an undivided interest in MBNA Master Credit Card Trust II (the "Trust"). The Trust has been formed pursuant to a pooling and servicing agreement between MBNA America Bank, National Association ("MBNA"), as seller and servicer, and The Bank of New York, as trustee. The property of the Trust will include receivables (the "Receivables") generated from time to time in a portfolio of consumer revolving credit card accounts (the "Accounts"), all monies due in payment of the Receivables and certain other property, as more fully described herein and, with respect to any Series, in the related Prospectus Supplement. MBNA initially will own the remaining undivided interest in the Trust not represented by the Certificates issued by the Trust and will service the Receivables.

Each Series will consist of one or more classes of Certificates (each, a "Class"), one or more of which may be fixed rate Certificates, floating rate Certificates or other type of Certificates, as specified in the related Prospectus Supplement. Each Certificate will represent an undivided interest in the Trust and the interest of the Certificateholders of each Class or Series will include the right to receive a varying percentage of each month's collections with respect to the Receivables of the Trust at the times, in the manner and to the extent described herein and, with respect to any Series offered hereby, in the related Prospectus Supplement. Interest and principal payments with respect to each Series offered hereby will be made as specified in the related Prospectus Supplement. One or more Classes of a Series offered hereby may be entitled to the benefits of a cash collateral account or guaranty, a collateral interest, a letter of credit, a surety bond, an insurance policy or other form of enhancement as specified in the Prospectus Supplement relating to such Series. In addition, any Series offered hereby may include one or more Classes which are subordinated in right and priority to payment of principal of, and/or interest on, one or more other Classes of such Series or another Series, in each case to the extent described in the related Prospectus Supplement. Each Series of Certificates or Class thereof offered hereby will be rated in one of the four highest rating categories by at least one nationally recognized rating organization.

While the specific terms of any Series in respect of which this Prospectus is being delivered will be described in the related Prospectus Supplement, the terms of such Series will not be subject to prior review by, or consent of, the Certificateholders of any previously issued Series.

Potential investors should consider, among other things, the information set forth in "Risk Factors" beginning on page 19 herein.

THE CERTIFICATES WILL REPRESENT INTERESTS IN THE TRUST ONLY AND WILL NOT REPRESENT INTERESTS IN OR OBLIGATIONS OF MBNA AMERICA BANK, NATIONAL ASSOCIATION OR ANY AFFILIATE THEREOF. A CERTIFICATE IS NOT A DEPOSIT AND NEITHER THE CERTIFICATES NOR THE UNDERLYING ACCOUNTS OR RECEIVABLES ARE INSURED OR GUARANTEED BY THE FEDERAL DEPOSIT INSURANCE CORPORATION OR ANY OTHER GOVERNMENTAL AGENCY.

THESE SECURITIES HAVE NOT BEEN APPROVED OR DISAPPROVED BY THE SECURITIES AND EXCHANGE COMMISSION OR ANY STATE SECURITIES COMMISSION NOR HAS THE COMMISSION OR ANY STATE SECURITIES COMMISSION PASSED UPON THE ACCURACY OR ADEQUACY OF THIS PROSPECTUS. ANY REPRESENTATION TO THE CONTRARY IS A CRIMINAL OFFENSE.

Certificates may be sold by MBNA directly to purchasers, through agents designated from time to time, through underwriting syndicates led by one or more managing underwriters or through one or more underwriters acting alone. If underwriters or agents are involved in the offering of the Certificates of any Series offered hereby, the name of the managing underwriter or underwriters or agents will be set forth in the related Prospectus Supplement. If an underwriter, agent or dealer is involved in the offering of the Certificates of any Series offered hereby, the underwriter's discount, agent's commission or dealer's purchase price will be set forth in, or may be calculated from, the related Prospectus Supplement, and the net proceeds to MBNA from such offering will be the public offering price of such Certificates less such discount in the case of an underwriter, the purchase price of such Certificates less such commission in the case of an agent or the purchase price of such Certificates in the case of a dealer, and less, in each case, the other expenses of MBNA associated with the issuance and distribution of such Certificates. See "Plan of Distribution."

This Prospectus may not be used to consummate sales of any Series of Certificates unless accompanied by the related Prospectus Supplement.

The date of this Prospectus is September 2, 1997.

MBNA cover page, core prospectus

After

Prospectus

MBNA Master Credit Card Trust II

Issuer

MBNA America Bank, National Association

Seller and Servicer

Asset Backed Certificates

Consider carefully the risk factors beginning on page 10 in this prospectus.

A certificate is not a deposit and neither the certificates nor the underlying accounts or receivables are insured or guaranteed by the Federal Deposit Insurance Corporation or any other governmental agency.

The certificates will represent interests in the trust only and will not represent interests in or obligations of MBNA or any MBNA affiliate.

This prospectus may be used to offer and sell any series of certificates only if accompanied by the prospectus supplement for that series.

The Trust—

- may periodically issue asset backed certificates in one or more series with one or more classes; and
- will own—
  - receivables in a portfolio of consumer revolving credit card accounts;
  - payments due on those receivables; and
  - other property described in this prospectus and in the accompanying prospectus supplement.

The Certificates—

- will represent interests in the trust and will be paid only from the trust assets;
- offered with this prospectus will be rated in one of the four highest rating categories by at least one nationally recognized rating organization;
- may have one or more forms of enhancement; and
- will be issued as part of a designated series which may include one or more classes of certificates and enhancement.

The Certificateholders—

- will receive interest and principal payments from a varying percentage of credit card account collections.

Neither the SEC nor any state securities commission has approved these certificates or determined that this prospectus is accurate or complete. Any representation to the contrary is a criminal offense.

February 27, 1998

Ample white space surrounds key information and makes page visually inviting.

Page layout highlights cross reference to risk factors.

Clear sentences are in active voice with concrete, everyday language.

No lengthy, block-like paragraphs

Information presented in three main categories:
- the trust
- the certificates
- the certificateholders

No defined terms

Common terms, like *classes*, are not capitalized.

Long sentences are put into bullet lists.

Left justified text and shorter line lengths are easy to read.

Serif typeface is easier to read than sans serif.

Legends in plain English and lowercase are easier to read than all capital letters.

Before — Premium Cigars International, cover page

Fully justified text creates a dense, block-like appearance.

Eliminate defined terms from cover page.

Is *no par value* helpful information for investors?

Key information, such as price per share, is not distinguished from general text.

Cross reference draws readers' attention away from key information.

All capital letters are hard to read.

Legend is in legalese.

Some legalese is used, like *set forth* and *when, as and if delivered.*

Offering table, references to footnotes, and paragraph following the table are legalistic.

Legalistic tone–does Item 501 require all this information?

Information contained herein is subject to completion or amendment. A registration statement relating to these securities has been filed with the Securities and Exchange Commission. These securities may not be sold nor may offers to buy be accepted prior to the time the registration statement becomes effective. This prospectus shall not constitute an offer to sell or the solicitation of an offer to buy nor shall there be any sale of these securities in any State in which such offer, solicitation or sale would be unlawful prior to registration or qualification under the securities laws of any such State.

PROSPECTUS

SUBJECT TO COMPLETION DATED JUNE 25, 1997

PREMIUM CIGARS INTERNATIONAL, LTD.

2,000,000 Shares

Premium Cigars International, Ltd. ("we" or "PCI"), distributes moderately priced premium cigars and other cigars, which are sold from our humidors placed primarily in convenience stores in the United States and Canada. By this Prospectus, we are offering you shares of PCI Common Stock, no par value ("Shares").

This is our initial public offering, and no public market currently exists for PCI's Shares. We estimate that the initial public offering price will be $5.01 per Share. The Offering Price per Share will be determined by negotiations between PCI and the Representative, and may not be indicative of the market price of Shares after the Offering. Factors used to determine the initial public offering price are set forth under "Underwriting."

We will apply to have our Shares listed on The Nasdaq SmallCap System under the symbol PCIG on completion of the Offering.

THIS INVESTMENT INVOLVES A HIGH DEGREE OF RISK AND IMMEDIATE AND SUBSTANTIAL DILUTION. YOU SHOULD PURCHASE UNITS ONLY IF YOU CAN AFFORD A COMPLETE LOSS. SEE "RISK FACTORS."

THESE SECURITIES HAVE NOT BEEN APPROVED OR DISAPPROVED BY THE SECURITIES AND EXCHANGE COMMISSION NOR HAS THE COMMISSION PASSED UPON THE ACCURACY OR ADEQUACY OF THIS PROSPECTUS. ANY REPRESENTATION TO THE CONTRARY IS A CRIMINAL OFFENSE.

	Price to the Public	Underwriting Discounts and Commissions (1)	Proceeds to the Company (2)
Per Share	$5.01	$.50	$4.51
Total (3)	$10,020,000	$1,002,000	$9,018,000

The Shares are being offered by the Underwriters when, as and if delivered to and accepted by the Underwriter and subject to various prior conditions, including their right to reject orders in whole or in part. W.B. McKee Securities, Inc. will act as representative of the Underwriters ("Representative"). We expect that Share certificates will be delivered in Phoenix, Arizona, on or about ______________, 1997.

W.B. McKEE SECURITIES, INC.

The date of this Prospectus is July __, 1997

Premium Cigars International, cover page

After

Initial Public Offering
Prospectus

PCI

PREMIUM CIGARS INTERNATIONAL

1,900,000 shares of Common Stock
$5.25 per share

Premium Cigars International, Ltd.
15651 N. 83rd Way, Suite 3
Scottsdale, Arizona 95260

The Offering

	Per Share	Total
Public Price	$ 5.25	$9,975,000
Underwriting discounts.........	$ .525	$ 997,500
Proceeds to PCI	$4.725	$8,977,500

We distribute moderately priced premium cigars and other cigars, which are sold from our humidors placed primarily in convenience stores in the United States and Canada.

This is our initial public offering, and no public market currently exists for our shares. The offering price may not reflect the market price of our shares after the offering.

Proposed Trading Symbols:
NASDAQ SmallCap Market^{SM} — PCIG
Boston Stock Exchange — PCI

This Investment Involves a High Degree of Risk. You Should Purchase Shares Only If You Can Afford a Complete Loss. See "Risk Factors" Beginning on Page 5.

Neither the Securities and Exchange Commission nor any state securities commission has approved or disapproved these securities, or determined if this Prospectus is truthful or complete. Any representation to the contrary is a criminal offense.

W.B. MCKEE SECURITIES, INC.

KASHNER DAVIDSON SECURITIES CORP.

August 21, 1997

Only key information on page

Offering information is clear and easy to read.

Ample white space is visually inviting and highlights key information.

Key information, like price per share, is highlighted.

Left justified text eliminates block-like appearance.

Two-column format is easier to read than text running across page.

Design and layout highlight market and trading symbols.

Short sentences use concrete, everyday terms.

Language is free from legalese, technical language, and unnecessary cross references.

Personal pronouns, while not required, enhance readability.

Legend is in plain English.

Before

General Motors Corporation, summary

Legalese and technical terms, like *pursuant to the terms and conditions set forth*, and *effected largely pursuant to transactions*, etc.

Cross reference to definition disrupts flow of information; meanings of terms in summary must be clear from context.

Terms like *certain* and *appropriate* are vague, not concrete.

Passive voice–who is completing these transactions?

Parenthetical phrases are legalistic and disrupt flow of information.

Little "i"s are legalistic; bulleted list would be easier to read.

Organization of information driven by mechanics of transactions rather than by information shareholders need to make a decision.

Transactions' effect on shareholders not discussed until column two.

Is detail about GM amending its certificate of incorporation necessary for the summary?

RAYTHEON

Raytheon is an international, high technology company which operates in four businesses: commercial and defense, engineering and construction, aircraft and major appliances. On July 11, 1997, Raytheon completed its acquisition of the business of Texas Instruments Defense. Immediately after the completion of the Hughes Transactions, Raytheon will merge with Hughes Defense.

For additional information regarding the business of Raytheon, see "Overview of Raytheon Business."

THE HUGHES TRANSACTIONS

Description of the Hughes Transactions

The Hughes Transactions will be completed through two principal steps:

(1) the Hughes Reorganization (consisting of several transactions which prepare Hughes Defense for the spin-off from General Motors, separate the businesses of Hughes Defense, Delco and Hughes Telecom and effect the transfer of Delco to General Motors); and

(2) the Spin-Off Merger (a merger transaction which effects the spin-off of Hughes Defense and the recapitalization and conversion of GM Class H Common Stock into New GM Class H Common Stock).

Step 1: The Hughes Reorganization. **Pursuant to the Hughes Reorganization, among other things, (i) certain assets and liabilities will be transferred among Hughes Defense, Delco and Hughes Telecom so that each entity will have the appropriate assets and liabilities for its business; (ii) Hughes Telecom will be separated from Hughes Defense (which we refer to as the "Hughes Telecom Spin-Off"); (iii) Delco will be transferred from Hughes Electronics to General Motors; and (iv) Hughes Defense will recapitalize its capital stock into Class A Common Stock and Class B Common Stock. The Hughes Reorganization will be effected largely pursuant to transactions described in the Master Separation Agreement and the agreements contemplated by that agreement. See "Description of the Hughes Transactions—General—Hughes Reorganization" and "Separation and Transition Arrangements."**

Step 2: The Spin-Off Merger. **Pursuant to the terms and conditions set forth in the Spin-Off Merger Agreement, a wholly owned subsidiary of General Motors formed in order to effect the Spin-Off Merger will merge with General Motors. General Motors will be the surviving corporation of the Spin-Off Merger. See "Description of the Hughes Transactions—General—Spin-Off Merger" and "—Spin-Off Merger Agreement."**

As a result of the Spin-Off Merger, the following will occur:

- **each outstanding share of GM Class H Common Stock will be recapitalized and converted automatically into one share of New GM Class H Common Stock and each GM Class H Common Stockholder will receive a distribution of the Per Share Class H Distribution (as defined under "Background—The Distribution Ratio") of Class A Common Stock;**
- **each outstanding share of GM $1⅔ Common Stock will remain outstanding and each GM $1⅔ Common Stockholder will receive a distribution of the Per Share $1⅔ Distribution (as defined under "Background—The Distribution Ratio") of Class A Common Stock; and**
- **the GM Certificate of Incorporation will be amended to delete provisions relating to the GM Class H Common Stock (including the provisions that require GM Class H Common Stock to be recapitalized into GM $1⅔ Common Stock at a 120% exchange ratio under certain circumstances) and to add provisions setting forth the terms of the New GM Class H Common Stock.**

For additional information regarding the Hughes Transactions, see "Description of the Hughes Transactions—General."

For a description of the methodology used to determine the allocation of Class A Common Stock between the two classes of GM common stockholders and a description of the post-closing payment to be made between Delco and Hughes Telecom, see "Background—Distribution Ratio."

General Motors Corporation, summary

After

...H Common Stock outstanding ... time. For most calculations ... ment which use the Class H Fraction, we have used the Class H Fraction as of September 30, 1997 (approximately 25.6%).

INTRODUCTION TO THE HUGHES TRANSACTIONS

THE HUGHES TRANSACTIONS

We are proposing three related transactions to enhance the value of the businesses operated by our Hughes Electronics subsidiary. We need your consent in order to accomplish these "Hughes Transactions."

(1) Hughes Defense

We propose to spin off the defense electronics business of Hughes Electronics to our common stockholders. We call this business "Hughes Defense." Immediately after the spin-off, Hughes Defense will merge with Raytheon Company. Based on the Recent Raytheon Stock Price, these transactions have an indicated value of approximately $9.5 billion.

The merged company will be the nation's third largest defense company and one of the largest providers of defense electronics in the world. The merger should enable it to compete more effectively in the U.S. defense industry, where significant consolidation has been occurring. We call the merged company "New Raytheon."

GM common stockholders will receive all of the Class A Common Stock of Hughes Defense, representing approximately 30% of the common stock of New Raytheon after the merger. This stock has an indicated value of approximately $5.2 billion based on the Recent Raytheon Stock Price. Approximately 58.7% of the Class A Common Stock would be distributed to GM Class H Common Stockholders and approximately 41.3% would be distributed to GM $1⅔ Common Stockholders based on the Recent Raytheon Stock Price.

Hughes Defense will be permitted to have approximately $4.3 billion of debt when it is spun off. Substantially all of the proceeds of this debt will be made available as new capital for Hughes Telecom. The obligation to repay this debt, however, will remain with New Raytheon (in which GM's common stockholders will have an approximately 30% equity interest).

The indicated transaction value of approximately $9.5 billion consists of the sum of (1) the value of the Class A Common Stock to be distributed to GM's common stockholders and (2) the amount of debt that Hughes Defense is permitted to have at the time of the spin-off. We believe that this amount represents a substantial premium to the enterprise value of Hughes Defense under its current ownership structure.

(2) Delco Electronics

We propose to transfer Delco Electronics, our automotive electronics business, from Hughes

3 CHAPTER 1: INTRODUCTION

Information organized from shareholders' perspectives—how transactions affect them addressed first.

Active voice helps shareholders follow the steps involved in the transaction more easily.

Summary is free of defined terms.

Concrete, everyday language replaces legalese like *pursuant to the terms and conditions set forth* and *effected largely pursuant to transactions*, etc.

Numbers are more reader-friendly than little "i"s.

Easy to read two-column format with left justified margins.

Personal pronouns, although not required, help engage shareholders' attention.

Before

Baltimore Gas & Electric Company

Section from body of prospectus

Paragraphs are lengthy and block-like.

Subheadings are helpful, but more would be better.

Defined below? Where is *below*? Cross reference not helpful.

Long sentence–85+ words

Many defined terms with definitions elsewhere. Can you make meanings clear from context?

Long sentence–90+ words

Lists embedded in text; complex presentation

Interest Rate

General

Each Note will bear interest from its date of issue at the fixed rate per annum or at the rate per annum determined pursuant to the interest rate formula, stated therein and in the applicable Pricing Supplement, until the principal thereof is paid or made available for payment. Interest will be payable on each Interest Payment Date (as defined below) and at Stated Maturity or, if applicable, upon redemption. Each payment of interest payable at Stated Maturity or, if applicable, upon redemption shall include interest accrued to, but excluding, the date of Stated Maturity or redemption. Interest will be payable generally to the person (which, in the case of Book-Entry Notes, shall be the Depositary or its nominee) in whose name a Note (or any predecessor Note) is registered at the close of business on the Record Date (as defined below) next preceding each Interest Payment Date; *provided, however,* that interest payable at Stated Maturity or, if applicable, upon redemption, will be payable to the person (which, in the case of Book-Entry Notes, shall be the Depositary or its nominee) to whom principal shall be payable. The first payment of interest on any Note originally issued between a Record Date and an Interest Payment Date or on an Interest Payment Date will be made on the Interest Payment Date following the next succeeding Record Date to the registered owner on such Record Date. Interest (other than interest payable at Stated Maturity or, if applicable, upon redemption) will be paid, at the Company's option, by check mailed to registered holders or by wire transfer to any holder of record. For additional information with respect to payments of interest on Book-Entry Notes, see "Book-Entry Notes" below. Interest rates, or interest rate formulas, will be subject to change by the Company from time to time, provided that any change in interest rates, or interest rate formulas, will not affect any Note previously issued or which the Company has agreed to sell. The interest rate on the Fixed Rate Notes and the Floating Rate Notes will in no event be higher than the maximum rate permitted by Maryland law, as the same may be modified by United States law of general application.

Fixed Rate Notes

The applicable Pricing Supplement relating to a Fixed Rate Note will designate a fixed rate of interest per annum payable on such Note. Unless otherwise indicated in the applicable Pricing Supplement, interest with respect to Fixed Rate Notes will be paid semi-annually each May 1 and November 1 and at Stated Maturity or, if applicable, upon redemption. If any Interest Payment Date or the Stated Maturity (or, if applicable, the date of redemption) of a Fixed Rate Note falls on a day that is not a Business Day, payment of principal, premium, if any, or interest will be made on the next Business Day as if it were made on the date such payment was due, and no interest will accrue on the amount so payable for the period from and after such Interest Payment Date or the Stated Maturity (or the date of redemption), as the case may be. The Record Dates for such Notes will be the April 15 and October 15 next preceding the May 1 and November 1 Interest Payment Dates. Unless otherwise indicated in the applicable Pricing Supplement, interest payments for Fixed Rate Notes shall be the amount of interest accrued to, but excluding, the relevant Interest Payment Date. Interest on such Notes will be computed on the basis of a 360-day year of twelve 30-day months.

Floating Rate Notes

The applicable Pricing Supplement relating to a Floating Rate Note will designate an interest rate formula for such Floating Rate Note. Such formula may be: (a) the Commercial Paper Rate, in which case such Note will be a Commercial Paper Rate Note, (b) the Prime Rate, in which case such Note will be a Prime Rate Note, (c) the CD Rate, in which case such Note will be a CD Rate Note, (d) the Federal Funds Effective Rate, in which case such Note will be a Federal Funds Effective Rate Note, (e) LIBOR, in which case such Note will be a LIBOR Note, (f) the Treasury Rate, in which case such Note will be a Treasury Rate Note, (g) the CMT Rate, in which case such Note will be a CMT Rate Note, or (h) such other interest rate formula as is set forth in such Pricing Supplement. The applicable Pricing Supplement for a Floating Rate Note also will specify the Spread and/or Spread Multiplier, if any, applicable to each Note. Any Floating Rate Note may also have either or both of the following: (a) a maximum numerical interest rate limitation, or ceiling, on the rate of interest which may accrue during any interest period (the "Maximum Interest Rate"); and (b) a minimum numerical interest rate limitation, or floor, on the rate of interest which may

5

Baltimore Gas & Electric Company

After

Section from body of prospectus

The interest rate on the notes will either be fixed or floating. The interest paid will include interest accrued to, but excluding, the date of maturity, redemption or repurchase. Interest is generally payable to the person in whose name the note is registered at the close of business on the record date before each interest payment date. However, interest payable at maturity, redemption, or repurchase will be payable to the person to whom principal is payable. The first interest payment on any note originally issued between a record date and interest payment date or on an interest payment date will be made on the interest payment date after the next record date. Interest payable other than at maturity, redemption or repurchase will be paid, at our option, by check or wire transfer.

Fixed Rate Notes

The applicable pricing supplement will designate the fixed rate of interest payable on a note. Interest will be paid May 1 and November 1, and upon maturity, redemption or repurchase. If any payment date falls on a day that is not a Business Day, payment will be made on the next Business Day and no additional interest will be paid. The record dates for such notes will be April 15 (for interest to be paid on May 1) and October 15 (for interest to be paid on November 1). Interest payments will be the amount of interest accrued to, but excluding, each May 1 and November 1. Interest will be computed using a 360-day year of twelve 30-day months.

Floating Rate Notes

General

Each floating rate note will have an interest rate formula. The formula may be based on:

- the commercial paper rate;
- the prime rate;
- the CD rate;
- the federal funds effective rate;
- the LIBOR;
- the Treasury rate;
- the CMT rate; or
- another interest rate index.

The applicable pricing supplement will also indicate the Spread and/or Spread Multiplier, if any. In addition, any floating rate note may have a maximum or minimum interest rate limitation.

Upon request, the Calculation Agent will provide the current interest rate and, if different, the interest rate which will become effective on the next Interest Reset Date.

Date of Interest Rate Change

The interest rate on each floating rate note may be reset daily, weekly, monthly, quarterly, semi-annually, or annually. The Interest Reset Date will be:

- for notes which reset daily, each Business Day;
- for notes (other than Treasury rate notes) which reset weekly, the Wednesday of each week;
- for Treasury rate notes which reset weekly, the Tuesday of each week;
- for notes which reset monthly, the third Wednesday of each month;
- for notes which reset quarterly, the third Wednesday of March, June, September and December;
- for notes which reset semi-annually, the third Wednesday of the two months of each year indicated in the applicable pricing supplement; and
- for notes which reset annually, the third Wednesday of the month of each year indicated in the applicable pricing supplement.

7

Paragraphs are short and readable.

Short sentences–longest sentence is 36 words.

Two-column format and left justified text, while not required, help make summary more reader-friendly.

More subheadings break up dense text and help readers navigate their way through information easily.

Defined terms are minimized, with meanings of terms clear from context.

Bullet lists help investors read and understand this information more quickly and easily.